ii

The Threshing Floor of Faith

iv

The Threshing Floor of Faith,
Enduring to the End

The Threshing Floor
Of
Faith

Enduring to the End

Part I

The Faith of the Fathers

Part II

Questions & Scriptural Answers

Bruce H. Porter

ISBN: 9781534609181
© Copyright 2016 Bruce H. Porter
Printed in the United States of America

Acknowledgements

I would like to acknowledge and recognize the generous sacrifice of time and energy provided by David and Laura Jones. Each selflessly labored for numerous hours to complete the transcription of the presented classroom material. David miraculously converted a vocal seminar and PowerPoint presentation into editable text. Likewise, Laura Jones expended diligent effort and talent in the process of turning the transcribed presentations into a readable form. Without both this work would not be possible. Aaron Brandley and Steven Smith must be given special notice and thanks for the preparation and editorial efforts to make this work worthy of print.

Dedication

This book and all others from my hand are dedicated to my wife Margaret and my children, my children's children, and so on. This, that they may know and understand that my faith and testimony is founded in: Jesus Christ my redeemer and Savior, Joseph Smith the Prophet of the Restoration, The Church of Jesus Christ of Latter-day Saints and the Priesthood which are the only earthly organizations that have the authority to administer the Gospel of Jesus Christ, and in scripture as the Standard of Doctrine which includes: The Bible, The Book of Mormon, The Doctrine and Covenants, and The Pearl of Great Price.

x

Contents:

Preface

This work is drawn from the transcripts of lectures and visual presentations spanning a length of time and was not intended to be a proper book. It is not, by any means, complete or perfect in scope and depth. Because the content and concepts covered here began in a physical classroom, it should not be considered perfect in its grammar or tense. A conscientious effort has been made to improve the readability and clarity of the ideas, but the organization is somewhat rudimentary. Some concepts and chapters may overlap and be repeated due to the reviews that were necessary to begin a new presentation in the sequence. Scripture passages may also be repeated within this work because of the reviews and to better present some answers to the important questions and chapters that might be read independent from the rest of the book. Please forgive the seemingly unnecessary repetition.

The ideas, concepts, and commentaries presented here do not represent official doctrine or policy of The Church of Jesus Christ of Latter-day Saints. The information, organization, and presentation of these materials are the sole responsibility of the author as an individual person, and not as any church official, teacher, or priesthood leader. Any copyrighted material that might be contained in this transcription has been used only for sources and reference materials. The information contained herein and referenced materials may be read and studied for personal use, and not for any financial gain without written permission of the author. Italics are used by the author throughout this book to emphasize concepts, and phrases within the text and scripture passages and will not be noted otherwise within the text.

Introduction

This book is a response to a troubling move of separation and disaffection with The Church of Jesus Christ of Latter-Day Saints by both youth and seasoned adults. This trend appears to be driven by questions arising from cultural trends and the dissemination of seemingly 'damning' information courtesy of the multiple voices found in cyberspace and in print. The questions that lie at the heart of this falling-away range from perceived historical inconsistencies and misgivings about doctrine and practices to questions that surround the translation of scripture – not only of the Book of Mormon, but more particularly, the Book of Abraham.

Because of the internet, a veritable warehouse of information both good and bad displaying the influence of modern cultural norms, many are taking issue with things based on a misunderstanding of both doctrine and scripture. These include: women and the priesthood; same sex attraction and marriage; plural marriage; and much more. Some stumble because of conflicting statements by priesthood leaders, past and present, while others see supposed doctrinal traditions that are not congruent with modern trends of science and supposed tolerance of cultural norms and liberal values. Most often the *filters of perception* that an individual has acquired by their experience, learning and education (or lack thereof) may often cause the greatest amount of misunderstanding.

This material was originally prepared as a PowerPoint and presented in a series of seminars over a number of months. This was done in an attempt to answer some of these questions and provide contextual evidence to increase an understanding of core doctrines as well as the purpose and function of the church and priesthood organizations. This work will examine some of the reasons for this falling away and the types of influences that are feeding the current phenomenon affecting the Latter-day Saint youth and those seasoned in the church and the gospel.

Some surveys indicate that approximately 50% of LDS youth are falling away because of the questions and misgivings they have. This has the potential to affect every family in the Church. Latter-day Saints need to arm themselves with knowledge that might help put these concerns to rest. There are answers – good, reliable, honest answers – but other points of view dominate the media and obscure the truth. Those that are falling away need answers they can trust, so the question becomes: How best to address these questions in a way that faith and testimonies are retained, restored, and strengthened? As always, knowledge is power. Before these questions are answered, core ideas about testimony and faith should be addressed.

Part One will address such topics as: the foundation of faith and testimony and the purpose and authority of priesthood leadership. It will include the role of the church in the member's life, the difference between tradition and doctrine, and why the scriptures are so important. It is hoped that this discussion may lay a foundation that will help resolve many of the issues causing good members to lose faith in their religion.

Part Two will address some of the historical factors that rank high in surveys as contributing to the recent trend toward disbelief. There are over fifteen "reasons," or questions linked to this phenomenon. However, when distilled, many of them relate to each other, leaving about five or six main issues.

Latter-day Saint families cannot afford to ignore what is happening. Turning a blind eye to the problem will cause this falling away to continue and increase. Nephi saw our day and declared that a sure sign of apostasy among the members of the church is the cry: "All is well in Zion; yea, Zion prospereth, all is well" (2 Nephi 28:21).

Within this text a 'relationship with Christ' is often mentioned. Not that anyone should ignore a relationship with any member of the

Godhead more or less than another; however, this phrase "relationship with Christ" is meant to underscore that the individual's personal responsibility is to 'work out their own salvation in fear and trembling" through the Atonement and Gospel of Jesus Christ. To "love" Him, "know" Him or "come unto Him" requires an understanding and realization of a necessary relationship with the Atonement and the grace and mercy offered by the Savior. All must exercise faith in Christ and His Atonement to receive eternal life. There is no other name wherein salvation may be found, as every knee shall bow and tongue will confess that Jesus is the Christ.

It is the hope of the author, that this information will provide members of the church with some of the information needed to understand and counter the mounting wave of disbelief that is destroying testimonies and crippling the faith of loved ones. This book is not meant to alter an individual's belief but to present a scriptural point of view of the concepts addressed, acting as an aid for improved faith and understanding.

Everyone has been given agency by a loving God to choose the path they wish to tread, to believe what they choose to believe. The words of Joseph Smith should be remembered as this agency exists and reigns supreme, and their right to personal belief is guaranteed without condemnation:

> "...If I esteem mankind to be in error, shall I bear down on them? No. I will lift them up, and in their own way too, if I cannot persuade them my way is better. I will not seek to compel any man to believe as I do, only by force or reasoning, for truth will cut its own way. Do you believe Jesus Christ and the gospel of salvation which he revealed? So do I. Christians should cease wrangling and contending with each other, and cultivate the principles of union and friendship. I am just as ready to die defending the rights of a Presbyterian, a Baptist, or a good man of any other denomination" (*TPJS* 313-314).

Chapter 1

The Threshing Floor

Anciently the Threshing Floor was a considered a central and sacred place that became important for the sustaining of both the physical life as well as the spiritual well-being of mankind. The most simple and practical purpose of the Threshing Floor was a place where the harvested grain would be broken down by animals that would tread on the collected grain separating the inedible chaff from the life giving protein and sustenance of the grain. The animals would not only tread on the grain but drag wooden sleds impregnated with pieces of flint to cut and break away the undesirable and useless stems and chaff. Once broken apart, the chaff and grain would be thrown into the air together. The lighter chaff would be blown away in the winds while the heavier and more important grain would fall to the bedrock or stone floor for gathering. This process of separating of the grain from the chaff on the threshing floor, is often used today to symbolize a separation of the good from the bad.

Life, in and of itself is similar to a Threshing Floor, with the destructive sledges and pounding hoofs of trials and tribulations that separate many from their religious faith that at one time may have provided a purpose of life and a belief in a loving God. Because the Threshing Floor is the place where the useful and useless are separated from each other, this common metaphor may be offensive to those

18

who consider the choice to separate themselves from the faith of their fathers to be an "enlightened" one. Therefore, the real symbol of the Threshing Floor should be viewed objectively and briefly discussed.

Anciently, threshing floors were usually found on a hill or high place where the wind could catch the chaff. They were usually round in shape, with pounded earth or flat stones making up the floor of the interior of the circle. The circular threshing floor was defined by a raised stone rim that held the grain and chaff together. Because of its location at a high, prominent spot, the Threshing Floor became a central place for sacrifice, and a sacred site where the creation of the world by the gods was acted out, the purpose of which was to explain the cultural beliefs and myths of the people and the community. Creating a perfect stage, the first theaters of Greece and Rome were fashioned around, and evolved from, the ancient Threshing Floors where the myths were acted out in the form of a creation drama.

The sacred nature of the Threshing Floor was so prevalent that altars were erected at the threshing sites and temples were often constructed near or over the Threshing Floors themselves. It was on the threshing floor that the battle of good and evil was acted out in the metaphor of threshing the grain. Sometimes the animals that worked on the threshing floor were sacrificed as they played the part of evil, symbolically trying to destroy the continuity and securities of life. The floor represented the place of good versus evil, death and resurrection, and the primal creation of the world. The circle of the Threshing Floor epitomized the world, and the rim around the edge symbolically represented the waters of creation surrounding the primordial mound of the hill and the stone floor.[1] This same example is seen on Mt. Carmel when Elijah builds the altar and surrounds it with water. This event in Biblical history no doubt took place at a Threshing Floor.

The spiritual drama of the creation was acted out on the circular floor so that the inhabitants of the local community could learn and actively participate in the creation drama. This was done to facilitate an

1. See B. H. Stricker, "The Origin of the Greek Theatre" in the "The Journal of Egyptian Archaeology," vol 41, December 1955, pp. 34-47

understanding of their relationship with their God and their fellow man. The Temple of Solomon was built on the Jebusite Threshing Floor, it being the place that David offered a sacrifice of the animals that helped in the threshing of the grain (2 Samuel 24:14-25; 1 Chronicles 21:13-30).

The Threshing Floor became a place of education and understanding rather than a simple place of separation of good and bad. It was a place to understand the plan of God for the life and salvation of mankind, assisting all to faithfully endure mortality to the end. This book is not to be considered a treatise on the wheat and chaff but a brief and simple work to help understand some eternal principles that are necessary for spiritual survival. Thus the title of this book: *The Threshing Floor of Faith, Enduring to the End* is meant to represent a place of learning and understanding, rather than separation; a place where truth and error might be discovered, and a place where an understanding of the sacred might be obtained. Ancient cultures believed that *Reality* existed only in the realm of the sacred. To emphasize this *Reality* and the connection between the world of the living, the world of the Gods, and the world of the dead, people would gather at the Threshing Floor to participate in an endowment of knowledge that would provide a personal power over the trials of life and a faith to endure to the end.

Chapter 2

Testimony and The Tree of Life

The spiritual goal of any active member of The Church of Jesus Christ should be to partake of the fruit of the Tree of Life—to taste that which is sweet and pure, finding "joy in the redemption," as mother Eve explains. Coming unto the tree is not enough. There must be faith to endure to the end, having the strength to not only pass through the mists of darkness but also become as the grain that is separated from the chaff on the threshing floor of life. This is a motif not only discussed by prophets but by the Savior Himself in the New Testament.

Every Parable in scripture is directed to members of the church i.e., those who know and understand the gospel. Each parable presents subtle and solemn warnings about personal faith and testimony while pointing out the connection between their activity in the gospel and salvation. There is a difference between one's activity in the Church and one's activity in the Gospel; therefore, the need for the parables. Like Lehi's dream of the Tree of Life, the Savior in the Parable of the Sower describes four types of church members. This parable is about internal spiritual depth and strength of faith and testimony, not one's level of activity in the church.

> 3 And he spake many things unto them in parables, saying, Behold, a sower went forth to sow;
> 4 And when he sowed, some seeds fell by *the way side*, and the fowls came and devoured them up:

5 Some fell upon *stony places*, where they had not much earth: and forthwith they sprung up, because they had no deepness of earth:

6 And when the sun was up, they were scorched; and because they had no root, they withered away.

7 And some fell among *thorns;* and the thorns sprung up, and choked them:

8 But other fell into *good ground*, and brought forth fruit, some an hundredfold, some sixtyfold, some thirtyfold. (Matthew 13:3-8)

"*The Seed*" is "the word" (Alma 33:1). *The Ground* is the heart. Faith and testimony of the individual is their relationship with the seed and "*The Word*" which is Christ (Alma 34:6).

Whether the seed of Christ finds fertile ground or not has less to do with one's activity in church (as with the Pharisees in Luke) than with one's activity in the Gospel, for it's the activity in the Gospel which leads to *the exercise of faith in Christ and his Atonement unto repentance.*

Lehi sees the identical types of believers in his dream of the Tree of Life. Both the Sower parable of Christ and the dream of Lehi explain why some members may fail in their testimony or fall away from the gospel. In every case, the loss of faith or falling away boils down to the individual's testimony and their relationship to the word, which is in Jesus Christ and His Gospel. Nephi said that all 'must liken the scripture unto themselves' (1 Nephi 19:23), so each member should be able to find themselves in the spiritual descriptions offered by Christ and His prophet Lehi. Below, the four groups found in the Parable of the Sower are compared to the four groups in Lehi's Dream.

The Way Side

Matthew 13	1 Nephi 8
19 When any one heareth the word of the kingdom, and understandeth it not, then cometh the wicked one, and catcheth away that which was sown in his heart. This is he which received seed by the way side.	21 And I saw numberless concourses of people, many of whom were pressing forward, that they might obtain the path which led unto the tree by which I stood. 22 And it came to pass that they did come forth, and commence in the path which led to the tree. 23 And it came to pass that there arose a mist of darkness; yea, even an exceedingly great mist of darkness, insomuch that they who had commenced in the path did lose their way, that they wandered off and were lost.

The "way side" represents those who have not taken the necessary time or effort to understand the gospel or develop a personal testimony founded in the Savior and His Atonement. Many individuals, and in particular the youth, rely on the borrowed or reflected light and testimony of parents and others to remain active. When alone and away from the reflected light of others, they will be faced with the trails and temptations of mortality. The "evil one" then finds it easy to "catch away that which was sown in their heart" because they were already lost by their personal lack of understanding of the doctrine of Christ. Lehi adds the insight that they evidently let go of—or didn't bother to use—the "iron rod" that might have helped them remain on the path. The Iron Rod represents the scriptures, which, being the word of God, become the standard of truth that will not fail while on the path toward the Tree of Life. In Lehi' dream, it is made clear that **no one** makes it to the Tree of Life without holding on to the Iron Rod.

Stony Places

Matthew 13	1 Nephi 8
20 But he that received the seed into stony places, the same is he that heareth the word, and anon with joy receiveth it; 21 Yet hath he not root in himself, but dureth for a while: for when tribulation or persecution ariseth because of the word, by and by he is offended.	24 And it came to pass that I beheld others pressing forward, and they came forth and caught hold of the end of the rod of iron; and they did press forward through the mist of darkness, clinging to the rod of iron, even until they did come forth and partake of the fruit of the tree. 25 And after they had partaken of the fruit of the tree they did cast their eyes about as if they were ashamed. 26 And I also cast my eyes round about, and beheld, on the other side of the river of water, a great and spacious building; and it stood as it were in the air, high above the earth. 27 And it was filled with people, both old and young, both male and female; and their manner of dress was exceedingly fine; and they were in the attitude of mocking and pointing their fingers towards those who had come at and were partaking of the fruit. 28 And after they had tasted of the fruit they were ashamed, because of those that were scoffing at them; and they fell away into forbidden paths and were lost.

The "stony places" represent those members who are converted to the church but not the gospel, who quickly and enthusiastically embrace the church culture only to slide back into old ways and habits when things get the least bit hard. Without a foundation in Christ and a conversion to the gospel, they lack the faith to persevere in the face of opposition and quickly find reasons to leave. Embracing their old ways, the pride of their hearts will often lead them to seek the success and honor of men rather than God.

The Thorns

Matthew 13	1 Nephi 8
22 He also that received seed among the thorns is he that heareth the word; and the care of this world, and the deceitfulness of riches, choke the word, and he becometh unfruitful.	31 And he also saw other multitudes feeling their way towards that great and spacious building. 32 And it came to pass that many were drowned in the depths of the fountain; and many were lost from his view, wandering in strange roads. 33 And great was the multitude that did enter into that strange building. And after they did enter into that building they did point the finger of scorn at me and those that were partaking of the fruit also; but we heeded them not. 34 These are the words of my father: For as many as heeded them, had fallen away.

Born in the church, these members are more concerned with the "cares of the world" (the fads, fashion, music and technology) than with developing a relationship with Christ. It has been said that the definition of God is: *The motivating force of one's life*. These members focus their energies on the gods of *this* world: the gods of wood and stone (grand homes), the gods of metal and money (cars and mammon), and the gods of pride and selfishness.

The Good Ground

Matthew 13	1 Nephi 8
23 But he that received seed into the good ground is he that heareth the word, and understandeth it; which also beareth fruit, and bringeth forth, some an hundredfold, some sixty, some thirty.	30 But, to be short in writing, behold, he saw other multitudes pressing forward; and they came and caught hold of the end of the rod of iron; and they did press their way forward, continually holding fast to the rod of iron, until they came forth and fell down and partook of the fruit of the tree.

Christ stated that: "Strait is the gate, and narrow is the way, which leadeth unto life, and few there be that find it" (Matthew 7:14). The 'rule of the remnant' taught throughout scripture implies that there will always be a remnant that will be saved; an unknown number who are listening and remain righteous and faithful in their testimony of Christ and His Atonement, regardless of difficulties and temptations. The faithful remnant are members of the Church who unconsciously display their love of God and their fellow man, it being a natural expression of their discipleship. This love is the fruit of a true faith and testimony in Christ and his redemption. For a testimony to grow and be strengthened, the 'good ground' *must be prepared* to receive the seed. Once there, it should be nourished with the 'good word of God' and the faith of the fathers. This nourishment—scripture, faith, and activity—will eventually lead one to the Tree of Life where the fruit of the Love of God lies waiting for those who are prepared to take and eat.

As the dream of Lehi and the parable of the Sower explains, the enduring and exalting power of true testimony lies in the individual's heart and conversion rather than something external. All that seek the presence of God must actively work to be 'born again' and embraced in the arms of mercy. Everyone who desires the salvation and the mercy offered by the sacrifice of the Savior must not only partake of the fruit of the Tree of Life but remain faithful and endure to the end in that salvation offered by the Son of God.

Chapter 3

An Unfortunate Perspective

A story is told about a man who became very ill. Not knowing what was wrong, his health continued to deteriorate. After a time, he was admitted into the hospital where they began to conduct numerous tests hoping to discover what his illness was and how to restore him back to health. The doctor consulted with the man and his wife and told them that yes, there were some problems, but they would require a few more tests to be run over the next few days. After the tests were completed, the doctor requested to speak with the man's wife...alone.

Taking the man's spouse into another room, the doctor began to explain that her husband could return home. However, the illness the man had was stress related and would lead to his eventual early death, *unless* he could be given time at home without stress of any sort. *If* this condition was met, her husband eventually could regain his normal health. To that end, the doctor recommended that when the husband returned home that she agree with everything he said and not make him want or wish for anything, give him the food he wanted to eat, let him watch his favorite TV shows, etc. In other words, she was to create a stress-free environment for her husband in order to prolong his life and help him recover.

The woman thanked the doctor for his counsel and returned to her husband's hospital room to prepare him for the trip home. The husband, naturally curious, asked his wife what she and the doctor talked about. She somberly looked at him for a moment and said, "You're going to die."

Everything is based on perspective: where you are, what you see, what you think you see, and what you might want to see. In order to make the best decisions, it is best to have multiple perspectives. To that end, the church is organized into presidencies, committees and councils, to present different points of view and experiences for a better decision. This broadened perspective will lead to a better delegation of responsibility.

The more an individual knows and understands about a given subject, the better perspective they will have. The greater the informed perspective, the better the decisions and actions should be.

The issue of disbelief and apostasy affects almost every family in the church today. For some, it already distresses immediate family members or extended families. Eventually, it may touch all. It is frustrating from a researcher's point of view to witness active members of the church question their faith and lose the testimony they once had (or thought they had) over issues that most often stem from a lack of knowledge and ignorance of scripture and doctrine.

Collecting "anti-Mormon" literature has been a personal hobby since the late 1960's, not to question faith or to become a self proclaimed 'apologist,' but to better understand which latter-day saint issues and beliefs are being attacked, and in what manner. What became clear, based on the examination of these attacks against LDS beliefs, is that the issues seldom change. However, the speed and availability with which they are presented to the public has changed considerably. Historically problematic issues are no longer invisible or difficult to find. They are presented to unwary latter-day saints with every turned page and keystroke of the computer. Hence, the need to discuss these matters and address these questions. Every member should be prepared for the intellectual attacks that will come from within and without the church. The purpose of presenting this material is to help parents and individual members of the church recognize the real focus and foundation of a true and lasting testimony. The accomplishment of this goal will require answers from a scriptural point of view that address the basic questions behind this falling away. It is hoped this information will arm adults and youth with the answers needed to pass through the dark mists of doubt.

Lost Sheep

All are familiar with the Parable of the Lost Sheep as taught by the Savior in the New Testament.

> 4 What man of you, having an hundred sheep, if he lose one of them, doth not leave the ninety and nine in the wilderness, and go after that which is lost, until he find it?
> 5 And when he hath found it, he layeth it on his shoulders, rejoicing.
> 6 And when he cometh home, he calleth together his friends and neighbors, saying unto them, Rejoice with me; for I have found my sheep which was lost.
> 7 I say unto you, that likewise joy shall be in heaven over one sinner that repenteth, more than over ninety and nine just persons, which need no repentance. (Luke 15: 4-7)

The "lost sheep" is a phrase used by many to refer to those who have fallen away from the Church and who seem unlikely to return. Everyone cares about family and friends who have begun to tread that path through "the mists of darkness." A sense of duty to support them, love them and build their faith is a major concern and worry for concerned loved ones. Yet all have their agency. And because of this personal agency, none should become too *overly stressed* or condemn or question themselves over an individual's or loved-one's personal choice and use of agency. A parent or family member cannot pray away the agency of a loved one. There is a big difference between the plot and cast of characters in the Parables of the "Lost Sheep" and that of the "Prodigal Son."

Based on the results of a recent survey of disaffected members, it was observed that there has not been as much apostasy or falling away within the Church since the years of apostasy in Kirtland from 1834-1835.[2] Any amount of falling away should cause all active members to stop and ask the questions: Why is this so? What is causing it? What are the issues or questions? Two even more important questions should follow those: 1) What should be done to help those who have already fallen away? 2) How do we pro-actively secure the testimonies of the rising generation?

Some statistics report that about 50% of members between the ages of 18-31 are falling away. Given these statistics, it must be asked: Are parents, grandparents, or even great-grandparents willing to watch half of their family members break away from the influence of the Church and gospel? Is it acceptable for family members to fall away over simple issues and questions, which, if properly understood, would not trouble them? This trend has the potential of leaving a big hole in the hearts of parents who have hoped to see their children become faithful members of the Church. Viewing this current reality, one can only wonder what the fallout will be like in five to ten years. Will whole families and even leaders become casualties?

So why are they leaving? What is really going on? The main issue that is causing good people to fall away from the faith of their fathers has to do with perspective. This more often than not is the result of ignorance, or trusting in their own flesh and education, which is a form of ignorance. Socrates put it clearly when he made the statement: "The only true wisdom is knowing that you know nothing." All too often men begin to trust in their own abilities and experience, even while in the darkened paths of youth. Often this misty path will not begin to clear until death's door is partly open at the end of a long life of learning and experience. Learning begins when the individual realizes how little they really know.

Like the teenager who believes a parent just does not know anything, those who are educated with letters and degrees often believe that they

---

2. Peggy Fletcher Stack "The Salt Lake Tribune" published February 3, 2012.

know better than those who have lived a long and faithful life full of experience. A common intellectual conceit by the spiritually ignorant is the belief that if a spiritual experience or religious manifestation personally hasn't happened to them, that it cannot happen to anybody else. Death is an event all will live through. This formidable door of the unknown will become the great equalizer, educator, and revealer of personal spiritual sacrifice, through which all mankind must pass.

Everyone has a personal outlook on life that becomes the filter through which they process the information and experiences that happen around them. This becomes a 'philosophy of life', which determines how they see the world—their ideas, their beliefs, their faith or lack of faith, their values and their morals. These views on life are not formed naturally at birth but are developed based on experience and the perspectives of those they accept and trust. The wisdom to make good choices is largely a result of experience. The experience that fosters this wisdom is often the result of the bad choices one has made.

This philosophy of life is formed in part by the examples and teachings of parents and teachers. Other significant influences are the books read, music heard and videos/TV watched. Thus the choices we make and the ideas we are exposed to form the lens through which life is viewed and defined. Through that lens, all the beliefs, values, and ideas that we use to make decisions are filtered. The problem is trying to determine which lens will provide the most correct view to live a purposeful life. Will it be the education, philosophies and filters of men, or the teachings of God, scriptures and the prophets? The fool's errand begins when one's own reflection in the mirror is chosen as the defining and ultimate authority.

The Intellectual

It is a well-known statistic that a belief in God decreases as an education of the world increases. As individuals place their trust in the philosophies of men and the two-dimensional reflection in the mirror, purer eternal realities appear out of focus. Today among graduates there is a greater movement away from a basic belief in God toward atheism. The traditional methods used in teaching the gospel to Bible believers may need to change to adapt to the popular philosophies of life embraced by the atheist and the agnostic.

Among the evangelical faiths, statistics show 80% of youth fall away from their faith by the time they graduate from high school, and of those, nearly 70% declare themselves to be atheists. As the world accepts and teaches the philosophies of the Anti-Christ Korihor, church missionaries will need to be better prepared to teach them. Ammon and Aaron, in Alma 18 and 22 respectively, both ask the Lamanite kings if they believe in God. This is done to know where to begin the gospel discussion.

Only mankind was created with a mind that can conceive of a God, the concept of life after death and a reward or punishment given after death for actions performed in this life. The ignorant and non-reasoning animal cannot do this. The dog may roll over for an immediate reward of a treat, but he doesn't roll over with the belief that he will receive the treat after death. The intellectual attainment of the atheist philosophy, which denies this larger picture, can reduce man's nature to that of an animal, with no real understanding of, or interest in, changing one's character for the better. Again, the philosophies of Korihor are worthy of reflection.

If one is to view life through the best lens it should be the lens of the one who created the world, man, and the cosmos. This lens should be the scriptures that a loving God and Father has provided for mankind. Any other philosophy that is not from the creator Himself will have at best a blurred and perhaps a blinded point of view. God is the same 'yesterday, today and forever.' His vision and view for what is best for individual happiness has not changed. This scriptural lens is spoken of in the Book of Mormon:

> 7 And behold, ye do know of yourselves, for ye have witnessed it, that as many of them as are brought to the knowledge of the truth, and to know of the wicked and abominable traditions of their fathers, and are led to **believe the holy scriptures, yea, the prophecies of the holy**

prophets, which are written, which leadeth them to faith on the Lord, and unto repentance, which faith and repentance bringeth a change of heart unto them—
8 Therefore, as many as have come to this, ye know of yourselves are firm and steadfast in the faith, and in the thing **wherewith they have been made free**. (Helaman 15:7-8)

This passage teaches that the understanding of life found in scripture and the lens through which one should view life leads to faith, repentance and a change of character 'wherewith they have been made free.' The understanding of God's perspective endows an individual with enlightenment and a power in this life over the problems of mortality. If those who provide another individual with a philosophy of life use the wrong lens, then the person who accepts those individuals as authoritative will be unable to view life, morals, and values correctly. A person cannot be any smarter than the individual they choose to believe or choose as their authority. If a person's viewpoint or lens is distorted, then their understanding and conclusions about life and eternity will also be out of focus.

Of all the knowledge, information, and truths that exist in the universe, mankind understands only a fraction. And of that fraction, the individual—no matter how smart or how long they may live—has a lifetime so short that only a small portion of available knowledge on the earth will ever be learned. This underscores the conceit of those who declare that they know everything about the temporal and spiritual worlds, that God does not exist, and/or that there is no life after death. These smug claims, and the confidence with which they are touted, make the modern-day intellectual atheist look as ridiculous as those who proclaimed and argued that the world was flat.

Many seek to become a victim of circumstance. They blame Satan or the devil for the wrongs committed in life. But Holy Scripture teaches us that Satan uses mankind to teach his philosophies and way of thinking. He uses people like Korihor, Sherem, Zeezrom, political leaders, judges, teachers and professors, Hollywood celebrities and other popular TV hosts to lead people away from the lens of the scriptures. The New Testament warns all about this:

> 8 Beware (be on guard) lest any man spoil you through philosophy and vain deceit, after the tradition of men, after the rudiments of the world, and not after Christ (Colossians 2:8).

A look at how Satan used the serpent to 'beguile' Eve, and the dialogue between them, will illustrate how her lens and view began to change as the serpent began to teach his philosophy.

> 5 And now the serpent was more subtle than any beast of the field which I, the Lord God, had made.
>
> 6 And *Satan put it into the heart of the serpent* (for he had drawn away many after him), and *he sought also to beguile Eve*, for he knew not the mind of God, wherefore he sought to destroy the world.
>
> 7 And he said unto the woman: Yea, hath God said—Ye shall not eat of every tree of the garden? (And he spake by the mouth of the serpent.)
>
> 8 And the woman said unto the serpent: We may eat of the fruit of the trees of the garden;
>
> 9 But of the fruit of the tree which thou beholdest in the midst of the garden, God hath said—Ye shall not eat of it, neither shall ye touch it, lest ye die.
>
> 10 And the serpent said unto the woman: Ye shall not surely die;
>
> 11 For God doth know that in the day ye eat thereof, then your eyes shall be opened, and ye shall be as gods, knowing good and evil. (Moses 4:5-11)

Eve's first inclination (point of view) was to obey, but the serpent began to convince her to think differently by adjusting words to make her out to be a victim of God. This change of thinking eventually led to partaking of the fruit.

> 12 And **when the woman saw** that the tree was good for food, and that it became pleasant to the eyes, and a tree to be desired to make her wise, she took of the fruit thereof, and

did eat, and also gave unto her husband with her, and he did eat (Moses 4:12).

The view or philosophy presented by Satan through the serpent the convinced Eve that the fruit was what she wanted. Satan seeks to infect the mind and heart by persuading one to believe in his (or his teacher's) philosophies and concepts that are not congruent with scripture and the word of God. Thus, Satan will use others, as he did with the serpent, to blind mankind from the fact that the truth can be found in the scriptures. Unaware, many 'reject the commandments of God to keep their own traditions' (Mark 7:9) thus, "making the word of God of none effect *through your tradition*" (Mark 7:13). Satan clearly understands, as do the atheist professors in the institutions of higher learning, that the first focused effort should be to '*infect*' one's way of thinking by causing one to use the wrong lens or point of view for life. "For as a man thinketh in his heart, so is he" (Proverbs 23:7). The characters that men and women develop is directly influenced by the choice of lens through which they view the temporal and spiritual aspects of life

The eyes and ears are the gateways into the mind. The music that is listened to, what is watched and read, will affect the choices that are made as these things become part of the lens through which life is viewed:

What you have been exposed to determines your thinking
The way you think determines how you feel,
How you feel will determine the decisions you make,
Your decisions will determine your actions,
Your actions will determine your habits,
Your habits will determine your character,
Your character will determine your destination.

To change a destination one must change one's life, and to change a life one must first change the way one thinks. To change the way one thinks, they must first change the lens through which truth is viewed. This is just another way of saying that life is a sum total of what is in the heart, which is based on one's thinking, which is made up of that which has entered the mind through the flood gates of the eyes and ears.

Latter-day Saints may fall from the faith as Satan, in his subtle and sure way, infects their way of thinking. He doesn't control people by making them float in the air or spin their heads. Always using other people, satanic control begins by the introduction of a new philosophy or thought to see if the individual will take *the suggestion,* then change their mind and eat of the forbidden fruit.

Ironically, when the mind is blurred because of the lens through which life is viewed, the supposed enlightened unbeliever will judge the spiritual experiences and the faith of friends, family members and loved ones as ignorance, tradition and the vain imaginations of a frenzied mind (Alma 30:16). Some of those who fall away claim they are free, blinded to the reality that they are now the spiritual captive of the being who seeks the 'misery of all mankind' (2 Nephi 2:8). This "captivity" is embraced by those who place their trust in the theories and traditions of men, secularism and the vast amounts of miss-information.

> 3 But if our gospel be hid, it is hid to them that are lost:
> 4 In whom the god of this world hath *blinded the minds* of them which believe not, lest the light of the glorious gospel of Christ, who is in the image of God, should shine unto them (2 Cor. 4:3-4).

The *spiritual* benefit of living gospel standards provides a power and lifestyle that can lead to eternal joy and exaltation. The *temporal* benefit alone of having a gospel-centered life is a happiness and joy in this life that will *never* be found in the symbolic bars and brothels nor the campuses and corporations of humanity.

Chapter 4

Questions and Control

Many years ago, Martin Luther was asked (as the story goes), "What was God doing before He created the earth?" He replied, "Creating a hell for those who ask that question!" It is well understood by many organizations including governments, military units, businesses, private corporations, religions and others, that the best way to control the masses is to control the quality and quantity of information dispensed. This has always been the case, and no doubt began in the family home as it was discovered that keeping children in the dark about certain things (where the candy is) promotes unity and control. It doesn't matter if it's in a business, at the home or within relationships; there exists specific information that is not always disclosed to others. This may be because it just doesn't matter, or because it really does. Thus, the best way to control the masses is to control the information they receive (be it right or wrong). As the old cliché simply states: "what they don't know won't hurt them." Often, the cost to correct the miss-information, instruction or direction outweighs the benefits of keeping the status quo.

In the early Church of Rome, *only* the Priests could read, interpret or give sermons on the scriptures. That gave them significant power over what was taught and believed. During the 1400's and 1500's in Europe and England, in order to maintain power over the masses, the priests, under the direction of the church, burned at the stake Christian scholars who translated the scriptures into English or German as well as the believers who dared to read them. The crime of possessing non-

Latin New Testaments that could easily be read and interpreted by the lay member was punishable by death. The early Roman church had a vested interest in preserving the status quo: no one but the priest, who had been "trained for the ministry" could deliver the real meaning and message of the scriptures. This way no individual could form a doctrinal conclusion based upon his or her own reading and understanding.

It works the same way in politics. Political candidates promise "transparency" but when elected, they often try to hide anything that might threaten their power and position. They seek to control the media and the electorate masses by controlling or 'spinning' their particular version of the truth. However, because of the Internet, it's much more difficult to hide information than it once was. The intellectual warehouse is open 24/7 and it is open to the public. Since most information can't be hidden any longer, the central question that now plagues the truth seeker is: What and who should be believed?

Questions

Every question is important to the person asking, so consequently there are no 'dumb' questions. Questions that seem trite and redundant to one person may be of huge import to another, and if possible, they ought to be addressed when in the right venue. Teachers have been instructed that when a student asks a difficult question, they should answer the question that the student *should have asked*. This is also the politician's first rule in his or her attempt to control and spin information.

Too often, when difficult questions are asked in a religious setting, the teacher's response is: "You don't need to know that right now" or, "That question is not important for your salvation" or, perhaps more discouragingly, "You just need to exercise a little bit more faith and not worry about that at this time." To the faithful and those with strong testimonies, these answers may be sufficient. The verbal deflections of ignoring questions may have worked in the past, but will not work anymore! Skirting around difficult questions cannot satisfy the inquiring mind today when all answers, right or wrong may easily be found with the stroke of a few keys or a tap on a screen. The deflections will not work without resentment, so parents and leaders need to be aware of the questions that students and family members are asking and be prepared with the answers that they are seeking.

The physical brain has been created with three very important internal traits. *First*, it must completely shut off for a few hours a day. *Second*, if there exists a question in the mind, it is driven to find an answer and will search until it finds one. *Third*, it can only think of one thing at a time. This is the way the mind of man is made and must operate, at least in mortality. God created humanity this way, purposely placing limits on the mind to help mankind seek answers to spiritual questions. The wonderful thing is, we have total control over this divine data processor. The *iPhone*, *iPad* and *iMind* all have a shut-off switch and a control button. If *an individual* doesn't want to think about something, they just have to think about something else. Everyone (excluding the mentally impaired) have control over all thought, making life a true probationary state where one's "words, works, and thoughts" may condemn them at the last day (Alma 12:14). When an important question arises, if the mind cannot find an answer in truth, then it will either make one up or continue to search until it finds a satisfactory answer (true or not) that the mind can understand and accept within its limited ability, knowledge and education. The great plan of salvation is connected to mortality. We all have an innate desire to seek for light and truth while living in this temporal, spiritual and mental probationary state, a state where all have control over their thoughts.

Unfortunately, when a person's relationship and belief in God is compromised by doubt and fear, they typically turn away from God for the answers to their questions. Instead of going to God in prayer seeking for faith, light, and truth, many instead rely on the informational internet god that is "without body, parts, or passions," one that is "everywhere but nowhere," that is so large that it can "fill the world" while at the same time, it is 'so small that it can fit in the palm of the hand.' The God of glory and intelligence; the God of light and eternal truth; the God from which Abraham sought and received his endowment of power, is often overshadowed by the god of this world, instantly viewed and seen in High Definition. The world has changed the name of the instantaneous source of supposed true information, from *"God" to "Google"* where religious concepts and truths about eternity are viewed with suspicion, suppression, and bigotry. Using these hand-held seer-stones the godless humanistic propaganda is heralded as the only real path to life and reason.

With all this information (some true and some false) that is instantly available at the stroke of a key or screen, the questions of our youth must be answered in a way that will strengthen their testimony and faith. The answers must come from a source that they can trust if they are to combat the onslaught that they will face from those seeking to destroy LDS beliefs. Make no mistake, this onslaught will come from all sides: friends, co-workers, and teachers, even from within the church and family.

The point is: if leaders, teachers, parents and grandparents are not answering the questions of the youth, they will find their answers on the Internet or from those who accept Internet answers. The best fortification is for our loved ones to understand the eternal truths that strengthen their faith and testimonies to such a degree, that the information presented by the "anti-Christ" will not affect them.

There was a poem published over 100 years ago called: "A Fence or an Ambulance" that illustrates this notion. The poem tells the tale of a path by a cliff that overlooks a beautiful panorama. Numerous people, while enjoying the view, would fall to their hurt. It is decided by the community to place an ambulance at the bottom of the cliff to be better prepared for the falls that inevitably occur rather than put a fence on the cliff to prevent people from falling in the first place. Their rationalization: it isn't the fall that hurts them, but the sudden stop at the bottom.

A final stanza from the poem:

Then an old sage remarked, "It's a marvel to me

That people give far more attention
To repairing results than to stopping the cause,
When they'd much better aim at prevention.
Let us stop at its source all this mischief," cried he.
"Come, neighbors and friends let us rally:
If the cliff we will fence, we might almost dispense
With the ambulance down in the valley."

The problem needs to be addressed. The intellectual warehouse is wide open. The questions have always been there, but information can no longer be controlled as before. Agency is a wonderful and terrible thing. The members of the church and especially the youth need to be prepared for the path that lies ahead, a path that all must walk to reach the tree of life. There is no spiritually safe detour. All must prepare for the path because the path that must be trod cannot be changed. This path, just as depicted in Lehi's dream, must and will lead through the mists of darkness, traverse along the river of filthy water, and around the great and spacious building where the inhabitants will mock and seek to destroy our faith. These 'mists of darkness' will include those questions that test faith and testimony, which only can be endured and overcome by grasping firmly and holding tightly to the iron rod. The instructions that will lead us through the dark mists of question and doubt have been given and all must prepare for that trek. As President Ezra Taft Benson stated: "It is better to prepare and prevent than it is to repair and repent."(Ezra Taft Benson, New Era, January 1988).

Chapter 5

The Perfect Storm

There are many reasons an individual may decide to leave the religion and faith of their family. However, this discussion will focus on four key elements that have primed the youth and young adults to question their church and faith. Each of these elements are interconnected, although some play a larger part in one's inactivity and apostasy than do others. The four cultural elements that are discussed in this chapter will not address the specific questions and issues that are often used as the reasons for people leaving the church (those will come later). These four concepts are more connected to the social time period in which we live and the basic ideas that provoke the questions that lead to a separation from faith and family.

It should be noted that the spiritual trajectory of a younger generation has the power to influence the spiritual health of preceding generations (see 3 Ne. 1:29, 30). Also, the spirit of apostasy may quickly move throughout a family because of the influence of one member on another. For this reason, there are two types of falling away happening in the church. Influences from *outside* the church seem to affect the youth and young adults more, as the 'good soil' has not yet been prepared for the seed of the gospel to be planted. Influences from *inside* the church tend to affect the older generation. For them, the gospel has already taken root, **but**—feeling intellectually unfulfilled— they sometimes look for someone to blame for a lack of spiritual experiences or knowledge to justify their rejection and unbelief. Some parents might even seek to blame the church or priesthood leaders as they search for reasons why their children might be forsaking the faith.

This chapter's discussion will first address the issues that seem to be affecting the thought process of the Millennials – the generation born between 1980 and the year 2000. Because of their influence, these four issues have also made their way into their parent's generation.

The four *Millennial* mindsets or issues are listed in order of the discussion that follows rather than in order of the greatest causes in the falling away. Some of these influences may affect an individual more than another yet all are somewhat present even if in the sub-conscience mind.

- Education
- Linear View of Time
- Saeculum
- Internet

Education

For the last 30 years, public schools have been teaching students at every level of education to question the authority and antiquated morals of their parents and religious leaders. The education system has been a primary force in promoting humanistic and socialistic philosophies, turning once immoral acts and actions into civil privileges, using terms such as "rights" and "choices." Schools and teachers adopt rules and agendas that are anti-religious, sowing seeds of doubt that overtly and covertly, consciously and subconsciously, cause students to question the morals and beliefs of their parents and religious leaders. Faith-based beliefs and family values based on spiritual laws and commandments are ridiculed and banned from discussion. Thus, as our culture seeks to do away with the concept of God and religious ideals, the Millennial minds have been taught to question the testimony and spiritual experiences of previous generations. Part and parcel of this phenomenon is the linear view of time.

A Linear View of Time

There are three mainstream views of the 'concept of time' that affect how individuals make decisions and form opinions. These are: the "chaotic" view of time, the "cyclical" view of time, and the "linear" view of time.

The *chaotic* view of time would suggest that the events of time are random and follow no pattern or reason. It's the view that one event in time follows another event without cause or effect. This view of time probably stems from ancient times when survival was a day-to-day experience. This view is compatible with the philosophy of life that repudiates the existence of a higher power to whom man must answer.

The *cyclical* view of time is based on patterns and cycles, creating a cause and effect: day/night, the phases of the moon, and seasons that repeat at specific times or intervals. The scriptures have a more cyclical outlook. This cyclical lifestyle was ordained by God to remind man of his relationship and dependence on God for his life and salvation. God even planned events around cyclical time. The Sabbath comes every seven days, marking weeks and months and years.

Smaller cycles may be used to determine larger or longer cycles that may be connected to a person's life. Because of cyclical time there are repeating anniversaries, birthdays, religious festivals and holy days that are renewed by cyclical repetition. These are often connected to some astral-cyclical event that might be sacred to a given culture. All give significance to the cyclical view of time.

Linear time is the view that everything progresses toward a positive perfection, like it does with technology. For example, from a technological linear time perspective, mankind has progressed from carving on stone to the reed and quill pen, and from there to the pencil and pen, then progressing to the typewriter and copy machine. Now, we just speak and the printed word arrives on the word processor ready for the laser printer. What took years of grueling labor copying texts in a monastery with a reed pen, now takes minutes with the copy machine and scanner.

This linear view of time is not limited to technology. Progressive and humanistic thought has applied this view to spiritual and moral issues. The practice of slavery was abolished as people fought for the equality of all men. In western culture, women have progressed from being treated as chattel to enjoying suffrage and equality in all areas. Our government now has laws protecting equal rights regardless of race, gender, color or creed. All of these things, it is argued, come from a linear view of time. However, this perspective is damaging to religious belief when morals and sacred practices of long standing are viewed as the moral relics of antiquity that are irrelevant to modern "enlightened" thinkers. In the linear time view, beliefs in the sacred are dismissed as the "traditions of the fathers" while old immoralities are recast as civil rights. Society has moved from viewing immoral acts as wrong to a liberal linear lifestyle that is bereft of the rules of morality and standards of scripture, fostering the absence of guilt.

What does the concept of linear time have to do with those who might be falling away from the Church today? This view is predicated on the belief that old ideas must give way to new more progressive beliefs. For example, it has been wrongly assumed that the priesthood was given to all worthy males in 1978 because of social pressure. Those holding to the ideas associated with linear time would believe that the Church bowed to the demands of political correctness, lifting all restrictions (In fact, the priesthood announcement came about because of prophecy and scripture, which will be explained in Part II). Since all worthy men now have the "right" to this priesthood, the linear view, being socially progressive, would demand that it's now time that women enjoy the same "right". This kind of thinking ignores the scriptural and doctrinal reasons the Melchizedek priesthood is limited to men in favor of pandering to modern sensibilities and emotions. In the same way, traditional marriage between a man and a woman has been deemed old fashioned. In other religious organizations, social pressure has resulted in the lifting of previously held taboos in the name of being "progressive". In the secular world, the common acceptance of same-sex relationships has been embraced to the point of becoming a cultural norm and civil right.

Members of the Church who hold to the linear view of time do not understand that God *cannot* change, and *does not* change to suit the politically-correct whims of the world. He doesn't live in linear time. There is no time where He lives. The plan of salvation is eternal and existed before the foundation of this world, having been prepared for this world and the next. The commandments are not restrictions but recipes for happiness, thus *"God is the same yesterday, today, and forever"* (Mormon 9:9, Hebrews 13:8, D&C 20:12, 2 Nephi 27:23, 1 Nephi 10:18, D&C 35:1, 2 Nephi 2:4, 2 Nephi 29:9, Moroni 10:19).

A **religion** must be founded upon a *standard of rules* and doctrines that cannot change. That unchangeable *standard is found in the scriptures* and the doctrines contained in them. Where there is no standard upon which truth may be founded, there exists no foundation upon which to build. Anything and everything goes. Those who want the church to "catch up with the times" do not understand the concept of religion. To think one can change religious doctrine that is founded on unchangeable scripture is to believe one can change the mind of God. God cannot change for the better because he is already perfect, and he will not change the perfect to make things worse. God does not conform His will to ours, as He is more concerned about eternal happiness rather than the simple pleasures of mortality. Therefore, a church that will change its fundamental doctrines because of vote, petition, vigil or personal will is not a church or religion based on faith, but a *club*.

Those who want an organization that can be "...tossed to and fro, and carried about with every wind of doctrine, by the sleight of men..." (Ephesians 4:14) should organize or belong to a club where the change of rules or doctrines might be accomplished by poll or vote. Everyone should know what is expected in action and belief before joining a religion. When one cannot, or does not want to adhere to the rules,

50

doctrines, or beliefs of an organized religion, they often remain—
kicking and screaming—in a futile effort to change the organization in
which they have lost, or never had, faith. Agency always prevails in an
individual's belief, and moving on is always an option when
disenfranchised.

In a church without a standard of truth, the linear Latter-day Saint
mindset will be the only rule. Without a standard, the congregation
could vote to make the overflow and cultural hall the smoking section
for Sacrament Meeting. Or perhaps sign a petition making adultery or
same sex relationships an accepted way of life for members and
priesthood leaders in the church. If there exists no unchangeable
standard, then wine tasting might, with a majority vote, be a part of
homemaking meetings. As ridiculous as this sounds, it illustrates the
point that religion must be founded on a standard of truth for salvation.
One who desires to update moral thought and law demanding doctrinal
changes for personal preference should join a club, not a religion.

The Bible implies that that there is a connection between *cyclical and
linear* time, as it opens with: "In the beginning", which indicates that
there *is a beginning* and therefore an end. *"In the end time"* is a phrase
found in the scripture in opposition to the opening words of Genesis.
This beginning and end are connected to the cycles of day and night,
the stars, sun, and moon which are created for times and seasons, days
and years. The 'holy days' of the Old Testament are based on a
cyclical lifestyle of planting and harvest, spring and fall all connected
to the phases of the moon. Yet at the same time, linear time is
connected in the life and progress of the individual: from birth to
death; milk to meat; movement from son to father; and from fallen
man to salvation, each a progression, moving toward the better.

Constantinian Christianity grasped hold of the religiosity of this linear
time concept that evolved out of the Judeo heritage. This view would
argue: *things and people should continue to get better.* Linear time
was wholly embraced by western culture. So much so that today, that
culture seeks to completely abort the cyclical connection that creates a
personal link to God and the sacred. This linear "progressive" view of

cultural practices and beliefs will increasingly cause some immoral acts to become civil rights as people embrace the idea that casting off the shackles of old cultural mores is the more enlightened way. This linear view of time is taught in the schools from kindergarten through the graduate degrees of college. The youth today are primed to accept this view of time as the lens of their culture and a fundamental system for their beliefs.

The Saeculum

A *Saeculum* is a length of time that generally equals the lifespan of a person. This *life's-time* has been defined as about 100 years. This span is basically divided into four equal parts or "ages" of about 22-25 years each. First used by the Etruscans, who were the cultural predecessors of the early Romans, it was believed that because of the four "ages" of man, there were different aspects in the Saeculum (or century) of contiguous generations that would cause similar events to happen at regular intervals. The Romans believed that there existed a specific number of Saeculum for the empire and that both external and internal conflicts and wars, as well as economic prosperity, were based on the Saeculum of contiguous generations.

What does the current falling away and the Saeculum have in common? One of the patterns found in the study of the Saeculum has to do with the pattern of *spiritual or moral revivals* (good and/or bad). This pattern is most apparent in the 40-55 year intervals, or half Saeculum. Here is a brief look at U.S. history in the 40-55 year increments of congruent Saeculum:

1770-1780

A spiritual and *national revival* that established a new country and nation set free from the national and state religions of Europe, with a Constitution based on religious freedom and the equality of mankind.

1825-1835

A great spiritual and religious revival enveloped the United States known as the "Great Revival" and described by Joseph Smith as "an unusual excitement on the subject of religion." The light from the heavens began to shine through the windows of *The Restoration* in the beginning years of this great revival age.

1870-1880

The *Industrial Revolution* forced open the doors of spiritual Babylon even wider as men, rather than nations, became rich at the expense of others. This was a time when morals and ethics were traded for money, which could only lead to spiritual corruption.

1920-1930

Commonly referred to as the *"Roaring Twenties"* the prosperity of the Industrial Revolution and the previous generation erupted into a time of vice and corruption and witnessed the rise of organized crime as Babylon (spiritual wickedness) took control of the hearts of men. Over the next decade, the Great Depression brought this corruption to a screeching halt, leaving the United States on the doorstep of a World War, a cycle outlined several times in the book of Mormon.

1960-1970

"Free Love" was the call of the day as the 'hippie' movement came into full swing, with youth rebelling against the organized "establishment" of government, religion and antiquated morals. On the beaches of Southern California, the **Jesus Movement** heralds a spiritual revival that establishes new 'Born Again' churches as a viable choice of faith.

2010-2020

The *Humanistic Revival, an amoral Saeculum born* of a liberal education and linear view of time, and well-oiled by the creation of the internet, creates *the perfect storm* for the falling away that's taking place in most Christian faiths today. (Humanism is a system of values and beliefs that are based on the idea that people are basically good and that problems can be solved using reason instead of religion, effectively doing away with the need for God.)

History does and will repeat itself without question. All scripture as well as world history reveals that when the evil past is ignored, or forgotten, and even purged by political correctness, secularism, and the linear view of time, the repetition of evil and destruction will be made sure.

These time patterns are also seen in the Old Testament and the Book of Mormon. For example, the length of time between King Benjamin and the wicked work of Alma the younger (Mosiah 26:1), as well as the amount of time after the visit of Christ and the falling away in 4 Nephi. The next big spiritual revolution: +/- 2065?

The Internet

At the time of this writing, the Internet has been around over two decades. Considering that the ages of those who are leaving the church at present and in the greatest numbers are between 18-31, might fuel the supposition there is a definite connection between the two? Where do the youth of today go to find their answers to their questions? They "Google it." When looking for the voice of authority, many reach for the Internet. Answers to almost every question is at our fingertips. While there are some great things contained on the Internet that are beneficial to the spirit and mind, the user must never fall into a false sense of security and trust. As with everything, it can be used for good and evil. In jest it is stated: "If it's on the Internet it must be true!" This is a comic reminder *to be mindful* of who or what becomes one's authoritative voice. In a day when **everyone** has a voice (thanks in large part to the Internet and social media), all must be wary of the calculated manipulation and impurity of others.

Many have begun to search for answers to difficult gospel questions by going to Internet sources. If one cannot (or is afraid to) find the answers from an easy, reliable and convenient human source, the Internet becomes the trusted 'private' source for answers. To assist us in seeking light and truth, God created the human mind to look for satisfying answers to the questions that are deemed important. It doesn't always matter to the organic computer of the mind if the acceptable answer is true or false, it just needs *an* answer that will satisfy the inherent desire to learn the truth. The answer will always be framed within the experience and learning of the individual to be accepted as valid. For this reason, many will accept as truth answers to some questions from sources that have as their objective a desire to distort truth and/or provide false or misleading information.

What once took hours of researching, pouring over encyclopedias and books to find answers to questions, may now be accomplished in an instant with a brief Internet search, bringing up thousands of possible responses that offer many answers and differing viewpoints. Some sites may have the right answers, while others will direct the user to sites that may provide false and incomplete information. Some sites will provide answers that are mostly true, but present them in a way that subtly provokes more questions, sowing seeds of doubt in the mind of the searcher, having the underlying objective of destroying one's faith. With answers so freely available, leaders, teachers, and parents should never respond to difficult questions asked by our youth by saying: "That is not pertinent to your salvation" or "You don't need to know that right now." Doing so will without doubt encourage the youth to go to the Internet.

Statistics show that the age groups with the highest Internet usage are (93%) the 18-30 years olds. That is not surprising since they are the first generation to grow up with the Internet. Today's school age students are taught to use the Internet to find answers to their questions, do research and complete homework assignments from the Internet. Anyone from that age group who has graduated from high school has already been taught to use Google to discover answers to difficult questions. The most difficult thing to remember when using the Internet for information is: *just because it is on the Internet does not mean it is true*. Most Internet sites are created with the objective to persuade, market, or manipulate the mind of the reader. That means the information found may or may not be true. Every individual should be taught that when going to the Internet to find answers to their questions, they should first question the sources, the context, and especially the objective of the site itself. A person will never be any smarter than the person (or website) they choose to believe. It behooves all to pay attention to the point of view and objective of the websites visited. Would one feel physically safe locked in a cage with a hungry tiger? *Of course not.* Then why would one feel spiritually safe believing the content found on websites that are calculated to devour and destroy one's faith and beliefs? Should the Latter-day Saint believe the explanations and statements of an organization or website that has as its objective the destruction of Mormonism? *Of course not*!

As a simple experiment, the words "Mormon Questions" were typed into a Google search, and within 0.2000 seconds, over 8,500,000—that's over eight and half million—different results appeared. How many of those do you think presented a pro-LDS view compared to those that were slanted against the church?

Since every website has an objective, purpose, goal, or opinion to offer the visitor, the user needs to be aware of those designs and purposes. All parents should teach their children to do the same. The Internet is the largest marketing tool that exists, and each website is designed to attract and persuade people that its products or ideas are *true and better than the rest.* These sites often present small truths to entice the visitor, explaining that the information presented is good and desirable and will make one wise, and then suggest that the reader should then go and get others to partake by pushing social media buttons that inform their friends what they believe and accept, inviting them to believe and partake also.

Satan's work is to *stop and destroy* the work of the Lord. However, he can only work through the words, works and marketing of others. There are people, organizations and websites that would do and say anything to destroy one's faith in Mormonism.

- Why would you want to trust a website whose very objective is to destroy the beliefs, teachings, and doctrines of a religion that would teach its members to become better fathers and mothers and more productive citizens?
- Why would you put trust in a website that seeks to destroy a religion that teaches that charity is the pure love of Christ, and that one demonstrates faith in Christ by serving and caring for their fellowmen?
- Why would one accept a website designed to destroy a faith and religion that seeks to help keep its members healthy physically, mentally and spiritually?

Nothing good may come from those who seek to destroy. Those who seek to destroy the Church from the inside or the outside should keep the following verses of scripture in mind. At a time when nonbelievers were seeking to destroy the first Church of Jesus Christ, Luke wrote:

> 35 ...Ye men of Israel, take heed to yourselves what ye intend to do as touching these men.
> 36 For before these days rose up Theudas, boasting himself to be somebody; to whom a number of men, about four hundred, joined themselves: who was slain; and all, as many as obeyed him, were scattered, and brought to naught.
> 37 After this man rose up Judas of Galilee in the days of the taxing, and drew away much people after him: he also perished; and all, even as many as obeyed him, were dispersed.
> 38 And now I say unto you, refrain from these men, and let them alone: for *if this counsel or this work be of men, it will come to naught:*
> 39 But *if it be of God, ye cannot overthrow it*; lest haply ye be found even to fight against God. (Acts 5:35-39)

Luke explains: 'It's a waste of time to try to destroy that which is of God, for if the work is of God it cannot be destroyed, and if not of God it will come to naught on its own, without any help from man.'

The liberal education being offered by the public schools and the linear view of time, coupled with the generational Saeculum and the profusion of questionable information on the Internet, all play a part in Satan's objective of destroying faith in God. The *perfect storm* of apostasy has arrived. Unaware, many who are falling away believe that the supposed true answers they have found to difficult questions in their electronic searches is what separates them from the faith of their fathers. The right and true answers to these questions do exist. There are answers that will strengthen their faith. The problem: many know not where to find the answers. This storm of faith affects almost every family in the church as the youth, young families, and even many older adults are choosing a different path of faith. The Book of Mormon teaches about the doctrine of agency and states multiple times that 'there was no law against a man's beliefs, only his crimes.' Religious freedom is based on the doctrine of equality and choice. Agency for the individual is the greatest gift God has promised and provided to man. That same individual agency often causes the greatest pain that a loving parent can endure.

Chapter 6

The Hope of Loved Ones

Those who believe they have eternally lost a loved one because of apostasy from the church and the gospel need to understand the concept of *agency* and how it works. Almost all of the emotional pain a person goes through in this life is because someone else is exercising his or her agency. Some teach that it was Satan's plan to stop all from sinning, but in reality God's plan of salvation was to guarantee that everyone could sin if they choose. The plan of Satan was to destroy the agency of man, which was an evil plan that made him unable to remain in the presence of God.

> 3 Wherefore, because that Satan rebelled against me, and sought to destroy the agency of man which I, the Lord God, had given him, and also, that I should give unto him mine own power; by the power of mine Only Begotten, I caused that he should be cast down (Moses 4:3).

When children are in the home, a parent can teach, discipline, and even force children to do things against their will. Once children are out of the home and on their own, the parents' role changes from *teacher* to *counselor*—and then, only when the children ask for it. Parental control has a time limit. Everyone has agency and eventually every child can and will make their own choices, decisions and actions.

One primary focus of the church is to do work for the dead in the context of providing the ordinances of salvation and exaltation. This activity exists because of the revelations received through Joseph Smith, found in the Doctrine and Covenants. Doing work for the dead is a valid endeavor because the spirit world is a continuation of our probationary state, where all will have the opportunity to work out their own salvation. If the spirit world were not a continuation of this probationary state, then work for the dead would be pointless.

Learning, faith and repentance continues beyond the veil. A perfect understanding of the Gospel and plan of salvation is required before one can be judged. Working out our salvation requires a perfect knowledge and understanding. Joseph Smith taught that a "person could gain salvation no faster than they gain knowledge" (*TPJS*, p. 217). A *perfect knowledge* is a requirement for true agency to exist.

All the spirits who have and will come to this earth could not make a choice in the council of heaven without first knowing how good *and* bad this life could be. Every spirit would be required to understand *perfectly* the potential of salvation and redemption as well as what it would *feel* like to suffer sicknesses, and illnesses such as cancer, leukemia, all manner of diseases, all physical abnormalities and pain. All spirits would have to know exactly what the emotional pain would be like to lose a spouse, or a child both physically and spiritually before a choice could be made to come to this earth. (That perfect knowledge could come from a loving God even without participating in the physical experience, for "all things are possible with God" especially in the environment of God.) Perhaps it was not required to know what specific experiences each individual would participate in during life, but every spirit *must have known and understood* the pain of life and how bad it *could* be. If this were not true, one could cry "foul" or "timeout" declaring that if they had known how bad it was going to be on earth they would have made a different choice. A *perfect* knowledge and *perfect* understanding of how bad life could be, would be required before an intelligent choice could be made based on agency. If this were not the case, then the 'agency' of mankind would have been compromised by God Himself, for it is the same exercise of agency for which Satan and his followers were cast out.

An individual who understands this perspective receives power and hope over mortality as they awaken to the realization that they don't have trials and tribulations—they have a life. This life, with its limitations and infirmities of body, mind, and spirit, were perfectly understood, and all spirits that receive a physical body willingly agreed to participate in this painful mortality. Understanding the potentials of futurity (exaltation) and the pain and suffering of life is the only way that the individual spirit could make an intelligent, informed choice to participate in the plan of salvation and happiness. Understanding this, God could never be blamed for the grievances and sufferings of mortality.

Likewise, the casting out of Satan and the third part of the spirits that were to come to this earth could not take place unless and until they understood *perfectly* the consequences of their actions and choices. Again, if this were not true, their punishment would be unjust, because their agency would have been compromised and God would cease to be God.

Agency's requirements apply to the hereafter as well. Once dead, if an individual spirit were to be judged or placed in any kingdom without first having a perfect understanding of the Atonement, the plan of salvation and the gospel of Jesus Christ, without any misunderstanding or misconception, their agency would be compromised and the judgment unjust. Therefore, every spirit must know and understand perfectly of Christ and his gospel before making a choice to accept or reject the plan (this is the reason why we do work for the dead). Having a perfect knowledge of the gospel is no guarantee one will choose to be redeemed, but a perfect knowledge is required to make a choice. As the pre-mortal Lord tells Alma: "And then shall they know that I am the Lord their God, that I am their Redeemer; but they would not be redeemed." (Mosiah 26:26). The perfect knowledge is first required to make an informed choice for agency to exist.

This complete and perfect understanding and comprehension of the gospel, plan of salvation and the Atonement cannot occur in mortality (Moses 1:5). Even those who understand the gospel on earth will still need to learn more on the other side of the veil. A perfect understanding is impossible here no matter the education, station or faith in life, and because of this Alma declares: "there *must needs be* space (time) betwixt the time of death and the time of the resurrection" (Alma 40:6, see also verses 9, and 21). This space or time is required so that all in the spirit world may come to a perfect understanding of the gospel of Jesus Christ without any misconception. This, that all may be judged with a perfect knowledge and bright recollection so that their agency will not be compromised and their judgment will not be unjust.

> 30 But behold, from among the righteous, he organized his forces and appointed messengers, clothed with power and authority, and commissioned them to go forth and carry the light of the gospel to them that were in darkness, *even to all the spirits of men*; and thus was the gospel preached to the dead.
> 31 And the chosen messengers went forth to declare the acceptable day of the Lord and proclaim liberty to the captives who were bound, *even unto all who would repent of their sins and receive the gospel.*
> 32 Thus was the gospel preached to those who had died in their sins, *without a knowledge of the truth, or in transgression, having rejected the prophets.*
> 33 These were taught faith in God, repentance from sin, vicarious baptism for the remission of sins, the gift of the Holy Ghost by the laying on of hands,
> 34 *And all other principles of the gospel that were necessary for them to know in order to qualify* themselves that they might be judged according to men in the flesh, but live according to God in the spirit.
> 35 And so *it was made known among the dead, both small and great, the unrighteous as well as the faithful,* that redemption had been wrought through the sacrifice of the Son of God upon the cross. (D&C 138)

This time "that must needs be" between death and the resurrection in the spirit world is required so that every spirit might use their agency to learn the gospel and develop the character that is capable of abiding in the glory and kingdom in which they will seek and be satisfied for eternity. It is not a timed test. The exaltation bus doesn't leave at 4:00 pm on Thursday. The process of changing our character takes as long as it takes. The individual will progress as fast as they choose to receive and be obedient to the light and truth available to them.

> 29 And this to the intent that whosoever will believe might be saved, and that whosoever will not believe, a righteous judgment might come upon them; and also if they are condemned they bring upon themselves their own condemnation.
> 30 And now remember, remember, my brethren, that whosoever perisheth, perisheth unto himself; and whosoever doeth iniquity, doeth it unto himself; for behold, ye are free; ye are permitted to act for yourselves; for behold, God hath given unto you a knowledge and he hath made you free.
> 31 He hath given unto you that ye might know good from evil, and he hath given unto you that ye might choose life or death; and ye can do good and be restored unto that which is good, or have that which is good restored unto you; or ye can do evil, and have that which is evil restored unto you. (Helaman 14:29-31)

With a perfect knowledge of the gospel's plan of salvation, all will be resurrected to the glory that they have chosen and prepared themselves for, no matter the kingdom: "...thus they stand or fall; for behold, they are their own judges, whether to do good or do evil" (Alma 41:7).

> 32 ...nevertheless, they shall return again to their own place, *to enjoy that which they are willing to receive, because they were not willing to enjoy that which they might have received.*
> 33 For what doth it profit a man if a gift is bestowed upon him, and he receive not the gift? Behold, he rejoices not in that which is given unto him, neither rejoices in him who is the giver of the gift. (D&C 88:32, 33)

As a parent I want my children to be as happy as they can be. That will be where they choose to be, not where I want them to be. Hell is where a person doesn't belong (and that could be the Celestial Kingdom); heaven is where one desires to be.

> 4 Behold, I say unto you that ye would be more miserable to dwell with a holy and just God, under a consciousness of your filthiness before him, than ye would to dwell with the damned souls in hell. (Mormon 9:4)

Once resurrected, possessed of the characters created by personal agency and the kingdom of glory they have chosen, all will be totally satisfied, never wanting more than they have, having reached their desired potential.

> 111 For they shall be judged according to their works, and every man *shall receive according to his own works, his own dominion,* in the mansions which are prepared; (D&C 76:111)

The pain and suffering for the choices made in life will take place in the spirit world as the spirits learn the plan of salvation. Here they will learn the doctrines and principles of repentance and change and come to a perfect understanding of the Atonement. Aided by a bright recollection of all their guilt and sin, without the fetters and limitations of an imperfect physical body, they will be taught the benefits of the gospel of repentance. All will have an opportunity to accept or reject the gospel and begin the process of changing their character. It is here in the spirit world that the tentacles of a loving God and loving parents will reach out to family members who either do not know of the gospel or have fallen away. Because no judgment can be made unless the gospel is understood perfectly, all will be taught the gospel by their families and loved ones who have already accepted Christ. The reason families are organized here on earth is to assist the spirits entrusted to parents (our children) in their progression toward salvation and exaltation (D&C 68:25). The same sociality will exist in the spirit world, and for the same reasons: It is within the bonds of family love that the gospel is best taught. In the spirit world those who have fallen away will be reminded of what they have been taught and perhaps knew at one time. It will require a broken heart and a contrite spirit provoked by that bright recollection of sin and guilt to help them understand. Nevertheless, all may choose for themselves and accept or reject the gospel truths even after death. Latter-day Saints have been taught by tradition that if the gospel is rejected here on earth, once presented, there will be no other chance for change and exaltation... This is simply not true (see D&C 138, even the righteous need to be taught, see verses 30, 35).

Any suffering for sin or choice will take place before the resurrection and will not endure for eternity (except for the sons of perdition).

> 14 Now this is the state of the souls of the wicked, yea, in darkness, and a state of awful, fearful looking for the fiery indignation of the wrath of God upon them; thus they remain in this state, as well as the righteous in paradise, *until the time of their resurrection.*
> 21 But whether it be at his resurrection or after, I do not say; but this much I say, that there is a space between death and the resurrection of the body, and a state of the soul in happiness or in misery *until the time which is appointed of God that the dead shall come forth*, and be reunited, both soul and body, and be brought to stand before God, and be judged according to their works. (Alma 40:14, 21)

Eventually the suffering of the wicked and those who have rejected the gospel on earth will end, and as explained in scripture, "all sin will eventually be forgiven" (Matthew 12:31).

> 5 Wherefore, I revoke not the judgments which I shall pass, but woes shall go forth, weeping, wailing and gnashing of teeth, yea, to those who are found on my left hand.
> 6 Nevertheless, *it is not written that there shall be no end to this torment*, but it is written endless torment (Because "endless and eternal" is God's name. Also see D&C 19:10-12).
> 7 Again, it is written eternal damnation; wherefore it is more express than other scriptures, *that it might work upon the hearts of the children of men*, altogether for my name's glory (D&C 19: 5-7)

According to God, there is an end to suffering (D&C 19). The only way that suffering could continue for eternity would be if we could remember what we might have had, or the relationships we may have had at one time. The Lord teaches us that after the resurrection our priorities will change and the memories of our former life will fade in importance. "For, behold, I create new heavens and a new earth: and the former shall not be remembered, nor come into mind" (Isaiah 65:17). This change in priority is not only merciful but ensures that all will be satisfied in whichever kingdom they choose. For every kingdom is a kingdom of glory wherein resurrected beings will be able to fill the measure of their creation and obtain their full potential.

Joseph Smith taught that progression requires character change—not only in this life but also in the spirit world as we prepare for the eternities.

> The work in which we are unitedly engaged is one of no ordinary kind. The enemies we have to contend against are subtle and well-skilled in maneuvering; it behooves us to be on the alert to concentrate our energies, and that the best feelings should exist in our midst; and then, by the help of the Almighty, we shall go on from victory to victory, and from conquest to conquest; our evil passions will be subdued, our prejudices depart; we shall find no room in our bosoms for hatred; vice will hide its deformed head, and we shall stand approved in the sight of Heaven, and be acknowledged as the sons of God.
> Let us realize that we are not to live to ourselves, but to God. By so doing, the greatest blessings will rest upon us both in time and in eternity. (*TPJS*, p. 179)

To be worthy of the Celestial kingdom the candidate will be required to love all mankind equally, without being a respecter of persons—in short, like God. As difficult as that seems, it would follow that the Celestial character could not love the children they may have had in mortality any more than *any other* child or person born in any other time and at any other place on earth.

Even though parents may experience emotional pain in mortality as the result of a child exercising his or her agency, parents need not fear for their offspring. We have been assured that all sin will be forgiven and that everyone will know and understand the gospel perfectly before any judgment can take place. It is reassuring to know that whatever happens will, in the end, be the result of choice, made with a *perfect* knowledge. Our children will receive a fullness of the joy for which they have prepared themselves. It is not the responsibility of the parent or priesthood leader to save an individual. The responsibility of both is to teach and make available all that is necessary for the individual to create their own relationship with Christ and the Atonement. This is only possible in the use of their own choice and agency, not the agency of parents and priesthood leaders. Every parent, should want their children to be as happy as they can be, and that will be the kingdom and glory where ***they choose*** and want to be, for hell is where one doesn't belong, and heaven is where one chooses to be.

Chapter 7

By Their Fruits

Christ declared that a true prophet could be determined by his "fruits" (Matthew 7:15-20). What fruits define a prophet? What are the fruits of the prophet Joseph Smith? The obvious ones include the Book of Mormon, latter-day scripture, the church and its priesthood organization and even prophecies and predictions. But the real fruits of a true prophet are described by Moroni in the Book of Mormon as a call to "believe in Christ."

> 16 ...for every thing which inviteth to do good, and to persuade *to believe in Christ,* is sent forth by the power and gift of Christ; wherefore ye may know with a perfect knowledge it is of God.
> 17 But whatsoever thing persuadeth men to do evil, and *believe not in Christ,* and deny him, and serve not God, then ye may know with a perfect knowledge it is of the devil; for after this manner doth the devil work, for he persuadeth no man to do good, no, not one; neither do his angels; neither do they who subject themselves unto him. (Moroni 7:16-17)

Moroni continues to speak of the "fruits" of good and evil:

> 10 Wherefore, a man being evil *cannot do that which is good*; neither will he give a good gift.
> 11 For behold, *a bitter fountain cannot bring forth good water; neither can a good fountain bring forth bitter water*; wherefore, a man being *a servant of the devil cannot follow*

> *Christ;* and if he follow Christ he cannot be a servant of the
> devil.
> 12 Wherefore, all things which are good cometh of God; and
> that which is evil cometh of the devil; for the devil is an
> enemy unto God, and fighteth against him continually, and
> inviteth and enticeth to sin, and to do that which is evil
> continually.
> 13 But behold, that which is of God inviteth and enticeth to
> do good continually; wherefore, every thing which inviteth
> and enticeth to do good, and to love God, and to serve him,
> is inspired of God.
> 14 Wherefore, take heed, my beloved brethren, that ye do
> not judge that which is evil to be of God, or that which is
> good and of God to be of the devil. (Moroni 7:10-14

The fruits of a prophet are not found in the prophet himself or in his character for "there are none righteous no not one" (Romans 3:10) and "none good but God" (Mark 10:18). The real fruit of a prophet is in his testimony and witness of Christ and the Atonement. The true prophet will stand as a witness of Christ at all times, in all things and in all places. John teaches "the spirit of prophecy is the testimony of Christ" (Revelation 19:10). The declaration of a true prophet, then, will be to "come unto Christ" through faith in the Atonement, faith unto repentance, baptism, and the gift of the Holy Ghost.

> 13 And the Lord God hath sent his holy prophets among all
> the children of men, to declare these things to every kindred,
> nation, and tongue, that thereby whosoever should believe
> that Christ should come, the same might receive remission of
> their sins, and rejoice with exceedingly great joy. (Mosiah
> 3:13)

Thus, the fruits of any true prophet are evidenced by his testimony and the resulting relationship converted believers have with the Atonement and the process of salvation. A prophet's fruit can be openly seen in the impact that his witness and testimony has on the character and understanding of the Atonement that his converts have. If the individuals and organizations that focused on destroying Mormonism spent the same time, energy and resources teaching about their faith and testimony of Christ instead of trying to destroy others, their success and conversions to Christ would be a hundredfold.

Latter-day Saints are commanded **not** to 'revile against revilers'. Apologetics, though popular with supposed intellectuals, are not the order of the day (Apologetics is the defense and justification of religious doctrine). The Prophet Joseph Smith taught:

> Let the Elders be exceedingly careful about unnecessarily disturbing and harrowing up the feelings of the people. Remember that *your business is to preach* the gospel in all humility and meekness, and warn sinners to repent and come to Christ. (*TPJS*, p.43)

> Avoid contentions and *vain disputes* with men of corrupt minds *who do not desire to know the truth*. Remember that "it is a day of warning and not a day of many words." If they receive not your testimony in one place, flee to another, remembering to cast no reflections, nor throw out any bitter sayings. If you do your duty, it will be just as well with you, as though all men embraced the gospel. (*TPJS*, p.43)

The truth has no need of defense. The true Christian character does not seek to destroy the faith of others or defend their own beliefs in an apologetic venue (D&C 31:9). A true Christian character loves others and seeks to bring all unto Christ and building their faith in the Atonement, not necessarily to Mormonism: "For all the law is fulfilled in one word, even in this; Thou shalt love thy neighbor as thyself. But if ye bite and devour one another, take heed that ye be not consumed one of another." (Galatians 5:14-15)

The fruits of a prophet are the "fruits of righteousness" (2 Corinthians 9:10; Philippians 1:11), and the fruits of the spirit will be found in the character of the truly converted.

> 16 This I say then, Walk in the Spirit, and ye shall not fulfill the lust of the flesh.

17 For the flesh lusteth against the Spirit, and the Spirit against the flesh: and these are contrary the one to the other: so that ye cannot do the things that ye would.

18 But if ye be led of the Spirit, ye are not under the law.

19 Now the works of the flesh are manifest, which are these; Adultery, fornication, uncleanness, lasciviousness,

20 Idolatry, witchcraft, hatred, variance, emulations, wrath, strife, seditions, heresies,

21 Envyings, murders, drunkenness, revellings, and such like: of the which I tell you before, as I have also told you in time past, that they which do such things shall not inherit the kingdom of God.

22 But the fruit of the Spirit is love, joy, peace, longsuffering, gentleness, goodness, faith,

23 Meekness, temperance: against such there is no law.

24 And they that are Christ's have crucified the flesh with the affections and lusts. (Galatians 5:16-24)

This means the fruits of Joseph Smith or Mormonism are not found in the human frailties of the leaders or the imperfections of history and the growing pains of organizational refinement, but in the *converted members*. The fruits of Joseph Smith and Mormonism are seen in the characters of its members as manifested by their desire to be better people and better Christians. These 'fruits' are evident in the life-changing relationships that exist among them, their God and their fellow man, as taught by the Church of Jesus Christ.

Anti-Mormon websites tend to *focus on historical inconsistencies and the human frailties, imperfections, and statements* of past leaders taken out of context. Their objective is, **first**: to *destroy faith in modern revelation,* and **second**: to *destroy belief in the plan of salvation and happiness.* These sites target personal histories and the policies of a young struggling church to convince the reader that 'Mormons' are brainwashed to believe what they do. Their intention is to snare the unwary and those who are easily swayed in the mistaken belief that "they" can't put anything on the internet that isn't true. The recent attacks are aimed at Joseph Smith and the statements of many of the priesthood leadership of the church. The impetuous apostle, Peter would have never been accepted as a church leader if his historical frailties and flaws were the focus rather than the changed lives that resulted from the divine message he brought.

The test of *classic* literature is always internal, not external. The circumstances under which something was written and the author's personality, habits or imperfections, are not nearly as important as the way the literature makes one feel and how it affects the heart and mind. The real fruits of Joseph Smith are the positive changes made in the Christian and (Mormon) character as their relationship with the Savior and Atonement is deepened by their faith and knowledge.

What is the message of The Book of Mormon? The text speaks for itself of the *internal* test:

> —Which is to show unto the remnant of the House of Israel what great things the Lord hath done for their fathers; and that they may know the covenants of the Lord, that they are not cast off forever—And also to *the convincing of the Jew and Gentile that Jesus is the Christ, the Eternal God, manifesting himself unto all nations*—And now, if there are faults they are the mistakes of men; wherefore, condemn not the things of God, that ye may be found spotless at the judgment-seat of Christ. (Title Page Book of Mormon)

> 25 …I shall deliver up these plates unto him, *exhorting all men to come unto God, the Holy One of Israel, and believe in prophesying, and in revelations*, and in the ministering of angels, and in the gift of speaking with tongues, and in the gift of interpreting languages, and in all things which are good; for there is nothing which is good save it comes from the Lord; and that which is evil cometh from the devil.
> 26 And now, my beloved brethren, I would that ye should *come unto Christ, who is the Holy One of Israel, and partake of his salvation, and the power of his redemption. Yea, come unto him, and offer your whole souls as an offering unto him*, and continue in fasting and praying, and endure to the end; and as the Lord liveth, ye will be saved. (Omni 1:25-26)

Moroni, the last prophet-teacher, sums up the whole purpose of the record as he concludes the history of his people and closes this inspired compilation for the next fourteen hundred years. Every honest and sincere reader can come to no other conclusion than: Christ, the Atonement, and man's relationship with Christ and His gospel are the central messages of the Book of Mormon, and by extension the message of the Prophet Joseph Smith.

> 32 Yea, come unto Christ, and be perfected in him, and deny yourselves of all ungodliness; and if ye shall deny yourselves of all ungodliness, and love God with all your might, mind and strength, then is his grace sufficient for you, that by his grace ye may be perfect in Christ; and if by the grace of God ye are perfect in Christ, ye can in nowise deny the power of God.
> 33 And again, if ye by the grace of God are perfect in Christ, and deny not his power, then are ye sanctified in Christ by the grace of God, through the shedding of the blood of Christ, which is in the covenant of the Father unto the remission of your sins, that ye become holy, without spot. (Moroni 10:32-33)

What is the message and testimony of Joseph Smith?

> The fundamental principles of our religion are the testimony of the apostles and prophets, concerning Jesus Christ, that He died, was buried, and rose again the third day, and ascended into heaven; and all other things which pertain to our religion are only appendages to it. But in connection with these, we believe in the gift of the Holy Ghost, the power of faith, the enjoyment of the spiritual gifts according to the will of God, the restoration of the house of Israel, and the final triumph of truth. (*TPJS*, p.121)

> 22 And now, after the many testimonies which have been given of him, this is the testimony, last of all, which we give of him: That he lives!
> 23 For we saw him, even on the right hand of God; and we heard the voice bearing record that he is the Only Begotten of the Father—

24 That by him, and through him, and of him, the worlds are and were created, and the inhabitants thereof are begotten sons and daughters unto God. (D&C 76:22-24)

Christ **has always been and will ever be** the foundation of Mormonism. Jesus Christ and the Atonement *is the central message* of not only the Prophet Joseph Smith's work but also all scripture, and is the central message of the Church and all priesthood leaders since the First Vision.

Chapter 8

Duped

Christ taught that evil cannot lead people to become good. This important notion should be understood, as many who have fallen away often believe that their parents, grandparents, and in some cases even their great-grandparents, have been duped or brainwashed. In essence, they are silently screaming that their faithful parents and family are ignorant in their faith, testimony and life experiences. Not surprisingly those who fall away always believe themselves more educated and enlightened. This begs the question: Are the *fruits of Mormonism* so difficult to see within their own families? How would their families be different if they were not Mormons? What kind of lifestyle would they be living, and what kind of family relationships would they have if they were not LDS and hadn't been for generations? Think about it! Can people who have been 'duped' or 'brainwashed' for generations produce the fruits of a true believer? In other words, can that which is evil lead people to become good? Not according to Christ:

> 22 And the scribes which came down from Jerusalem said, He hath Beelzebub, and by the prince of the devils casteth he out devils.
> 23 And he called them unto him, and said unto them in parables, How can Satan cast out Satan?
> 24 And if a kingdom be divided against itself, that kingdom cannot stand.
> 25 And if a house be divided against itself, that house cannot stand.

26 And if Satan rise up against himself, and be divided, he cannot stand, but hath an end. (Mark 3:22-26)

17 Every good gift and every perfect gift is from above, and cometh down from the Father of lights, with whom is no variableness, neither shadow of turning. (James 1:17)

18 And I would exhort you, my beloved brethren, that ye remember that every good gift cometh of Christ.... For if there be one among you that doeth good, he shall work by the power and gifts of God. (Moroni 10:18, 25)

There are different levels of inactivity, falling away from the faith, and apostasy. There are those who have embraced an advanced stage of apostasy, becoming so anti-Mormon that they cannot leave the faith of other members alone, even within their own family. Some claim that they have a newfound freedom to "love everyone" but at the same time they harbor anger at the organization that has purportedly "brainwashed" and led their family members astray. It becomes their mission to "save" loved-ones and friends by pointing out the error of their faith and belief. They show their "love" by hacking away at doctrine and dredging up the personal failings of past leaders in an attempt to destroy faith. Spiritual experiences only come to those who are living a life worthy of revelation. Many unbelievers seem not to understand testimony and faith or they would realize that personal spiritual experiences might be the basis for an active member's testimony and faith.

Given that mankind understands only the tiniest portion of all the laws and forces that operate in our universe, it is reasonable to conclude that what any of us know for sure is an infinitesimal part of the whole. In other words, what we know and understand perfectly compared to the knowledge and truth that exists in the universe is minuscule. Yet many assume they know enough about temporal and spiritual domains, dimensions, and unseen realities to make informed decisions about the experiences of other individuals.

No one can judge the spiritual experiences of another. Feelings generated from such an experience are personal and it is foolish to say or deduce that another's spiritual witness or experiences are the effect of a frenzied mind.

The real question is: Who are the ones duped? Those who have the faith and commitment to change their lives for the better, or the one who seeks to destroy the faith of their loved ones? The basis for this rebellion is often, but not always, the desire to live a lifestyle that is incongruent with accepted morality of the Church and their family. The effort by the nonbeliever to enroll and proselyte other family members in this rebellion may stem from loneliness and a desire to not be the only outsider; but more often than not, they seek to satisfy a need to justify their choice. The ego of the natural man must protect itself, seeking some type of justification for falling away. Some become spiritual victims, blaming their disaffection on the supposed wrongs perpetrated against them by ignorant priesthood leaders.

Those who are miserable will seek the misery of those around them (2 Nephi 2:18). Look at the fruits of the active Latter-day Saint and the fruits of the anti-Mormon.

> 16 Wo unto them that turn aside the just for a thing of naught and revile against that which is good, and say that it is of no worth! For the day shall come that the Lord God will speedily visit the inhabitants of the earth; and in that day that they are fully ripe in iniquity they shall perish.
> 20 For behold, at that day shall he rage in the hearts of the children of men, and stir them up to anger against that which is good.
> 22 And behold, others he flattereth away, and telleth them there is no hell; and he saith unto them: I am no devil, for there is none—and thus he whispereth in their ears, until he grasps them with his awful chains, from whence there is no deliverance. (2 Nephi 28:16-23)

The spiritual manifestations that a loving God provides will only come to the prepared heart. Signs and testimonies follow the faith of a believing heart, but only on God's time-table and within the framework of His restrictions and rules. To say or conclude that a believer is 'duped' in their spiritual witness is the epitome of ignorance and arrogance. When an intellectual says that the spiritual realm doesn't exist or that messengers from the other world are not real (because it hasn't happened to them), it is as foolish as saying that the country of England doesn't exist because they have never been there and then scorning the reports of those who have. The weakest of men may be inspired to initiate the greatest of changes.

> 19 The weak things of the world shall come forth and break down the mighty and strong ones, that man should not counsel his fellow man, neither trust in the arm of flesh—
> 20 But that every man might speak in the name of God the Lord, even the Savior of the world;
> 21 That faith also might increase in the earth;
> (D&C 1:19-21)

Only one has walked the earth without sin or imperfection. The Lord has chosen to work with the human frailties' and weakness of mind, body and spirit. God can and does use humanity in their weakness to serve others, and in particular He uses those who have spiritually prepared themselves for the tasks that lie ahead. In truth, those who believe they can judge the reality of the spiritual preparation and experiences of another individual are the ones who are duped.

Chapter 9

The Barriers to Exaltation

Within the pages of The Book of Mormon at least nine (9) different "barriers to exaltation" are found. These are natural and emotional barriers that separate humanity from God and His presence. These barriers often contribute to the cause (hence the word 'barriers') of inactivity, or a falling away from an active life in the church and gospel. Apostasy on the other hand is a complete rejection of doctrine, faith or belief. Often, a complete rejection of the truth and of the church will turn into an *aggressive apostasy*. Aggressive apostates are not satisfied with being inactive, finding a faith in another religion, nor in just having their names removed from the records of the church. Aggressive apostates must attack and destroy the faith of others, and their first targets are usually family members. Why does this aggression exist? Why does it turn into a hatred of history and doctrine? Why is this hatred (by both apostate Mormons and non-Mormons) directed more specifically against Mormonism than against any other faith? What would cause someone to have a spirit that seeks to destroy?

Curiously, the vitriol seems reserved almost exclusively for the Latter-day Saints. Why not attack other Christian churches or non-Christian faiths like Hindu, Islam, Judaism or Buddhism? Would there not be non-conciliatory issues of doctrine, history and leadership statements within these other faiths? Though most apostates of the Church deem it inappropriate to attack the beliefs, faith and doctrine of other religions, they feel no such restraint when it comes to attacking the faith of loved ones. In essence, apostates attack the organization and family unit that made them the people they are. The big question is: Why can't they just leave it alone? If one doesn't believe in the LDS faith, doctrine and principles, why is it so hard to simply walk away?

The scriptures teach us that conflict and contention is of the devil and does not come of God. An LDS fundamental belief is that of *agency*, the ability and freedom to choose one's belief. The good Christian and a true disciple of Christ will not devote time or energy trying to destroy another person's faith in Christ. So why do the malcontents persist? Is it so true that misery loves company and the ego needs justification? Joseph Smith made an interesting observation about apostasy:

> The Messiah's kingdom on earth is of that kind of government, that there has always been numerous apostates,....Strange as it may appear at first thought, yet it is no less strange than true, that notwithstanding all the professed determination to live godly, *apostates after turning from the faith of Christ, unless they have speedily repented, have sooner or later fallen into the snares of the wicked one, and have been left destitute of the Spirit of God,* to manifest their wickedness in the eyes of multitudes. From apostates, the faithful have received the severest persecutions. Judas was rebuked and immediately betrayed his Lord into the hands of His enemies, because Satan entered into him. There is a superior intelligence bestowed upon such as obey the gospel with full purpose of heart, which, if sinned against, the apostate is left naked and destitute of the Spirit of God, and he is, in truth, nigh unto cursing, and his end is to be burned. *When once that light which was in them is taken from them, they become as much darkened as they were previously enlightened, and then, no marvel, if all their power should be enlisted against the truth, and they, Judas like, seek the destruction of those who were their greatest benefactors.* What nearer friend on earth, or in heaven, had Judas than the Savior? And his first object was to destroy Him.... *From what source emanated the principle which has ever been manifest by apostates from the*

true Church to persecute with double diligence, and seek with double perseverance, to destroy those whom they once professed to love, with whom they once communed, and with whom they once covenanted to strive with every power in righteousness to obtain the rest of God? Perhaps our brethren will say the same that caused Satan to seek to overthrow the kingdom of God, because he himself was evil, and God's kingdom is holy. (*TPJS,* p.66. Italics added for emphasis)

What seems clear: When the spirit and testimony of truth is rejected, the heavens withdraw, and when left unto themselves a person will "kick against the pricks, persecute the saints and fight against God."

The Nine Barriers

Before one can begin to repair the rejection of the faith and testimony of a loved one, the reason for the falling away must first be determined.

There are nine barriers to exaltation that are specifically addressed in the Book of Mormon. Some of these barriers are natural events that have separated man from God. Others are based on the pride of mankind, while the last three *Guilt, Willfulness* and *Uncertainty / Ignorance* seem to rise to the top as elements that may cause a willful inactivity and falling away. These three will be discussed in detail following a brief explanation of the first six elements.

1. **The Fall**
   2 Nephi 9:6, The separation between man and God as a result of the First parents partaking of the forbidden fruit.
2. **Physical Distance** (between Heaven & Earth)
   Alma 5:33-35 John 14:21,23, The distance or physical separation between this lone and dreary temporal world and the world of the Gods.
3. **Pride and Vanity**
   3 Nephi 6:15, Pride and vanity is the sin of the Book of Mormon that became a catalyst, leading to destruction.

84

4. **Weaknesses of the Flesh**
2 Nephi 2:29, Galatians 5:16, The flesh and the 'evil therein' that causes man to seek the satisfaction of his desires, appetites and passions.

5. **The Cares of the World**
3 Nephi 13:25, Many are consumed by the concern about being accepted of the world and the supposed securities of a temporal life.

6. **The Deceitfulness of Riches**
Mormon 8:38-39, Men trust in Mammon and the wealth that provides a supposed happiness and security.

7. **Guilt**
8. **Willfulness**
9. **Uncertainty / Ignorance**

Guilt results from understanding the doctrines of truth and righteousness and then acting in opposition to what you know is right.

> 17 Now, how could a man repent except he should sin? How could he sin if there was no law? How could there be a law save there was a punishment?
> 18 Now, there was a punishment affixed, and a just law given, *which brought remorse of conscience unto man.* (Alma 42:17-18)

Without knowledge of right and wrong there can be no guilt or remorse for thoughts or actions. Guilt and remorse, like pain, may be useful and corrective.

> 22 But there is a law given, and a punishment affixed, and a repentance granted; which repentance, mercy claimeth; otherwise, justice claimeth the creature and executeth the law, and the law inflicteth the punishment; if not so, the works of justice would be destroyed, and God would cease to be God.
> 23 But God ceaseth not to be God, and mercy claimeth the penitent, and mercy cometh because of the Atonement; and the Atonement bringeth to pass the resurrection of the dead; and the resurrection of the dead bringeth men back into the presence of God; and thus they are restored into his

> presence, to be judged according to their works, according to
> the law and justice. (Alma 42:22-23)

Guilt is good the same way that pain is good. If humans did not feel pain most would die an early death. A person with appendicitis who felt no pain would just suddenly die. Pain is the body's way of signaling when something is wrong with the workings of the physical body. In the same way, guilt was built into man so that he would be able to know when he needs spiritual correction. When Adam was created, the Lord pronounced him to be "very good." After the primal father did something he had been commanded not to do, Adam tried to hide from God, indicating that he felt guilt. This single passage in Genesis reveals that guilt or remorse was placed in him by God. Unfortunately, the discomfort and shame that accompanies guilt may keep some from participating in church activities and meetings.

> 3 Then will ye longer deny the Christ, or can ye behold the Lamb of God? Do ye suppose that ye shall dwell with him under a consciousness of your guilt? Do ye suppose that ye could be happy to dwell with that holy Being, when your souls are racked with a consciousness of guilt that ye have ever abused his laws?
> 4 Behold, I say unto you that ye would be more miserable to dwell with a holy and just God, under a consciousness of your filthiness before him, than ye would to dwell with the damned souls in hell. (Mormon 9:3-4)

Remember, Hell is where you don't belong (and that could be the Celestial Kingdom), but a *bright recollection of guilt* will cause one to shrink away from God, creating an eternal separation from those unlike themselves.

Willfulness is open rebellion. To knowingly sin without any conscious feelings of guilt or remorse is open and willful rebellion. Many choose to participate in a lifestyle that is contrary to that outlined by scripture and commandment. Essentially, the desire to live this lifestyle is greater than their commitment to gospel principles. In order to minimize the chance of feeling guilt, they often remove themselves from any environment that would place moral restrictions—real or imagined—on their actions. The person who does not want to change or does not have a desire to believe in truths that will inspire this change will continue to rebel and resist reform. The choice is always theirs.

> 29 And this to the intent that whosoever will believe might be saved, and that whosoever will not believe, a righteous judgment might come upon them; and also if they are condemned they bring upon themselves their own condemnation.
>
> 30 And now remember, remember, my brethren, that whosoever perisheth, perisheth unto himself; and whosoever doeth iniquity, doeth it unto himself; for behold, *ye are free; ye are permitted to act for yourselves; for behold, God hath given unto you a knowledge and he hath made you free.*
>
> 31 *He hath given unto you that ye might know good from evil, and he hath given unto you that ye might choose life or death;* and ye can do good and be restored unto that which is good, or have that which is good restored unto you; or ye can do evil, and have that which is evil restored unto you. (Helaman 14:29-31)

The desire to sin without guilt is nothing more than the degradation of human potential to that of an animal. Being acted upon by the environment reduces a godlike nature to that of animal instinct. That which separates man from the animal kingdom is the ability to "act in futurity." This is the ability to make a decision or perform an action in view of a reward or punishment that will not take place until after death. To 'act in futurity' requires one to realize that reality exists only in the realm of the sacred, and to acknowledge an accountability to God that transcends this life.

Those who willfully rebel often question the standards of Mormonism as a way of justifying their inactivity and lack of participation in the Church. The willful maverick is generally not an aggressive apostate, just one who doesn't want to be found in the LDS record system. They don't want to participate or to be active because that would require them to change their lifestyle in a way they are not yet willing to do.

Uncertainty / Ignorance is the barrier that is seen in those who just don't know or understand the gospel of Jesus Christ. Sometimes this is because of family traditions, interpretations and opinions with which they have grown up. When confronted with challenges to their beliefs, these are they who want to know something but don't know how or where to find the answers. They often don't understand how to view what has been presented to them and after consulting the Internet, they feel lost in the whirlpool of anti-Mormon websites and teachings. These members are usually sincere in their desire to know more and they are the easiest to teach light and truth to once they begin to seek for it. Many will have what the scriptures call a "broken heart and a contrite spirit" which is the Lord's requirement of a personal spiritual preparation necessary for learning light and truth.

A cardinal rule of teaching, in or out of the Church, is that it is virtually impossible to teach those who do not want to know. Seeking further light and truth requires a broken heart and a contrite spirit. Before learning can take place, one has to come to an honest recognition of one's ignorance. This recognition of the need for further light and truth is the first step to spiritual enlightenment. Nevertheless, some people will *fanatically* choose to remain uncertain or ignorant, verifying the missing beatitude: "Blessed are the ignorant in thinking they know everything." A fanatic was aptly defined by Winston Churchill as "one who will not change their mind and will not change the subject." It has been said that: it's not what you don't know that gets one in trouble, it's *what one knows for sure, that isn't true* that causes the problems.

Guilt, Willfulness and Ignorance are often the main elements that lead to inactivity. Most of the falling away today is because of ignorance and the lack of an understanding of the responsibilities of the priesthood and the purpose for the organization of the Church. To blame God, the priesthood or the church for a lack of spiritual experiences is an overt manifestation of one's ignorance of scripture and doctrine. There is always only one to blame for the lack of a relationship with Christ and the Atonement. Guilt is the byproduct of the willful sins of the flesh, while ignorance coupled with tradition and opinion can cause many to be led astray. As simple as it seems to correct, ignorance lies at the cause of many who are falling away from the church. As the old saying goes: 'Samson slew a thousand Philistines with the jawbone of an ass, and many a testimony has been slain the same way.'

Chapter 10

Satan's Control

According to the Book of Mormon there are two specific ways by which Satan gains control over mankind; the first is the will of the flesh and the second is ignorance. Both are obviously based on the *agency* that mankind has been guaranteed by God. The choice to satisfy the desires, appetites and passions of the flesh develops a character described by King Benjamin as the "natural man."

To seek for light and truth, with a *desire* for understanding, requires a broken heart and contrite spirit. This *desire* is another choice that is made by the same agency. The desires of the flesh and the desires of the mind are the two appetites of life an individual has total control of, making this life a truly probationary state. Because of this, the Book of Mormon declares that all will be judged according to one's words, works and thoughts (unless physically or mentally handicapped).

The Flesh

After Lehi describes our dual natures and the need for opposition in all things, he concludes his discussion on agency and choice and the evil of the flesh:

> ...and not choose eternal death, according to the *will of the flesh and the evil which is therein, which giveth the spirit of the devil power to captivate*, to bring you down to hell, that

he may reign over you in his own kingdom. (2 Nephi 2:29)

Everyone inherits at birth a physical machine called a body, which in its infancy is created to seek satisfaction for every need and want of body and mind. As the infant begins to grow, so does the desire and sometimes the ability to manipulate others to satisfy every appetite, desire, or passion. The natural man becomes awakened and begins to develop a character that must be overcome. By the time the age of accountability is reached, every trick in the book has been learned and perfected. When 8 years old, the child of record is baptized, receives the Gift of the Holy Ghost and is confirmed a member of the Church of Jesus Christ. After years of sharpening manipulative skills, this new Christian will spend the rest of his or her life trying to stop thinking about themselves, learning respect for others, and exercising self-control and restraint. Moving from this pride to humility turns out to be harder than it sounds because the 'machine' (the natural man running the show in the background) wants what it wants. There seems to be no way out of this dilemma because we live in a physical world with a physical body that has its own physical needs and desires. This wonderful body, hardwired with natural man inclinations from youth and a prideful nature, is vulnerable to temptations of the flesh, which Satan exploits. Lehi teaches his children about agency and the "will of the flesh and the evil which is therein" which will give the "devil power to captivate" our bodies, our spirits, and our minds. The only way out is through the action of choice. For the rest of our mortal lives—a choice at a time—all must learn how to bridle their physical passions and submit their will to God (Alma 38:12) for exaltation requires all to eventually develop the same will that God has.

Ignorance

The second way Satan gains power over us is *ignorance.* Spiritual ignorance may be the result of our own choices. However, it can also be the result of evil designs by others who seek control over us. When Nephi sought to understand the vision his father had, it was revealed to him how Satan gains power over mankind when they are intentionally left ignorant of the truth. Speaking of spiritual ignorance, the verse below discusses the plain and precious things that were removed from the Bible:

> And after these plain and precious things were taken away it goeth forth unto all the nations of the Gentiles... thou seest—because of the many plain and precious things which have been taken out of the book, which were plain unto the understanding of the children of men, according to the plainness which is in the Lamb of God—and *because of these things which are taken away out of the gospel of the Lamb, an exceedingly great many do stumble, yea, insomuch that Satan hath great power over them.* (1 Nephi 13:29)

As this verse explains, Satan began to have power over the people because they did not have the true points of the Lord's doctrine and His word. Without plain and precious truths, many are vulnerable to error, giving Satan power over them. The control of information and truth can only lead to a 'non-belief' or 'wrong-belief' and therefore a fall from the truth. Since Satan was a liar from the beginning, and is the 'father of all lies' (2 Nephi 2:18) the control of information, and the ignorance it inevitably leads to, may cause some to fall away. Without an understanding of truth, by choice or by design, there will eventually be problems.

People who harden their hearts against the truth when it is presented (pride), believing they already know it all (the definition of ignorance), are described by Alma as being in the "chains of hell."

> 10 And therefore, he that will harden his heart, the same receiveth the lesser portion of the word; and he that will not harden his heart, to him is given the greater portion of the word, until it is given unto him to know the mysteries of God until he know them in full.
> 11 And *they that will harden their hearts, to them is given the lesser portion of the word until they know nothing concerning his mysteries; and then they are taken captive by the devil,* and led by his will down to destruction. Now *this is what is meant by the chains of hell*. (Alma 12:10-11)

"The only good is knowledge and the only evil is ignorance," said Socrates. "The wisest among us (concerning God's understanding) are only fools until they learn to recognize their ignorance." A person cannot expect to know the mysteries of God until they first realize just how little they know (a broken heart and contrite spirit). One cannot even begin to understand the processes of knowing and learning if they believe they already know it all. "A man cannot be saved any faster than he gains knowledge," taught Joseph Smith (*TPJS* pp. 217, 357). Thus, beside one's righteousness, the surest path to *exaltation* is the conscientious and continued search for light and truth. At the opposite end of the spectrum, those who believe they have already acquired all of the spiritual knowledge they need, or who are complacent in their spiritual ignorance, are setting themselves up to have the *end of their progression made sure.* All need to be seeking for further light and knowledge, just like Abraham, whose desire for more led to the covenants and knowledge of the fathers being given to him. For Abraham, good was not good enough—he wanted *more* light and truth. He understood that if he only knew what God knows, he would act the way God acts and do what God does. Abraham saw the link between righteousness and the obtaining of knowledge.

> 2 And, finding there was greater happiness and peace and rest for me, I sought for the blessings of the fathers, and the right whereunto I should be ordained to administer the same; *having been myself a follower of righteousness, desiring also to be one who possessed great knowledge, and to be a greater follower of righteousness, and to possess a greater knowledge,* and to be a father of many nations, a prince of peace, and *desiring to receive instructions, and to keep the commandments of God,* I became a rightful heir, a High Priest, holding the right belonging to the fathers. (Abraham 1:2)

Because Abraham was "perfect in his generation," the Lord's command to Latter-day Saints in this generation is to "go and do the works of Abraham" (D&C 132:32; John 8:39). As the "Father of the Faithful," Abraham represents every man, as every man *should be.*

A statistic has shown the higher an education one has, the less religious one becomes in their demonstration of faith and belief in God. This is because the educated often place their confidence in their own education and knowledge (their own arm of the flesh), making them less teachable. Jacob warns us about the pride of education:

> 28 O that cunning plan of the evil one! O the vainness, and the frailties, and the foolishness of men! *When they are learned they think they are wise, and they hearken not unto the counsel of God,* for they set it aside, supposing they know of themselves, wherefore, their wisdom is foolishness and it profiteth them not. And they shall perish.
> 29 *But to be learned is good if they hearken unto the counsels of God.* (2 Nephi 9:28-29)

With insight born of experience, Hugh Nibley remarked: "it was better to be in the company of a smart baby than a stupid department dean," as one might more successfully teach a crying baby than an arrogant professor. As this dispensation began, Joseph Smith was told by the Lord that one purpose of the restoration was to teach man that he "should not counsel his fellow man, neither trust in the arm of flesh" (D&C 1:19). Our trust should always be in the Lord's counsel and not on our own understanding (Proverbs 3:5).

There is nothing wrong with obtaining an education. The warning in scripture is about the *pride* that often accompanies education, letters and degrees. The more one knows and understands about a given subject, the better and more correct one's decisions and choices about that particular subject will be. Mortal life is but a fleeting moment and dream compared to eternal life. What subjects and truths will be relevant through the eternities? What knowledge will do the most good in immortality? Remember, *reality exists only in the realm of the sacred.*

There are some in the Church who believe if they haven't heard it before that it can't be true, and that everything that should be known is found in the manuals. There are others who cannot be taught because of their trust in the arm of flesh belonging to themselves or others.

The rejection of light and truth is a perilous decision. Joseph Smith stated that a man would be "held more accountable for what he doesn't believe than what he does believe" (*TPJS* p 374). The desire for further light and truth is a character trait that separates the prophets and patriarchs from all others.

> 29 Wo be unto him that shall say: We have received the word of God, and we need no more of the word of God, for we have enough!
>
> 30 For behold, thus saith the Lord God: I will give unto the children of men line upon line, precept upon precept, here a little and there a little; and blessed are those who hearken unto my precepts, and lend an ear unto my counsel, for they shall learn wisdom; for unto him that receiveth I will give more; and from them that shall say, We have enough, from them shall be taken away even that which they have.
>
> 31 Cursed is he that putteth his trust in man, or maketh flesh his arm, or shall hearken unto the precepts of men, save their precepts shall be given by the power of the Holy Ghost. (2 Nephi 28:29-31)

Some may say, "A Quad, a Quad, I have a Quad...we need no more." Others might believe, "If it does not come from Deseret Book, it cannot be true and should not be read." Brigham Young once said that if there were truth in Hell that he would go there to get it (JD 14:160). Even the Thirteenth Article of Faith teaches that we should be seeking for all that is praiseworthy and of good report. The LDS bookstore does not have a monopoly on all truth or righteousness!

The tendency among members is to feel satisfied and secure in the knowledge they have, crying "all is well." To shut one's ears, heart and mind to the issues of today that affect our children or grandchildren is the apathy of apostasy. All should be looking for ways to strengthen the testimonies of Christ and the Atonement in ourselves and every member of our family, not turning a blind eye to the questions and issues that plague this generation. Nephi warns about the attitude and apathy of apostasy:

21 And others will he pacify, and lull them away into carnal security, that they will say: All is well in Zion; yea, Zion prospereth, all is well—and thus the devil cheateth their souls, and leadeth them away carefully down to hell. (2 Nephi 28:21)

24 Therefore, wo be unto him that is at ease in Zion!
25 Wo be unto him that crieth: All is well!
26 Yea, wo be unto him that hearkeneth unto the precepts of men, and denieth the power of God, and the gift of the Holy Ghost! (2 Nephi 28:24-26)

Nephi's prophetic warning to all believers is to not let their spiritual guard down. None should think they are safe just because they might live in Happy Valley or any other part of Zion. The evil one never sleeps nor does he take vacations. No one, from prophet to pauper, can afford to become complacent because of prosperity, ease, or education. The location of a Temple and working therein is no indication of the righteousness and spiritual security of the members in that area. This same problem and issue caused the Children of Israel to be taken captive as they began to trust in the 'lying words' of complacency and security:

4 Trust ye not in lying words, saying, The temple of the Lord, The temple of the Lord, The temple of the Lord, are these.
5 For if ye thoroughly amend your ways and your doings; if ye thoroughly execute judgment between a man and his neighbor;
6 If ye oppress not the stranger, the fatherless, and the widow, and shed not innocent blood in this place, neither walk after other gods to your hurt:
7 Then will I cause you to dwell in this place, in the land that I gave to your fathers, for ever and ever.
8 Behold, ye trust in lying words, that cannot profit.
9 Will ye steal, murder, and commit adultery, and swear falsely, and burn incense unto Baal, and walk after other gods whom ye know not;

10 And come and stand before me in this house, which is called by my name, and say, We are delivered to do all these abominations?
11 Is this house, which is called by my name, become a den of robbers in your eyes? Behold, even I have seen it, saith the Lord.
12 But go ye now unto my place which was in Shiloh, where I set my name at the first, and see what I did to it for the wickedness of my people Israel.
(Jeremiah 7:4-12)

The Lord told Jeremiah to tell the children of Israel not to trust that all was well in Zion just because there was a Temple across the street, or close by. Their attitude was not unlike ours today: "We are not only in Zion, we *are* Zion, and His temple is here so we are safe, and there is no need to worry." By way of warning Jeremiah told them to remember what happened in Shiloh (v14), *(Shiloh was the spiritual capital of the nation, in the land of Ephraim; the place where the Tabernacle and the Ark of the Covenant was, until the wickedness of Israel caused the Ark to be lost (Bible Dictionary p 773).*

Nephi's and Jeremiah's warning was and is directed to those who know the gospel law. Their message and warning is as valid today as anciently since the 'nature and disposition of man has not changed'. The Saints in Far West, Nauvoo, and Independence fell into the same complacent trap as the Israelites did in the Old Testament and The Book of Mormon. Spiritual security exists only for a little season, because the gospel is new to every generation.

Chapter 11

The Foundation of Testimony

Testimonies are not inherited. Children will not have the same testimony their parents have, nor will the rising generation have the same knowledge of truth the previous generation had. The experiences that build and strengthen testimony are different for every generation and are individually acquired. Opportunities for learning, the pool of friends and peers, and the community where one is raised can all influence the strength of a testimony. The testimony of one spouse may be different than the partner because of learning and education. The experiences of a mission or service, even the friends and social circles can make a difference within a marriage. The time period in which one is born, and the young men and young women that our children may grow up with, will influence the testimonies of our youth. One age group in a ward may all go on missions while few or none will go in the next year.

The scriptures teach over and over that the gospel is new to each generation. They also teach that faith is individually acquired, the same as a testimony of the gospel of Christ and His Atonement. Parents should not expect children to have the same testimony and faith that they have. A testimony is not genetic nor can it be wrapped in boxes to be presented to children on their eighth birthday. Therefore parents should seek to provide an environment where their children can have the spiritual experiences that will be the basis of their own testimony. As children have experiences that help them recognize the difference between spiritual feelings and emotions, they will develop a confidence in their own testimony that will help them stand strong in the face of opposition and doubt As the youth grow mentally and spiritually they will have questions that are unique and specific to their personal spiritual needs and problems. They will always seek answers to their questions in their quest and search for faith and truth. Just as there is a period of growth physically, there is also a time for spiritual growth and the development of their faith and testimony. The gospel is new to every generation, and the parents, adults, and priesthood leaders need to be ready for it.

The strength of a testimony is only revealed in the face of challenges and opposition. Someone who basks in the security of 'borrowed light' will not have developed the spiritual strength to stand strong under spiritual attack. For the youth to survive the wickedness and calamities of the last days, it will require more than just making sure they are in church every Sunday. Parents and teachers will need to put more energy into the youth's spiritual upbringing than even they received. The second law of thermodynamics is alive and well in all aspects of one's faith and testimony.

Because of entropy (a gradual decline in order) in today's world of greater temptation and distraction, the parents should be more exact in keeping the commandments, and more committed to living the gospel than the previous generation. If not, entropy wins, and all could lose ground. An increase of energy, example, faith and testimony is the only way to offset the decay of entropy. If parents are telling their children what to do while modeling something contrary, they are in effect pointing their children toward heaven while leading them to hell.

There are reasons that righteousness (and wickedness) only lasts until the third and fourth generations (D&C 98:30). An example from the Book of Mormon adds insight about how the decline in obedience and faith in the rising generation even had a negative and contaminating effect on the faith of the older generation.

29 And there was also a cause of much sorrow among the Lamanites; for behold, they had many children who did grow up and *began to wax strong in years, that they became for themselves,* and were led away by some who were Zoramites, by their lyings and their flattering words, to join those Gadianton robbers.

30 And thus were the Lamanites afflicted also, and *began to decrease as to their faith and righteousness, because of the wickedness of the rising generation.* (3 Nephi 1:29-30)

The righteous Lamanites had been raising their children in the Gospel. However, when the "rising generation" became the new leaders and started making their own lifestyle choices, they were led away by the popular views of an organization that promised progressive thinking and freedom from the old norms and morals of their parents. With the support of an organization that promised to provide all they would need without honest work, the rising generation was seduced into accepting the Gadianton agenda.

This Gadianton philosophy and government is described in scripture:

38 And it came to pass on the other hand, that the Nephites did build them (the Gadianton robbers) up and support them, beginning at the more wicked part of them, until they had overspread all the land of the Nephites, and had *seduced the more part of the righteous until they had come down to believe in their works and partake of their spoils,* (entitlements) and to join with them in their secret murders and combinations.

39 And *thus they did obtain the sole management of the government,* insomuch that they did trample under their feet and smite and rend and turn their backs upon the poor and the meek, and the humble followers of God.

40 And thus we see that *they were in an awful state, and ripening for an everlasting destruction.* (Helaman 6:38-40)

The Gadianton agenda succeeded because of a sure-fire formula: First, teach their philosophy of wealth distribution, taking from those who have, and giving it to themselves; and Second, getting the righteous to "partake of the spoils" through promises and entitlements. Being taught to believe in this kind of progressive and popular way of thinking, it was just a matter of time before the rising generation was in "an awful state." *The one and only requirement for the law of entropy* (see page 130) *to work its destructive force is the dimension of time.*

A question often asked is: Why have there been changes in the Temple presentation? I am not privy to the actual answers—and therefore any answer I give is nothing more than guess work. Some have suggested that many of the changes were the result of the complaints people had over particular movements that seemed disturbing or strange, as well as the personal contact required in some ordinances. If this is the case, there now exists more than one generation that does not know what a penalty is (an integral part of oath making). There is a whole generation now living who have lost light and truth, which made some passages of scripture more clear and understandable. Once truths are lost they may never return. Just as the testimony of the generation that personally knew the prophet Joseph passed away, those experiences in the temple are now only second hand, and are soon to be forgotten. Why do the changes take place? Could it be because there is "a rising generation" that decided they didn't like the old ways; that progress requires being more sensitive to personal feelings than doctrinal insights, light, and truth? There may not be another generation who will have the information that has been lost; in fact, we might well plan on losing more. Thus light, truth, and understanding once offered in the Temple has already been lost to the "rising generation."

> 30 For behold, thus saith the Lord God: I will give unto the children of men line upon line, precept upon precept, here a little and there a little; and blessed are those who hearken unto my precepts, and lend an ear unto my counsel, for they shall learn wisdom; *for unto him that receiveth I will give more; and from them that shall say, We have enough, from*

them shall be taken away even that which they have. (2 Nephi 28:30)

The Lord has a *perfect will* and a *permissive will*. For example: The Lord's *perfect will* was not to give the 116 pages of the Book of Mormon manuscript to Martin Harris. *His permissive will* was just that: permission contrary to His *perfect will*. The same is true regarding the Law of Consecration: there is a *perfect will* and a *permissive will* in this dispensation. The important question to ponder is: To which *will* are the blessings "irrevocably decreed"? The blessings come to those who are "willing *and* obedient", not just to those who are willing. Because of agency we will receive that which we are *willing to receive*; it may be more, or less. The hinges are well oiled on the wondrous windows of heaven and they are always primed to be easily opened, or quickly closed. The Lord awaits our preparation and decision. There is no stirring in the heavens above *until* there is a stirring in the hearts below.

After the Children of Israel came into the Land of Canaan and began to have children that "became for themselves," the generational lack of testimony made itself manifest during the time of the Judges:

> 10 And also all that generation were gathered unto their fathers: and *there arose another generation after them, which knew not the Lord*, nor yet the works which he had done for Israel.
> 11 And the children of Israel *did evil in the sight of the Lord*, and served Balaam:
> 12 And they *forsook the Lord God of their fathers*, which brought them out of the land of Egypt, *and followed other gods, of the gods of the people that were round about them*, and bowed themselves unto them, and provoked the Lord to anger. (Judges 2:10-12)

The Book of Mormon also explains why the gospel is new to every generation:

> 1 Now it came to pass that there were *many of the rising generation that could not understand the words of king Benjamin, being little children at the time he spake unto his people; and they did not believe the tradition of their fathers.*
> 2 *They did not believe* what had been said concerning the resurrection of the dead, neither did they believe concerning the coming of Christ.
> 3 And now *because of their unbelief they could not understand the word of God;* and their hearts were hardened.
> 4 And they would not be baptized; neither would they join the church. And they were a separate people as to their faith, and remained so ever after, even in their carnal and sinful state; for they would not call upon the Lord their God. (Mosiah 26:1-4)

Each generation must discover its own faith and testimony. As the scripture above makes clear, unbelief was and is the reason many people may not understand the word of God. Alma teaches that a particle of faith must be injected to begin the process of understanding:

> 27 But behold, if ye will awake and arouse your faculties, even to an experiment upon my words, and *exercise a particle of faith,* yea, *even if ye can no more than desire to believe,* let this desire work in you, even until ye believe in a manner that ye can give place for a portion of my words. (Alma 32:27)

Alma explains how the unbeliever may begin to discover light and truth, faith and testimony. Faith is meaningless unless founded in something that cannot fail. Scripturally speaking, the only thing that cannot fail is Jesus Christ, His gospel and the Atonement. He is the Lamb *slain before the foundation of the world.* His Atonement is the sacrifice *that was, is, and shall be infinite and eternal*, a sacrifice that "cannot fail." Thus, if an individual's faith is placed in a man or an organization, they will eventually fail, and that person's faith will have been in vain. Since a testimony should be grounded in the substance of one's faith, it must also be placed in that which cannot fail.

Chapter 12

The Gospel of Jesus Christ

There are two recorded earthly ministries of Jesus Christ: one account in the New Testament before His crucifixion and the second account found in the Book of Mormon. Following His resurrection, Christ appeared to the people in Bountiful and ministered to them, teaching the same gospel He had taught in the old world. Each scriptural record clearly shows that Christ did not organize the church while He ministered in Judaea or to the descendants of Lehi. Given that a necessary part of the gospel of Christ is the authority to administer the same, the Savior, during both ministries, taught the gospel and then organized the priesthood, providing the authority and keys required to administer His gospel. The priesthood leadership, then, in both cases, organized the church to effectively facilitate that administration. What is His gospel? According to scripture, the gospel of Jesus Christ is: Faith; Repentance; Baptism; and the Gift of the Holy Ghost.

A reporter once asked President Harold B. Lee, "Why do you claim that the fullness of the gospel of Jesus Christ was contained in the Book of Mormon when it does not have any information about baptism for the dead, or temple work, or sealings? In fact, it does not contain most of the things you believe as a church about the gospel. Why then do you claim it has the fullness of the gospel of Jesus Christ?" President Lee answered the reporter's question by quoting modern-day scripture:

> 11 Yea, *repent and be baptized*, every one of you, for a remission of your sins; yea, *be baptized* even by water, and *then cometh the baptism of fire and of the Holy Ghost.*
> 12 Behold, verily, verily, I say unto you, *this is my gospel*; and remember that they shall *have faith* in me or they can in nowise be saved;
> 13 And *upon this rock I will build my church*; yea, upon this rock ye are built, and if ye continue, the gates of hell shall not prevail against you. (D&C 33:11-13)

The Doctrine and Covenants declare that the gospel of Jesus Christ is Faith, Repentance, Baptism and the Gift of the Holy Ghost.

> 5 And verily, verily, I say unto you, he that receiveth *my gospel receiveth me*; and he that receiveth not *my gospel* receiveth not me.
> 6 And *this is my gospel—repentance and baptism* by water, and then cometh *the baptism of fire and the Holy Ghost*, even the Comforter, which showeth all things, and teacheth the peaceable things of the kingdom. (D&C 39:5-6)

The Book of Mormon may not have everything that the Latter-day Saints believe as "doctrine" but it does contain a "fullness of the Gospel," since by scriptural definition, faith, repentance, baptism, and the gift of the Holy Ghost constitute the fullness of the Gospel of Jesus Christ. (D&C 20:9; D&C 42:12)

The first instructions Christ gave to the Nephites after his resurrection (3 Nephi 11) was an explanation about His gospel or doctrine. In verses 31 through 40, the Savior makes sure that His gospel would be understood to avoid contention (verse 29). The concluding message of Christ as his ministry comes to a close is found in 3 Nephi 27. The Savior again reinforces an understanding of the principles and ordinances of the gospel of Jesus Christ in such a way that no mistake should be made. This last sermon was addressed to the priesthood leadership [his General Authorities] where He declared that if the church that they organized was built upon His gospel as explained, *then* the Father would show forth his works in it (3 Nephi 27:10).

Everything Christ taught the Nephites in Bountiful is couched between these two discourses about faith, repentance, baptism, and the gift of the Holy Ghost. The Savior's Nephite ministry is structured in such a way that the latter-day reader can make no mistake about what constitutes "the gospel or doctrine" (Jacob 7:6) of Jesus Christ.

3 Nephi 11 - The First Gospel Instruction:

> 31 Behold, verily, verily, I say unto you, *I will declare unto you my doctrine.*
> 32 And *this is my doctrine*, and it is the doctrine which the Father hath given unto me; and I bear record of the Father, and the Father beareth record of me, and the Holy Ghost beareth record of the Father and me; and I bear record that the Father commandeth all men, everywhere, t*o repent and believe in me.*
> 33 And whoso *believeth in me, and is baptized,* the same shall be saved; and they are they who shall inherit the kingdom of God.
> 34 And whoso believeth not in me, and is not baptized, shall be damned.
> 35 Verily, verily, I say unto you, that *this is my doctrine,* and I bear record of it from the Father; and whoso believeth in me believeth in the Father also; and unto him will the Father bear record of me, for *he will visit him with fire and with the Holy Ghost.*
> 36 And thus will the Father bear record of me, and the Holy Ghost will bear record unto him of the Father and me; for the Father, and I, and the Holy Ghost are one.
> 37 And again I say unto you, ye must repent, and become as a little child, and *be baptized in my name*, or ye can in nowise receive these things.
> 38 And again I say unto you, *ye must repent, and be baptized in my name*, and become as a little child, or ye can in nowise inherit the kingdom of God.
> 39 Verily, verily, I say unto you, *that this is my doctrine*, and whoso buildeth upon this buildeth upon my rock, and the gates of hell shall not prevail against them.
> 40 And *whoso shall declare more or less than this, and establish it for my doctrine, the same cometh of evil,* and is

not built upon my rock; but he buildeth upon a sandy foundation, and the gates of hell stand open to receive such when the floods come and the winds beat upon them.

3 Nephi 27 - The Last Gospel Instruction:

13 Behold I have given unto you my gospel, and *this is the gospel which I have given unto you*—that I came into the world to do the will of my Father, because my Father sent me.

14 And my Father sent me that I might be lifted up upon the cross; and after that I had been lifted up upon the cross, that I might draw all men unto me, that as I have been lifted up by men even so should men be lifted up by the Father, to stand before me, to be judged of their works, whether they be good or whether they be evil—

15 And for this cause have I been lifted up; therefore, according to the power of the Father I will draw all men unto me, that they may be judged according to their works.

16 And it shall come to pass, that *whoso repenteth and is baptized* in my name shall be filled; and if he *endureth to the end,* behold, him will I hold guiltless before my Father at that day when I shall stand to judge the world.

17 And he that endureth not unto the end, the same is he that is also hewn down and cast into the fire, from whence they can no more return, because of the justice of the Father.

18 And this is the word which he hath given unto the children of men. And for this cause he fulfilleth the words which he hath given, and he lieth not, but fulfilleth all his words.

19 And no unclean thing can enter into his kingdom; therefore nothing entereth into his rest save it be those who have washed their garments in my blood, because of their *faith, and the repentance* of all their sins, and their faithfulness unto the end.

20 Now this is the commandment: Repent, all ye ends of the earth, and come unto me and be baptized in my name, that ye may be sanctified by the reception of the Holy Ghost, that ye may stand spotless before me at the last day.

21 Verily, verily, I say unto you, ***this is my gospel;*** and *ye know the things that ye must do in my church;* for the works which ye have seen me do that shall ye also do; for that which ye have seen me do even that shall ye do;

Christ explains that anyone who declares more or less than "faith, repentance, baptism and the Gift of the Holy Ghost" as His gospel is not of God (3 Nephi 11:40). *The Encyclopedia of Mormonism,* Page 556; defines "The Gospel of Jesus Christ" in these terms:

Even though Latter-day Saints use the term "gospel" in several ways, including traditional Christian usages, the Book of Mormon and other latter-day scriptures define it precisely as the way or means by which an individual can come to Christ. In *all* these scriptural passages, the gospel or doctrine of Christ teaches that salvation is available through his authorized servants to all who will (1) believe in Christ; (2) repent of their sins; (3) be baptized in water as a witness of their willingness to take his name upon them and keep his commandments; (4) receive the Holy Ghost by the laying-on of hands; and (5) endure to the end. All who obey these commandments and receive the baptism of fire and of the Holy Ghost and endure in faith, hope, and charity will be found guiltless at the last day and will enter into the kingdom of heaven (Alma 7:14-16, 24-25; Heb. 6:1-2).

The gospel and Atonement of Jesus Christ should be founded on faith and testimony, not necessarily on the organization and administration of the church. The doctrinal concept of testimony will be discussed in more depth below. The relationship that the individual may have with Christ should be the focus of any organized religion. All need to participate in the gospel of Jesus Christ, but the reality of that participation is only accomplished by the relationship of "receiving Him and His Gospel" (D&C 39:5).

The Gospel incorporates two principles—faith and repentance, and two ordinances—baptism and the Gift of the Holy Ghost. Faith, according to scripture, may only be faith if it lies in Jesus Christ and His Atonement. Of the 350 plus times the word faith appears in scripture, only three are not associated with Christ and the Atonement. Amulek explains how to *exercise faith* in Christ and the Atonement using a single phrase multiple times in just a few verses:

> 15 And thus he shall bring salvation to all those who shall believe on his name; this being the intent of this last sacrifice, to bring about the bowels of mercy, which overpowereth justice, and bringeth about means unto men that they may have *faith unto repentance.*
> 16 And thus mercy can satisfy the demands of justice, and encircles them in the arms of safety, while he that *exercises no faith unto repentance* is exposed to the whole law of the demands of justice; therefore only unto him that has *faith unto repentance* is brought about the great and eternal plan of redemption.
> 17 Therefore may God grant unto you, my brethren, that ye may begin to *exercise your faith unto repentance*, that ye begin to call upon his holy name, that he would have mercy upon you; (Alma 34:15-17)

The way to exercise faith in Christ and the Atonement is to change one's character. In other words, faith without the works of *repentance* (the change of character) is dead. (This being the "intent of this last sacrifice" and Atonement: "to bring about the bowels of mercy, which overpowereth justice, and bringeth about means unto men that they may have *faith unto repentance. "*) The faithful are those who are repenting; the unfaithful are those not repenting. What is repentance? It is the process of changing character, to stop doing one thing and start doing another. It is to take aim again because one has missed the mark. Repentance is not something to be feared, or embarrassed about, it is a recognition of a need for change, and then going through the processes that will help make that change. Repentance is nothing more than the process of changing character with a hope and view of salvation and exaltation through the grace and mercy of Jesus Christ.

Contrary to common belief, every parable taught by Christ was directed to the members of the church—those who knew and understood the law and the gospel of Jesus Christ. Therefore, they are directed to us. The inspired messages in the parables were not intended for non-members or non-believers. The normal LDS ego will often project the character and attitudes of those in the parables onto non-members as a way of protecting itself, but all parables are directed to those who have the light and truth of the gospel. They were meant for the saints anciently and for the Latter-day Saint today in the process of likening the scriptures to themselves.

Chapter 13

The Two Conversions

A parable about the Pharisee and the Publican found in Luke 18 explains that there is a difference in the conversion process. The Pharisee, an active member of the Jewish religion, and the publican, considered a sinner by the same faith, also represent the members of the church in our day. The Pharisee foolishly thought that his salvation was based on his activity in the 'works' of the church.

> 9 And he spake this parable unto certain which trusted in themselves that they were righteous, and despised others:
> 10 Two men went up into the temple to pray; the one a Pharisee, and the other a publican.
> 11 The Pharisee stood and prayed thus with himself, God, I thank thee, that I am not as other men are, extortioners, unjust, adulterers, or even as this publican.
> 12 I fast twice in the week, I give tithes of all that I possess.

As evidence of personal righteousness, the Pharisee, considering himself faithful and obedient, lists his outward actions that could be seen of men. With pride he boasts of his righteousness in his temple attendance, his fasting, and his comprehensive tithes and offerings. Perhaps he brought two dishes to every potluck. In Zoramite fashion (Alma 31:12-18), the Pharisee proudly gives thanks to God that he is not like all the other sinful people, as he is the shining example of righteousness!

> 13 And the publican, standing afar off, would not lift up so much as his eyes unto heaven, but smote upon his breast, saying, God be merciful to me a sinner.
> 14 I tell you, this man went down to his house justified rather than the other: for every one that exalteth himself shall be abased; and he that humbleth himself shall be exalted.

In clear and simple words, the Savior teaches that there is a difference between activity in the church and activity in the gospel of Jesus Christ. The Pharisee was active in the Jewish church of his day, but the publican (the sinner) was active in the gospel. According to Christ, this sinner was more righteous than the Pharisee because he recognized the need for change and was actively trying to change his character.

The strength of faith and the resolve to repent is not always as visible as the rote actions of activity in checking the boxes of righteousness. Repentance might be seen in subtle changes of character stimulated by one's personal faith in Christ and the Atonement. A person may be totally active in the church of Jesus Christ—attending every meeting, doing all that is asked, obedient in every outward display—and yet may be internally inactive in the gospel of Jesus Christ. Members that are converted to the church rather than the gospel may become disillusioned by leaders or offended by doctrines due to their weakness in faith and gospel understanding. Salvation and exaltation is dependent on the inner activity in the gospel rather than the outer activity in the church. When converted to the gospel and Atonement of Christ *first*, activity in the Church will be a natural consequence. Without exception, every example *in scripture* of teaching and conversion—Ammon, Aaron, Alma, King Lamoni etc.—reveals that the conversion is always *first* to Christ and the Gospel, and *never* to the administrative elements of prophets, priests, and a church organization. Remember, the faith and testimony required for salvation must be in Christ and the Atonement because it cannot fail.

Checking the Boxes

When parents seek to teach their children the gospel and provide testimony-building experiences, Latter-day Saints should recognize the difference between activity in the Church and activity in the Gospel. The *religion* (the Church organization) is an aid that helps to foster and strengthen the *relationship* an individual should have with Christ, His Gospel, and the Atonement. Many believe that checking the boxes of church activity is a sure sign of spiritual activity and security. It is not uncommon to hear the following statements and questions when a once active individual falls away from the church: *I don't understand why they would leave the church! He attended all his meetings and went on a mission, and was a leader in all his priesthood quorums, and didn't his parents serve in every position?'* As if the outward actions insured an inward conviction. The terrible question is: How can this apostasy, inactivity, or even divorce happen when all the boxes have been checked. The scriptures teach that the Christian character developed by church activity on earth should be the same character developed for heaven (Alma 34:34).

The Doctrine and Covenants makes a connection between the church and kingdom on earth and that of heaven:

> 5 Call upon the Lord, *that his kingdom may go forth upon the earth, that the inhabitants thereof may receive it, and be prepared for the days to come*, in the which the Son of Man shall come down in heaven, clothed in the brightness of his glory, *to meet the kingdom of God which is set up on the earth.*
> 6 Wherefore, *may the kingdom of God go forth, that the kingdom of heaven may come*, that thou, O God, mayest be glorified in heaven so on earth... (D&C 65:5-6)

The purpose that the "kingdom of God" (the Church) should go forth is so that the "Kingdom of heaven" may come. The Church organization and the priesthood is to prepare the saints for the glory and kingdom of heaven when it does come. This personal preparation does not lie exclusively in one's physical activity in the Church.

During his mortal ministry, even Christ taught that there must be a
connection between the activity on earth and the activity of heaven, as
he explains in the first restorative sermon: "Thy will be done on earth
as it is in heaven" (3 Nephi 13:10). In this sermon the Savior makes
an obvious shift from the lesser Law of Moses (performances and
ordinances) to the higher law of character development and change.

The activity that connects these two environments is not just the
leadership boxes of the Mosaic Law, which focused on the temporal
and visual performances and ordinances, but the boxes of character
change. A brief but serious look at the boxes that need to be checked
for the signs of activity on earth and heaven should be looked at. The
list below is not comprehensive in any way, but presented as a
comparison between the outward and inward signs of activity and
conversion. Remembering always that there can be a difference
between activity in the Church and activity in the Gospel.

Outward Activity
Attend your meetings
Pay a full tithing
Pay a generous Fast Offering
Family Home Evening
Attend the Temple
Personal and family prayer
Living the Word of Wisdom
Honest in your dealings
Living the Law of Chastity
Read the scriptures
Serve when called
Sustain all your leaders

These necessary questions asked by leaders are the boxes that are used
(checked or unchecked) to determine one's activity in the Church or
Kingdom of God on earth. The answers to these questions, even if
favorable, will not satisfy the Celestial requirements to be in the
presence of God and endure His Glory. The character or 'celestial

spirit' ensures a celestial resurrection (D&C 88:22-28). King Benjamin taught that one must not only act like a saint but must 'become a saint through the atonement of Christ' (Mosiah 3:19). If going to the Temple is symbolic of entering into the presence of God, then not only the questions above must be answered correctly to determine one's activity in the church, but the following character traits should also be connected to the same interview if one hopes to dwell with God. If the Outward Activity doesn't lead to the Inward Character Change required to check the Celestial Boxes, then the primary activities have been a failure.

The Celestial Boxes

Inward Activity and Character

Exodus 20
>No other gods before me,
>No graven image or any likeness,
>Not take the name of the Lord in vain,

Matthew 5:2
>Poor in spirit,
>Meek,
>Hunger and thirst after righteousness,
>Merciful,
>Pure in heart,
>Peacemakers,
>Persecuted for righteousness sake,
>Love your enemies,
>Do good to them that hate you,
>Bless them that curse you,
>Pray for them which despitefully use you and persecute you,

Matthew 22:36-40
>Love God with all thy heart, and with all they soul, and with all thy mind,
>Love thy Neighbor as thyself,

John 13:34-35
>Love one another as Christ loved you,

Doctrine and Covenants 82:19
>Every man seeking the interest of his neighbor,
>Doing all things with an eye single to the glory of God,

2 Nephi 25: 26-27
>Rejoice in Christ,
>Preach of Christ,

Mosiah 3:19
>Become a saint,
>Submissive,
>Meek,
>Humble,
>Patient,
>Full of love,
>Willing to submit to all things

Mosiah 5:2
>No more disposition to do evil,
>Do good continually,

Mosiah 18:8-10
>Mourn with those that mourn,
>Comfort those that stand in need of comfort,
>Stand as a witness of God; at all times, in all things, in all places,

Alma 13:12
>Cannot look upon sin save it were with abhorrence,

Moroni 7:45-48
>Suffereth long,
>Is kind,
>Envieth not,
>Not puffed up,
>Seeketh not her own,
>Not easily provoked,
>Thinketh no evil,
>Rejoiceth not in iniquity but rejoiceth in the truth,
>Beareth all things,
>Believeth all things,
>Hopeth all things,
>Endureth all things.

Charity is the pure love of Christ, and it endureth forever; and whoso is found possessed of it at the last day, it shall be well with him. Wherefore, my beloved brethren, pray unto the Father with all the energy of heart, that ye may be filled with this love, which he hath bestowed upon all who are true followers of his Son, Jesus Christ; that ye may become the sons of God; that when he shall appear we shall be like him, for we shall see him as he is; that we may have this hope; that we may be purified even as he is pure. Amen. (Moroni 7:48-49)

A lengthy amount of time has been spent converting the youth, prospective and new members to the church and programs that exist to help administer the gospel of Jesus Christ. Today, unlike examples in scripture, there is a tendency to focus on the church and the priesthood leadership, which constitute the organization and vehicle created for the administration of the gospel. Without doubt, the inspired administration of the gospel by the church and priesthood leadership is *required and needed* by the general membership. This administration of the gospel and the accompanying responsibilities of the priesthood, such as the 'perfecting of the saints and the work of the ministry' are aided by the programs of the church. Family Home Evenings, Relief Society, Young Men's and Young Women organizations, are all a necessary part of building individual faith and testimony.

Albert Einstein once stated: "I just want to know the thoughts of God; all the rest are just the details." The "immortality and eternal life of man" (Moses 1:39) is the work and glory of God, and thus His thoughts. This "work" of God is to provide for *the individual spirit*, without compulsion, an opportunity for a relationship with Christ as their Savior, forging the kind of personal relationship with Him that makes the Atonement real and effective in their life, eventually creating a character that is worthy to return to the presence of God. If these are the thoughts and works of God, the details alluded to by Einstein could be the church's organization, programs, auxiliaries, and policies. The priesthood leaders, through that authoritative inspired organization of administration, provide the help and support that *the individual* may need to gain light and truth, participate in Gospel ordinances, and learn to develop a character that loves God and his or her fellow man (i.e. to repent).

Current church policies, programs, and auxiliaries are intended to assist members to come unto Christ. An individual relationship with Christ and His Atonement is the underlying goal of every program and auxiliary in the church. The programs themselves should not become the focus. This is not to say that these programs are wrong. Christmas programs, Easter pageants, ward dinners, etc. can be useful in introducing investigators to the fellowship of the church, however, these should be used as an aid and not as a substitute for the meaningful gospel instruction of coming unto Christ.

Unfortunately, the tendency to push programs over Christ-centered-content extends to the youth as well. There are many LDS young adults whose conversion and testimonial strength is no greater than that of a "baseball baptism" [referring to a practice many years ago in some mission fields to invite local youth to play baseball, insisting they get baptized if they wanted to continue to play. This was a baptism without any conversion to the Gospel]. Unintentionally, many have taught the youth to focus their faith in the church, the programs, and priesthood leaders more so than faith in Jesus Christ, the gospel, and the scriptures. Parents and leaders seek to have their children and young adults "active" in every aspect of the church organization, but some have not remembered the fundamental purpose of church organizations, which is to teach and encourage the individual to "come unto Christ" (Moroni 10:30, 32). Like an automobile, the active participation in the programs and auxiliaries become a valuable vehicle that should be used as a means to assist in the arrival to a specific destination or goal.

Understanding this distinction helps answer the question of why the youth retention in some evangelical churches seems so high, and conversions away from those churches are so difficult, even when their doctrines may not be correct. These evangelical churches have a singular converting focus—Christ—and little else. In more ways than one, the greatest threats to the LDS youth are the Christ-centered "Born Again" faiths. One successful example, though incorrect in doctrine, is the scripture and Christ-centered Calvary Chapel.

There is an unassailable truth manifested in scripture and life, which is this: When a conversion is centered on Christ and is coupled with an awareness of man's fallen nature and need for the gospel of Christ, the activity and retention of converts is a hundred fold. When the converted have "received his image in their countenances" (Alma 5: 14), and begin to "sing the song of redeeming love" (Alma 5:26; 26:13), their faith, testimony and conversion will be more lasting and true than those who are merely converted to a church organization, program, activity or social network.

Before "coming unto Christ", the individual needs to understand *why* they need a Savior. This was the main message of King Benjamin in the Book of Mormon. He realized that *understanding why* must precede the testimony of *action*. Seldom does anyone run into the street in the middle of the night in their pajamas until they first realize the house is on fire, and when they do, proper attire is not a primary concern. The testimonies of youth are often borrowed from those around them. Like the moon reflecting the light of the sun, the youth often reflect the testimonies of their parents and teachers. This reflected testimony is a necessary part of testimony development; however, the time must come when, through trials and experience and life's problems and disappointments, a personal testimony must be developed. A reflected testimony cannot endure to the end.

Once, while attending ward fast and testimony meeting, seventeen people approached the pulpit to share their testimony. Fifteen of those 17 were *not* baptized members of the church—they were all under the age of 8 and technically non-members because they had not yet been confirmed as members. Children are the echoes of their parents, teachers and environment. Their testimonies overtly revealed the focus and teachings they were receiving. Each said, "I know the church is true and I know President Monson is a prophet." This statement is not bad or wrong. But none stated that they knew or believed in Jesus as the Christ, or that they knew the gospel of Jesus Christ was true. Subtly and quite unintentionally children and youth are taught to place their faith in the church and leadership more than in the Savior. Often the pictures, statements, and primary songs are more about the leadership and church than Christ. Sacrament talks are chosen from Conference talks rather than from the words of God found in the scriptures, with the constant injunction to "follow the leaders." While this is good and proper counsel, it silently implies the infallibility of past and present leadership. This practice of placing a *primary* faith and testimony in leadership rather than in Christ has been a significant factor in the falling away that is currently taking place.

The label "Mormon" often indicates a way of life that revolves around the church and organization of administration rather than a relationship with Christ. This way of life, the Mormon culture, is often mistaken for the Mormon religion. Unfortunately, there may be a difference between *religion* and *relationship*. Technically, organized religion should exist to facilitate the relationship one has with Christ. Yet in many faiths (including the LDS), the religious culture can become the focus, to the detriment of a relationship with Christ, as faith and repentance take a back seat.

In a way, those born in the church are born to be a Mormon. When parents are active members, there is the expectation that their children will be baptized and confirmed a member of the church when eight years of age. There's no way out of it; it's a rite of passage for an eight year old. However, none are necessarily born a Christian or a disciple of Christ despite their baptism at eight years of age. This relationship with the Savior and Christian character must be personally developed over time. While this relationship is fostered with the help of the church organization, being active in a church culture doesn't automatically translate unto becoming a Christian. For instance, one may live in a Mormon community and be involved in the Mormon culture, attend the Mormon Church and participate in all aspects of the Mormon religion. But only those who have taken the necessary steps in the gospel can begin to develop a personal *relationship* with Christ *as their Savior*. The reality of becoming a disciple of Christ will then be manifest in the works of their character.

A testimony founded upon the vehicle of administration (the church) will always leave the believer wanting. Many young adults who are coming of age today and even some older adults have placed their faith and testimony in the vehicle of the administration of the church rather than in Christ *without even realizing it*. This vehicle, even with Divine guidance, is the organization and leadership, which has as its primary responsibility the administration of the gospel of Jesus Christ.

Today the "mists of darkness" have rendered a zero visibility for the path that leads to the tree of life (1 Nephi 8:23). The tree cannot be reached, nor the fruit tasted, unless there is a standard that can be "grasped firmly and held tightly" (1 Nephi 8:24), leading all of us safely through the black fog of doubt and temptation. The wise and faithful will seek a standard surer than themselves. The arm of flesh, educated or not, can and will fail. Anchored to bedrock, the "rod of iron" that leads to the tree *cannot fail*. It is the "word of God" and the "word is in Christ" (Alma 34:5).

As the scriptures make clear, there is no other name than Christ that has the *power to save*—no priesthood leader, no prophet; not Moses, Abraham, or Adam; not Kimball, Hinckley, or Monson.

> 4 ...while one saith, I am of Paul; and another, I am of Apollos...
> 5 Who then is Paul, and who is Apollos, *but ministers by whom ye believed* (1 Corinthians 3:4-5)

> 12 Is Christ divided? was Paul crucified for you? or were ye baptized in the name of Paul? (1 Corinthians 1:12)

> 11 For another foundation can no man lay than that which is laid, which is Jesus Christ. (1 Corinthians 3:11)

> 26 For ye are all the children of God by faith in Christ Jesus.
> 27 For as many of you as have been baptized into Christ have put on Christ.
> 28 There is neither Jew nor Greek, there is neither bond nor free, there is neither male nor female: for ye are all one in Christ Jesus.
> 29 And if ye be Christ's, then are ye Abraham's seed, and heirs according to the promise. (Galatians 3:26-29)

> 17 And moreover, I say unto you, that there shall be no other name given nor any other way nor means whereby salvation can come unto the children of men, only in and through the name of Christ, the Lord Omnipotent. (Mosiah 3:17)

The misdirection of faith and testimony is only one of the key elements and contributing reasons that underlie the apostasy or falling away seems rampant among many Christian faiths today.

Chapter 14

Responsibility of Parents

The goal of every faithful parent is to have their children embrace the same gospel that means so much to them. Unfortunately, almost *all* emotional pain that righteous parents feel is because others, in particular their children, exercise their own agency to their detriment. Satan was cast out of heaven because of rebellion and because he sought to "destroy the agency of man." He wanted to control and guarantee the salvation of mankind. Many a parent seeks to do the same with their children. Children in time will have their own agency. All that a good parent can hope to accomplish is to teach them how to use it correctly and righteously. Of course that requires understanding what it means to "act in futurity;" understanding why each individual must 'come unto Christ;' understanding what it means to have faith in Christ; understanding that their faith testimony should be in Christ and His Atonement; and understanding that they may use their agency to choose freedom and eternal life or captivity and death. All must understand that freedom and agency is the *power of exaltation* **or** *the power of damnation*. These powers are initiated by the act of choosing good or evil—even (and perhaps especially) while in the presence of the other. There are good and evil forces that surround each person, pulling opposite directions, enticing us toward good or toward evil in a struggle that cannot be greater in one direction than the other. The *tie of good and evil* is broken only by the power of agency as choices are made that propel the individual toward the freedom of exaltation or towards captivity and spiritual death.

> 13 There hath no temptation taken you but such as is common to man: but God is faithful, who will not suffer you to be tempted above that ye are able; but will with the temptation also make a way to escape, that ye may be able to bear it. (1 Corinthians 10:13)

The faith and testimony of the sons of Helaman first required the faith and testimonies of the **parents** of the sons of Helaman. The faith of these young men could not exist without the teachings and examples of their parents. This was a commitment and covenant so sacred that their fathers suffered death rather than fail in their commitment and covenant to God. When coupled with the same faith and testimony of their mothers, they *'could not doubt.'* This responsibility cannot be passed on to the Scout Leader, the Sunday School Teacher, or the Young Women and Young Men's leader. The salvation of a child is not a responsibility that can be passed on to the Bishop, Stake President, or any other priesthood leader or teacher. A parent cannot leave the responsibility of building the faith and testimonies of their children to somebody else. Every individual must discover his or her own faith and testimony. Every member of the church should be a convert to Christ, His gospel, and the Atonement. Parents should help provide opportunities for children to discover and strengthen their own faith, founded in Christ. The sons of Helaman gave the credit for their faith and testimonies to their mothers, not to their Young Men's leader.

Notice the Lord's directive about what parents are to teach their children:

> 25 And again, inasmuch as parents have children in Zion, or in any of her stakes which are organized, *that teach them not to understand the doctrine of repentance, faith in Christ the Son of the living God, and of baptism and the gift of the Holy Ghost* by the laying on of the hands, when eight years old, the sin be upon the heads of the parents. (D&C 68:25)

This is an admonition for parents to teach their children *to understand* the gospel, placing their faith and testimonies in *"Christ the Son of the*

Living God"—not in the vehicle of the administration of the gospel, but in the Son of God and His Plan of Salvation. Of course, this passage assumes that the parents also understand the doctrine. Notice that the requirement is to teach children to understand so that they (the children) may find their faith and testimony.

The Savior, introducing the verses that follow, gives this instructional command to the parents in Zion. He (the Lord) is about to describe some of the problems facing every generation, explaining why a testimony founded in Christ must be taught.

> 31 Now, I, the Lord, am not well pleased with the inhabitants of Zion, for there are idlers among them; and their children are also growing up in wickedness; *they also seek not earnestly the riches of eternity,* but their eyes are full of greediness. (D&C 68:31-32)

An Ancient and Latter-day Problem

The Lord explains in Section 68 that because the youth "seek not earnestly the riches of eternity," the falling away has already begun. Likewise Isaiah, seeing our day, explains that eventually music will become more important than things sacred, as the children in every dispensation will begin to focus on things temporal in nature.

> 12 And the harp, and the viol, the tabret, and pipe, and wine, are in their feasts: but they regard not the work of the Lord, *neither consider the operation of his hands.*
> 13 Therefore my people are gone into captivity, *because they have no knowledge*: and their honorable men are famished, and their multitude dried up with thirst. (Isaiah 5:12-13)

Inspired, Isaiah warns that in the last days music will become more important than "*the works of the Lord*" and the "*operation of his hands.*" The neglect of the 'work of God' will lead to famine and captivity because of a lack of knowledge and understanding. As noted in an earlier chapter, the spiritual focus of the youth, be it right or wrong, will eventually affect the older generation as parents begin to

126

fail in their faith because of the sins of the rising generation (3 Nephi 1: 30).

After being 'driven' out of the Garden of Eden the first parents of this temporal and probationary world received a command similar to that of D&C 68. According to tradition, *not* canonized scripture, many teach that Adam and Eve knew and understood the gospel before they were driven out of Eden. This traditional understanding is usually based on the belief that Eve's actions in the Garden were motivated by an understanding of the gospel plan that required her to do 'x' in order for 'y' to happen. However, a careful reading of Moses 5 reveals that there were at least three generations living outside the Garden of Eden *before* Adam and Eve received any knowledge about the gospel of Jesus Christ and the plan of salvation. Before the Fall there was no death or separation from God in the garden, thus no need for the gospel or the plan of salvation. They were in an immortal state of innocence. It is explained that *"if"* they partook of the fruit, *"then"* a Savior would be provided to restore that which would be lost in their transgression and fall: their immortality and the presence of God. After the Fall, Adam and his wife Eve were driven out of the Garden of Eden to begin their life in a new and terrifying environment. Only then, after several generations, were they taught the gospel and the plan of salvation.

> 2 And Adam knew his wife, and *she bare unto him sons and daughters, and they began to multiply and to replenish the earth.*
> 3 And from that time forth, *the sons and daughters of Adam began to divide two and two* in the land, and to till the land, and to tend flocks, and *they also begat sons and daughters.*
> 4 And Adam and Eve, his wife, called upon the name of the Lord, and they heard the voice of the Lord from the way toward the Garden of Eden, speaking unto them, and they saw him not; for they were shut out from his presence.
> 5 And *he gave unto them commandments*, that they should worship the Lord their God, and should *offer the firstlings of their flocks*, for an offering unto the Lord. And Adam was obedient unto the commandments of the Lord.

6 And *after many days an angel of the Lord appeared unto Adam, saying: Why dost thou offer sacrifices unto the Lord?* And Adam said unto him: I know not, save the Lord commanded me.

7 And then the angel spake, saying: *This thing is a similitude of the sacrifice of the Only Begotten of the Father, which is full of grace and truth.*

8 Wherefore, *thou shalt do all that thou doest in the name of the Son, and thou shalt repent and call upon God in the name of the Son forevermore.* (Moses 5:2-8)

The details of what Adam and Eve were taught when they received the light and truth they were seeking is found in Moses 6:51-68, where Enoch quotes from the Book of Adam:

56 And it is given unto them to know good from evil; wherefore they are agents unto themselves, and I have given unto you another law and commandment.

57 Wherefore *teach it unto your children*, that all men, everywhere, must repent, or they can in nowise inherit the kingdom of God, for no unclean thing can dwell there, or dwell in his presence; for, in the language of Adam, Man of Holiness is his name, and the name of his Only Begotten is the Son of Man, even Jesus Christ, a righteous Judge, who shall come in the meridian of time.

58 Therefore I give unto you a commandment, to *teach these things freely unto your children, saying:*

59 That by reason of transgression cometh the fall, which fall bringeth death, and inasmuch as ye were born into the world by water, and blood, and the spirit, which I have made, and so became of dust a living soul, even so ye must be born again into the kingdom of heaven, of water, and of the Spirit, and be cleansed by blood, even the blood of mine Only Begotten; that ye might be sanctified from all sin, and enjoy the words of eternal life in this world, and eternal life in the world to come, even immortal glory;

60 For by the water ye keep the commandment; by the Spirit ye are justified, and by the blood ye are sanctified;

62 And now, behold, I say unto you: *This is the plan of salvation* unto all men, through the blood of mine Only

Begotten, who shall come in the meridian of time. (Moses 6:56-62)

Notice: The main responsibility Adam and Eve had after receiving the gospel was to teach it to their children:

> 57 Wherefore *teach it unto your children,* that all men, everywhere, must repent...
> 58 Therefore *I give unto you a commandment, to teach these things freely unto your children...* (Moses 6:57-58)

When Adam receives the gospel he is commanded *twice* to teach these things (the gospel) *freely* (all the time) to his children. Their testimony needs to be in Christ and in His gospel and nothing else. How are parents supposed to teach Christ and the gospel *freely* to their children? Moses was given a testimony-building exercise that was directed toward the youth and the rising generation:

> 6 And these words, which I command thee this day, shall be in thine heart:
> 7 And thou shalt *teach them diligently unto thy children,* and shalt talk of them when thou sittest in thine house, and when thou walkest by the way, and when thou liest down, and when thou risest up.
> 8 And thou shalt bind them for a sign upon thine hand, and they shall be as frontlets between thine eyes.
> 9 And thou shalt write them upon the posts of thy house, and on thy gates. (Deuteronomy 6:6-9)

In other words, children should be taught the gospel "freely" or *ALL THE TIME,* so that they can begin to come to an understanding of *why* they need a Savior, who that Savior is, and how their salvation depends upon their relationship with Him and the Atonement. D&C 93 states that it was given to know how and who we should worship:

> 19 I give unto you these sayings that you may understand and *know how to worship, and know what you worship,* that you may come unto the Father in my name, and in due time receive of his fullness.

Each Sunday during the sacrament meeting, participants covenant to "always remember Him." There is a good reason why Moses was commanded to teach the parents to *always discuss* the works of the Lord, and why we make the same covenant at the symbolic sacrificial altar of the Lamb of God. Again, the gospel is new to every generation, and testimonies are not passed on genetically nor are they purchased cheaply or by proxy.

Not only is the gospel new to each generation, the sins of Israel (those who know the gospel) are the sins of Israel in every generation and every dispensation. The evil and sins that plagued one generation will plague each generation, and the problems that exist in the first dispensation will show up in every dispensation. As the prophet Joseph Smith explained, the "nature of man has not changed since the beginning" (*TPJS*, p. 60).

One of the primary responsibilities of parents is to teach the gospel of faith, repentance, baptism, and the gift of the Holy Ghost to each generation, with the divine injunction to teach the children to *understa*nd the gospel of Christ so that they will, when converted, place their faith and testimony in Christ and His Atonement. The same focus is mentioned by Nephi in the Book of Mormon. Living under the Law of Moses, Nephi explains that the educational thrust of the parents and church organization should be centered in Christ.

> 23 For *we labor diligently to write, to **persuade our children**, and also our brethren, **to believe in Christ**, and to be reconciled to God; for we know that it is by grace that we are saved, after all we can do.*
> 24 And, notwithstanding *we believe in Christ*, we keep the law of Moses, *and look forward with steadfastness unto Christ*, until the law shall be fulfilled.
> 25 For, for this end was the law given; wherefore the law hath become dead unto us, and *we are made alive in Christ because of our faith*; yet we keep the law because of the commandments.
> 26 And *we talk of Christ, we rejoice in Christ, we preach of Christ, we prophesy of Christ, and we write according to our*

*prophecies, **that our children may know** to what source they may look for a remission of their sins.*

27 Wherefore, *we speak concerning the law **that our children may know*** the deadness of the law; and they, by knowing the deadness of the law, may *look forward unto that life which is in Christ,* and know for what end the law was given. And after the law is fulfilled in Christ, that they need not harden their hearts against him when the law ought to be done away. (2 Nephi 25:23-27)

Entropy

There are many theories in science, but very few laws. A scientific law must be "observable and repeatable." One of those "laws" is that of *Entropy,* or the Second Law of Thermodynamics. The law of Entropy states that:

> Everything moves from a state of order to a state of disorder, *unless an independent source of outside energy is infused.* Otherwise, everything will continue to deteriorate, decompose and otherwise move from a state of order to a state of disorder.

The law of entropy is at work not only in the biological and physical world. It affects language, speech, the written word, faith, religions, and testimonies. Entropy is alive and well in the lives of the members of the church today, both adults and youth. As mentioned earlier, parents who do not put more spiritual energy into their children than was put into them risk raising children who will become less active in the gospel. To ensure that the testimonies of our members and children are stronger, there must be *more outside energy* put into gospel instruction and practice than was offered the older generation or faith will wane and testimonies will fail.

To review: The gospel is new to every generation and testimonies are not genetic. Faith does not pass from one generation to another without increased energy. Because of this entropy (which is illustrated over and over in the Book of Mormon), righteousness and wickedness (i.e.

the traditions of the fathers) lasts only until the third and fourth generation (2 Nephi 26:9-10).

> 9 But the Son of righteousness shall appear unto them; and he shall heal them, and they shall have peace with him, *until three generations shall have passed away, and many of the fourth generation shall have passed away in righteousness.*
> 10 And when these things have passed away, a speedy destruction cometh unto my people; for, notwithstanding the pains of my soul, I have seen it; wherefore, I know that it shall come to pass; and they sell themselves for naught; for, for the reward of their pride and their foolishness they shall reap destruction; for because they yield unto the devil and choose works of darkness rather than light, therefore they must go down to hell. (2 Nephi 26:9-10)
>
> 12 Yea, and this because they shall dwindle in unbelief and fall into the works of darkness, and lasciviousness, and all manner of iniquities; yea, I say unto you, that because *they shall sin against so great light and knowledge,* yea, I say unto you, that from that day, *even the fourth generation shall not all pass away before this great iniquity shall come.* (Alma 45:12)

In time, every organization will experience some sort of spiritual complacency. Nephi warned that the church should be careful not to cry "all is well in Zion, yea Zion prospereth", for history shows that its not until the fourth and fifth generation (almost when it is too late) that people will begin to question it. This is a historical fact, observed over and over again in history and scripture. Based on generational life spans, called the *Saeculum* (as discussed earlier), a study of the past becomes a reflective *Saeculum* of the future. Thus, the Book of Mormon, when viewed as a *prophetic history,* warns all readers that this sacred record of a fallen people (entropy) has the potential to become a *historical prophecy* for all saints in all dispensations.

The Book of Mormon is a witness and testimony of this concept as the cycles of faith and falling away are only overcome by faith and testimony in Christ and His Atonement. The personal cure and outside energy required to overcome *spiritual entropy* is knowledge, coupled with the action of active faith. Abraham, in his statement about the connection between activity and knowledge, taught his readers how he, and thus all, might overcome spiritual entropy:

> 2 ...having been myself *a follower of righteousness, desiring also to be one who possessed great knowledge,* and to *be a greater follower of righteousness, and to possess a greater knowledge,* and...*desiring to receive instructions, and to keep the commandments of God,* I became a rightful heir, a High Priest, holding the right belonging to the fathers. (Abraham 1:2)

Chapter 15

Repentance and Character

The religious leaders in the Book of Mormon – priests, teachers, even the 12 disciples – were called and authorized to assist the individual in developing a spiritual relationship the Savior. The intent of priesthood leadership, from the days of Adam, has always been to help promote the change of character that activates the power of the gospel in the lives of believers. This power of the Gospel has the ability to prepare them to eventually dwell in the presence of God. Likewise, membership in an organized Christian *religion* should be motivated by that desire for a *relationship* with the Atonement as one seeks to come unto Christ. To review again:

> 26 And we *talk of Christ, we rejoice in Christ, we preach of Christ, we prophesy of Christ,* and we write according to our prophecies, *that our children may know* to what source they may look for a remission of their sins. (2 Nephi 25:25-26)

This verse makes it clear that the spiritual purpose of the scriptures, parents, priesthood leaders, and the church, should be "that our children may know to what source they may look for a remission of their sins." The importance of a sure and faithful foundation in Christ stretches above and beyond that of the organization that administers the gospel. This faith expands beyond the simple "activity" and participation in church programs, and lies in the quality of heart and character. What sets a faithful Christian apart from an unfaithful one? The faithful Christian is "exercising faith unto repentance." Repentance is nothing more than the process of changing one's character, and the character that must be developed by the true disciple of Christ is the character and nature that has learned to love God and humanity. The last commandment that Christ gave the apostles before His crucifixion was:

> 34 A new commandment I give unto you, that ye love one another; as I have loved you, that ye also love one another.
> 35 By this shall all men know that ye are my disciples, if ye have love one to another. (John 13:34-35)

Christ informs the reader that to be a disciple of Christ (a Christian) one must love one another as He has loved. A Christ centered faith and testimony is founded in the "pure love of Christ" (Moroni 7:45-47), rather than how many church meetings one has endured throughout their life. Not all Christians are Mormons, but all Mormons **should** become Christians and disciples of Christ.

Consider these statements from the Prophet Joseph Smith about the individual's responsibility to initiate that change of character:

> If you wish to go where God is, *you must be like God,* or possess the principles which God possesses, for *if we are not drawing towards God* in principle, we are going from Him and drawing towards the devil. (*TPJS,* p 216)

> Here, then, is eternal life – to know the only wise and true God; and *you have got to learn how to be a God yourself –* and to be kings and priests to God, the same as all Gods have done before you, namely, *by going from one small degree to another, and from a small capacity to a great one; from grace to grace, from exaltation to exaltation,* until you attain to the resurrection of the dead, and are able to dwell in everlasting burnings, and to sit in glory, as do those who sit enthroned in everlasting power. (*TPJS,* p 346-347)

> . . . so it is with the principles of the Gospel – you must begin with the first, and go on *until you learn all the principles of exaltation.* But it will be a great while after you have passed through the veil before you will have learned

them. It is not all to be comprehended in this world; it will be a great work to learn our salvation and exaltation even beyond the grave. (*TPJS*, p 348)

The best preparation for exaltation is to develop a character that loves all mankind as Christ loved them. "Upon two commandments hang all the law and the prophets," taught Christ, which are: to "love God and love your fellowman" (Matthew 22:36-40). It would follow that the surest way to develop that kind of character (and love) lies in obedience to all commandments. All commandments, laws, and even ordinances (Alma 13:16) are not restrictive in nature, but are calculated to help mankind develop the kind of character that will enable an individual to one day stand in the presence of God with a confidence that will wax strong.

If all the law and prophets hang upon these two commandments, it stands to reason that all judgment will hang upon the same. "By their works" shall all men be judged. The "works" of life can't help but reflect the character developed. If sin is defined as "the breaking of commandments," one could define sin as: *any word, work or thought that distracts or inhibits one from developing the character that loves God and all others*. Scripture declares that this life is a "probationary state." Sin then, is the misuse of the time that is allotted to mankind to develop that character.

Every Christian religious organization should have this as their primary focus: providing the assistance the individual might need to create a loving relationship with themselves, their fellowman, and Christ. Like the Sabbath, (Mark 2:27) organized religion exists for the spiritual benefit of man, not the other way around. If this focus is missing in any denomination, that church has no authority, no purpose, and no power to save man.

Sometimes it might be easier to teach youth the joy of giving and serving others than it is to convince them why they should go to church and actively attend all their meetings. Because love is borne of service (they go hand-in-hand), teaching them to love and serve one another does more to help them develop a character worthy of exaltation than sitting through every single sacrament meeting during their lifetime. All should keep an eye on the big picture. And that eye must become single to the glory of God. Every true and enduring relationship with Christ is predicated on our learning to love one another.

The importance of this relationship with Christ and His Atonement is a central theme in the Book of Mormon. A quick review from Nephi to Moroni:

Nephi states that our faith and testimonies should be in Christ:

> For we labor diligently to write, to persuade our children, and also our brethren, to believe in Christ... for we are made alive in Christ because of our faith...and we talk of Christ, we rejoice in Christ, we preach of Christ, we prophesy of Christ, and we write according to our prophecies, that our children may know to what source they may look for a remission of their sins. Wherefore, we look forward unto that life which is in Christ...for the right way is to believe in Christ and deny him not; for by denying him ye also deny the prophets and the law....and Christ is the Holy One of Israel; wherefore ye must bow down before him, and worship him with all your might, mind, and strength, and your whole soul; and if ye do this ye shall in nowise be cast out. (2 Nephi 25:23-29)

King Benjamin taught that this relationship is most important:

> ...if ye have come to a knowledge of the goodness of God, ... and also, the Atonement which has been prepared from the foundation of the world, that thereby salvation might come to him that should put his trust in the Lord, and should be diligent in keeping his commandments, and continue in the faith even unto the end of his life, I mean the life of the mortal body—this is the man who receiveth salvation, through the Atonement which was prepared from the foundation of the world for all mankind, which ever were since the fall of Adam, or who are, or who ever shall be,

even unto the end of the world. And this is the means whereby salvation cometh. And there is none other salvation save this which hath been spoken of; neither are there any conditions whereby man can be saved except the conditions which I have told you. (Mosiah 4:6-8)

Alma the Younger describes the character change we are to seek:

...I have repented of my sins, and have been redeemed of the Lord; behold I am born of the Spirit. And the Lord said unto me: Marvel not that all mankind, yea, men and women, all nations, kindreds, tongues and people, must be born again; yea, born of God, changed from their carnal and fallen state, to a state of righteousness, being redeemed of God, becoming his sons and daughters; and thus they become new creatures; and unless they do this, they can in nowise inherit the kingdom of God. (Mosiah 27:24-26)

Behold, he sendeth an invitation unto all men, for the arms of mercy are extended towards them, and he saith: Repent, and I will receive you.
He saith: Come unto me and ye shall partake of the fruit of the tree of life; yea, ye shall eat and drink of the bread and the waters of life freely...come unto me and bring forth works of righteousness, and ye shall not be hewn down and cast into the fire. (Alma 5:33-35)

Christ explains the need for the relationship:

If ye will *come unto me* ye shall have eternal life. Behold, mine arm of mercy is extended towards you, and whosoever will come, him will I receive; and *blessed are those who come unto me.*

Behold, I am Jesus Christ the Son of God. I created the heavens and the earth, and all things that in them are. I was with the Father from the beginning. I am in the Father, and the Father in me; and in me hath the Father glorified his name...as many as have received me, to them have I given to become the sons of God; and even so will I to as many as

shall believe on my name, for behold, by me redemption
cometh...Behold, I have come unto the world to bring
redemption unto the world, to save the world from sin.
Therefore, whoso repenteth and cometh unto me as a little
child, him will I receive, for of such is the kingdom of God.
Behold, for such I have laid down my life, and have taken it
up again; therefore, repent and come unto me ye ends of the
earth, and be saved. (3 Nephi 9:14-22)

Moroni ends the Book of Mormon with his last lecture and most
important message:

32 Yea, come unto Christ, and be perfected in him, and deny
yourselves of all ungodliness; and if ye shall deny yourselves
of all ungodliness, and love God with all your might, mind
and strength, then is his grace sufficient for you, that by his
grace ye may be perfect in Christ; and if by the grace of God
ye are perfect in Christ, ye can in nowise deny the power of
God.
33 And again, if ye by the grace of God are perfect in Christ,
and deny not his power, then are ye sanctified in Christ by
the grace of God, through the shedding of the blood of
Christ, which is in the covenant of the Father unto the
remission of your sins, that ye become holy, without spot.
(Moroni 10:32-33)

These messages from the Book of Mormon are just a few of the
hundreds that are found in this sacred record that focus on the
relationship one should have with Christ and the character change of
the believer. The Title Page itself proclaims that the record is for the
"convincing of Jew and Gentile that Jesus is the Christ." Those who
assume that Joseph Smith was a fraud and a charlatan who concocted
or copied this work—putting himself, his friends, and his family in
harm's way without ever denying its divine origin—are ignorant of its
message. This book contains the "fullness of the gospel of Jesus
Christ", and the central message is "come unto Christ". The only sure
test of the truth and value of a book will be the changes that unfold in
the life of the reader because of the message found between its covers,
not in the weaknesses of the man behind the translation. The fruits of

the Book of Mormon are openly visible in the character of its believers.

Faith and repentance (the principles of Salvation) are self-directed in nature. That means they are actions that cannot be done for one individual by another. One cannot "repent" another person! Salvation, then, is an individual process, aided by the community of saints.

In scripture, the power and authority of the priesthood is an administrative authority. What is the power that makes gospel ordinances effective in one's life? Even though a person might be baptized a thousand times or participates in any saving ordinance over and over: The "power" of the ordinance's promise is in the individual's agency and character. If a person has not changed their character by exercising faith in Christ "unto repentance" then that priesthood ordinance has no saving power in their life! This is what Nephi, Benjamin, and Alma, among others, are all trying to explain. There is no miracle or ordinance that will change our character into the character of God, or perfect our thinking and actions. The power within any ordinance lies within the individual through the exercise of agency, choice, action, and character.

The ordinances associated with the gospel are administered to assist in that change of character as they (the ordinances themselves) point the mind to Christ and the Atonement. The power and purpose of a priesthood ordinance is explained by Alma:

> 16 Now these ordinances were given after this manner, that *thereby the people might look forward on the Son of God,* it being a type of his order, or it being his order, and this *that they might look forward to him for a remission of their sins, that they might enter into the rest of the Lord.* (Alma 13:16)

Alma explains that the ordinances of the gospel exist as a ***hope** of a future reality*, based on one's commitment to the requisite *change of character*. That means the individual receiving the ordinance holds the power to make the promised blessing of the ordinance a reality. The power behind the reality does not lie in the officiator nor his authority

140

or position. It is true that a designated administrator with the proper authority must administer the ordinance, but the priesthood itself does not hold any "power" to force the reality of the blessing connected to the ordinance. The *power* to make any ordinance a reality lies within the recipient, based on their righteous desires, agency, choices and character change. As Joseph Smith explained, "God would not exert any compulsory means, and the devil could not" (*TPJS*, 187).

Conversion

The account of King Lamoni, found in the Book of Mormon, is a prime example of *what should be taught and how it should be taught* (see Alma 18: 36, 39). Ammon did not convert King Lamoni to the programs and activities of the church. He first taught the King the need for the Atonement and then the gospel of Jesus Christ. The three pillars of the gospel must be understood to begin this change of heart. They are: 1) The Creation; 2) The Fall; and 3) The Atonement.

> 36 Now when Ammon had said these words, he began at the *creation of the world*, and also the creation of Adam, and told him all the things *concerning the fall of man*, and rehearsed and laid before him the records and the holy scriptures of the people, which had been spoken by the prophets, even down to the time that their father, Lehi, left Jerusalem.
> 39 But this is not all; for *he expounded unto them the plan of redemption*, which was prepared from the foundation of the world; and *he also made known unto them concerning the coming of Christ*, and all the works of the Lord did he make known unto them. (Alma 18:36-39)

Aaron, like Ammon, first explains the need for a relationship with Christ, and then explains that the Gospel of faith and repentance are the first steps toward that sacred relationship.

> 12 And it came to pass that when Aaron saw that the king would believe his words, *he began from the creation of Adam, reading the scriptures unto the king—how God created man after his own image, and that God gave him*

commandments, and that because of transgression, man had fallen.

13 And Aaron did *expound unto him the scriptures from the creation of Adam, laying the fall of man before him, and their carnal state and also the plan of redemption, which was prepared from the foundation of the world, through Christ, for all whosoever would believe on his name.*

14 And *since man had fallen he could not merit anything of himself; but the sufferings and death of Christ atone for their sins, through faith and repentance, and so forth; and that he breaketh the bands of death, that the grave shall have no victory, and that the sting of death should be swallowed up in the hopes of glory*; and Aaron did expound all these things unto the king.

15 And it came to pass that after Aaron had expounded these things unto him, the king said: *What shall I do* that I may have this eternal life of which thou hast spoken? *Yea, what shall I do that I may be born of God,* having this wicked spirit rooted out of my breast, and receive his Spirit, that I may be filled with joy, that I may not be cast off at the last day? Behold, said he, I will give up all that I possess, yea, I will forsake my kingdom, that I may receive this great joy.

16 But Aaron said unto him: *If thou desirest this thing, if thou wilt bow down before God, yea, if thou wilt repent of all thy sins, and will bow down before God, and call on his name in faith, believing that ye shall receive, then shalt thou receive the hope which thou desirest.* (Alma 22:12-16)

The conversions of King Lamoni and his father were complete. They discovered their faith and testimony in the understanding of their need for a redeemer and the Atonement provided by Christ. This understanding opened the door to the relationship with Christ through a spiritual rebirth. They were not converted to the programs and activities of a religious organization, but were taught an understanding of the fundamental concepts or pillars of the gospel: The Creation, the Fall, and the Atonement. Their conversion and participation in the gospel (upon the principles of faith and repentance) will have the power to initiate a relationship with Jesus Christ and the Atonement that will precipitate a lasting change of character.

Chapter 16

The Church and Priesthood

The foundation for an enduring and lasting testimony will always lie in the relationship one develops with the Savior and not with the religious organization designed to administer the Gospel. There exists no 'Mormon Church' in the Spirit World. The only righteous congregation will be the faithful believers and followers of the gospel of Jesus Christ. As established earlier, the gospel is comprised of 1) Faith in Jesus Christ and His Atonement; 2) Repentance, the process of changing your character, which is made possible through faith in the Atonement and the hope of a celestial resurrection; 3) Baptism, a covenant of obedience that must precede progression in the gospel; and 4) the Gift of the Holy Ghost, which will testify of the Father and the Son, to those who have entered into the "covenant of obedience" and are "exercising faith unto repentance." Eventually all who actively participate in the first principles and ordinances of the gospel may receive a remission of sins as they are "wrought upon and cleansed by the power of the Holy Ghost" (Moroni 6:4; 2 Nephi 31:17).

The Lord's *organization of administration* for His gospel is the priesthood leadership and The Church of Jesus Christ of Latter-day Saints. This *organization of administration* is the only church that has the authority through the restoration of the priesthood to administer the Gospel of Christ.

During the personal ministries of Christ in both ancient Palestine and the promised land of Lehi's descendants, the Savior taught His Gospel, but did not organize the church. In both areas, the Savior restored the higher law that the Children of Israel lost at the time of Moses, teaching His gospel of faith, repentance, baptism, and the Gift of the Holy Ghost. Christ then organized the priesthood leadership with the commission and authority to administer the gospel He taught. The Savior provided the necessary instructions and authorization (priesthood and keys) to these inspired administrators to make the gospel available for all who would like to participate.

Then as now, the priesthood was organized to administer the gospel of Jesus Christ. This began on an individual level. But as the number of believers increased, the leadership recognized the need to create a church (organized congregation) in order to provide the necessary ordinances and teachings to larger groups in a more productive, orderly, and organized way.

The word "church" is used two different ways. The broad definition is: a congregation of similar believers. However, it is sometimes used to denote the voice of the highest priesthood leadership that administers the gospel. In this instance, the *organization of administration* [purposely phrased in this manner] *is* the Church of Jesus Christ of Latter-day Saints. For example, when the leaders issue a statement, or discuss church policy, "the church" is understood to be the voice of the priesthood leadership whose responsibility it is to administer the gospel. When the term *organization of administration* is used, it is meant to underscore that only The Church of Jesus Christ of Latter-day Saints and its priesthood leadership has the divine authority to administer the gospel.

The organizing of believers into congregations makes it easier for the leadership of the church to administer the gospel effectively and keep records of members' activity and participation in all ordinances. Besides administering the gospel, the priesthood leadership and the church organization provide opportunities to teach and serve one another. In their responsibility to 'perfect the saints,' the teachings and counsel of those who are chosen as priesthood administrators will help members learn how best to make necessary character changes that will help free them from the sins of their generation. The main responsibility of the priesthood leadership is to make sure that every individual (able by law) who may desire to "come unto Christ" has every opportunity to participate in the gospel of Jesus Christ.

Priesthood leaders are chosen by the "common consent" of the general membership, who sustain, recognize and accept them as gospel administrators within their stewardship. In the stakes and wards the members themselves provide the authorization to administer the gospel with its respective "keys" (the authority to make decisions) for the administration of the gospel in the given location and area (ward and stake) of their responsibility. Priesthood leaders, general and local, are *not* sustained to teach mysteries, provide secret ordinances, expound deep doctrines, or to teach those things that are not elemental and essential to the gospel of Jesus Christ. Their call and authority is to administer the ordinances (Baptism and the Gift of the Holy Ghost) and teach faith and repentance. To expect more is foolishness. To condemn priesthood leadership for what they did or didn't do in their life, or what they taught or didn't teach, or to find fault in their character when they have been faithful in their responsibility to administer the gospel, is even more foolish. There is *only one person to blame* for a lack of spiritual experiences and enlightenment and it is NOT the Church or priesthood leadership.

Most of the issues causing some members to question their faith have little to do with the teachings of and about Christ that are found in ancient and modern scripture. However, many of the concerns and questions causing members to question their faith have to do with something a priesthood leader, past or present, may have personally said or did not say, or taught, or believed. It is important to remember that what they may have said or believed is separate and distinct from their call and responsibility in the administration of the gospel. Priesthood leaders cannot claim infallibility in their personal knowledge, opinions, tradition, or interpretation of scripture. Accordingly, faith and testimony should be in Christ and His gospel, not in the vehicle of administration. The church and leadership exists as an aid for the individual to come unto Christ and participate in the necessary ordinances administered with the correct and authorized authority.

The definition used in this work for the church and priesthood leadership is *the organization divinely authorized to administer the gospel.* The priesthood leadership's responsibilities, as outlined in the scriptures, are two-fold: 1) to administer the gospel of Jesus Christ (which includes the work of the ministry, and the perfecting of the saints); and 2) to protect the interests of the church and the faith of the members. In every reference in scripture where the Savior calls and sets apart His priesthood leadership, He first teaches the gospel to the leadership and then gives them their commission and responsibility concerning that gospel. The priesthood organization is established and designed for the ease of the administration of the gospel. This church organization is the vehicle that will assist the priesthood in that administrative responsibility.

The Savior called and commissioned the twelve disciples at the beginning of His ministry among the Nephites:

> 21 And the Lord said unto him: [Nephi] I *give unto you power that ye shall baptize* this people when I am again ascended into heaven.
> 22 And again the Lord called others, and said unto them likewise; and he *gave unto them power to baptize.* And he said unto them: On this wise shall ye baptize; and *there shall be no disputations* among you.
> 23 Verily I say unto you, that *whoso repenteth of his sins through your words, and desireth to be baptized in my name, on this wise shall ye baptize them—Behold, ye shall go down and stand in the water, and in my name shall ye baptize them.*
>
> 41 Therefore, *go forth unto this people, and declare the words which I have spoken,* unto the ends of the earth. (3 Nephi 11:21-23, 41)
>
> 1 And it came to pass that when Jesus had spoken these words unto Nephi, and to those who had been called, (now

the number of them who *had been called, and received power and authority to baptize*, was twelve) and behold, he stretched forth his hand unto the multitude, and cried unto them, saying: Blessed are ye if ye shall give heed unto the words of these twelve whom I have chosen from among you *to minister unto you*, and *to be your servants*; and unto them *I have given power that they may baptize you with water*; and after that ye are baptized with water, behold, I will baptize you with fire and with the Holy Ghost; therefore blessed are ye if ye shall believe in me and be baptized, after that ye have seen me and know that I am. (3 Nephi 12:1)

Christ *ensures* that the disciples understand their responsibility in the church that will later be organized in His name, as Mormon explains in his editorial comments.

17 And it came to pass that *the disciples whom Jesus had chosen began from that time forth to baptize and to teach as many as did come unto them; and as many as were baptized in the name of Jesus were filled with the Holy Ghost.*
18 And many of them saw and heard *unspeakable things, which are not lawful to be written.*
19 And *they taught, and did minister one to another;* and they had all things common among them, every man dealing justly, one with another.
20 And it came to pass that they did do all things even as Jesus had commanded them.
21 And *they who were baptized in the name of Jesus were called the church of Christ.* (3 Nephi 26:17-21)

18 But this much I know, according to the record which hath been given—they did go forth upon the face of the land, and *did minister unto all the people, uniting as many to the church as would believe in their preaching; baptizing them, and as many as were baptized did receive the Holy Ghost.* (3 Nephi 28:18)

The calling of the twelve apostles in this dispensation restored the same responsibilities that the twelve disciples and apostles had in the Meridian of Times.

27 Yea, even twelve; and the twelve shall be my disciples, and they shall take upon them my name; and the twelve are they who shall desire to *take upon them my name with full purpose of heart.*

28 And if they desire to take upon them my name with full purpose of heart, *they are called to go into all the world to preach my gospel unto every creature.*

29 And they are they who are *ordained of me to baptize in my name,* according to that which is written;

30 And you have that which is written before you; wherefore, you must *perform it according to the words which are written.*

31 And now I speak unto you, the twelve—Behold, my grace is sufficient for you; you must walk uprightly before me and sin not.

32 And, behold, *you are they who are ordained of me to ordain priests and teachers; to declare my gospel, according to the power of the Holy Ghost which is in you,* and according to the callings and gifts of God unto men;

33 And I, Jesus Christ, your Lord and your God, have spoken it. (D&C 18:27-33)

When the converted masses become larger, congregations are organized creating the Church of Christ as discussed in 3 Nephi 27. The priesthood organization and leadership can then more efficiently teach believers and baptized converts how and why it is necessary to come unto Christ. Priesthood leaders can also more efficiently officiate in the performance of ordinances such as the sacrament, baptism, and the Gift of the Holy Ghost if members are organized into groups or 'churches' rather than going into every individual home to minister. Connected to this responsibility and organization is the keeping of records for the sake of efficiency and the reduction of redundancy.

Paul explains in Ephesians that the organization for administration must be built upon "apostles and prophets," which is the priesthood leadership with the responsibility to assist in the individual need to come unto the "chief corner stone" of Christ.

> 19 Now therefore ye are no more strangers and foreigners, but fellow citizens with the saints, and of the household of God;
> 20 And are built upon the foundation of the apostles and prophets, Jesus Christ himself being the chief corner stone; (Ephesians 2:19, 20)

Paul teaches in the same Chapter that the organization of administration is essential, not only to come unto Christ, but to become like Him:

> 11 And he gave some, *apostles; and some, prophets; and some, evangelists; and some, pastors and teachers;*
> 12 For the *perfecting of the saints, for the work of the ministry,* for the edifying of the body of Christ:
> 13 Till we all come in the *unity of the faith,* and of the knowledge of the Son of God, unto a perfect man, *unto the measure of the stature of the fullness of Christ:*

These scriptures make clear that the purpose of the church organization is the same in every dispensation. The responsibility of priesthood leadership is to *assist the individual* to come unto Christ. It is not the responsibility of the church or priesthood to ensure a relationship with God, nor to make sure the individual will come to Christ, but only to provide the necessary teachings, ordinances programs, auxiliaries, and opportunities so that those who have a desire may come unto Him and work out *their own* salvation in fear and trembling (Philippians 2:12, Mormon 9:27). One cannot blame others, not even priesthood leaders, for a personal lack of spiritual experiences or gospel understanding. All are victims of themselves. The lack of a relationship with the Savior is due to one's own choice and negligence.

Regarding the calling of Latter-Day apostles, Joseph Smith made the following statement about their responsibilities:

> They are the twelve apostles, who are called to the office of the Traveling High Council, who are to preside over the churches of the Saints, among the Gentiles, where there is no

> presidency established; and they are to travel and preach among the Gentiles, until the Lord shall command them to go to the Jews. *They are to hold the keys of this ministry, [preach the Gospel] to unlock the door of the kingdom of heaven unto all nations, and to preach the gospel to every creature. This is the power, authority, and virtue of their apostleship.* (*TPJS.* p 74, italics added for emphasis)

The twelve's responsibility, according to this description by the prophet Joseph, is inseparably connected to the gospel of Jesus Christ and making it available to all mankind.

The apostles are to:

- •preside over the churches,
- •preach among the Gentiles,
- •hold the keys of this ministry,
- •unlock the door of the kingdom of heaven unto all nations,
- •preach the gospel to every creature.

According to the Prophet Joseph, this responsibility is "the power, authority and virtue of their apostleship." In a nutshell, the Quorum of 12 Apostles are to *make available* the gospel (through the priesthood and Church organization) to *all who might seek* that personal relationship with Jesus Christ. This they do through the ordinances and principles of the gospel administered and taught in The Church of Jesus Christ of Latter-day Saints. This responsibility and authority is the power of the priesthood, office, and position they hold.

The restored priesthood organization and church is the only vehicle that may, under the order and authority of Christ, administer the gospel of salvation to mankind. That administration is usually accomplished through the inspired teachings of priesthood leaders and the gospel ordinances made available to those who seek after these things.

There are multitudes of people who have an enduring faith in Christ, his Atonement and resurrection who are not Latter-day Saints. Eventually everyone will receive all the necessary teachings and ordinances of salvation and exaltation. The *organization of administration* exists to ensure that all mankind, alive or dead, have available *if they choose*, all the ordinances necessary for their desired spiritual progression.

To review: The priesthood leadership and its organization exist for the administration of the gospel and to protect the interests of the church and the faith of the members. It is:

- *Not* for the teaching of so called "mysteries;"
- *Not* for expounding scripture and providing *deep doctrine;*
- *Not* for the dissemination of secret doctrines;
- *Not* for the performing of secret ordinances;
- *Not* for answering the questions of detractors or unbelievers.

The first principles and ordinances of the gospel are faith, repentance, baptism, and the Gift of the Holy Ghost. The first two principles are the responsibility of the individual as the church or priesthood cannot "faith" someone or "repent" someone. Exercising one's faith unto repentance is singular to the individual in their personal quest for a relationship with Christ and His Atonement. The authorized administration of the ordinances of baptism and the Gift of the Holy Ghost are the responsibility of the priesthood organization. These ordinances are made available, with authority, to all who desire to participate, enhancing the individual hope and ability to strengthen that personal relationship founded upon their faith and repentance.

A common goal among detractors, like Korihor and others in the Book of Mormon is to make their listeners feel like duped victims of negligent priesthood leaders. Vocal apostates teach that the priesthood leadership has held back powerful ordinances or special knowledge of doctrines and mysteries. These individuals often claim that there is lost knowledge, authority and power, which, if believed, spawns a "gospel victim" mentality. Thus, blaming others eliminates a personal responsibility for their own inadequacies and salvation. These modern-day agitators, like Korihor, Zeezrom, and Sherem, use scriptural manipulation and elaborate oration to seduce the faithful. They convince the elect that their doctrinal ignorance, lack of knowledge, and lack of spiritual experiences is not their own fault, but the fault of church leadership.

It has never been a church or priesthood responsibility to "save" the individual, or ensure that personal relationship with Christ. Priesthood responsibility lies in the injunction to administer and make available the gospel in principle and in ordinance by assisting the sincere seeker in the spiritual journey that will lead them to Christ. Everyone who sincerely seeks a relationship with Christ may have it. Everyone who exercises faith in Christ, repents of their sins, is baptized and receives the gift of the Holy Ghost, initiates the process to obtain that personal relationship with the Atonement and salvation. The success of this quest is individual and personal, as is its failure.

The sacrament prayer is not a blessing for the bread or water, but a blessing for those who partake, as these emblems might become "sanctified *to the souls of those who partake* of it" and are sincerely seeking that personal relationship. As Section 27 of the Doctrine and Covenants makes clear, what's important is not what we partake of, but the state of our heart as we do so:

> 2 For, behold, I say unto you, that it mattereth not what ye shall eat or what ye shall drink when ye partake of the sacrament, *if it so be that ye do it with an eye single to my glory—remembering unto the Father my body which was laid down for you, and my blood which was shed for the remission of your sins.* (D&C 27:2)

To recap: A relationship with Christ, the Atonement, and the gospel is a personal accomplishment—not a priesthood or church responsibility. The priesthood cannot "faith" a member, nor can the church "repent" a person. However, these two (the Church and Priesthood) can and do assist the individual by providing the ordinances of baptism and Gift of the Holy Ghost, as well as inspired instruction and council (through auxiliaries classes and conferences) for those who seek that relationship and opportunity of redemption.

Chapter 17

Authority

When Moses met face to face on the Mount with the only true and living God, the Children of Israel convinced Aaron to forge (from the fires of idolatry) a golden calf as their deity (Exodus 32). Returning to camp, Moses in anger drew a line in the sand and asked, "Who is on the Lord's side?" (Exodus 32:26) The Levites were the only ones to stand with him, and because of this, the "Sons of Levi" were chosen to bear the ministry and priesthood. This opportunity to serve God and man in this capacity was henceforth limited to a single family and restricted from all others. The Levites were told to consecrate themselves for the upcoming blessing of *service and administration* (Exodus 32:29). Prior to this time the responsibilities of service and priesthood leadership were borne by the firstborn male of every family and every tribe of Israel (Numbers 3:41, 45). In consequence of the Children of Israel's faithlessness, the service and ministry was restricted to one blood line, that of Levi. The High Priest of that priesthood was to be a direct descendant of Aaron within that chosen family.

The Levites were brought before the assembly of the Children of Israel and sustained as the priesthood linage that would be the ministers unto the Lord for the "service of Israel" (see Numbers 8:9-25). Notice, it was not a *power* that the Levites were given but a *privilege and responsibility* to serve others. (See also Numbers 18:1-7).

Long before the time of Moses and Aaron, under the Patriarchal Order, the patriarch of each family was responsible for the temporal and spiritual welfare of his family. The patriarch (or father) acted in his own right and authority as a *prophet, priest and king* to his family. As *prophet,* he would provide the inspired direction and guidance to those for whom he was responsible. As *priest,* he was to stand as a mediator between man and God, officiating in the ordinances of salvation and exaltation for those in his care. Finally, as *king* he was to protect his family from temporal and spiritual intruders and provide for their temporal needs. Father Abraham, described in scripture as the "friend of God," was endowed with the knowledge and responsibility of being a Grand Patriarch as others before him. He was the exemplar of a righteous parent and priesthood holder of both the Melchizedek and Patriarchal responsibilities. Thus, all are commanded to "go and do the works of Abraham" (John 8:39; D&C 132:32).

The blessings connected to the Covenant of Abraham include three key elements. Abraham explains that these blessings did not originate with him, but were given to Adam, the first man (Abraham 1:2-4). These eternal concepts include the elements of *priesthood, posterity, and inheritance.* By accepting the gospel, the faithful convert *inherits* a responsibility (as the *posterity* and seed of Abraham) to administer the gospel of Jesus Christ to all the nations of the earth. Abraham is every man as every man should be. The covenants the Lord made with the "Father of the Faithful" are directly connected to the priesthood leadership and the administration of the gospel.

The blessing and covenant of Abraham:

> 9 And I will make of thee a great nation, and I will bless thee above measure, and make thy name great among all nations, and thou shalt be a blessing unto *thy seed* after thee, that *in their hands they shall bear this ministry and Priesthood unto all nations. (*Abraham 2:9)

The seed of Abraham, i.e. those who accept the gospel of Christ, have an inherent "ministry", which is the right and responsibility to *administer* the rites (ordinances) of the gospel of Jesus Christ. This authority of administration is called the priesthood and will reside in

Abraham and the hands of his righteous posterity who are accounted as his seed.

> 10 And I will bless them through thy name; for *as many as receive this Gospel shall be called after thy name, and shall be accounted thy seed*, and shall rise up and bless thee, as their father. (Abraham 2:10)

The seed of Abraham have this responsibility to administer the gospel to the world in perpetuity. For "as many of the Gentiles as will repent are the covenant people of the Lord," teaches Nephi. He adds: "for the Lord covenanteth with none save it be with them that repent and believe in his Son, who is the Holy One of Israel" (2 Nephi 30:2).

Because of his righteousness, Abraham is told that the authority of administration (the "right" to administer) will be part of the promise and covenant that God will endow upon him and his posterity:

> 11 And I will bless them that bless thee, and curse them that curse thee; and *in thee (that is, in thy priesthood) and in thy seed (that is, thy priesthood)*, for I give unto thee a promise that *this right shall continue in thee, and in thy seed after thee* (that is to say, the literal seed, or the seed of the body) *shall all the families of the earth be blessed, even with the blessings of the gospel, which are the blessings of salvation, even of life eternal*. (Abraham 2:9-11)

The Lord's covenant to Abraham is that this administrative right is protected and guaranteed by God in such a way that anybody who accepts or rejects the priesthood responsibility of Abraham and his seed (literal or adopted) will be blessed or cursed respectively. The cursing is not directed at Abraham or the posterity but at those who condemn the gospel and who seek to hinder or stop the administration of the gospel by the seed of Abraham. This is best explained in the Doctrine and Covenants:

> 16 *Cursed are all those that shall lift up the heel against mine anointed*, saith the Lord, and cry they have sinned when they have not sinned before me, saith the Lord, but

have done that which was meet in mine eyes, and which I commanded them.

17 But those who cry transgression do it because they are the servants of sin, and are the children of disobedience themselves.

18 And those who swear falsely against my servants, that they might bring them into bondage and death—

19 Wo unto them; because they have offended my little ones *they shall be severed from the ordinances of mine house.*

20 Their basket shall not be full, their houses and their barns shall perish, and they themselves shall be despised by those that flattered them.

21 *They shall not have right to the priesthood, nor their posterity after them from generation to generation.*

22 It had been better for them that a millstone had been hanged about their necks, and they drowned in the depth of the sea.

23 Wo unto all those that discomfort my people, and drive, and murder, and testify against them, saith the Lord of Hosts; a generation of vipers shall not escape the damnation of hell. (D&C 121:16-23)

The promise of innumerable seed was not based on Abraham's desire for large family and numerous progeny. In seeking for a son, his desire (because of his *love of God and his fellow man*) was to have a posterity that would be worthy to *administer* the ordinances and "blessings of salvation and life eternal" to all mankind. This is why the parenthetical phrases are inserted in verse 11:

> *"bless them that bless thee, and curse them that curse thee; and in thee (that is, [meaning] in thy priesthood [responsibility of administration]) and in thy seed (that is, [meaning] thy priesthood [responsibility]), for I give unto thee a promise that this **right** shall continue in thee, and in thy seed after thee." (Abraham 2:11)*

The priesthood organization today is an organization of those who have accepted the gospel of Christ and are considered the righteous seed of Abraham. As Saviors on Mt. Zion, the seed of Abraham will bless all the "families of the earth" through the administration of the gospel. By virtue of the covenant made with Abraham, these are those recognized and sustained by God to receive the authority to serve, administer, and bless mankind.

Joseph Smith taught this about the priesthood authority to administer the ordinances of the gospel:

> "Whenever men can find out the will of God and find an **administrator** *legally authorized from God*, there is the kingdom of God; but where these are not, the kingdom of God is not. All the ordinances, systems, and administrations on the earth are of no use to the children of men, *unless they are ordained and authorized of God*; for nothing will save a man but a **legal administrator**; for none others will be acknowledged either by God or angels." (*TPJS,* p 274)

This statement indicates that there are certain "authorities" (or keys) that leaders must possess for the kingdom of God and the gospel to exist. Again from the Teachings of the Prophet Joseph Smith:

> Christ was the head of the Church, the chief corner stone, the spiritual rock upon which the church was built, and the gates of hell shall not prevail against it. He built up the kingdom, chose apostles, and *ordained them to the Melchizedek Priesthood, giving them* **power to administer** *in the ordinances of the gospel.* (*TPJS,* p 318)

The apostolic responsibility is to make the gospel available to the entire world, while the keys and the authority they receive give them an *authoritative power* to administer the gospel. Those who have "keys" are those who have the authority to make decisions that will affect the administration of the gospel for those under their responsibility. Thus, the prophet and president of the church holds all keys necessary for the administration of the gospel for the whole church, while the Deacons quorum president has the keys to make decisions for the priesthood activity and service for those under his leadership and quorum.

The Prophet Joseph explains:

> There is no salvation between the two lids of the Bible *without a legal administrator.* Jesus was then the legal administrator, and *ordained His apostles.* (*TPJS*, 319).

Every priesthood holder will have a *line of authority.* This line of authority traces a priesthood holder's authority of administration from the person ordaining him back to the Lord. This ensures that the priesthood holder has been duly authorized to administer in the responsibility of the priesthood order to which they have been conferred and set apart. Therefore "no man taketh this honor unto himself, but he that is called of God, as was Aaron" (Hebrews 5:4). This verse is teaching that any priesthood calling or authoritative position **cannot be self-proclaimed**, but must come from a legal administrator who has been given the authority within the priesthood organization to ordain others (see D&C 18:32). Hence the *line of authority* is the order of heaven. It is this line of authority that connects them to the "rights" and blessings of Abraham and his descendants.

Part of this order of heaven is the *law of witnesses,* that "in the mouth of *two or three witnesses* shall *every word be established.*" (see: D&C 6:28, D&C 128:3; Deut. 17:6, Deut. 19:15; Matt. 18:16; 2 Cor. 13:1) At the beginning of this dispensation when the priesthood was conferred and keys given, there was always at least two present to bear witness of the event. Why is this important? The charlatan will claim manifestations and authority without the required second witness, for who then can argue or disagree? However, this is not the order of heaven, as "no man taketh this honor to himself", nor by himself. All ordinances of record and the transmission of divine priesthood "authority and keys" requires and invokes the law of witnesses, as outlined by the Savior in D&C 128:3, for the sake of order and faith.

Moses had the authority to call and set apart Aaron because of his line of authority through Jethro, which, when it comes to Melchizedek administrative authority, is even more important than bloodline genealogy.

6 And the sons of Moses, according to the Holy Priesthood which he received under the hand of his father-in-law, Jethro;

7 And Jethro received it under the hand of Caleb;

8 And Caleb received it under the hand of Elihu;

9 And Elihu under the hand of Jeremy;

10 And Jeremy under the hand of Gad;

11 And Gad under the hand of Esaias;

12 And Esaias received it under the hand of God.

13 Esaias also lived in the days of Abraham, and was blessed of him—

14 Which Abraham received the priesthood from Melchizedek, who received it through the lineage of his fathers, even till Noah;

15 And from Noah till Enoch, through the lineage of their fathers;

16 And from Enoch to Abel, who was slain by the conspiracy of his brother, who received the priesthood by the commandments of God, by the hand of his father Adam, who was the first man—

17 Which *priesthood continueth in the church of God in all generations*, and is without beginning of days or end of years. (D&C 84:6-17)

Verse 17 above reveals that this administrative authority will be in the "church of God in all generations." This is not to imply that the church is on the earth in all generations, but that this organized administrative authority, called 'priesthood', will be present when the church of God is on the earth. Today, this authority from God is not given personally by God, but conferred by authorization and under the hand of righteous men who previously received it. The authority to administer the gospel must come through an earthly and physical line because the administration of the gospel for the temporal and spiritual salvation of man is linked to this earth. None can "minister to this earth but those who do belong or have belonged to it" (D&C 130:5). There are specific righteous men who were foreordained with authorities, keys and responsibilities before the foundation of the earth. As the holders of these responsibilities and keys, these select righteous men have the authority to restore them in orderly succession. This is why John the Baptist, Moses, and Elias [Elijah] appeared to Joseph Smith and Oliver Cowdery, just as they appeared to Peter, James, and John on the Mount of Transfiguration to transfer keys and authority.

God declares that His "house is a house of order...and not a house of confusion" (D&C 132:8). Therefore, the ordaining of priesthood authority (i.e. the authority to administer the gospel) must be done in an orderly fashion (via the line of authority) in order to know who has, and who doesn't have, the authorization to administer the gospel. The Doctrine and Covenants outlines this order as given by Christ. Notice: it is not power that is given authorizing him to perform the duties of his calling, but "license."

> 64 Each priest, teacher, or deacon, who is ordained by a priest, may take a certificate from him at the time, which certificate, when presented to an elder, shall entitle him to a *license*, which shall *authorize* him to perform the duties of his calling, *or he may receive it from a conference.*

> 84 All members removing from the church where they reside, if going to a church where they are not known, may take a letter certifying that they are regular members and in good standing, which certificate may be signed by any elder or priest if the member receiving the letter is personally acquainted with the elder or priest, or it may be signed by the teachers or deacons of the church. (D&C 20:64, 84)

These certificates and licenses establish membership, activity, and priesthood office of responsibility in an orderly way so that there can be no claim of authority without due process. Records are also kept of ordinances and ordinations to prevent confusion and redundancy. To claim baptism and authority without witnesses of record and license would be a sure sign that the authority did not come from God.

Those who claim authority unto themselves without witnesses do so because they have no authority other than their own personal proclamation. Often they believe that the priesthood is a *power* rather than an *organization of administration*, leading to claims that they have Godly power, authorization, special knowledge, and manifestations that are given to them alone, thus creating a supposed *authority ex nihilo* (out of nothing). In contrast, the Lord mandates within a restoration that *"every word"* shall be established in the mouth of two or three witnesses, and the witnesses must physically see and participate for themselves, according to the scriptural patterns established anciently and by the modern revelations given to Joseph Smith from the Lord.

Outside the opening of a dispensation, the authority to administer the gospel, and the keys to do so, must be restored with witnesses. This, that no man taketh this honor unto himself, nor by himself. Thus, in this dispensation, following this mandate:

- There were Three Witnesses and then Eight Witnesses of the Nephite National Treasures
- The Aaronic and Melchizedek Priesthoods were restored to Joseph and Oliver Cowdery
- The Keys of Melchizedek were restored in Kirtland to Joseph Smith and Oliver Cowdery

162

Chapter 18

A Personal Responsibility

Within the Church there is a dichotomy between individual responsibility and the responsibility of priesthood leadership. On the one hand, individuals must *act for themselves* to develop a relationship with Christ. On the other hand, the priesthood has a responsibility to make sure that everything, including authorized ordinances, are made available to assist the individual in their quest for such a relationship. Some members find it hard to separate the two responsibilities. There is a tendency by some who have not established a relationship with Christ to blame the priesthood leadership for failing to provide it.

A Mental Picture

Adam's fall initiated a physical and spiritual death; therefore all are going to die. Let's pretend for a moment that there is a "medicine" that would cure these two deaths:

> "if they partake of the fruit, then a Savior shall be provided."

The patent holder of this life-saving medicine is the Savior. He wants all to have the chance to live again so He authorizes a corporation to market and distribute the medicine in order to better succeed in meeting the objective of saving lives. As always, opposing competition appears, offering knock-offs and other products to distract consumers. Ad campaigns are launched with spurious claims targeting the need for and efficacy of the medicine. Websites are created with opposing viewpoints and claims against the purity or quality of the real and pure product. The success of the corporation ultimately depends on educating the public so that they are willing to *give it a try*, placing enough trust in the claims of the corporation to experience for themselves that the medicine works as claimed. Once this has happened their *faith is in the product that saved their lives, not the corporation that administered it*, or the packaging it came in.

What's the purpose of a medicine bottle? The bottle protects the medicine, maintains its purity, and identifies what's in it and how to administer the medicine in the proper manner. The label might explain what the ingredients are, and the benefits of using it and how often to take it. Perhaps the label describes the physical symptoms that would necessitate the use of the medicine, providing warnings against taking it improperly.

If the Atonement and the Gospel of Jesus Christ is the life-saving medicine, then Christ is the active ingredient; His Atonement and resurrection is the medicine that will save all from the terminal illness of physical and spiritual death. The instructions and proper dosing are repeated at the Sacrament table every Sunday: "Always remember Him, that you might have His spirit to be with you."

When an illness or disease is recognized, and the medicine prescribed, it is not the bottle that should be swallowed. Rather it is the active ingredients of the medicine that will save the patient.

If you want to become better spiritually, it is up to you to take the medicine—it cannot be force-fed. The priesthood organization is vital in the administration of this medicine, but it is still up to you to take what is being offered. To refuse it because one does not like the packaging would be foolish, since it's what's in the bottle that saves your life, not the bottle itself.

It's important to remember that the "medicine" presented and ordinances offered by the Church of Jesus Christ of Latter-day Saints is a relationship with Jesus Christ and the Atonement. This relationship is the healing product that should be sought after. Many of the issues that are leading members to fall away are the result of faith and testimonies being placed in the vehicle of the administration (the bottle), and not in the Gospel of Jesus Christ (the medicine).

Everyone who seeks to progress spiritually through their faith and repentance must eventually become free from the blood and sins of the generation in which they live. This goal establishes the need for the prophet, apostles and other leaders of the priesthood to declare what those sins are. The goal of every prophet has been (and still is) to establish Zion. This can only be accomplished when individuals choose to become pure in heart. This goal has failed in every dispensation (except for the people of Enoch and Melchizedek) because those who should know better (i.e. those who have the gospel) have embraced spiritual Babylon. Zion is character! Zion cannot be established by a command or proclamation from the church office building, but *only* by the change of heart and character of the individual. If it takes a natural or economic disaster for people to have "all things in common", you can be sure "Zion has fled" from the heart. The desire to live those laws must grow from the seeds of the love of God and man in the good ground of the heart and character, not from the necessity of survival. This may only be accomplished by the use of agency, never by force, be it destructive, economic, or by proclamation or command. If there is no choice but to be good then being good is not a choice. Righteousness cannot exist in this scenario, as Lehi and Alma explain.

The priesthood and church organization work for the individual. The church is organized expressly to facilitate a personal relationship between God and the individual.

The Church is organized for two reasons: to show our love of God and our love of our fellow man. *First,* one demonstrates their love of God through worship and a willingness to *sincerely* participate in the church and in the ordinances of the gospel (the sacrament, baptism, receiving the gift of the Holy Ghost, etc.), in an organized and orderly manner. [Records are kept of specific ordinances a member might participate in to prevent redundancy of performing those ordinances over again, as in relocations (see, D&C 20:64, 84; D&C 72:17, 25).] *Second,* the church is organized so that the individual may have an opportunity to serve other people. Service is the key to developing the character of loving God and loving our fellowman. This is the command of Christ to all believers, and upon these two commandments hangs all of the commandments, all of the law and all that the prophets have taught (and will teach) (Matthew 22:40). The church organization provides the opportunity to serve (minister to) others in the administration of the gospel, thereby helping the faithful develop the necessary character trait of charity, the pure love of Christ.

Everyone should participate in the ordinances necessary for salvation, which will simultaneously develop the traits of love and service. Home teaching and visiting teaching does not exist for the sole purpose of taking care of others. The more important end result may well be the love that is developed for others in the commission of this service. These assignments provide the individual who is faithful in their home or visiting teaching an opportunity to develop a character required for exaltation: a character that will love all others. Developing this type of love is the real fruit of activity and obedience that can be developed through the gospel and church. No one has the authority to take away the right and privilege of learning to love others. Those who refuse to do their home and visiting teaching harm no one but themselves.

Remember: There is no "church" on the other side—there is only the gospel of Jesus Christ, which will still be taught and administered by a priesthood organization. The Savior did not organize the church when he was in Jerusalem or in Bountiful; He taught His gospel. He then organized the priesthood giving them the authority to administer the Gospel. The priesthood leadership determined that the best way to administer the gospel in an effective manner was to set up an administrative organization (wards and stakes). That is the purpose of the organization: to administer the gospel in an efficient and orderly manner, which includes record keeping. It's the priesthood organization that creates and organizes the church. That's why Christ says in 3 Nephi 27, verse 10:

If it so be that the church is built upon my gospel then will
the Father show forth his own works in it. (3 Nephi 27:10)

Priesthood leaders (like every individual) have their own opinions,
traditions, and interpretations of scripture and doctrines. These exist
outside of their authorized responsibilities as ministers and
administrators of the gospel. Members of the church should not expect
the leaders to expound deep doctrines or reveal mysteries. Nor should
they be expected to be correct or perfect in their understanding of
scripture or doctrine. Leaders are not called because they know more
about the scriptures than anyone else; they are called to administer the
gospel and protect the interests of the church. Regardless of what they
know or don't know, say or don't say; despite any decision, discussion,
discourse, opinion, or interpretation of life or scripture they might
make, their primary responsibility is to make sure that the gospel of
Jesus Christ and its ordinances are available to all who seek it. The
mission of the church and its priesthood leadership is to provide all
that is necessary for the individual who desires to come unto Christ to
do so. Some have supposed that the responsibility of the priesthood is
to *make sure that all members come unto Christ*. This is not so.
Leaders, like everyone, may only lead by example and encouragement,
not by force.

> 41 No power or influence *can or ought* to be maintained by
> virtue of the priesthood, [or priesthood position] only by
> persuasion, by long-suffering, by gentleness and meekness,
> and by love unfeigned; (D&C 121:41)

As always, the responsibility for the quality of the relationship that is
developed with Christ and the Atonement rests solely on the
individual, not the church or the priesthood.

Chapter 19

Sustaining the Priesthood

In the deepest layers of Catholicism, the Pope is considered infallible on certain issues. So much so, that when he makes a pronouncement on these issues, that statement supersedes anything that was previously established and accepted in the canon of belief. Many Latter-day Saints, because of *tradition*, labor under the assumption that latter-day church leaders are *infallible* no matter what they may say or teach. Consequently, some feel that if a priesthood leader or general authority says something that conflicts with scripture, then the words of the priesthood leader, like the Pope, are more binding and correct. Latter-day Saints are taught, and rightly so, that the prophet and president of the church will never be allowed by God to lead the church astray. However, this *divine default* refers *only* to the prophet and president of the church, not any other general authorities or local priesthood leadership. No doubt this Godly default is true, because in D&C 107:21-32, the Lord set up a system of checks and balances within the presiding priesthood organizations to maintain the purity of administration.

The church and priesthood leadership is led by the prophet and a quorum that functions as the Presidency of the Melchizedek Priesthood to ensure there will be no mistake in the *direction* of the Church. Mistakenly, many believe that every general authority will never say anything that might be wrong or untrue. Seldom do the priesthood leaders teach anything that would step beyond the inspired council that leads to a better understanding of the gospel and a Christ-like character change. But occasionally today, and especially in times past, leaders have been known to offer their personal commentary or opinions on scripture or doctrines that, filtered by their education and understanding, may or may not be correct. Many of the questions causing members to lose faith are based on statements or teachings arising from the *opinions* of current or past priesthood leaders. When a testimony is securely founded in Jesus Christ, and *not* the organization of administration, the contradictions and differing opinions and interpretations about scripture, science or any other subject, by any *local or general* priesthood leader, should not threaten one's faith or testimony. The obligation of the member is to determine if the statements made by the leadership are directed by the spirit and agree with the *standards* of the scripture, the words of Joseph Smith, and the statements of living prophets given to the church.

A Standard

So what is the standard of truth? As discussed earlier: if there is no standard then anything goes; everything could be correct and everything may be wrong at the same time. The scriptures counsel to "trust not in the arm of flesh" and to trust in the doctrine of no man. This would seem to include one's teachers, professors, lawyers, politicians, and even our personal opinions. Yet a standard must be chosen, and in the Lord's church, *scripture is the standard by which all doctrine should be determined and the standard by which all truth should be judged.* To this end, the scriptures have been designated as the 'Standard Works' from which to determine true doctrine, containing the necessary principles and doctrines of salvation and exaltation. The quality of intelligence and truth that one may have is dependent upon the source chosen to be that standard of truth. The individual cannot be any smarter than the source that is believed, and if that source is one's self, failure is assured. The one who recognizes their own nothingness before God and continues to seek for light and truth will receive the witness and revelation—not the one who believes they already know.

The educated atheist might only believe in that which they have experienced, thinking if it has not happened to them, it can not happen to anyone else. To the learned, the spiritual experience of a believer is defined as nothing more than an emotional situation. The line is thin between emotion and a spiritual experience. Nevertheless, there is a line. There is a difference. A beautiful piano concerto to one may invoke an emotion so strong that tears form, not only in the eyes, but in the spirit also. Yet to another person, the same music may be a chaotic pounding on the keys of a piano, creating emotions of anger and distress. The latter could claim that beautiful music doesn't exist and can't exist, because he hasn't yet experienced it. The educated fool might believe there can be no life after death, because it has not been experienced personally, nor have they known anyone who has come back from the dead (nor do they believe the *scriptural reports and testimonies of others*). This logic is as foolish as if one were to say that the land of Australia can't exist because they haven't ever seen it with their own eyes. Of course, even a home-bound person might have confidence that Australia does exist because of the *special reports and testimonies* of others they feel are trustworthy.

Korihor, a man of education and letters, had great success convincing the followers of God that they were duped using the logic and understanding of his own mind to judge spiritual matters:

> 12 And this Anti-Christ, whose name was Korihor, (and the law could have no hold upon him) began to preach unto the people that there should be no Christ. And after this manner did he preach, saying:
> 13 O ye that are bound down under a foolish and a vain hope, why do ye yoke yourselves with such foolish things? Why do ye look for a Christ? For no man can know of anything which is to come.
> 14 Behold, these things which ye call prophecies, which ye say are handed down by holy prophets, behold, they are foolish traditions of your fathers.
> 15 How do ye know of their surety? Behold, ye cannot know of things which ye do not see; therefore, ye cannot know that there shall be a Christ.

16 Ye look forward and say that ye see a remission of your sins. But behold, it is the effect of a frenzied mind; and this derangement of your minds comes because of the traditions of your fathers, which lead you away into a belief of things which are not so.

17 And many more such things did he say unto them, telling them that there could be no Atonement made for the sins of men, but every man fared in this life according to the management of the creature; therefore, every man prospered according to his genius, and that every man conquered according to his strength; and whatsoever a man did was no crime.

18 And thus he did preach unto them, leading away the hearts of many, causing them to lift up their heads in their wickedness, yea, leading away many women, and also men, to commit whoredoms—telling them that when a man was dead, that was the end thereof. (Alma 30:12-18)

In Korihor's limited spiritual experience (and pride), he sought to become the source of the spiritual knowledge, testimony, and experience for others. Korihor felt that he was not only qualified to know for himself, but also to know and judge the spiritual experiences of everyone else. Korihor, like many detractors today, began to trust in his own flesh, his own learning and his own experiences. Convinced he was right, and perhaps reveling in the power and influence his words had over others, he sought to destroy their testimonies using his gift for argument and logic. Notice: In the verses above Korihor first intellectually attacks the spiritual experiences of the believer, and then attacks the organized church and priesthood.

Like many today who discount faith and testimony based on spiritual manifestations, Korihor had no use for scriptures or the testimony of others, or for any beliefs that were not 'provable' according to the standards of men. Accordingly, many of those who have become the prey and victims of modern Korihors become so spiritually blunted that past experiences—spiritual truths they once knew—are lost to them. In that state spiritual darkness they begin to believe they are enlightened and free from the shackles of faith and religion. As they begin trusting in the arm of flesh, they come to believe that their lack of faith and belief is a result of superior education, knowledge and experience, which is directly out of the Korihorian Encyclopedia of Faith and Religion. In their pride they are essentially saying they know more about faith and testimony than the generations who gave their whole life for their faith and their God. To justify their disbelief, they insinuate that parents and family are the ignorant and uneducated ones who have been manipulated and brainwashed by emotion and church leaders.

Fruits of Faith

Those who are struggling with their faith might consider what their life and family might be like now if the three generations previous to them had no faith and no belief. What if their fathers, grand and great, had felt the same as they do? There would be no commandments to shackle physical desires as one begins to make choices that create character. There might be no moral code or restrictive morality; families might not be important or even necessary. Those falling away today might not even exist because of the pro-choice agenda. Imagine the generational trajectory of a family whose values went no deeper than "eat, drink, and be merry, for tomorrow we die". The fruits of Joseph Smith are the members of the church today; not so much who they are or how many there are, but what they are. This alone should be a spiritual witness of the reality of God and goodness, of faith and family. Only a fool would declare that the absence of a faith in God and morality is the better way.

Korihor, trusting in his own arm of flesh, became the epitome of pride and selfishness. In his arrogance, the anti-Christ then demanded a sign:

> 43 And now Korihor said unto Alma: If thou wilt show me a sign, that I may be convinced that there is a God, yea, show unto me that he hath power, and then will I be convinced of the truth of thy words.
> 44 But Alma said unto him: Thou hast had signs enough; will ye tempt your God? Will ye say, Show unto me a sign, when ye have the testimony of all these thy brethren, and also all the holy prophets? The scriptures are laid before

174

> thee, yea, and all things denote there is a God; yea, even the
> earth, and all things that are upon the face of it, yea, and its
> motion, yea, and also all the planets which move in their
> regular form do witness that there is a Supreme Creator.
> (Alma 30:43-44)

Oh, say what is truth? This is a question that is best answered in the scriptures and reinforced by the witnesses of prophets and apostles. The need to understand the scriptures in order to understand doctrine has taken a secondary position, leading to the teaching of traditions and opinions as doctrine. This is not the fault of the church, as the manuals are based on the scriptures, and are intended to help members of the church begin the process that will bring them to Christ and initiate that change of character. Printed in the introduction of each manual is the instruction that it should be used as an aid in teaching or studying the scriptures. However, the prepared lesson material and sometimes the teacher's traditions often supersede the importance of the scriptures, in the classroom **and** from the pulpit. Seldom are the scriptures, or a passage or topic from the scriptures, used as a primary source for a talk. It is much easier to use church magazines or a conference talk as the first choice and major source. This is not bad or wrong, but because of this, the scriptures have migrated to a lesser position, often taking a back seat in the teaching, learning, and discovery of truth and doctrine. In consequence of this, disputes, arguments and rationalizations for a lack of faith are often focused on what someone in a position of authority has said, right or wrong, rather than on the doctrines and truths found in the scriptures. Of course, one must read and study the scriptures to know what truths they contain.

Scripture is the standard by which all doctrine should be determined, by member and priesthood leader alike. They are the standard by which all truth should be judged. It follows then that all opinions, interpretations and statements of the General Authorities, in General Conference or any other setting, should *square with the scriptures*.

Below are a few statements about the importance of scripture that should be remembered as one weighs the statements of past or present priesthood leaders. Notice that all doctrine must be founded upon the four standard works. Joseph Smith implied the same in a statement about the importance of scripture and his opinion:

> If any man will prove to me, by one passage of Holy Writ, one item I believe to be false, I will renounce and disclaim it as far as I promulgated it. (*TPJS*, p 327)

Joseph Fielding Smith explained that the teachings and statements of all, including the leading brethren, should agree with the scriptures:

> It makes no difference what is written or what anyone has said, if what has been said is in conflict with what the Lord has revealed, we can set it aside. My words, and the teaching of any other member of the church, high or low, *if they do not square with the revelations, we need not accept them.* Let us have this matter clear. We have accepted *the four standard works as the measuring yardsticks, or balances, by which we measure every man's doctrine.*
> (*Doctrines of Salvation*, Vol.3, p.203)

President Harold B. Lee echoed the same as he emphasized the importance of scripture:

> We have the standard church works. Why do we call them standard? If there is any teacher who teaches a doctrine that can't be substantiated from the standard church works—and I make one qualification, and that is unless that one be the president of the church, who alone has the right to declare new doctrine—then you may know by that same token that such a teacher is but expressing his own opinion. (*Stand Ye In Holy Places*, p.109-110)

Notice the one qualification to scripture that President Lee mentions: The president of the church "alone, has the right to declare new doctrine" or change doctrine—not his counselors, nor any of the twelve apostles. If the president of the church declares new doctrine or makes a change of existing doctrine, it must be made by *revelation* and then canonized by *declaration*.

A "declaration" of *new* doctrine or a *change* of doctrine will require the church as a body to first sustain the president of the church as a prophet, seer, and revelator. Following the sustaining vote, the new revelation or doctrine (or the change in old doctrine) will be read to the church. The body of the church then, by show of hand, accepts and sustains the revelation as the mind and will of the Lord, as all things must be done by common consent according to scripture. Remember, it is only the president of the church who has the right to declare or change doctrine.

• *Revelations* are scripture if canonized by official declaration.
• *Declarations* are those which change scripture or add new revelation to the standard works.
• *Proclamations* are official statements that explain church position, policy and doctrine that is based on existing scripture.

The scriptures, then, are binding. As the supreme standard of truth, the doctrines and principles that the prophets and the apostles teach must agree with those found in the scriptures. Scriptures are called "The Standard Works" for a reason. This idea of a "standard" that is unchangeable will be expanded upon in the first chapter of Part II.

The general leadership should rely on scripture as their standard both when speaking to the church membership and when discharging their responsibility to administer the gospel. On all other subjects, the priesthood leadership may have their opinions, filtered by their own education and learning. Thus, a prophet may speak as a prophet when required by ecclesiastical responsibility, and still voice an opinion as any man on other subjects that would not necessarily be binding on the general membership. Joseph Smith took pains to make the following distinction clear:

> "This morning I read German and visited with a brother and sister from Michigan who 'thought a prophet is always a prophet.' But I told them that *"a prophet was a prophet only when he was acting as such."* (TPJS page 278)

Below are a few references and quotes about the statements and teachings of priesthood leadership:

George Q. Cannon, Member of the First Presidency stated:

> The First Presidency cannot claim, individually or collectively, infallibility.[3]

J. Reuben Clark, Member of the First Presidency made the comment about the fallibility of leaders:

> Even the president of the church has not always spoken under the direction of the Holy Ghost.[4]

Spencer W. Kimball, President of the Church stated:

> I make no claim of infallibility.[5]

In 2007 a published statement by the church on Mormon doctrine was made available to all:

> Not every statement made by a church leader, past or present, necessarily constitutes doctrine. A single statement made by a single leader on a single occasion often represents a personal, though well-considered, opinion, but is not meant to be officially binding for the whole church. With divine inspiration, the First Presidency (the prophet and his two counselors) and the Quorum of the Twelve Apostles (the second-highest governing body of the church) counsel together to establish doctrine that is consistently proclaimed in official church publications. This doctrine resides in the four "standard works" of scripture (the Holy Bible, the Book of Mormon, the Doctrine and Covenants and the Pearl of Great Price), official declarations and proclamations, and the Articles of Faith. Isolated statements are often taken out of

3. George Q. Cannon, *Gospel Truth: Discourses and Writings of President George Q. Cannon*, 1957, 1:206
4. Elder J. Reuben Clark, quoted in *Faithful History: Essays on Writing Mormon History*, p. 82
5. Spencer W. Kimball, "Improvement Era," June 1970, p. 9

context, leaving their original meaning distorted.
(LDS Newsroom, "Approaching Mormon Doctrine")

In the October 2013 General Conference Elder Uchtdorf, a counselor in the First Presidency made this statement about the leaders and the mistakes of imperfect people:

> And, to be perfectly frank, there have been times when members or leaders in the church have simply made mistakes. There may have been things said or done that were not in harmony with our values, principles, or doctrine.
> It is unfortunate that some have stumbled because of mistakes made by men. But in spite of this, the eternal truth of the restored gospel found in The Church of Jesus Christ of Latter-day Saints is not tarnished, diminished, or destroyed.
> As an Apostle of the Lord Jesus Christ and as one who has seen firsthand the councils and workings of this church, I bear solemn witness that no decision of significance affecting this church or its members is ever made without earnestly seeking the inspiration, guidance, and approbation of our Eternal Father. This is the church of Jesus Christ. God will not allow His church to drift from its appointed course or fail to fulfill its divine destiny.[6]

In spite of these public disclaimers from the pulpit, many members still expect infallibility from their leaders. The belief of infallibility may stem from years of sustaining the leaders as prophets, seers, and revelators. The nonverbal and subconscious implication is: as "prophets, seers, and revelators" the leaders cannot say or do anything wrong. Another contributing factor is the conditioning to be obedient to the voice of leadership. Members of the church are taught to follow the leaders, as they will not lead you astray. It is true, they do not and will not intentionally lead the members in a wrong direction or down the wrong path. Still, in the belief that obedience (The first law of heaven) is better than questioning, it is considered a *sin* to turn down a calling despite personal circumstances. To some, the act of sustaining implies that these leaders are *always* inspired, and all words they speak

---

6. 2013 October Conference, p 21, "Come Join with Us"

are given them directly from God. This position foolishly and unrealistically presupposes that these priesthood leaders no longer have *their* own personal interpretations, opinions, or traditions, and that their word and will is always the same as God's. The leadership's responsibility is the ministry and the administration of the gospel, that the individual may come unto Christ. Priesthood leaders are not commissioned to provide scriptural commentary or an unfettered oration on the mysteries.

This practice of the improper faith and confidence in priesthood leaders worried Brigham Young:

> I am more afraid that this people have so much confidence in their leaders that they will not inquire for themselves of God whether they are led by him. I am fearful they settle down in a state of blind self-security, trusting their eternal destiny in the hands of their leaders with a reckless confidence that in itself would thwart the purposes of God in their salvation. Let every man and woman know, by the whispering of the Spirit of God to themselves, whether their leaders are walking in the path the Lord dictates, or not.[7]

In a letter for the Millennial Star in 1887, B. H. Roberts made a statement that addresses the fallibility of individual views:

> Relative to these sermons [Journal of Discourses] I must tell you they represent the individual views of the speakers, and the church is not responsible for their teachings. Our authorized church works are the Bible, Book of Mormon, Doctrine and Covenants, and the Pearl of Great Price. In the church very wide latitude is given to individual belief and opinion, each man being responsible for his views and not the church; the church is only responsible for that which she sanctions and approves through the formal actions of her councils. So it may be that errors will be found in the sermons of men, and that in their over zeal, unwise

---

7. *Journal of Discourses*, 14:205

expressions will escape them, for all of which the church is not responsible.[8]

All leaders speak, make decisions, and take actions based on *their learning* and understanding of all subjects, including the meaning of scripture. While they may be inspired in the counsel and advice they give to church members, seldom today do leaders publicly speak of doctrine outside of the basics. This has rankled some members who blame priesthood leadership for their spiritual and scriptural ignorance. Nevertheless, there exists a very good reason for the presentation of basic doctrines in the church.

There exists Three Doctrinal 'M's or levels of doctrine discussed in the scriptures: *Milk, Meat,* and *Mysteries*. By necessity and design there is a dairy department in every ward and stake of the church. The church must provide a never-ending supply of milk products through a fourth 'M', the *Manuals*. ALL manuals must teach to the lowest common denominator in the church, from the Primary youth to the newly baptized member. All spiritual knowledge must be built on the solid foundation of the gospel of Jesus Christ: Faith, Repentance, Baptism, and the Gift of the Holy Ghost. Thus the basic milk products must be available to all ages and all levels of understanding.

Some complain about the monotony of the milk, and wonder why the church doesn't serve steak now and then. The church *cannot* teach the meat. Without the foundation of the milk, the meat will choke the unprepared. This meat must be actively and personally pursued by the individual who "hungers and thirsts after righteousness." All must learn by "study and also by faith" and do so *"line upon line, precept upon precept, here a little and there a little."* Providing the meat is not the responsibility of the church or its leaders; that responsibility rests upon the individual. The Gospel Doctrine class, at best, should stimulate an appetite for the Bar-B-Que. Sustained by the milk, the meat is extracted from the scriptures by personal initiative and study. It's from the scriptures that the doctrinal depth and discovery of the

---

8. Millennial Star 49. 48 (November 28, 1887): 760-763; A Letter written by B. H. Roberts November 4, 1887

eternal truths are offered, and they are found only by those who have expended the effort and sacrificed the time to seek and study more.

There are two reasons why the church should not be condemned for the menu of milk products offered in church meetings and the manuals. *First*: the church's responsibility is to lay the foundation for that newest member of the church and gospel. Each lesson and manual is geared to offer the basics, and to inspire and direct the individual to seek for an in-depth understanding in their personal study of the scriptures. *Second*: the lack of scripture knowledge by some, mixed with tradition and doctrinal speculation by many members, would render every class a smorgasbord of beliefs and feelings. This would result in destructive time tangents and perhaps perpetuate false traditions or opinions that may be taught and believed as doctrine.

A lay ministry has a tendency to make everyone an expert on doctrine, no matter how active or inactive they may be or have been. This is one important reason manuals are prepared, so that tangents are controlled and basic and true doctrines are taught. This means that the meat that is found in the scriptures should be *individually sought but restrictively taught*. Unfortunately, those who make no effort to find the meat rarely have the teeth and muscles to chew it. Like life, the 'milk' can and should be the springboard into 'meat' of the scriptures. Those who want more than the 'milk' they get in church *are not* victims of a failed church correlation, but victims of their own laziness and rationalizations. The 'meat' is of no value to those who will not use their own energy to find it. The demand that others, in particular the church, provide the 'meat' without any personal preparation will only cause them to choke on the most tender of cuts.

On the other side of the instructional spectrum, there are those who believe kosher law applies to learning, insisting that milk and meat cannot be mixed. Firm in their belief that all members should ingest only milk products, they cough and sputter whenever a little meat broth is introduced in the Gospel Doctrine class. Having never been outside the dairy section (believing that true spiritual insights must be

182

composed of only milk), they are openly suspicious of non-dairy products and insist everyone get back to the safety of the dairy aisle.

The *Mysteries*, (whatever they are) on the other hand, come from God to the *prepared* individual who seeks further light and truth. Further light and knowledge always comes with increased accountability, and in the case of mysteries, there are certain restrictions. As scripture makes clear, mysteries come only to those who are prepared to receive them, and they are for the individual's own knowledge and enlightenment—not the body of the church in any setting—and therefore should not be shared with those who lack the same preparation. Those who have been blessed with an understanding of important truths (mysteries) will not talk about them, while those who discuss them often don't know what they're talking about. Those who receive revelation must be prepared not only to ask the question but also be just as prepared to receive the answer. Those who receive light and truth are not only accountable for it but also restricted in how it might be used.

There is a divine rule of order for the reception and dissemination of revealed knowledge and manifestations. Joseph Smith warned of the "impropriety" of listening to those who claim to have manifestations, visions, and special knowledge who then seek to correct the church organization that God has set up. Joseph explains this restriction by stating:

> I will inform you that it is contrary to the economy of God for any member of church, or any one, to receive instruction for those in authority higher than themselves; *therefore, you will see the impropriety of giving heed to them*; but if any person have a vision or a visitation from a heavenly messenger it must be for his own benefit and instruction; for the fundamental principles, government, and doctrine of the church are vested in the keys of the kingdom. *(TPJS,* p. 21)

Alma teaches about the restrictions placed on those who may receive insights into what are called 'mysteries,' as did Joseph Smith above:

And now Alma began to expound these things unto him, saying: *It is given unto many to know the mysteries of God; nevertheless, they are laid under a strict command that they shall not impart* only according to the portion of his word which he doth grant unto the children of men, according to the heed and diligence which they give unto him. (Alma 12:9)

One can be assured that when a person begins to declare special visions, visitations, assignments, and authorities, crying 'lo here, or lo there!' that they are seeking to deceive the very elect. Invariably, these events lack the requisite witnesses and fail the tests outlined in scripture, defying the economy and order of God. The words of Christ should be heeded as He commands, "believe him not" (JS Matthew 24:21, 25).

So what is our responsibility when a priesthood leader makes a statement or acts in a way that seems incongruent with our learning and education? Some will question whether the leaders were really inspired or worthy opening the door to doubt. The real question that should instead be asked is: Are they fulfilling their responsibility in the administration of the gospel?

Remember, the primary responsibility of priesthood leadership lies in the administration of the gospel of Jesus Christ. That is their job and the purpose for which they are called. Under the guidance and direction of the Lord, they are empowered (inspired) to discharge their duties within the scope of their call. At all other times, they are human and must make their own decisions and speak their own opinions. One need not worry if their opinions and traditions are incongruent with accepted theories of science, or don't agree with the scriptural interpretations of other priesthood leaders. All may be assured that their counsel on spiritual matters will *point to the path* that leads to God. From there, it is *an individual* responsibility to grasp the iron rod and make one's own way toward the Tree of Life.

Salvation is not only an individual responsibility; it is also a joint effort with the Divine. The sacrifice has been provided and Christ stands at the door and knocks. Those who hope to be embraced by God, however, must individually be prepared to open that door, and then act upon the knowledge that is received. Priesthood leaders have been called and set apart to help those within the scope of their responsibility reach that door with the spiritual strength to initiate a personal relationship with the Savior. Their help (counsel, teachings, ordinances) means nothing if the individual refuses to come unto Christ through the fruits meet for repentance and character change.

To recap: That faith which keeps one active in the gospel is a faith centered in Jesus Christ. All general authorities and priesthood leaders are sustained in their specific responsibility in the ministry and administration of the gospel of Jesus Christ. They are not sustained because they have read the scriptures more than someone else, nor are they called to expound the mysteries, answer every question, or explain and give commentary on the scriptures. They are not sustained because of their exceeding righteousness, nor with the expectation that they will be perfect in every action, work, word, or thought.

If the local priesthood authorities (under the direction of the general leadership) ensure that the baptized member (me, the individual) has been provided every opportunity to participate in the ordinances of the gospel, they have succeeded. When every opportunity to develop and strengthen that relationship with God and man through the gospel and church organization has been provided, the priesthood leaders have then fulfilled their responsibility to the individuals that have sustained them. If each week the sacrament is prepared, blessed, and passed at sacrament meeting by those authorized, and the baptismal font is filled when someone desires to be baptized, a record is kept, and witnesses provided, the leaders have succeeded in their responsibility. It is to this end that they are sustained.

The personal weaknesses and faults of priesthood leaders can be overlooked if they do not affect their ability to administer the gospel. Every man has faults, and there is "none good but one, and that is God" (see Matthew 19:17; Mark 10:18; Luke 18:19). It doesn't matter who they are or the calling they have—all men have faults, weaknesses of the flesh, pride, and intellect. To expect perfection and infallibility from any man but Christ is foolish. Yet God will work with and inspire men in their weaknesses and imperfections.

Of course, our leaders should be men of good character, as Jethro explains to his son-in-law Moses:

> 21 Moreover thou shalt *provide out of all the people able men, such as fear God, men of truth, hating covetousness; and place such over them, to be rulers* of thousands, and rulers of hundreds, rulers of fifties, and rulers of tens: (Exodus 18:21)

Moses was instructed by Jethro to choose good men that "fear God", placing character, faith and testimony as primary traits in that choice. They must be "men of truth" and "hating covetousness". In the opening of this dispensation the Lord instructed Joseph Smith and Oliver Cowdery what traits to look for in the men that would become apostles in the restored priesthood.

> 27 Yea, even twelve; and the Twelve shall be my disciples, and they shall take upon them my name; and the Twelve are they who shall desire to *take upon them my name with full purpose of heart.*
> 28 And if they desire to take upon them my name with full purpose of heart, they are *called to go into all the world to preach my gospel* unto every creature.
> 29 And they are they who are *ordained of me to baptize in my name, according to that which is written*;
> 30 And you have that which is written before you; wherefore, *you must perform it according to the words which are written.*
> 31 And now I speak unto you, the Twelve—Behold, my grace is sufficient for you; *you must walk uprightly before me and sin not.*
> 32 And, behold, *you are they who are ordained of me to ordain priests and teachers; to declare my gospel, according to the power of the Holy Ghost which is in you, and*

*according to the callings and gifts of God unto me*n; (D&C 18:27-32)

Oliver was instructed to find men that would:

- Take upon my name with "full purpose of heart"
- "Go into all the world to preach my gospel"
- "baptize in my name"
- Do their work "according to that which is written"
- "Walk uprightly"
- "Sin not"
- Ordain others to priesthood responsibilities
- Do their work "according to the power of the Holy Ghost"
- Do their work "according to the callings and gifts of God unto men"

These few verses in the Doctrine and Covenants outline three important aspects of those chosen to become apostles: *who* they are, *what* they should do, and *how* they are to do it. First is *who*, the kind of men they should be in relation to their character and testimony: the apostolic priesthood leaders should be good men with a commitment to God and righteousness. Second is *what* their responsibilities are going to be that they should be prepared to accomplish. They must preach the gospel throughout the world and baptize and ordain others to the work. Third and last is *how* they are to accomplish this important work. Verses 29 and 30 both stipulate that what they do must be according to scripture ('that which is written'), as it is the standard. The second aspect of *how*, is that all that they do *within this responsibility* (not every aspect of their life) should be done under the inspiration and power of the Holy Ghost, which is a gift of God given to all the good and righteous, not just priesthood leaders. Every priesthood leader should seek the guidance of the Holy Ghost in discerning the gifts of those who might best serve in any calling. No individual leader or teacher is perfect. All must do their best using their personal judgment and education coupled with the inspiration of the Holy Ghost.

God can and does use men and women in their weaknesses and can use everyone who is willing to serve. Even so, the judgments of mankind and even priesthood leaders are based on personal opinions of righteousness and the fences that may have been placed around specific laws and commandments. Would or should it be an issue that Christ drank wine or that Christ chose Judas for an apostle? Did He not know about Judas' character? Would it make a difference that Peter, who walked with the Savior daily and who was chosen to become the president of the church, denied Christ three times? These are not issues that affect the administration of the gospel. The rule is taught to Peter and every other leader: "when thou art converted, strengthen thy brethren."

Joseph Smith said this about recognizing the quality of the leaders we sustain:

> The servants of God teach nothing but principles of eternal life, by their works ye shall know them. A good man will speak good things and holy principles, and an evil man evil things. ... I exhort you to give heed to all the virtue and the teachings which I have given you. (*TPJS*, p 367)

This statement by Joseph Smith would indicate that outside of the administration of the gospel and priesthood responsibilities, the church leadership can and do have their own activities, opinions and interpretations. Nevertheless, in their assigned responsibility as chosen ministers and administrators, I as an individual can and do sustain them as the Doctrine and Covenants teach:

> 65 Wherefore, it must needs be that one be appointed of the High Priesthood to preside over the priesthood, and he shall be called President of the High Priesthood of the Church;
> 91 And again, the duty of the President of the office of the High Priesthood is to preside over the whole church, and to be like unto Moses—
> 92 Behold, here is wisdom; yea, to be a seer, a revelator, a translator, and a prophet, having all the gifts of God which he bestows upon the head of the church. (D&C 107:65, 91-92)

Author's Note:

I accept and sustain the President and Prophet of the Church of Jesus Christ of Latter-day Saints, the Quorum of the First Presidency, and the Quorum of the Twelve Apostles in their responsibility as outlined in the Doctrine and Covenants. I sustain them in their position and responsibility, recognizing their inspiration and authority, along with the "gifts of God" that He bestows on the leaders that are called as the authorized administrators of the gospel of salvation and eternal life.

I can and do support and sustain all my priesthood leaders, general and local! It is my understanding and belief (from scripture) that the most important role of priesthood leadership is the administration of the gospel of Jesus Christ. Priesthood leaders exist to *assist me*, the individual, in the improvement of my character, and to provide the opportunities and ordinances to strengthen my relationship with Jesus Christ, and His gospel. Their responsibility of service is to *assist me* in developing a better understanding of the Atonement of Christ in order to make it more effective in my life. However, coming unto Christ and having that personal relationship is *my* responsibility, not the responsibility of my priesthood leaders.

I do not expect the priesthood leadership to expound deep doctrines or reveal mysteries, nor do I expect them to always be correct or perfect in their understanding and teaching of scripture or doctrine. I realize that priesthood leaders are not called because they know more or studied more about the scriptures than anyone else. They have been called and set apart to administer the gospel of Jesus Christ for the

190

benefit of my family and myself. According to scripture, that gospel is: Faith, Repentance, Baptism, and the Gift of the Holy Ghost— nothing more.

My priesthood leaders are not expected or required to ensure that I have a relationship with Christ. Nor are they required to teach the gospel to my family or myself (that is my responsibility). However, I recognize that the priesthood organization has the authority to provide opportunities through the activities and auxiliaries of the church to *assist me* in my responsibility. As a parent and individual I have a personal responsibility to learn more and teach my family the Gospel of Christ.

My weekly gospel need as I develop a relationship with my Savior is to partake of the Sacrament which has been prepared, blessed, and *administered* by authorized ministers. In this ordinance, I covenant "to keep his commandments and always remember him," seeking for that relationship with my God and Redeemer each week. Simply put, if the sacrament is prepared, blessed, and passed by the priesthood authority required, and the ordinances of salvation are made available to myself and my family as needed, then the priesthood leaders have fulfilled their responsibility. I expect no more.

Thus, what my priesthood leaders (general and local, past or present) know, or think they know, or don't know, about particular aspects of doctrine and scripture will not affect my sustaining of them. I can and do sustain them even if they have the weaknesses and frailties of man and mortality—whether it be of the flesh, mind, culture, or education—as long as they are faithful in the administration of the gospel of Jesus Christ. I sustain them in their call to administer the gospel and make it available to myself and my family, not in their perfection or infallibility.

Bruce H. Porter

The Threshing Floor of Faith
Enduring to the End

Part II

Questions & Scriptural Answers

Part II

A Second Introduction

The articles and chapters presented in this book are presented as food for thought and do not in any way represent official doctrine or policy of the Church of Jesus Christ of Latter-day Saints. As the author, I sustain and support all general and local priesthood leaders and authorities. I have total respect and honor for their position in the priesthood organization, as also, for the responsibilities, authority and keys that these leaders hold for the spiritual development and salvation of every individual in the church and in the world.

Even though this work may present a different point of view from accepted opinion or the traditional interpretation of scripture, it does not constitute a non-sustaining attitude toward the leadership of the church. The ideas presented in this book represent only a point of view or alternative way of looking at a concept, topic or scripture. Over time, many opinions have been generally accepted as church doctrine. However, when explored through the lens of scripture, these supposed doctrines are often revealed to be "tradition, opinion, or interpretations" that have been presented by a leader or teacher. Examples include the requirement to wear white shirts and ties to administer and pass the sacrament, or the teaching that the sacrament should be taken with the right hand. Some stakes will not allow men with facial hair to hold any leadership positions. These are just a few of the traditions and policies that have taken on the weight of doctrine, which if they were requirements or doctrines would be found in *The General Handbook of Instructions*. True doctrines are found in the gospel of Jesus Christ as taught and outlined by the Savior and in scripture.

As a reminder, the chapter discussions in this book are not meant to correct any doctrine or church leader; but to demonstrate how certain doctrines that are often misunderstood are nevertheless consistent with scripture. Latter-day Saints should *not* be looking for discrepancies between teachings and scripture, or finding fault in doctrines and principles that may be taught. The focus of any study of this sort should be on the discovery and understanding of how and why supposed contradictions exist, rather than crying 'foul' before one understands the rules. Supposed doctrinal contradictions within scripture are usually nonexistent when time is taken to study. Nevertheless, questions are often created in the mind of those who may not know to use the scriptures as a standard; therefore, opinions often become more important than scriptures. Skeptics and sometimes even the well-intentioned reader are often quick to cry 'contradiction!' rather than seek for clarification within the pages of scripture. The light of day is nothing more than darkness until the eyes are opened. Truths and answers are difficult to find in the shadows of darkness until the light of scripture illuminates the mind and heart.

The Doctrine and Covenants mandates that all should *"seek learning even by study and also by faith"* (D&C 88:118). This means that a spiritual *learning* and education requires both study and faith as part of the recipe. When searching scriptures or doing research (by study) and a supposed contradiction or doctrinal difference is found, doubt will not be an issue *if* faith becomes the next step in research. Just because an individual doesn't understand an idea or doctrine doesn't mean that there is not an answer to be found. Too often, because of educational indoctrination or belief, a person may trust in their own 'arm of flesh' and understanding, supposing of themselves that there is no answer to their questions. Some have not spent sufficient time in the scriptures and in reading the words of Joseph Smith to add the ingredients of knowledge, light, truth, and 'faith' to the process of a spiritual education.

Sometimes it is difficult to determine what constitutes church doctrine, as there is not always agreement on the interpretation of scripture. This is further complicated by the statements and opinions of leaders about subjects that may be only opinions. The topics presented in this work are not necessarily "doctrines" per se, even though tradition may give them the force of doctrine. The chapters that follow discuss specific doctrinal issues that reflect the author's thoughts, opinions, and interpretations of scripture, using the scriptural standard to explain and define a topic. For example, recently it was reported by the church that the restriction of the priesthood from a particular race was a *policy* rather than a doctrine. At one time, however, this *policy* was considered a doctrine, with many books written about this supposed doctrine. Even though the race restriction is now considered a policy rather than a doctrine, there is a doctrine found in scripture that spawned the policy, be it right or wrong, which will be explored here.

This begs the question: What is real doctrine? How should tradition be separated from doctrinal truth? The answer: the scriptures contain the standards of truth. The other unassailable sources that should not be ignored are the teachings of Joseph Smith and the words of other prophets while they are acting as prophet and president of the church. Remember, only one man, the president of the church, has the authority to change doctrine or scripture, which is done by official declaration following a revelation or change of doctrine.

The topics presented here are formulated from questions that are more often asked than they are answered. Some of the topics in this collection address concerns that are rarely brought up or voiced because personal opinions and interpretation may not agree with scripture and the teachings of Joseph Smith. This material as presented is just food for thought and should not be considered as doctrine, policy, or the official belief of the Church of Jesus Christ of Latter-day Saints. It is important to read every chapter, as particular elements of one discussion or chapter might apply tangentially to another chapter focusing on a different topic. As Part I concluded with a brief discussion about the standard of scripture, the beginning of Part II will continue that discussion in more depth.

Because some may read only the chapter that answers a question that interests them, some concepts have been repeated within the surrounding chapters. This is done that each chapter may be read and understood independently based on interest from the rest of the book.

The uses of italics and bolded font in text and quotes have been used for emphasis throughout the book, and may or may not be noted as such.

Chapter 20

A Standard of Doctrine

It is hoped that the ideas and scriptural discussions presented in this work might help explain some of the questions that are often generated between the traditional teachings of the church and the prescribed teachings of the manuals, the scriptures, and the words of Joseph Smith. This work is not trying to present new doctrine or teach mysteries of any sort. There is neither goal nor presumptuous idea in this work that seeks to change the church or any accepted position, doctrine, or tradition espoused or taught by its general leadership. However, traditions are strong and sometimes become more important than true doctrine and scripture.

Every business and organization must determine which problems or traditions can be changed without much effort or cost, and which issues cannot be improved because of a cost so high it might prohibit the modification. These costs and repercussions might require better machinery or the rewriting of the many manuals of instruction and publications. This process may require correcting the public statements of executives, which correction might cause a disruption within an organization, creating a lack of faith or trust in leadership that would be better left alone. In the same way, many traditions and policies in the church are perpetrated gradually over time, so that eventually the 'traditions of men' assume the force of doctrine. As these traditions become accepted as doctrines, they become more difficult to change with each passing generation. This is because the cost of change may outweigh the benefits of making the correction. These doctrinal traditions are not perpetuated intentionally, but they nevertheless become accepted by all who are exposed to the traditions or interpretations over time.

The scriptures are the best commentary on the scriptures and all members of the church should rely on the doctrines and teachings found in the "standard works" or canonized scriptures. The words of the prophets and apostles at general conference are those issues and ideas that members of the Church need to know and understand to survive the spiritual and temporal calamities of the last days. The talks of leaders help individual members recognize the need for change in their character and lifestyles. Even though policies and programs may change to better administer the gospel to the general membership of the church, true and eternal principles and doctrines do not change. Doctrines that need to be changed or scripture that needs to be added will be accomplished by revelation. This change can only come only through the *prophet and president* of the church. It is then presented as Declaration with the sustaining vote of the general membership of the church. The two examples of doctrinal changes are the Declarations on "The Plurality of Wives" and "The Priesthood to All Worthy Males" found in the Doctrine and Covenants. This is the standard: *revelation* is scripture. A *declaration* is a change of revelatory position or doctrine within scripture. A *proclamation* establishes or emphasizes the position of the church on a given issue or subject based on existing revelation or scripture.

The scriptures are often referred to as the "Standard Works." However, for many reasons they have not remained the standards of doctrine and truth among the general membership of the church. Because of our lay ministry, what is taught is generally filtered by the teachers' opinions and understandings, which is a product of their education, upbringing, and traditions. This is one reason prepared manuals of instruction are needed. These manuals have been written under the direction of the leaders of the church to help teachers understand basic principles and doctrines using the scriptures. Since the leaders have stressed that teachers 'stick with the manual' rather than open the scriptures, traditions have sometimes morphed into doctrines, creating questions in the minds of many members.

Sadly, the scriptures as a standard have taken second place to the Ensign, the Church News and other sources of information. Many members have found it more convenient and entertaining to quote books, talks, and articles using church authorities as sources rather than quoting straight from the scriptures. In a classroom setting, when scriptures are quoted or read that teach something different than tradition, the first cry is, "but Elder 'so-and-so' said—". Many teachers and speakers scramble to find quotes from publications, Internet blogs, or websites from self-appointed saviors of gospel doctrine teachers, which perpetuates the acceptance of traditions rather than rely on the prepared manuals and the scriptures. Many years ago, *Especially for Mormons* was the source book for almost every talk in church rather than the scriptures. Sacrament talks today are drawn more from the words of church leaders than they are from scripture. Not that this is wrong, but the scriptures are the "standard" of truth and should be the primary source when it comes to doctrinal learning or teaching.

Some members feel that the Ensign should take the place of the scriptures, and that the scriptures should only be used as a secondary source rather than as the primary word of God. The words of modern priesthood leaders are important for the day and age in which we live, and their counsel is needed and invaluable as we plod through the struggles of daily life seeking to become free from the sins of our times. Nevertheless, the scriptures set the doctrinal standards and *should be* the primary source of light, truth, and doctrine, rather than opinion, tradition and personal interpretation. God is the same yesterday, today and forever and His word, found in scripture, is for every dispensation, as the nature and sins of mankind have never changed.

The scriptures have been neglected because it takes effort and time to study them well enough to learn the doctrines contained in them, much less where to find them. Everyone has their favorite scripture verse and quote to pass along in Gospel Doctrine class, but to know the scriptures requires constant effort and study. There are only a few times that the word "read" is used in reference to what should be done with the scriptures. More often, words like: *hold tightly, seek to obtain my word, grasp firmly, feast upon, ponder in your hearts, seek diligently and study*, is found. All these words and phrases imply more than simple rote reading. Many members check the obedience box by reaching the goal of an allotment of time, or reading a set number of verses or chapters in order to fulfill the perceived requirement of scripture reading. The scriptures should be *read consecutively* by chapters, verses, or time. However, one should *study the scriptures topically*—searching, pondering and feasting in addition to the reading that one might accomplish.

The importance of the scriptures or 'Standard Works' are easily seen in a few quotes from church leaders as they explain that, not just priesthood leaders, but even the prophets themselves are held accountable to the doctrines and teachings found in scripture. This means that scriptural accountability rests upon all, from prophet to primary teacher.

Joseph Fielding Smith

> It makes no difference what is written or what anyone has said. If what has been said is in conflict with what the Lord has revealed, we can set it aside. My words, and the teaching of any other member of the church, high or low, *if they do not square with the revelations, we need not accept them.* Let us have this matter clear. We have accepted the four standard works as the measuring yardsticks, or balances by which we measure every man's doctrine. (Joseph Fielding Smith, *Doctrines of Salvation,* Vol.3, p.203)

> You cannot accept the books written by the authorities of the church as standards in doctrine, only in so far as they accord with the revealed word in the standard works. (Joseph Fielding Smith, *Doctrines of Salvation*, Vol.3, p. 203)

The Lord has given us the four Standards which lie at the foundation of our faith. Each member of the church should be so well versed that he or she, would be able to discern whether or not any doctrine taught conforms to the revealed word of the Lord. . .The fact remains, however, that too many of the members have not taken advantage of their blessings and obligations, and therefore they are unable to distinguish between truth and error. *The "lay" members of the Church are under obligation to accept the teachings of the authorities, unless they can discover in them some conflict with the revelations and commandments the Lord has given. There are times when the leading brethren have expressed their own opinions on various subjects. This they have a perfect right to do.* They have divided on political questions; some belong to one political party and others to another. This they have a perfect right to do. (Joseph Fielding Smith, *Answers to Gospel Questions,* Vol.2, p.113)

Harold B. Lee

We have the standard church works. Why do we call them standard? *If there is any teacher who teaches a doctrine that can't be substantiated from the standard church works*—and I make one qualification, and that is unless that one be the president of the church, who alone has the right to declare new doctrine—*then you may know by that same token that such a teacher is but expressing his own opinion. If, on the other hand, you have someone teaching a doctrine that cannot be substantiated by the scriptures, and more than that, if it contradicts what is in the standard Church works, you may know that that person is teaching false doctrine, no matter what his position in this church may be.* The president of the church alone may declare the mind and will of God to His people. No officer nor any other church in the world has this high and lofty prerogative. When the president proclaims any such new doctrine, he will declare it to be a revelation from the Lord. (Harold B. Lee, *Stand Ye In Holy Places,* p.109-110)

It is not to be thought that every word spoken by the General Authorities is inspired, or that they are moved upon by the

Holy Ghost in everything they write. *I don't care what his position is. If he writes something or speaks something that goes beyond anything that you can find in the standard church works,* unless that one be the prophet, seer, and revelator—please note that one exception—*you may immediately say, "Well, that is his own idea." And if he says something that contradicts what is found in the standard church works, you may know by that same token that it is false, regardless of the position of the man who says it.* (Harold B. Lee, *Stand Ye In Holy Places*, p.162-163)

Ezra Taft Benson

We know that Satan has great power to deceive, and because of this, we must be aware. The safeguard against his sophistry and deception has been specified by revelation. We are to give heed to the words of eternal life. In other words, we must understand and live by the revelations the Lord has granted to His prophets. These are contained in the four standard works and the written and public declarations of our current prophet. (*Teachings of Ezra Taft Benson*, p.404-405)

Bruce R. McConkie

The books, writings, explanations, expositions, views, and theories of even the wisest and greatest men, either in or out of the church, do not rank with the standard works. Even the writings, teachings, and opinions of the prophets of God are acceptable only to the extent they are in harmony with what God has revealed and what is recorded in the standard works. (Bruce R. McConkie, *Mormon Doctrine*, p.764)

As these quotes make clear, the standard works are the standards of doctrine and truth, and modern day prophets and apostles are held accountable to these standards of truth.

As mentioned earlier, if scriptures are to be added to, or doctrines changed, it can only be done by the President of the Church, not by any other general authority or church leader. The scriptures are the standards for prophet and apostle alike, and only the Prophet and

President of the Church has the authority to make any changes by revelation.

A common motif in the heavenly visitations of God and angels is that a manifestation of the divine is almost always accompanied by scripture being quoted as the sources of the central message. Christ quoted and explained scripture in his teaching during his life and often answered questions using scripture. The Sermon on the Mount is based on the fulfilling the law given to Moses. In the Book of Mormon, Christ quoted Malachi and Isaiah and commanded that their words be added to the record. When the Father and Son appeared to Joseph Smith in the First Vision, Christ quoted scripture. Joseph's account of Moroni's visit reveals that the angel quoted the same passage of scripture multiple times and throughout the night. If the scriptures are important enough for God and angels to use, then they should be important enough for all to study and talk about in every meeting.

Everyone has a favorite General Authority to quote and rely on for insights and teaching. However, the scriptures are the standard for the prophets and should be for all priesthood leaders. Without a standard there is no basis for doctrine and truth. God is the same yesterday, today and forever. The priesthood leaders teach, when they speak in local and general settings, how to become better saints. They instruct the members using concepts and principles that will help listeners develop a better character as they seek for that relationship with God. Leaders must adhere to their call of perfecting the saints, the work of the ministry, and edifying the body of Christ. In order to accomplish this great work of teaching and ministering, the scriptures must always be the standard of truth and doctrine.

Every spiritual revival that has occurred in the history of the world has revolved around the scriptures—every one. From Adam teaching his children the words of God to Enoch quoting from the Book of Adam to establish his city; from Moses coming down from the Mount with the Law to Josiah finding the record of the Law. The early Christian church relied on the Law and the Prophets of Judaism along with the

Gospels and the letters of the apostles to help set the religious and moral standard. The reformation that began with Luther and his interpretation of scripture spawned the Protestant faiths. The publication of the Bible in German and then English fostered a religious awakening that led to the Puritans and Pilgrims moving to a new land for religious freedom and the private interpretation of scripture. The Book of Mormon and other modern scripture from a living prophet was pivotal in the rise of the Latter-day Saint faith. Every spiritual revival was founded in, on, and around sacred texts. It may be that the next spiritual revival, when it comes, will of necessity revolve around scriptures once again.

Growing Pains

History teaches that every organization, nation, government, or religion will have some growing pains, even if the leadership was chosen by God and the prophet leaders are inspired. Moses continued to learn after he led the Children of Israel out of Egypt. It is evident that those who founded this nation were inspired by God to do so, and they still had to go through the growing pains of a new nation. The same is evident as the church moved from Palmyra to Kirtland, from Kirtland to Far West, then from Far West to Nauvoo, and shortly thereafter from Nauvoo to Salt Lake City. Even today, as the membership snowballs, the church still has growing pains along the way, as the gospel is *always new* to every generation. That which keeps the church or any other organization together and solid through these growing pains is an *unalterable standard.* Where would the United States be today without its Constitution to set the rules of freedom and rights?

The growing pains of any organization are sometimes met with inside opposition, especially when a supposed doctrine is only tradition or policy. Likewise, there is opposition when some do not know the doctrine or the standard that sets the doctrine apart from policy, opinion, or tradition.

There are members of the church that are trying to convince others that some specific and current doctrines are *not correct or 'fair'*. These individuals believe that these doctrines are just policies, and that doctrine can and should change with the times (the linear view of time). Policy may need to change often, to reflect the needs of the church, but doctrine cannot change because doctrine is established in scripture. Understanding the difference between doctrine and policy requires one to accept the standard as an irrevocable standard. Thus, many "do err, not knowing the scriptures" (Matthew 22:29). A church without a standard of truth in God's word is not a church. Without a standard, every member would be "tossed to and fro and carried about with every wind of doctrine" based on the whim or wish of the arm of flesh.

When the rules and doctrines of an organization are open to change by petition, vigil, vote, or pressure, it is not a religion—it is a social club. If doctrines can change with every social movement because the standards of salvation and truth are fluid, then that religion has no power of salvation, authority, or eternal truths upon which one might build an enduring faith. To be considered a religion, the organization's articles of faith and doctrines of truth cannot change, and therefore must be founded on a written standard that will not change. The individual that does not like the rules of an organization that is founded on unchangeable doctrine and scripture will discover there are many other options. There exists clubs and organizations and even other churches where the petition and vote of a committee have the power to change the rules without the burden of a scriptural standard.

Thus, when any activist declares that the church needs 'changing', what they are really saying is that the organization is not a religion, that the doctrines are not founded on scripture, and that the church is not directed by Christ. They are subtly insinuating that the church is just a social club that can be changed by petition or vigil. Those who seek to change doctrine are also asserting that the priesthood leaders are no longer inspired and that God needs to change His mind to conform to personal opinions and desires of special interest groups. In short, they do not believe the church is true.

9 For do we not read that God is the same yesterday, today, and forever, and in him there is no variableness neither shadow of changing?

10 And now, if ye have imagined up unto yourselves a god who doth vary, and in whom there is shadow of changing, then have ye imagined up unto yourselves a god who is not a God of miracles. (Mormon 9:9-10)

Religion and Scripture

The word **Religion** is defined as *"A set of beliefs concerning the cause, nature and purpose of the universe. A religion explains why things are, especially when considered as the creation of a superhuman agency or agencies, usually involving devotional and ritual observances often containing a moral code governing the conduct of human affairs."* A religion or system of beliefs will answer questions about the purpose of the universe, about the creation, the Creator, and will establish rituals and a written moral code.

The word **Scripture** is defined as: *"A definitive collection of sacred books regarded as given by the inspiration of God, with the purpose to perpetuate His revealed will."* Scripture is the way God makes known His will to man. This He does by raising up men from time to time to commit to writing an infallible record [His revelations]. He then places His seal of authority on these divine collections as given by inspiration.

A religion must be founded upon the revealed word of God that is unchangeable or it cannot be considered a religion. Everyone within a religion or denomination should understand that God-given rules cannot and should not be changed but by divine revelation. The scriptures are the standards—not the cultural beliefs or practices of the time or generation in which one lives, nor the standards of political correctness currently in vogue. Someone who seeks to force a change in church doctrine does not know the difference between doctrine and policy, or scripture and opinion.

There is a standard to which the church and the doctrine *MUST* adhere. This standard will not change and cannot change without the heavens opening. The scriptures are the standard, because God is the "same today, yesterday and forever."

Chapter 21

Joseph Smith and Translation

Over the last century, the translation of the Book of Abraham has been the source of major controversy, within and out of the church. [This controversy and scrutiny now extends to the translation of the Book of Mormon]. The Book of Abraham has been the target of critics and anti-Mormons as well as a rationalization for unbelief by some Latter-day Saints ever since its first publication in the *Times and Seasons* in 1842-43. The problem for the detractors is that the Book of Abraham is still here. There are even members of the church who do not understand the spiritual process of translation, and being ill-informed, would like to see the Book of Abraham removed from Latter-day Saint scripture. This is unfortunate because the Book of Abraham stands solidly as proof that Joseph Smith was a Prophet of God and inspired in the restoration of scripture, doctrine, priesthood, and even the Church of Jesus Christ. The information found in the Book of Abraham is of such a sacred nature that the unbeliever and spiritually bereft are self-blinded as if staring directly at the sun trying to determine the source of its light. Unable to focus on the spiritual benefits and truths of the Book of Abraham, these detractors are able only to see darkness through the blind eyes of ignorance.

The primary question that is raised about the Book of Abraham is: "Why doesn't the Book of Abraham translation match up with Egyptologist translations?" Another written objection found ad-infinitum is paraphrased as:

The arguments to defend the Book of Abraham would not stand up to peer review by recognized Egyptologists. The church has had parts of the papyri since 1967 and they have been translated by Egyptologists. They are no more than magical funerary texts, often buried with the dead, and nothing to do with the purported translation by Joseph Smith.

Before this question can be addressed from a scriptural and historical point of view, it is helpful to understand what the word 'translation' means. Many critics focus on the intellectual abilities of Joseph Smith rather than "the gift and power of God" as described by the prophet.

A Spiritual Translation

Every ancient record that the Prophet Joseph Smith provided to the Saints *that was an ancient record at one time*, he called a "translation." Understanding what a "translation" is will first be discussed as it appears in the scriptures and the works of Joseph Smith.

In the introduction to The Book of Mormon, written by Joseph Smith, he explains that:

> The ancient record thus brought forth as the voice of the people speaking from the dust and *translated into modern speech by **the gift and power of God**.*

The real query here should be: What does that phrase mean, "translated by the gift and power of god?" There are two additional questions connected to this query: First, What does the word "translated" mean? And Second, in two parts, How and why is the "gift and power of God" connected to translation?

One answer is found in the introduction of section seven of the Doctrine and Covenants:

> Revelation given to Joseph Smith the Prophet and Oliver Cowdery, at Harmony, Pennsylvania, April 1829, when they

inquired through the Urim and Thummim as to whether John, the beloved disciple, tarried in the flesh or had died. *The revelation is a translated version* of the record made on parchment by John and hidden up by himself. (*HC* 1: 35–36)

The pattern is easily seen in these two examples: if there was an ancient record at one time, Joseph called it a "translation" —even when the translation came by revelation rather than from any intellectual ability he might have had. In other words, rendering a once ancient record into "modern speech", no matter the mode, constitutes a "translation".

Look at the introduction to the Book of Moses in the *Pearl of Great Price*:

An extract from *the translation of the Bible as revealed* to Joseph Smith the Prophet, June 1830—February 1831.

The Book of Moses comes from a *"translation of the Bible as revealed"* to Joseph Smith. This is commonly referred to as "The Joseph Smith Translation" or "Inspired Version" (IV) of the Bible. **Question:** Did Joseph have access to the original Hebrew and Greek manuscripts and documents from which he could "translate" the Bible? Of course not. He had a copy of the English Bible. He would read passages in his Bible and "by revelation," give us an inspired "translation" of the Bible—hence the "Joseph Smith *Translation.*" Because it *was* an *"ancient record"* it did not matter if it was in Hebrew, Greek, Egyptian, or reformed Egyptian. The Prophet gave us an English version of an ancient record that was not originally written in English. Therefore, it is a translation.

The term or use of the word 'translation' does not have to involve a direct translation from one record in one language to another record. An example, though simple and crude, is worth looking at as an explanation:

Pablo, who only knew and spoke Spanish, needed to communicate information that was written only in Spanish to

Bob who only understands English. Pablo found Jose, a 'mediator translator' who could speak and understand both English and Spanish. Pablo, reading aloud in Spanish to Jose the mediator translator, communicates the Spanish message from Pablo to Bob in his native tongue, English. Bob then writes down the written message from Pablo through Jose. Bob now has a written translation of a Spanish document. Even though Bob didn't translate it himself, the fact it came through a mediator translator, it is still a translation.

Cannot the Spirit of God or the Holy Ghost provide the words of an ancient text "by the gift and power of God" in any language necessary for the text to still be considered a translation? Joseph Smith was merely the inspired recipient.

As with the Book of Moses, the introduction of the Book of Abraham implies the same revelatory inspiration is behind the translation. Here is what it says in the introduction to the Book of Abraham:

A *Translation* of some ancient Records, that have fallen into our hands from the catacombs of Egypt. —The writings of Abraham while he was in Egypt, called the Book of Abraham, written by his own hand, upon papyrus.

This phrase from the introduction: "The writings of Abraham while he was in Egypt, called the Book of Abraham, written by his own hand, upon papyrus," is a colophon. This is a term that doesn't mean much to most people, but is important when writing on papyrus, and is often found in ancient scrolls. At the beginning or at the end of a scroll or document there would be a few phrases or paragraphs that would describe the contents of the scroll, allowing the reader to see what the scroll was about without having to open the entire scroll to read it. This is very common in middle-eastern cultures. Even in the Book of Mormon we see Nephi's colophon in the first 3 verses:

1 I, Nephi, having been born of goodly parents, therefore I was taught somewhat in all the learning of my father; and having seen many afflictions in the course of my days,

> nevertheless, having been highly favored of the Lord in all
> my days; yea, having had a great knowledge of the goodness
> and the mysteries of God, therefore I make a record of my
> proceedings in my days.
> 2 Yea, I make a record in the language of my father, which
> consists of the learning of the Jews and the language of the
> Egyptians.
> 3 And I know that the record which I make is true; and I
> make it with mine own hand; and I make it according to my
> knowledge. (1 Nephi 1:1-3)

A colophon reveals who wrote the record, what the record is about, and that it is a true record. These first verses in the Book of Mormon follow the same ancient colophonic method. The first 4 verses in the Book of Abraham, chapter one, and the last verse of the same chapter are also colophons (see Abr. 1: 1-4, 31). In ancient records or scrolls, this was common practice for identifying the contents of the document. This is something that Joseph Smith could not have known and would not have included were it not an actual record at one time, given to him by the Gift and Power of God.

Joseph calls the Book of Abraham a "translation" because it was an ancient text. Even if the translation was given to him by the gift and power of God, which could include revelation or inspiration, it was *still* a translation. The fact that it was an ancient record that existed at one time made it by definition a "translation" as it was written into English. Joseph Smith, with a fourth grade education, did not have the education to translate from one language into another, as do those trained in ancient languages. He could not have translated as they do. Nor did he claim to have the intellectual ability to do so. His own words verify his lack of ability: He states that it was 'by the gift and power of God' that he was able to provide the translations of these ancient records. He was well aware of his lack of education and his limitations. In any case, Joseph would not be able to "translate" the same as one trained in ancient languages if it were a revelation of an ancient text.

Translation by Education

To translate an ancient record there are a number of steps that one might take to render an acceptable translation. Ancient Egyptian, hieroglyphics can be written from left to right, or right to left, and top to bottom being read right to left or left to right within the vertical column.

Translating an Egyptian text would first require the translator to make sure it was reading from left to right, as that is how the final translation would be printed or discussed. The steps for translation of an ancient text are below. Of course, no matter what the language, a dictionary would be required to render a correct translation.

1. Change from right to left to left to right
2. Create a transliteration of the text into the correct sounds
3. Translate the transliteration into English
4. Provide a grammatical translation

A translation was made from one of the columns in the Chapel of Anubis connected to the outside of the Funerary Temple of Hatshepsut. The columns have on each side a vignette that is called the "ritual embrace." In this ritual embrace, the Pharaoh embraces the deity. The embrace is recognized by the unusual stance and close proximity of the god with the Pharaoh. The feet of each participant are always touching each other, while one hand of the god is touching or resting on the shoulder or head of the Pharaoh. The Pharaoh's hand is on the shoulder of the god at the same time. The faces are close together with an implied equality as god and man are now foot-to-foot, eye-to-eye and the hands are on the shoulders of each other. This is sometimes called the "mutual embrace."

To begin the translation of the text that is connected to this ritual embrace, the text written right to left should be turned around to correspond to the English translation.

Now that the text can be read from left to right the next step would be the Transliteration:

mert di ank djed waas snb re mtt jdtt taa

Following the transliteration, would be the first English Translation:

"beloved give eternal life, stability and endurance, power, eternal health, Re, like eternity"

The next step would be the English Grammatical Translation:

"My Beloved, I endow thee immortality, and endurance (through your posterity) I bestow priesthood, and eternal health, like God has for eternity."

It can be seen that if Joseph was expected to translate the text from the original text or document he would have to do it based on his education and knowledge. This type of intellectual translation would have to move word for word from text to translation. This he could not do as he was not trained in ancient languages. It was **only** by the gift and power of God that he could give us translations of the Book of Mormon, Moses, Abraham, Bible and The Parchment of John. A translation done by the gift and power of God would not even require the translator to look at the text, for it would do no good other than verify the reality of the record. In such cases the text often becomes the catalyst for translated revelation. (More on that below)

There is a precedent for this style of spiritual translation. Bible scholars of all faiths accept the premise that Moses provided the first book of the Pentateuch, Genesis, thousands of years after the fact by that same "gift and power of God". From the creation, to Joseph being sold into Egypt, Moses recorded the events found in the book of Genesis by the same power of inspiration that Joseph Smith received from God to translate Moses, Abraham, the Book of Mormon, the parchment hid up by John as well as the Joseph Smith Translation of the Bible.

A Law of Revelation

The Law of Revelation, as made plain in scripture and church history is: That revelation cannot precede the prepared question. In coming before God, seeking enlightenment, one must be *as prepared to ask the question as they are to receive the answer*. Knowledge can only come line upon line and precept upon precept (D&C 98:12). Likewise, light and truth, once received, demands obedience (D&C 132:3).

In Moses chapter five, Adam has been "obedient to the commandments he received offering sacrifices" for "many days" seeking for further light and knowledge. He doesn't know why he is offering sacrifice and seeks greater light and knowledge. He first needed to be obedient to the light and knowledge he had received before messengers were sent from the presence of God. Obedience precedes revelation. And greater light and knowledge then demands a greater obedience to receive more light. (See Moses 5: 5-7)

All revelation requires a catalyst. To Adam, the catalyst was the sacrifice and the desire to know why he was required to make the offerings. God does not, and cannot, reveal knowledge without preparation and a thoughtful and sincere question. Revelatory translations also require a catalyst to open the heavens. An old Jewish proverb in the Talmud states that: There is no stirring above until there is a stirring below. One does not seek or pronounce a blessing on the food until it has been prepared.

The doors of heaven will only open after the door is opened below. A brief look at scripture and church history will show the reality of this principle. Joseph Smith's questions and specific catalysts lead to his revelations and the restoration. Sometimes the question is the catalyst and sometimes the catalyst creates the question. But in the end, the revelation only comes after the preparation and the question. Often, the Lord will put the catalyst in front of the prophet to inspire the question.

The great exhortative challenge in Moroni chapter ten describes the process of revelation in the search for light and truth. Moroni, directing those seeking for truth, teaches that revelation only comes *after* one has been prepared to ask the question.

Moroni 10:3-5

3 Behold, I would exhort you that when ye shall

The Catalyst (The Book of Mormon)

read these things,

if it be wisdom in God that ye should read them,

The Preparation and Focus

that *ye would remember*

how merciful the Lord hath been unto the children of men, from the creation of Adam even down until the time that ye shall receive these things, and

ponder it in your hearts.

4 And when ye shall

The Catalyst (The Book of Mormon)

receive these things, I would

The Question

exhort you that ye would ask God, the Eternal Father, in the name of Christ,

if these things are not true; and if ye shall ask

The Preparation and Focus

with a sincere heart, with real intent, having faith in Christ,

The Revelation

he will manifest the truth of it unto you, by the power of the Holy Ghost.

5 And *by the power of the Holy Ghost* ye may know the truth of all things. (Moroni 10:3-5)

This process of revelation is easily seen in the history of Joseph Smith and the events that led to the restoration of the Church and modern scripture. Every revelation begins with a catalyst and question. There is no stirring above until there is a stirring below.

First Vision

"An unusual excitement on the subject of religion" in the area where Joseph lived, became the catalyst that created the question: "Which church is right?" in the mind of the young prophet. Pondering this question and searching the scriptures for answers led him to go into the grove of trees to petition the Lord for an answer to his question. This process led to the First Vision.

The Lord didn't interrupt the daily life and appear unannounced to an unprepared youth. The revelation and First Vision required a thoughtful preparation, asking in faith, with real intent, and a sincere heart before the heavens were opened. The question and concern became the catalyst that led to the First Vision. Joseph then *acted in faith* by putting forth the effort to go the Lord in prayer.

Moroni

Joseph's first vision became the catalyst for him to seek further knowledge. Joseph Smith records:

> I betook myself to prayer and supplication to Almighty God for forgiveness of all my sins and follies, and also for a manifestation to me, that I might know of my state and standing before him; for *I had full confidence in obtaining a divine manifestation, as I previously had one.* (JS-H 1: 29)

Joseph wanted to know if he was still worthy. He had more questions and this focus on the catalyst and prayer resulted in the visitation of Moroni. It was not until he pondered his worthiness and mission as he came before the Lord in prayer that he received the manifestation of Moroni coming into his room. Heaven's windows were not opened until after Joseph opened his heart and mind.

John The Baptist

When Joseph and Oliver were in the work of translating the record, they came across the passages respecting baptism for the remission of sins. On a certain day they went into the woods and began to pray. (*DHC,* 1:39). John the Baptist appeared to them. The heavens were opened and the Aaronic priesthood was restored (D&C 13).

The Catalyst: during the translation of the plates, the question about baptism for the remission of sins resulted in going into the woods to seek an answer. The Revelation: the heavens were opened again and John the Baptist appeared to Joseph and Oliver. The preparation and asking took place before the revelation.

The Inspired Version of the Bible

Almost sixty percent (60%) of the Doctrine and Covenants was received during the Kirtland Period. It was in Hiram and Kirtland that Joseph was commanded to continue the translation of the Bible. This translation is key to the restoration of the priesthood and temporal organization of the church. During this time, the questions that formed in Joseph's mind about the church organization and Gospel came from the work of the translation of the Bible. A loving God awaits the personal preparation of even the prophets before the heavens are opened. The Lord, awaiting Joseph's personal preparation, counseled and encouraged Joseph multiple times to continue and to finish his work on translating the Bible. Always, He waited for Joseph to ask the question before opening the heavens. In section forty-five of the Doctrine and Covenants, the Lord explains that much of the restoration is awaiting his questions—questions that cannot be formulated until he is working on the translation of the Bible.

> 60 And now, behold, I say unto you, *it shall not be given unto you to know any further concerning this chapter, until the New Testament* be translated, and in it all these things shall be made known;
> 61 Wherefore I give unto you that ye may now translate it, *that ye may be prepared for the things to come.*
> 62 For verily I say unto you, that *great things await you*;

Many of the revelations in the Doctrine and Covenants are a direct result of the 'inspired version' of the Bible. The questions that arose in

Joseph's mind while doing the Biblical translation led the prophet to seek for answers in supplication to God, which led to some of the most important revelations in this dispensation.

The inspired version of Genesis led to a *"translation"* of the Book of Moses. The Gold Plates became the catalyst for the *"translation"* of the Book of Mormon. The inspired version of the Book of John led to the *"translation"* of the revelation of John on the Parchment. Likewise, the Egyptian Papyri served as a catalyst for the *"translation"* of the Book of Abraham and the Book of Joseph.

Speaking of translating ancient records that have 'been hid up,' the Lord informs Oliver Cowdery about the preparation of faith that must take place to *translate* by the gift and power of God; or the 'manifestation of my Spirit.'

> 1 Oliver Cowdery, verily, verily, I say unto you, that assuredly as the Lord liveth, who is your God and your Redeemer, even so surely shall you receive a knowledge of whatsoever things you shall *ask in faith, with an honest heart, believing that you shall receive a knowledge concerning the engravings of old records, which are ancient, which contain those parts of my scripture of which has been spoken by the manifestation of my Spirit.*
> 2 Yea, behold, I will tell you in your mind and in your heart, by the Holy Ghost, which shall come upon you and which shall dwell in your heart.
> 3 Now, behold, *this is the spirit of revelation...*
> 9 And, therefore, whatsoever you shall ask me to tell you by that means, that will I grant unto you, and you shall have knowledge concerning it.
> 10 Remember that *without faith you can do nothing; therefore ask in faith.* Trifle not with these things; do not ask for that which you ought not.
> 11 **Ask** *that you may know* the mysteries of God, and *that you may translate and receive knowledge **from all those ancient records which have been hid up,** that are sacred; and according to your faith shall it be done unto you. (D&C 8)*

Verse eleven is speaking of records that existed and were hid up, but which they did not physically have.

When Joseph acquired the mummies and papyrus from Michael Chandler, he focused on those ancient prophets that were in Egypt: Abraham, Joseph who was sold in Egypt, and Moses. All three were prophets who no doubt kept records, as all righteous patriarchs and prophets have done. Like the Gold Plates, the papyrus becomes that catalyst which leads to the revelation of the Book of Abraham. It did not have to be the actual ancient record for this to be possible. This is the same way that Moses was able to write the book of Genesis and record the words of the patriarchs, for he also translated by the gift and power of God. Joseph Smith did not have the learning or skill to translate ancient languages, especially *Hieroglyphics;* therefore, the *translations* had to come through him by the gift and power of God.

The catalyst: the question (asked in faith) and the ability to focus the mind (with a sincere heart and real intent) are the key elements preparatory for revelation. When a translation comes by revelation, there is no need to physically *use* the "catalyst." Joseph did not need to look at the Gold Plates to translate them. That's why Emma could say that when Joseph was translating the Book of Mormon at their table—Martin Harris on one side, Joseph on the other—the plates sat wrapped in a napkin sitting on the center of the table, while Joseph peered at a seer stone (a way to focus) placed in his Hat (a way to block out the world). There are numerous accounts of Joseph translating the record this way, and the remarkable thing is that when he stopped or finished and began again the next day, or the next week or month, he did not ask to see where he left off previously or request the scribe to read the last line of the manuscript so he would know where to begin. He did not need to do that. He would begin with the next word because it was a translation by revelation, not intellectual abilities.

The fact that Joseph did not ask to be reminded of the last thing that he had translated after an extended period of time is a sure indication that the Book of Mormon was not a fictional fabrication nor intellectual translation from Joseph himself, but rather, God's translation of this ancient record. He could not have done it in any other way. The "translation" is a revelation. Joseph claims over and over that it was accomplished by the gift and power of God. The Book of Mormon, like the Book of Abraham, is a revelatory translation, and as such, Joseph did not have to physically touch or view the plates or papyri (the physical catalysts) to complete the translation.

The papyri Joseph acquired served as the catalyst that prompted Joseph to begin to ask the questions about who was in Egypt. These questions led to the revelation that gave us the translation of the Book of Abraham and the Book of Joseph (ancient records that existed at one time). When the fragments of the Joseph Smith Papyrus were recovered from the New York Metropolitan Museum in 1967, many Latter-day proponents boasted that, 'finally, the anti-Mormons will now know that Joseph Smith was a true prophet because the papyrus was found,' in the mistaken assumption that the original Book of Abraham manuscript was found. They were wrong. Again, it was the papyri itself, not the text on the papyrus, that acted as the catalyst that led to the revelation. Without that catalyst, there would be no revelation. Therefore, the scholastic translations should not and will not be the same as the revelatory translations. It had to be revelatory, because Joseph could not have done it any other way.

The Seer Stone

When Joseph received the plates he also received the *Urim & Thummim* to help him learn how to focus his mind for the revelatory process and translation. They were essentially tools to help him learn how to focus and receive revelation. When the *Urim & Thummim* were no longer available after the loss of the 116 pages, he was able to continue the translation by using a similar translucent stone. Placing a seer stone in his hat facilitated the revelatory translation by helping him focus his mind. As Joseph became exercised in receiving revelation, the seer stone was no longer used. This is how personal prayer works too. When we pray we try to focus our minds on the catalysts of the day. The catalysts could be our flocks, our herds, or families. We may not block out the world by placing our face in a hat, but we close our eyes, or retire to a bedroom, closet, or even a grove of trees where we can be alone and away from distractions. The prayerful individual will try to block out the world to focus on the issues (the catalysts) and problems in order for the Spirit to give us them the inspiration or revelation needed. It is the same process.

The Facsimiles in the Book of Abraham

Joseph Smith provided *"translations"* of the ancient records and texts. Included with the Book of Abraham are three Egyptian Facsimiles. These Facsimiles or vignettes are connected to the Abraham text in multiple ways. Abraham uses them as examples or *"representations"* as well as in a conceptual way within the text itself. The first four verses of chapter one explain that this text is a record of Abraham's desire to receive and bestow what may be called his endowment or the covenants and rights of the fathers with their associated blessings. The Three Facsimiles represent this very idea within the Egyptian Religion.

The ancient coronation ceremony had three major components within the kingship rituals. These rituals were copied and 'earnestly imitated' from the religion of the earliest patriarchs. The three main elements of this ritual are: 1. The death of the God, 2. The Resurrection and Ascension of the God, and 3. The Enthronement of the God. In ancient Egypt, these elements were required to be in the order listed above in order to convey the meaning of the ritual and initiation into the world of the Gods. It is no coincidence that the Facsimiles presented in the Book of Abraham (representing the blessings and endowment for which Abraham so earnestly sought) are presented in just that order.

The Coronation Ceremony

Research on ancient and modern coronation ceremonies is most enlightening when viewed from an LDS perspective. It becomes evident that the coronation ceremony and ritual evolved from the religion of the patriarchs and the blessings that Abraham desired and then received. These are the same blessings that Adam, the first man, received from the Lord and then passed down through his righteous posterity (Abraham 1:2-3).

Christ and His sacrifice provided a power to become the sons and daughters of God (John 1:12) that all might become kings and queens and priests and priestesses unto God. As a consequence of apostasy, the ordinances of this ancient endowment of power became the coronation or enthronement ceremony throughout the ancient world. The Book of Abraham is a record of Abraham's endowment as seen in chapter one, beginning in verse two. As with the ancient coronation ceremony, there are three important aspects to the ancient endowment (coronation) that point back to a connection with and relationship to God. (1) The Death of the God, (2) The Resurrection and Ascension, and (3) The Enthronement.

Two (non-LDS) works stand out as the accepted sources for ancient coronation ceremonies: the research of Tor Irstram[9] and A. M. Hocart.[10] Irstram's research focused on sixty-two coronation ceremonies in various parts of Africa. Hocart looked at Kinship Rituals that included ancient and contemporary traditions around the world. Each came to the conclusion that there were common elements found in every ceremony. In fact, in the lists of the common elements of each author, an astounding theme becomes visible.

Provided below is an explanation of the events taking place along with the lists containing the numbers and letters of Irstram and Hocart's works on the ancient and modern coronation ceremonies. These rituals were and are connected to the temple and ordinances and teachings performed there. Nimrod and Pharaoh were descendants of Egyptus and Ham, and being unable to hold the priesthood, took the endowment of which they were familiar and turned it into a public ritual to justify their kingship over mankind. Just as the real endowment will make the participant a king and priest unto God, these imitated ceremonies legitimized the king and his position in the eyes

9. Irstam, Tor, The King of Ganda: *Studies in the Institutions of Sacral Kingship in Africa.* (Stockholm, 1944).
10. Hocart, A. M., *Kingship*, (London 1927).

of the people by portraying him as the son of God on earth. To better understand the endowment of Abraham and the ancient coronation ceremony, below is a table showing Hocart's, Irstram's and the author's explanation of the common elements found in almost all enthronement rituals.

Porter	Irstram	Hocart
1. The coronation must symbolize (1) the Death of the God, (2) the Resurrection and Ascension, and (3) the Enthronement. These are the fundamental meanings of Facsimiles 1, 2, and 3 of Abraham	(1) Ceremonies that symbolized the King's death and rebirth.	A. The theory is that the king (1) dies; (2) is reborn, (3) as a god.
2. Participants must have an invitation or Recommend. See Psalms 15 and 24. "Who may ascend the hill of the Lord?"	(19) Not all were allowed to be present at the most important ceremonies.	C. (1) Persons not admissible to the sacrifice are not allowed to know anything; (2) an armed guard prevents prying eyes.
3. Must wear the robes and clothing of the Gods. The witnesses are the Angels and Gods.	(23) Those taking part dressed themselves as gods.	X. Those taking part in the rites are dressed up as gods. Y. Which may be those of animals.
4. Must be ready to continue both intellectually and spiritually.	(4) Entrance dialogue and proclamation.	B. By way of preparation he fasts and practices other austerities.

Porter	Irstram	Hocart

Facsimile # 1 - The Death

Porter	Irstram	Hocart
5. Must descend below all things in order to rise above all things.	(22) The King was made the butt of the people	H. The people indulge at one point in obscenities, or buffoonery.
6. The battle of good against evil, light and darkness, death and resurrection, Christ and Satan.	(5) Ritual fight.	E. The King must fight a ritual combat (1) by arms, (2) by ceremony, (3) come out victorious.
7. The death of the God or King was often portrayed by a human substitute King during the ritual combat. The substitute could be the sacrifice of the King's enemy or those who may present a threat to the throne.	(24) Human sacrifices.	
	(25) The King's brothers were killed.	
	(26) Substitute King is killed	

Porter	Irstram	Hocart

Abraham was a substitute for Nimrod, as Christ became the infinite and eternal sacrifice for all the world and the substitute for Caesar during the coronation rituals.

Facsimile # 2 - Resurrection and Ascension

After the symbolic combat and death of the King, he must go into the basement of the Temple for three days representing being in the world of the dead.

Porter	Irstram	Hocart
8. The King (god) must go into the world of the dead for three days. This becomes a time of chaos before the recreation when darkness reigned upon the face of the deep. All fires are to be extinguished for the three days	(6) The King went into retirement for a certain period. (3 days)	D. A kind of Sabbath is observed; The people are silent and lie quiet as at a death.
9. During the three days there is no light, no creation chaos reigns.	(17) All fires are extinguished	

While in the Basement of the Temple or the World of the Dead, the King must prepare himself for the glorious resurrection.

Porter	Irstram	Hocart
10. The King must be cleansed from evil to come forth in the resurrection as the anointed King and God.	(8) The King was washed or baptized with water	
11. The anointing is an ordinance of the resurrection as those parts of the body are anointed to function proper and perfect	(12) The King was anointed with oil.	K. He is anointed with oil,
12. Robes are changed to show the progression toward King and God.	(2) The King was dressed in special robes.	I. The King is invested with special garments.
13. Every new life, or station requires a new name to signify the new creation and new creature. In exaltation you receive a new name that only the recipient knows.	(3) The King received a new name.	U. He receives a new name
14. The ritual and sacral meal. Life comes from death, sustenance and nourishment to both body and spirit comes from the sacrifice, death and resurrection of the God.	(7) The King receives a Communion or Sacrament	G. He receives communion

Coming out of the Temple or underworld after three days, order is now established. Life and light may continue. A new Son of God is the New King.

Porter	Irstram	Hocart

Facsimile # 3 - The Enthronement

15. Part of the ritual dress to "trod upon the footstool of god" having your feet shod with the gospel.	(13) The King put on shoes as part of the coronation	P. He puts on shoes as part of the Coronation
16. The scepter, or "wa'as" scepter signifies the authority and power to rule and reign as king and the son of God on earth.	(14) The King received certain regalia. (emblems of authority)	Q. He receives other royal regalia such as a sword, a scepter, and a ring.
17. The covenant making process must take place accompanied with the oath formulary, as with Abraham.	(11) Admonitions and promises.	F. The King is (1) admonished to rule justly and (2) promises to do so.
18. The crown signifies the acceptance of the King from the gods and the masses. It is an earthly and heavenly crown.	(16) The King was crowned.	O. The King is crowned

Porter	Irstram	Hocart
19. The throne is the "mercy seat" where justice and judgment are rendered. The throne is the primordial mound, the center of creation.	(15) The king sat on the throne.	R. Sits upon a throne.
20. The King cannot be crowned without a Queen. Ascension and exaltation can only come to the righteous pair.	(27) The Queen was crowned at the same time as the King.	The Queen is consecrated with the King. W. So are the vassals or officials.
21. The rising sun on the primordial mound. A new day, and a new creation as light fills the earth.	(9) The King mounted a hill	S. The King takes three ceremonial steps in imitation of the rising Sun
22. Only the King can plant, prune, harvest and dispense the fruit from the tree of life.	(10) The King planted his life tree.	
23. With the new King comes the New Creation, as all creation sings the creation hymn (poem). The heavens and the earth rejoice.	(21) Festivities were held.	N. A feast is given.
24. Blessings are given to the masses signifying that all life and health, prosperity, and fertility is dispensed by the King and god, as the multitudes scramble for the blessings. Christ sweat drops of blood: the gift of mercy.	(18) The King scattered beans, etc. among the people.	M. The people rejoice with noise and acclamations.
25. As Abraham traveled around his God-given inheritance, so the King must see and accept his kingdom as the kingdom accepts him.	(20) After the coronation the King traveled around his domain and received homage.	T. He goes the round of his dominion, and receives the homage of the vassals.

232

Porter	Irstram	Hocart
Commencement is progression traveling up the scale or ladder of exaltation, being found true and faithful in one level and then progressing to the next. From Telestial to Celestial.		Z. The King may be consecrated several times, going up each time in the scale of kingship.

The Three Facsimiles in the Book of Abraham not only belong there, but they are in the proper order and place in the printed text. Abraham was trying to explain why and how he received the 'blessings of the fathers' by his using the Egyptian records and religion as "representations" (Abraham 1:12). Abraham himself explains that the facsimiles are "representations", not the text or a translation. In Egypt, the 'representations' refer to the same aspects of Christ's life as in the myth of Osiris and the religion of Egypt. Osiris the God Son is slain and sacrificed by an evil brother and then ascends into the world of the Gods and becomes a God as a resurrected being. He then becomes the God and power of exaltation, with whom all Pharaohs identified themselves in their quest for, and claim to, the Divine son-ship of deity and their eventual enthronement in the heavens as a God.

The Death of the God	The Resurrection and Ascension	The Enthronement

Purpose of the Book of Abraham

The Book of Abraham is a record or journal account, as is all scripture, about his receiving his covenant and blessing from God. The opening verses of the book explain what the book is about and why Abraham is writing the record.

> **2** And, finding there was greater happiness and peace and rest for me, *I sought for the blessings of the fathers,* and the *right whereunto I should be ordained to administer the same;* having been myself a follower of righteousness, desiring also to be one who possessed great knowledge, and to be a greater follower of righteousness, and to possess a greater knowledge, and *to be a father of many nations, a prince of peace,* and desiring to receive instructions, and to keep the commandments of God, *I became a rightful heir, a High Priest, holding the right belonging to the fathers.*
> **3** *It was conferred upon me from the fathers;* it came down from the fathers, from the beginning of time, yea, even from the beginning, or before the foundation of the earth, down to the present time, *even the right of the firstborn,* or the first man, who is Adam, our first father, through the fathers unto me.
> **4** *I sought for mine appointment unto the Priesthood* according to the appointment of God unto the fathers concerning the seed. (Abraham 1:2-4)

Abraham explains that his record is an abridgment of other records and all was written for the benefit of his posterity.

> **31** But the records of the fathers, even the patriarchs, concerning the right of priesthood, the Lord my God preserved in mine own hands; therefore, a knowledge of the beginning of the creation, and also of the planets, and of the stars, as they were made known unto the fathers, have I kept even unto this day, and I shall endeavor to write some of these things upon this record, for the benefit of my posterity that shall come after me. (Abraham 1:31)

234

Joseph Smith provided this ancient record through inspiration using the papyrus that was bought from Michael Chandler as the catalyst. This revelatory record led to the instruction and ordinances that comprise the endowment in the Latter-day Temples. As discussed above, the papyri, like the plates, acted as a catalyst and became an integral part of the 'gift and power of God,' since they initiated the *revelatory process of the translation* of an ancient text of Abraham. Since the time of Joseph Smith there have been other texts discovered that are attributed to Abraham that verify the translated information and concepts found in the Joseph Smith Abraham.

Discovered and translated after the death of Joseph Smith, two texts are found in Volume One of *The Old Testament Pseudepigrapha*, edited by James H. Charlesworth. One being the "Testament of Abraham" (considered an Egyptian text in origin) and the other being the "Apocalypse of Abraham." Each of these texts, unavailable to Joseph Smith, have many of the same concepts: the creation, Abraham seeking further light and knowledge from God, the blessings of the Fathers, and angels taking him away, as depicted in the Facsimile 1 explanation. The Apocalypse of Abraham also contains a

discussion of the spirits before the world was created and how some were more prepared to become the leaders on earth after the creation of the earth. In 1975 Janet H. Johnson translated and published a newly discovered Greco Egyptian vignette depicting an individual on a lion couch identified in the text to be Abraham.[11]

What all this means to latter-day saints is this: The actual age and content of the papyri that Joseph Smith acquired does not matter. Again, the papyri became the catalyst for the revelation that became the Book of Abraham. Because there existed an ancient text of

11. Johnson, Janet H. OMRM 56(1975): 44-45, col I,ll. 1-5, 12; and E.N. O'Neil (ll. 140-45) following Preisendanz, PGM XII. 474-79

Abraham, the Book of Abraham could be translated by revelatory (not intellectual) means.

The few fragments of papyri that the church has would easily fit on the top of an ordinary desk top. Joseph recorded that the papyri he acquired from Michael Chandler "covered the floor of the parlor of the Mansion House," indicating that today the church may only have about a tenth of what was originally in the possession of Joseph Smith. The fact remains, Joseph could not translate ancient Egyptian by intellectual means; it could only be done by the Gift and Power of God and was therefore revelatory in nature, as was the Book of Mormon, the Book of Moses, the Inspired Version of the Bible and the parchment hid up by John.

Many will use Facsimile #2 as a point of contention, declaring that the translation by Egyptologists do not agree with the explanation provided by Joseph Smith. According to Hugh Nibley, when Klaus Behr, an Egyptologist, looked at Facsimile # 2, he stated, as other Egyptian scholars have: "I can tell you what it says, but I cannot tell you what it means." Joseph did not call the facsimiles translations; he called them "*explanations*." In other words, Joseph is stating within the text, "I can tell you what it means—but not what it says." Translating hieroglyphs is easy work compared to revelation, while explaining the meanings of the Facsimiles and Egyptian traditions is a more difficult task. Joseph is not providing a *translation* but an *explanation,* as stated at the head of each Facsimile. Within the text, Abraham calls them "*representations*", which means they are not meant to be used as a translation; but a symbol to convey meaning. Although, when Facsimile # 2 is translated, it has much to do with the text and message of Abraham. This facsimile is an ordinance of resurrection and ascension through the heavens as a 'justified' or redeemed person that becomes an Osiris or an exalted Son of God in the temple of God. It is stated in the hieroglyphics of this facsimile that the person has become "so exalted and so glorious...a mighty God in the first Temple of God." This was the goal and blessing that Abraham sought for as described in his record.

236

Those that seek to discredit the church and Joseph Smith because of the Book of Abraham do not understand the revelatory process. This record of Abraham, like the Book of Mormon, becomes a testament of its own reality. Joseph Smith could not create either book of his own accord or intellectual knowledge. The prophet never claimed an ability to translate intellectually, but recognized that it was the "gift and power of God" that gave him the ability to produce this scripture. The test of a classic is internal. Inspiration is revealed in the fruit, rather than living in the intellect. Despite his lack of education, Joseph became an instrument in the hands of God to begin a process that led to a spiritual and scriptural restoration of the church and gospel of Jesus Christ. Paul talks of the men that are used by God to fulfill His will:

> 26 For ye see your calling, brethren, how that not many wise men after the flesh, not many mighty, not many noble, are called:
> 27 But God hath chosen the foolish things of the world to confound the wise; and God hath chosen the weak things of the world to confound the things which are mighty;
> 28 And base things of the world, and things which are despised, hath God chosen, yea, and things which are not, to bring to naught things that are: (1 Corinthians 1:26-28)

The test of truth is within the text, not in Joseph Smith and his abilities or lack thereof. For "all things are possible with God."

Chapter 22

Cain, Abel and the Priesthood

Priesthood is often defined in LDS circles as the power and authority to act in God's name. This definition of priesthood is correct, but should be expanded in its meaning and understanding. Many assume that even God has priesthood. That being the case, the definition above would not necessarily be true. Therefore, the term 'priesthood' itself should be defined before moving forward.

Priest-hood is an "authority" given to, or placed upon an individual, hence the term 'hood.' This authority is the right to act as a priest, which is an earthly mediator or "*servant.*" It is defined in the dictionary as "*a devoted and helpful follower or supporter*" for God's love and care for others. Priesthood is *the authority to represent God* (as a servant) in His love and salvation offered to man. Accepting this responsibility and sustained by those whom the individual will serve, the Lord promises his support and inspiration to those called and sustained. Enoch is told this when he questions his calling from God as a servant:

> 31 And when Enoch had heard these words, he bowed himself to the earth, before the Lord, and spake before the Lord, saying: Why is it that I have found favor in thy sight, and am but a lad, and all the people hate me; for I am slow of speech; *wherefore am I thy servant*?
> 32 And the Lord said unto Enoch: Go forth and do as I have commanded thee, and no man shall pierce thee. Open thy mouth, and it shall be filled, and I will give thee utterance,

for all flesh is in my hands, and I will do as seemeth me good. (Moses 6:31-32).

Omnipotent and omniscient as God is, He has no priest-hood that He receives from someone else. He is Deity, thus the power is inherent within Him and His glory. This "inherent power" is the power, authority, knowledge, glory, and honor to rule as a God and creator in the eternities. This is the honor Satan sought for in the beginning, as recorded in scripture. Lucifer did not seek to take the place of Christ, but to obtain the Father's power and position. Thus Satan sought to do away with the necessity of Christ and the Atonement. This he would do, as scripture explains, by saving everyone and consequently taking away their agency.

From the beginning, there has always been a conflict between legitimate priesthood authority and the illegitimate leader who rules or demands that "*right*" by confiscating the "*rites*" to rule. This exercise of pride was manifest in the pre-earth life as the Son of Morning sought for the Father's *honor* which is His *power*.

> And it came to pass that Adam, being tempted of the devil— for, behold, the devil was before Adam, for he rebelled against me, saying, *Give me thine honor, which is my power;* and also a third part of the hosts of heaven turned he away from me because of their agency. (D&C 29:36)

> And I, the Lord God, spake unto Moses, saying: That Satan, whom thou hast commanded in the name of mine Only Begotten, is the same which was from the beginning, and he came before me, saying—Behold, here am I, send me, I will be thy son, and I will redeem all mankind, that one soul shall not be lost, and surely I will do it; *wherefore give me thine honor.* (Moses 4:1)

The honor and power of God that Satan demanded included his position as the supreme ruler. Having failed in his endeavor, Satan and those that followed him were cast from the pre-earth abode to continue their work of spiritual destruction through temptation. In his misery, the devil seeks the misery of all mankind, as all humanity has the *potential* to obtain the power, glory and honor that he has lost for eternity.

Mormon records in 3 Nephi that the fall of the Nephite nation came because of the "temptations of Satan," which temptations have been the same from the time of Cain. Mormon lists four primary temptations that Satan uses to overthrow the individual and the culture (a warning for our time and culture, Mormon and non-Mormon alike). Nephi gives the same four elements in prophecy for the last days (1 Nephi 22:23).

> Now the cause of this iniquity of the people was this—Satan had great power, unto the stirring up of the people to do all manner of iniquity, (1) and to the puffing them up with pride, (2) tempting them to seek for power, and authority, (3) and riches, (4) and the vain things of the world. (3 Nephi 6:15)

These temptations are innate tendencies of the 'natural man' in the attempt to satisfy the lusts and demands of the flesh. These are the temptations that Paul so often speaks of in the Epistles as he describes the battle that rages between the spirit and the flesh. These four character traits of spiritual depravity are the essential elements of today's entertainment. Without these, there would be no mental captivity to draw the interest and money for the big screen, primetime television and so-called "reality shows" that steal life's time and induce stupors of thought like a narcotic or drug that numbs the mind.

The great conflict between man and God described throughout scripture is connected to the four temptations listed above. These four elements become the moving force behind the person who *wants* to be the leader, competing with the legitimate priesthood authority whose right it is to reign as God's mouthpiece on earth: Moses versus Pharaoh; Abraham versus Nimrod; and Christ versus Herod and the High Priest, etc. Like Satan in the pre-earth life, the conflict is between the one who *wants to rule* and the one who is *chosen to rule*. Often this conflict is between the older son (usually the firstborn son) who is not worthy for the responsibilities of the birthright, and the younger

240

and more righteous sibling that is chosen to become the new patriarchal leader for the family. This is a pattern seen in the Old Testament and the many ancient texts that discuss pre-earth conflicts. This motif is seen in the sibling rivalries of Michael and Lucifer (Adam and Satan), Cain and Abel, Ishmael and Isaac, Joseph and his brothers, Esau and Jacob, Laman and Nephi and others.

The Shabbakah Stone is the oldest written document in the world. It is an Egyptian temple text dating to abt. 3500 b.c.e. which also makes it the oldest written religious instruction.[12] Inscribed on a large stone, the text outlines the 'Memphite Theology' that was performed as a play

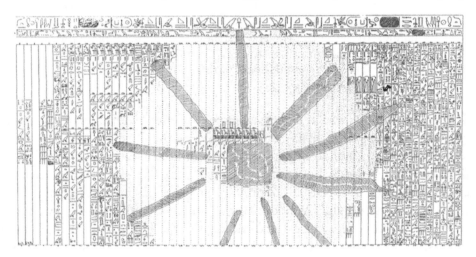

which included stage directions and dialogue. This drama, presented in the first ancient temples, focused on the pre-earth council of gods and the creation of the earth, and details the first conflict between the two sons of the creator over which son was to rule the new creation. In this text, as in other ancient epochs, the god finishes the creation and ponders the choice of which divine son to place in charge of the new world. The wicked son tries to usurp the authority bestowed upon the favored or "most beloved son" of the god of creation. This is the same

12. See: Gaster, Theodor H., *Thespis; Ritual, Myth, and Drama in the Ancient Near East.* W.W. Norton Co, New York, New York. 1977. p. 399.

motif which is outlined in Moses chapter four, which Joseph Smith would have known nothing about.

It appears within the text of Moses, that the conflict in the pre-earth was not just a conflict between Satan and Christ. Lucifer "*rebelled*" against God (not Christ) so by the "*power of mine Only Begotten* (the Melchizedek Authority) I caused that he should be cast down" (Moses 4:3). Satan's plan to save all, that 'not one soul would be lost,' was also motivated by the desire to *eliminate the necessity of the Atonement* and the need for a redeemer, effectively eliminating the role of Christ and the Gospel. Satan not only desired to take away the agency of man but also wanted the honor and glory of the Father. This act of pride, if fulfilled, would have placed Satan in a position that would be above that of Christ.

Almost singular to Mormonism is the doctrine of the pre-earth life and a grand council in heaven. However, there are many ancient texts that discuss the pre-earth existence that also speak of the conflict between Satan and Michael (the Archangel), who later becomes Adam. This confrontation is caused when Adam is chosen to be the first man to be placed on the earth and is given the authority to hold all the priesthood keys of all dispensations, becoming a prophet, priest and king to all mankind. One ancient text describes Satan's rebellion as he refused to recognize Adam as God's choice as the first father and head of the human race (see note # 13). After putting the breath of life into Adam, the Father required all spirits to recognize (sustain) and honor Adam as the father of our bodies and the keeper of all the authority and priesthood keys. In this document Lucifer is irate, and argues that he existed as one with authority before Michael, and that it was his (Lucifer's) right as an angel of power and position (D&C 76) to be the first man and patriarch on earth, his right to rule over Michael and all of humanity. This same idea (that Lucifer felt it was his right to be the first man and patriarch; that he should rule over Michael because Michael was "younger" than he) is found in D&C 29:36.

Many of these texts go on to describe that with a body (created in the pre-earth environment) and priesthood keys, Michael (Adam) was given the responsibility and authority "by the power of Christ" to cast Satan out of the presence of our Father to the newly created earth. In the April 2000 General Conference, Elder Russell M. Nelson referred to an apocryphal document he read while visiting London.[13] This ancient non-canonical text, entitled "The Discourse on Abbatôn", stated that before Lucifer/Satan was cast down, Adam "removed the writing from his hand", which means he lost all his priesthood and authority.

In the statues of Egyptian pharaohs this 'writing in the hand' is seen as a rolled papyrus in the hand, and represents his legitimate ancestral right to reign as the prophet, priest, and king. In the Latter-day Saint vernacular this would be called a "line of authority." The *"Discourse"* explains that Satan's power to move about was restricted by limiting "his bounds to the horizon" (to this earth only). He also was cut from "shoulder to shoulder through to the vertebrae" with a sickle. These acts represent physical restrictions that would govern or limit the abilities that Satan could use against mankind.

A great part of the conflict between Adam and Satan was over who was chosen to become the 'grand patriarch', with the inherent right to hold and administer the keys of the priesthood by which the inhabitants of the world would receive glory and exaltation. One of the key responsibilities of the Arch-angel Michael is to "detect" and *control Satan* when he appears as an angel of light to the righteous as he did with Joseph Smith in D&C 128:20 [See also the *Apocalypse of Abraham*, where Satan appears as an angel of light and is detected by Michael]. Michael also holds the keys of the bottomless pit, and will eventually bind and cast Satan into outer darkness in the end time (D&C 88:112-115; Revelation 20:1-3).

Satan, who was cast out of heaven for rebellion, was bound to the same earth to which he should have come had he kept his first estate (Abraham 3:26). Though restricted in his abilities and limited by laws

---

13. "Ensign," May 2000, p. 84

that govern his actions, Satan seeks the "misery of all mankind". Hence his plan to thwart the plan of salvation of which he will have no part.

> 18 And because he had fallen from heaven, and had become miserable forever, *he sought also the misery of all mankind.* Wherefore, he said unto Eve, yea, even that old serpent, who is the devil, who is the father of all lies, wherefore he said: Partake of the forbidden fruit, and ye shall not die, but ye shall be as God, knowing good and evil. (2 Nephi 2:18)

After the earth was created and prepared for Adam and Eve, they were placed in the Garden of Eden to begin their 'physical' yet immortal life. After partaking of the 'forbidden fruit' from the Tree of Knowledge of Good and Evil, our first parents were cast or driven out of the security of their garden home. The first parents began a new life and lifestyle in the physical existence of mortality with all its pain, suffering, and eventual death. Having been blessed with the ability to have posterity, subdue the earth, and have dominion over every living thing, the first couple begin to fulfill their potential 'blessings' with the abilities given to them at the time of their creation (Moses 2: 27-29). Adam and Eve begin to labor for their sustenance as they subdue the earth, having dominion over the animals, and begin the process of multiplying and filling the earth.

> 1 And it came to pass that after I, the Lord God, had driven them out, that *Adam began to till the earth, and to have dominion over all the beasts* of the field, and to eat his bread by the sweat of his brow, as I the Lord had commanded him. And Eve, also, his wife, did labor with him.
> 2 And Adam knew his wife, and she bare unto him sons and daughters, and *they began to multiply and to replenish the earth.* (Moses 5:1-2)

Expelled from the Garden of Eden, the gospel was introduced to Adam and Eve after three generations of their posterity were on the earth (Moses 5:1-3). Their children and grandchildren rejected the gospel (Moses 5:12, 13), being seduced by Satan's counterfeit "gospel" which was introduced at the same time. Nevertheless, understanding the plan

of salvation, the primal parents continued to have hope in the children
that were yet to be born.

> 16 And Adam and Eve, his wife, ceased not to call upon
> God. And Adam knew Eve his wife, and she conceived and
> bare Cain, and said: *I have gotten a man from the Lord;*
> *wherefore he may not reject his words.* But behold, Cain
> hearkened not, saying: Who is the Lord that I should know
> him?17 And she again conceived and bare his brother Abel.
> And Abel hearkened unto the voice of the Lord. And Abel
> was a keeper of sheep, but Cain was a tiller of the ground.
> (Moses 5:16-17)

Cain

Chapter Five of the Book of Moses teaches that Cain and his brother
Abel were the first sons born to Adam and Eve *after* they receive the
gospel. Cain, the firstborn in the gospel, is now in first position to
become the birthright son. Cain should also be the one chosen as the
new patriarch (under his father Adam) and set apart to help administer
the gospel to all of Adam's posterity, becoming their prophet, priest
and king. Eve is excited about the birth of her son Cain because he will
be raised in the gospel that his older brothers and sisters rejected and
"believed it not" (vs. 12, 13). Cain is the first of Adam's posterity
'born in the covenant', unlike his older siblings, and he will be the first
child to be taught the gospel from his youth. He will, in effect, go to
primary, young men's, seminary, institute, family home evenings, and
priesthood meetings with his father; thus Eve declares, "I have gotten a
man from the Lord; *wherefore he may not reject his words*" (Moses
5:16) as his older brothers and sisters had done. Adam, and Eve
especially, recognize that there is now offspring to carry on the
patriarchal order and priesthood line. Cain should become the prophet,
king and priest to the posterity of Adam, having all power, authority
and possessions of his father Adam.

The Prophet Joseph Smith taught, as do the scriptures, that Cain held
the priesthood, providing him the authority to function and officiate in

its ordinances.[14] Cain received the priesthood from his father and no doubt participated in the ordinances of salvation and exaltation for himself. Cain and his brother Abel prepared themselves to officiate in all the ordinances of the priesthood. His righteousness and priesthood activity would be manifested to his father and to God as he participated in priesthood ordinances, which would include those of sacrifice. The priesthood responsibility that Adam held was an authority that functioned under both the Patriarchal and Melchizedek priesthoods. The lesser, or Aaronic Priesthood, did not exist as a separate authority or responsibility at that time because each patriarch was responsible for their family's spiritual and temporal needs. Cain was the first in line to become the new *Grand Patriarch* to all of Adam's posterity, holding and having all of the priesthood keys and authorities of his father.

In scripture there are patriarchs (family fathers restricted to immediate family lines) and *Grand Patriarchs* (holding a responsibility for all their father's children in their extended family lines). The book of Genesis is the priesthood manual of the Patriarchal Priesthood. Every sealed patriarch and matriarch entered into 'that order of the priesthood' which was patriarchal, the father becoming the patriarch to his own immediate family. A father is naturally responsible for the temporal and spiritual wellbeing of his family. The *Grand Patriarch* held all the keys and authority necessary to provide the *temporal* (today's Aaronic) and *spiritual* (Melchizedek) welfare to *his father's* family, (the brothers, sisters and their children etc.) thus, becoming a prophet, priest and king for them as well as for his own family.

The Melchizedek authority given to man is the power inherent in Christ as the firstborn and anointed birthright son of God. This Melchizedek authority is called the "Holy Priesthood, after the Order of the Son of God" (D&C 107:3). Christ is the only begotten in the flesh and the firstborn of the spirit. This inherent power, plus his position as the firstborn and birthright son of God, uniquely qualifies Christ to provide for the temporal and spiritual welfare of all His Father in Heaven's children. Thus, only Christ can be the Savior. As

---

14. *TPJS*, pp. 58-59; 169

the birthright and firstborn son, the Anointed Messiah provides for the *temporal welfare* (creator of the world) and the *spiritual welfare* (the Atonement and resurrection) of *all* the children of His Father.

> That by him, and through him, and of him, the worlds are and were created, and the inhabitants thereof are begotten sons and daughters unto God. (D&C 76:24)

This authority is inherent within Christ as the firstborn and birthright son, and the same responsibility and authority is bestowed on each of the birthright sons of Adam and Eve. This birthright and firstborn authority is "without father or mother" (JST Hebrews 7:3) which legitimately provides the necessary temporal and spiritual salvation outside a direct family line. Hence, the Melchizedek authority may function without father or mother, unlike one holding the patriarchal authority and priesthood only (D&C 107:39-41).

The *Grand Patriarchs* (those holding both Patriarchal and Melchizedek authority) are listed in scriptures as the first born of the first born: Adam, Seth, Enoch, etc., down to Abraham, Isaac, Jacob, Joseph, and Ephraim. The *Grand Patriarch's* authority to administer the gospel and its ordinances resides in the authority of Christ, the Firstborn, and is an authority to administer outside the immediate family for the benefit of his Father's children. The Melchizedek authority steps in as an aid to the family patriarch and becomes a substitute for the families that may not have a father or patriarch to provide for them. Hence the command throughout scripture to take care of the temporal and spiritual needs of the "fatherless, widows, and orphans."

The common element among the "fatherless, widows, and orphans" is the absence of a patriarch to physically and spiritually provide and protect. Thus the Melchizedek authority and responsibility is to provide for the temporal and spiritual needs of those who are without a patriarch or priesthood leader in the home. For this reason, the Melchizedek priesthood is given to the male, as this responsibility is to become an assistant—and a replacement if necessary—for the authority and responsibility of the father of the family.

The Patriarchal Law of Inheritance in the Old Testament put forth that the first *'righteous'* son would receive the birthright, becoming the Grand Patriarch with Melchizedek authority. The book of Genesis discusses both a *firstborn son* and a *birthright son*. In most cases, these should be the same son, but the birthright responsibility is to be passed to the first righteous son, as in the case of Jacob or Israel and his sons. Ruben was the firstborn son but Joseph became the birthright son. Esau was the firstborn son of Isaac, but Jacob became the birthright son. Ishmael was the firstborn of Abraham, but Isaac became the birthright son. The firstborn son of Joseph (who was sold into Egypt) was Manasseh, but the birthright son was Ephraim. Cain was the firstborn in the gospel (who had accepted it) but Abel was chosen to be the *Grand Patriarch*, the priesthood leader and birthright son. This righteous and chosen *Grand Patriarch* was to *lead and direct* his father's family as a *prophet*, stand as a *priest* in providing and *performing the ordinances* of salvation and exaltation that were required, and act in the responsibilities of a *king* in providing for the *temporal needs and the protection* of his father's family.

Eve, excited to see the patriarchal line in the birth of Cain declares: "I have gotten a man from the Lord; wherefore he may not reject his words" as their previous sons and daughters had done. However, in the 'process of time,' "Cain hearkened not, saying: Who is the Lord that I should know him?" (Moses 5:16, 19) Eventually the *'rights'* and the *'rite'* of a *Grand Patriarch* was conferred to Abel, the more righteous second-born son in this gospel-centered home. This is made clear in Moses 5:20-21, as the "Lord had respect" for Abel's offering, and had "not respect" for Cain's sacrifice. Because of his faith, the service, sacrifice, and faithful priesthood activity of Abel was accepted by God as more righteous than the bloodless offerings Cain made without faith in Christ and at the behest of Satan (Moses 5:18).

It is important to understand that this is not the first time they offered sacrifice. They both had to prove themselves in priesthood activity over years of growing in either faith or pride. Of this particular offering the scripture states that it was *"in process of time"* that it came to pass that Cain brought the fruit of the ground" (Moses 5:19). This particular account in scripture is about the decision to choose another Grand Patriarch, someone who is qualified to carry on the priesthood authority and responsibility of the "birthright son" to provide for the temporal and spiritual welfare of all his father's posterity. It was now time to choose the righteous son who would become the prophet, priest, and king to all the posterity of Adam, and eventually to all of mankind.

The Prophet Joseph spoke of three priesthoods, one being the Patriarchal Priesthood as given anciently to the patriarchs and matriarchs (See *TPJS* p.323). Today, this priesthood is entered into by way of the sealing (marriage) ordinance, wherein one is anointed and blessed on earth to be a *prophet, priest and king* to their family.

> In the celestial glory there are three heavens or degrees; And in order to obtain the highest, a man must enter into *this order of the priesthood* [meaning the new and everlasting covenant of marriage]; (D&C 131:1-2)

This "order of the priesthood" is intimately connected to the marriage and sealing ordinance of a husband and wife. This sealing is the entrance into that "order of the priesthood" or the "patriarchal priesthood", becoming a patriarch and matriarch to their family and posterity. Anciently, to become the birthright son, one must not only be sealed to a matriarch but also have the authority of the Melchizedek Priesthood (the inherent authority of Christ) to function as the *'prophet, priest and king'* for all his father's posterity when a worthy patriarch may be absent.

Cain received the priesthood, as did his brother Abel. However, Cain, being the oldest son (after Adam and Eve had received the gospel), felt he was entitled (in his mind) to not only the double inheritance of the firstborn, but also the birthright authority to "rule" over all the posterity of his father. [Anciently, the firstborn son received a double portion of the inheritance as part of his responsibility to provide for the widows and orphans in the extended family.]

Cain, like his brother Abel, participated in and received all the blessings and ordinances of salvation and exaltation. This is something required to become Perdition (D&C 76:31-34) as described in Moses, chapter five. To emphasize again, this account of Cain and Abel is rehearsed in the scriptures because it was the time to choose the worthy son to be the Grand Patriarch of the family line for all mankind.

Oaths and Covenants

It is generally taught that the Oath and Covenant of the Priesthood has a singular reference to those young men and brethren who receive the priesthood in their respective quorums and orders. Let's expand the term of Oath and Covenant of the Priesthood into the definitions that the scriptures provide. There have been many articles published by L.D.S. authors and scholars about the meanings of the terms "oath" and also "covenant" which will not be reviewed at this time. It would be of greater benefit to provide the meanings of these words as defined by the original language and in the lexicons of the Bible. In the Old Testament, the word or words used to "*make, establish* or *enter*" into a covenant is comprised of two words: "karath b'irth" which literally translated means to "*cut a covenant.*" These two words are connected because anciently a sacrificial death or a cutting (symbolic or real) was involved in the making of a covenant. The cutting is the "oath" in the covenant making process. This 'cutting a covenant' may be seen in Genesis as Abraham receives the covenant from God that will significantly impact his descendants for the rest of time. Notice that the large animals are cut in two and the smaller were not, but no doubt their throats were cut. The word "oath" is the cutting that is implied in the making of a covenant anciently.

> 6 And he believed in the Lord; and he counted it to him for righteousness. 7 And he said unto him, I am the Lord that brought thee out of Ur of the Chaldees, to give thee this land to inherit it. 8 And he said, Lord God, *whereby shall I know that I shall inherit it*?

9 And he said unto him, Take me an heifer of three years old, and a she goat of three years old, and a ram of three years old, and a turtledove, and a young pigeon.

10 And *he took unto him all these, and divided them in the midst, and laid each piece one against anoth*er: but the birds divided he not.

11 And when the fowls came down upon the carcasses, Abram drove them away.

12 And when the sun was going down, a deep sleep fell upon Abram; and, lo, an horror of great darkness fell upon him.

13 And he said unto Abram, Know of a surety that thy seed shall be a stranger in a land that is not theirs, and shall serve them; and they shall afflict them four hundred years;14 And also that nation, whom they shall serve, will I judge: and afterward shall they come out with great substance.

15 And thou shalt go to thy fathers in peace; thou shalt be buried in a good old age.

16 But in the fourth generation they shall come hither again: for the iniquity of the Amorites is not yet full.

17 And it came to pass, that, when the sun went down, and it was dark, behold a smoking furnace, and a burning lamp that *passed between those pieces.*

18 In the same day the Lord *made (cut) a covenant* with Abram, saying, Unto thy seed have I given this land, from the river of Egypt unto the great river, the river Euphrates. (Genesis 15:6-18)

In verse eighteen above, it is the Lord that "cut a covenant" with Abram, symbolized by the animals that were cut in two. This cutting acted as a witness and token of that covenant, stressing the importance of obedience to the stipulations, with the implication of perpetuity. The covenant between Jacob and Laban in Genesis 31:51-55 is also ratified by a sacrifice on the mount. These two examples set an interpreting precedent for the 'law of sacrifice' that existed in the patriarchal period centuries before the Law of Moses was instituted. The patriarchal sacrifices represented the oath portion of the personal covenants that the individual was entering into with God. Each sacrifice was, by nature, establishing a commitment and covenant between God and the one offering the sacrifice. Through the 'cutting of a covenant' the initiate becomes indelibly connected to the Atonement and sacrifice of Christ, as the messenger explained to Adam when he was offering sacrifice:

> 7 And then the angel spake, saying: This thing is a similitude of the sacrifice of the Only Begotten of the Father, which is full of grace and truth.8 Wherefore, thou shalt do all that thou doest in the name of the Son, and thou shalt repent and call upon God in the name of the Son forevermore. (Moses 5:7-8)

In the Book of Ruth, Naomi is told by her daughter-in-law that she will remain with her:

> 16 And Ruth said, Entreat me not to leave thee, or to return from following after thee: for whither thou goest, I will go; and where thou lodgest, I will lodge: thy people shall be my people, and thy God my God:17 Where thou diest, will I die, and there will I be buried: *the Lord do so to me, and more also,* if ought but death part thee and me. (Ruth 1:16-17)

Ruth is making a promise (i.e. a covenant) with Naomi to remain with her. In verse seventeen Ruth makes the statement, "*the Lord do so to me, and more*" and then states that only death will part her from this promise to Naomi. This phrase "Lord do so to me and more" was, as Edward F. Campbell states in the *Anchor Bible Series* on *Ruth* an "oath formulary."

> This solemn oath formulary appears only here and in eleven passages in Samuel and Kings. The first part of it was *presumably accompanied by a symbolic gesture, something like our index finger across the throat.* Deep behind this lay, in all probability, a ritual act involving the slaughter of animals, to whom the one swearing the oath equated himself. The slaughtered and split animals represent what the oath-taker invites God to do to him if he fails to keep the oath.[15]

The Interpreters Dictionary of the Bible defines the word "oath" as:

15. Campbell, Edward F. Jr., *Anchor Bible: Ruth*, Vol. 7, Doubleday, 1975. p.74.

> ...an ancient and universal means of impressing this obligation on the responsible parties in an agreement or an investigation. The oath as a holy act was properly pronounced in a sacred place or administered by a holy person. An oath must be kept through to one's hurt (Ps. 15:4) *The oath is accompanied by symbolic acts. The gesture of the oath was to raise the hand toward heaven...both hands, or the right hand. Sacrifices accompanied the oath in connection with a covenant.* In Jeremiah 34:18, those who break the covenant with the Lord are told that they will be made like the calf which they cut in two and passed between its parts. This suggests that the oath which bound the parties to a covenant may have stipulated in the conditional curse that the violator should be treated like the sacrificial animal.[16]

This 'oath formulary' has been passed down through the ages and has been participated in by almost all modern day youth. The familiar juvenile promise of secrecy is often accompanied with the well-known phrase "*cross my heart and hope to die*" by those involved. The crossing of the heart is not the cross of Christianity, but the 'dividing asunder' or the cutting in two—making a commitment to die before breaking the promise.

Zoram's fears were silenced when Nephi promised "*with an oath* that he need not fear; that he should be a free man like unto us if he would go down in the wilderness with us" (1 Nephi 4:33). It would have been understood by Zoram that Nephi promised to put his life on the line with a symbolic act of death or sacrifice, ensuring the safety of Laban's servant by oath and covenant.

This cutting and oath formulary will be discussed later in connection with Cain and the oaths that he entered into. The oaths of Cain are also discussed in the Book of Mormon, but should be viewed in respect to "secret oaths and combinations", which differ from the "oaths and covenants" of the priesthood.

---

16. *The Interpreter's Dictionary of the Bible*, Vol 3, "Oath" New York, Abingdon Press, 1962. pp. 575-576.

The Covenant Pattern

A covenant is defined as "a solemn promise made binding by an oath, which may be either a verbal formula or a symbolic action. Such an action or ritual is recognized by both parties as the formal act which binds the actor to fulfill his promise."

The covenant pattern found in the ancient Middle East and the 'treaty pattern' found in the Hittite records reflect the same elements in the covenantal process. These elements of the treaty covenant pattern are:

a. *The Preamble*: Lists the parties involved or opens with the statement: "These are the words of ..." followed by the identification of the individuals involved, whether suzerain to vassal or God to man.

b. *The Historical Prologue*: This consists of a description of the previous relationships between the two parties. Many Temples incorporated the Historical Prologue as the Creation epic.

c. *The Stipulations:* Contain the obligations to which the vassal binds himself to in accepting the covenant.

d. *The Deposit and Public Reading:* The covenant process is deposited, and then repeated at the Temple or sanctuary multiple times a year.

e. *The Witnesses:* Ancient legal documents normally ended with a list of witnesses. Usually God or divine beings are invoked as witnesses and are mentioned beside those who are present.

f. *The Blessings and Curses:* This consists of a list of goods and calamities which the divine witnesses were called upon to bring upon the individual for obedience and disobedience respectively.[17]

This covenant pattern is solemnized by the "oath" or the cutting (an actual sacrifice or symbolic act of death or cutting) would indicate that the covenant or promise was more important than death. This did not necessarily mean that the individual could be slain if he didn't keep the

---

17. *The Interpreter's Dictionary of the Bible*, Vol 3, "Covenant" New York, Abingdon Press, 1962. pp. 214-215.

stipulations, but that the commitment was more important than life itself. Antithetical to the sacred traditions are those secret combinations of 'blood Atonement' that would place the individual in peril of his life if the stipulations were not kept. Both righteous and unrighteous covenants existed with an oath or cutting, and are reflected in the scriptures as the 'oath and covenant of the priesthood' and 'secret oaths and combinations' respectively.

The Oath and Covenant of the Priesthood

Using the ancient treaty and covenant pattern as described above, it can be seen that the Oath and Covenant of the Priesthood found in Section 84 of the Doctrine and Covenants fits into this ancient pattern. Using the lettered elements of this covenant pattern, Section 84 may be viewed as an endowment or covenant of knowledge and power.

a)   *The Preamble*: Lists the parties involved or opens with the statement: "These are the words of . . ." followed by the identification of the individuals involved.   Suzerain to vassal, or God to Man.

D&C 84:1-2, The "revelation and words" of Jesus Christ to Joseph Smith, the Elders and the Church.

b)   *The Historical Prologue*: This consists of a description of the previous relationships between the two parties. Many Temples incorporated the Historical Prologue as the Creation epic.

D&C 84:6-26, comprise the *Historical Prologue* which is the history of the priesthood including those patriarchs and prophets through which the authority passed. The purpose and loss of the higher or greater Melchizedek Priesthood is outlined with the brief history of the Aaronic Order and when the Melchizedek would return.

c)   *The Stipulations:* Contain the obligations to which the vassal binds himself in accepting the covenant.

D&C 84:31-32, The *Stipulations* are outlined in the responsibility of the sons of Moses and of Aaron: "whoso is faithful unto the obtaining these two priesthoods... and the magnifying their calling."

    d)   *The Deposit and Public Reading:* The covenant process is deposited, and then repeated at the Temple or sanctuary multiple times a year.

This whole section is a discussion about the Temple, the New Jerusalem and the endowment. Verses 19-22 discuss the ordinances of the priesthood that are required to receive the "mysteries" and how to pass through the veil into the "rest of the Lord" or the "fullness of his glory" as described in the text. This is a direct reference to the ordinances of Exaltation that can only be received in the Temple. The organization of the priesthood was to have a regular meeting at the Temple twice a year as required for all males in ancient Israel, which was to take place at Passover (April) and Yom Kippur (October).

    e)   *The Witnesses:* Ancient legal documents normally ended with a list of witnesses. Usually the God or divine beings are invoked as witnesses and are mentioned beside those present.

The *Witnesses* of any ordinance are not just those present or designated, but also God and Angels.

    f)   *The Blessings and Judgments:* This consists of a list of goods and calamities that the divine witnesses were called upon to bring upon the individual for obedience and disobedience respectively. This could be connected to life and or property

D&C 84:33-42, The Blessings and Judgments or Curses are discussed in verse 33, "For whoso (are) faithful are sanctified by the Spirit unto the renewing of their bodies."

The two priesthoods are the Melchizedek and the Aaronic. Each priesthood has connected to it particular laws that are promised to be kept by covenant. The Aaronic requires the temporal care of the church and membership through the laws of 'sacrifice and the gospel.' The Melchizedek order requires that one be obedient to the more spiritual laws of 'virtue' or that of being chaste in all relationships, and the 'consecration' of one's life and blessings for the good of the whole. One who magnifies their responsibilities in these priesthoods will receive the blessings stipulated by the covenant of obedience.

> 34 They become the sons of Moses and of Aaron and the seed of Abraham, and the church and kingdom, and the elect of God.
> 35 And also all they who receive this priesthood receive me, saith the Lord; (D&C 84:34-35)

The obedient can have all the rights, powers (authorities) and privileges of the Melchizedek order just as with the Aaronic order. Included in these 'rights' is the covenant that they may become the "seed of Abraham and the elect of God." This oath and covenant of the priesthood also contains the opportunity and blessing of receiving Christ and the servants of Christ, who are the presidency of that 'greater priesthood.'

There exists in the Doctrine and Covenants a reverse line of authority, which is singularly unusual within scripture. This reverse line of authority is found in D&C 27:5-12. To quickly summarize, it begins with Moroni (abt. 400 A.D.) and moves to John the Baptist and his father of the Aaronic priesthood (abt. 30 A.D.). It then moves to Elijah (abt. 800 B.C.) and then to the patriarchs who are listed in an unusual reversed way: "And also with Joseph and Jacob, and Isaac, and Abraham, your fathers, by whom the promises remain" (D&C 27:10), which push it back to about 1700 B.C. It continues back to "Michael, or Adam, the ancient of days" (abt. 4000 B.C.) and then concludes with the *presidency* of the authority of Christ in all ages, and perhaps even before this world: "And also with Peter, and James, and John, whom I have sent unto you." (D&C 27:12). These are the servants responsible for the Melchizedek Order, it's ordinances, and endowments. Section 84 continues with the blessings of the initiate if he has magnified his responsibilities in these two priesthoods:

> 36 For he that receiveth my servants receiveth me;
> 37 And he that receiveth me receiveth my Father;
> 38 And he that receiveth my Father receiveth my Father's kingdom; therefore, all that my Father hath shall be given unto him. (D&C 84:36-38)

By receiving the instruction from the servants of Christ, one may receive Him, and if the relationship with the Savior is acceptable, then the Father is also received (John 14:23). Verse 38 concludes that those righteous and valiant receive all that the Father hath. This would include becoming an heir and joint heir with Christ, as one qualified may pass through the veil and enter into the presence of the Father prepared to receive all that the Father hath.

This endowment of blessings is according to the "oath and covenant" of the priesthood which cannot be broken.

> 39 And this is according to the oath and covenant which belongeth to the priesthood.
> 40 Therefore, all those who receive the priesthood, receive this oath and covenant of my Father, which he cannot break, neither can it be moved. (D&C 84:39-40)

The actual Oath and Covenant of the Priesthood appears to be an endowment of power when understood correctly. Whenever the ordinances of exaltation are discussed, explained, or referred to in the scriptures, it is considered to be in 'real time' and not to become such by one's faithfulness. The reality is always described in scripture. Some would call this a 'calling and election, second anointing, more sure word of prophecy or sealing by the Holy Spirit of Promise.' Because of this, the "oath" (the cutting or cursing) is explained in the text.

> 41 But whoso breaketh this covenant after he hath received it, and altogether turneth therefrom, shall not have forgiveness of sins in this world nor in the world to come.

> 42 And wo unto all those who come not unto this priesthood which ye have received, which I now confirm upon you who are present this day, by mine own voice out of the heavens; and even I have given the heavenly hosts and mine angels charge concerning you. (D&C 84:41-42)

When this oath and covenant of the priesthood (endowment) is entered into, and one receives its fullness and *"altogether turneth there from,"* they "shall not have forgiveness of sins in this world nor in the world to come" (D&C 84:41). These are they who become the sons of perdition, who knew God's power and had been made partakers thereof (D&C 76:31). This is not referring to those who promised 'to become such, *if*' true and faithful in their obedience and change of character.

Back to Cain

Joseph Smith, speaking of Adam, Cain and Abel, states, "if they offered sacrifices they must be authorized by ordination."[18] The Prophet Joseph continues by teaching that "Cain, also being authorized to offer sacrifice" did so without the faith that was required of the righteous priesthood holder.[19]

Cain, after he received the priesthood and his endowment of power ("in process of time"), "hearkened not, saying Who is the Lord that I should know him" (Moses 5:16, 18), and "Cain loved Satan more than God." As it came time to choose the new Grand Patriarch who would be the 'birthright' son, the character, desires, and priesthood activity of Cain and Abel were made manifest. As these sons of Adam offered sacrifice, their righteousness and worthiness became evident to Adam and the Lord.

> 19 And in process of time it came to pass that Cain brought of the fruit of the ground an offering unto the Lord.

---

18. *TPJS.* p.169.
19. *Ibid.*

> 20 And Abel, he also brought of the firstlings of his flock, and of the fat thereof. And the Lord had respect unto Abel, and to his offering;
> 21 But unto Cain, and to his offering, he had not respect. Now Satan knew this, and it pleased him. And Cain was very wroth, and his countenance fell. (Moses 5:19-21)

Because of Cain's attitude, pride, and wickedness the "Lord had not respect" for Cain's offering. This statement would indicate that the deliberate disrespect by Cain's offering (he knew the rules) disqualified him from being the accepted and rightful priesthood authority. "Satan knew this" (v. 21) "and it pleased him" but Cain was "wroth" and he was depressed.

Cain had prepared his offering under the direction of Satan (Moses 5:18) and therefore it was not an offering of righteousness. Again, the Prophet Joseph Smith gives added insight into this event by explaining that since Cain did not offer his "offering in righteousness, he was cursed."[20] The Prophet Joseph continues:

> Abel offered to God a sacrifice that was accepted, which was the firstlings of the flock. Cain offered of the fruit of the ground, and was not accepted, because he could not do it in faith, he could have no faith, or could not exercise faith contrary to the plan of heaven. It must be shedding the blood of the Only Begotten to atone for man. Cain could have no faith and whatsoever is not of faith, is sin. But Abel offered an acceptable sacrifice, by which he obtained witness that he was righteous. The mere shedding of the blood of beasts or offering anything else in sacrifice, could not procure a remission of sins, except it were performed *in faith of something to come.*[21]

The righteousness of Abel is discussed in a passage of scripture quoted by Joseph Smith about the offering of Abel by stating:

---

20. *TPJS.* p. 169
21. *TPJS.* pp.58, 59.

> We read in Genesis 4:4, that Abel brought the firstlings of the flock and the fat thereof, and the Lord had respect to Abel and to his offering. And, again "by faith Abel offered unto God a more excellent sacrifice than Cain, by which he obtained witness that he was righteous." [Hebrews 11:4][22]

Because of faith and righteousness, Abel, the younger brother of Cain, is chosen to be the Grand Patriarch. He is chosen and set-apart to assist his father in caring for the spiritual and temporal welfare of all his father Adam's posterity (remember there were three generations alive before Adam received the gospel). Abel, now chosen to be the 'prophet, priest and king' to the family of his father, also becomes Cain's priesthood and patriarchal leader. The scriptures summarize the calling of Abel and the rejection of Cain as the Grand Patriarch stating: "Now Satan knew this, and it pleased him. And Cain was very wroth, and his countenance fell" (Moses 5:21).

The Lord addresses Cain giving him another chance to exhibit the faithful responsibility of the birthright son:

> 22 And the Lord said unto Cain: Why art thou wroth? Why is thy countenance fallen?
> 23 If thou doest well, thou shalt be accepted. And *if thou doest not well, sin lieth at the door, and Satan desireth to have thee*; and except thou shalt hearken unto my commandments, I will *deliver thee up*, and it shall be unto thee *according to his desire*. And thou shalt rule over him. (Moses 5:22-23)

The Lord explains that if he (Cain) would remain faithful and 'do well' that he would still be accepted, while at the same time warning him that Satan desires to have control over him. It is explained to Cain that if he doesn't keep and live up to the laws, commandments, and covenants he entered into—including no doubt the oath and covenant of the priesthood—he would be in Satan's power. (See also D&C 104:5-9)

---

22. *TPJS*. p. 169.

Character is of even greater importance than that of obedience to law, as all commandments are given to create the character that loves God and their fellow man. Cain's question "Am I my brother's keeper?" is descriptive of his inner nature and lack of worthiness for the responsibility of the temporal and spiritual welfare of all his brothers and sisters that he knew, and all the posterity of Adam that he would never know.

The attitude or character of loving God through obedience is more important than the performances of ordinances. Obedience and ordinances without a resulting character change is useless. Nonetheless obedience to the Lord's commands and the connected ordinances are imperative in that character change. In the example below, it is the individual's obedience and love of God that makes them worthy of the leadership, recognition and blessing of God in that calling.

> 22 And Samuel said, Hath the Lord as great delight in burnt offerings and sacrifices, as in obeying the voice of the Lord? Behold, to obey is better than sacrifice, and to hearken than the fat of rams.
> 23 For rebellion is as the sin of witchcraft, and stubbornness is as iniquity and idolatry. *Because thou hast rejected the word of the Lord, he hath also rejected thee from being king.* (1 Samuel 15:22-23)

To "obey and hearken" *by natural inclination* is the character required to be accepted by God. It is the heart and character that is important, not the ordinance. The action of ordinances, such as sacrifice, baptism, and other ordinances are to assist in the necessary change of character by providing a hope of a future reality. Without the requisite change of character, however, ordinances are of no value or power. The ordinance that identified the Lord's chosen people and seed of Abraham was the law of circumcision. The prophet Jeremiah explained that obedience to law without change of heart does not ensure acceptance by the Lord. Again, the ordinance means nothing without the change of heart and character. Obedience to this 'law of ordinance' *requires* the change of heart for the ordinance itself to be validated and accepted by God. The Lord explains through Jeremiah that being "uncircumcised in the heart" renders the circumcision of the lineage of Abraham worthless.

> 24 But let him that glorieth glory in this, that he understandeth and knoweth me, that I am the Lord which exercise lovingkindness, judgment, and righteousness, in the earth: for *in these things I delight,* saith the Lord.

> > (This is the character of God and should be the character of those that love Him, for this is His delight.)

> 25 Behold, the days come, saith the Lord, that *I will punish all them which are circumcised with the uncircumcised;*

> > (Without the change of heart, those who participate in ordinances will be condemned with those who have rejected God.)

> 26 Egypt, and Judah, and Edom, and the children of Ammon, and Moab, and all that are in the utmost corners, that dwell in the wilderness: for all these nations are uncircumcised, and *all the house of Israel are uncircumcised in the heart.* (Jeremiah 9:24-26)

Perdition

In Moses 5, the Savior explains that if he (Cain) continues down this path with Satan, he will become, "the father of his (Satan's) lies", and *"thou shalt be called Perdition*; for thou wast also before the world" (Moses 5:24). Many assume that means Cain was perdition before he came to this earth. However, the last phrase could be understood differently when considering the whole picture. Cain 'was before the world:' he was in the Council of Heaven. The fact that he was born here on earth indicates that he chose not to follow Satan's plan, i.e. he kept his 'first estate', and so was added upon and came to this 'second estate' of mortality (Abraham 3:26). Cain, like all who are born on this earth, existed 'before the world was' and chose to participate in mortality and the plan of salvation. Because of that choice in the pre-earth life, Cain moved into this 'second estate,' coming to a knowledge of the gospel and receiving the fullness of the priesthood, participating and functioning in the ordinances. Only *because* he had taken upon himself the oath and covenant of the priesthood and received the fullness of the priesthood ordinances, (meaning his calling and election) could he become perdition as described in D&C 76. Cain eventually made spiritual decisions based on pride and followed Satan, and "altogether turned therefrom", eventually committing murder and shedding innocent blood. Cain cannot receive a forgiveness of sins in this world or the world to come (D&C 132:27); therefore he may be called Perdition.

There are three "sons" that are discussed in scripture: 1) The *"sons of men"* are those who have not heard of, nor ever embraced, the gospel; 2) The *"sons of God"* are those who have accepted Christ, embraced the gospel, and are worthy to receive the ordinances and blessings of salvation and exaltation; and 3) The *"sons of perdition"* are those who have accepted the gospel and have known his "power and been made partakers thereof" (D&C 76:31), being guaranteed exaltation by ordinance and/or manifestation, only to then altogether turn from it (D&C 84:41).

Since Cain had participated in the fullness of the priesthood and knew the oaths and covenants, and the signs and tokens of the priesthood, he would become the father of his Satan's lies. "For of him unto whom much is given much is required; and he who sins against the greater light shall receive the greater condemnation" (D&C 82:3). Cain qualified to be called "perdition" because he altogether turned from those exalting ordinances and promises. Because of this, he would not receive forgiveness in "this world or the world to come."

The required process to become perdition is explained by the Lord in Section 76 of the Doctrine and Covenants.

> 31 Thus saith the Lord concerning all those who know my power, and have been made partakers thereof, and suffered themselves through the power of the devil to be overcome, and to deny the truth and defy my power.

> 32 They are they who are the sons of perdition, of whom I say that it had been better for them never to have been born;
>
> 33 For they are vessels of wrath, doomed to suffer the wrath of God, with the devil and his angels in eternity;
>
> 34 Concerning whom I have said there is no forgiveness in this world nor in the world to come—
>
> 35 Having denied the Holy Spirit after having received it, and having denied the Only Begotten Son of the Father, having crucified him unto themselves and put him to an open shame.
>
> 36 These are they who shall go away into the lake of fire and brimstone, with the devil and his angels—
>
> 37 And the only ones on whom the second death shall have any power;
>
> 38 Yea, verily, the only ones who shall not be redeemed in the due time of the Lord, after the sufferings of his wrath.
> (Doctrine and Covenants 76:31-38)

The requirements to become perdition are listed in verses 31-35. They must:

1) "know my power"
2) "been made partakers thereof"
3) "suffered themselves to be overcome by the power of Satan"
4) "deny the truth"
5) "defy my power"
6) "denied the Holy Spirit after having received it"
7) "denied the Only Begotten Son of the Father"
8) "crucified him unto themselves and put him to an open shame"

These requirements make it clear that Cain would have to have "known the power of God and been made a partaker thereof." Moses 5 explains that Cain suffered himself to be overcome by the power of Satan and cites each point from the above list, confirming that he is worthy of being called 'perdition.'

The verses just quoted in Section 76 also list the cursing or consequences of becoming perdition. These are found in verses 32-34, 36-38, 44-46 of that same Section.

1) "It had been better for them never to have been born"
2) "They are vessels of wrath"
3) "Doomed to suffer the wrath of God"
4) "With the devil and his angels in eternity"
5) "No forgiveness in this world nor in the world to come"
6) "Go away into the lake of fire and brimstone"
7) "The only ones on whom the second death shall have any power"
8) "The only ones who shall not be redeemed in the due time of the Lord, after the sufferings of his wrath"

As Verse 34 makes clear, these sons of perdition shall not have "forgiveness in this world nor in the world to come." This is the same phrase used in D&C 84:41 in relation to those who receive the 'oath and covenant of the priesthood' and 'altogether turneth therefrom', for they must also become sons of perdition. The requirements to receive the judgment of "not having forgiveness of sins in this world nor the world to come" would appear to be the same. Thus the "oath and covenant of the priesthood" is connected to the fulfilling of the endowment of power, where one would "know my power and been made partakers thereof" before qualifying for this judgment.

Verses 44-46, wraps up the vision of the sons of perdition in this Section.

> 44 Wherefore, he saves all except them—they shall go away into everlasting punishment, which is endless punishment, which is eternal punishment, to reign with the devil and his angels in eternity, where their worm dieth not, and the fire is not quenched, which is their torment—
> 45 And the end thereof, neither the place thereof, nor their torment, no man knows;
> 46 Neither was it revealed, neither is, neither will be revealed unto man, except to them who are made partakers thereof; (D&C 76:44-46)

Continuing to speak with Cain, the Lord not only counsels him, but prophesies that his covenant with Satan and his influence of evil will affect the rest of mankind. The Lord continues to warn Cain by prophecy, providing him an opportunity to repent and change:

> 25 And it shall be said in time to come—That these abominations were had from Cain; for he rejected the greater counsel which was had from God; and this is a cursing which I will put upon thee, except thou repent. (Moses 5:24-25.)

The Lord explains that "*these abominations*" will become the 'oaths and combinations' that would be passed to and through wicked men in the future. The Lord also states that this evil would be said to be "from Cain." This is fulfilled and identified in the Book of Mormon as the abominations of Cain are directly attributed to him and his followers. These secret oaths and combinations ravaged the Nephite culture as the government fell into their hands due to the apathy of the righteous and the selling of the sacred for the spoils of wickedness.

> 15 And it came to pass that thus they did agree with Akish. And Akish did administer unto them the oaths which were given by them of old who also sought power, which had been handed down even from Cain, who was a murderer from the beginning. (Ether 8:15)

> 26 Now behold, those secret oaths and covenants did not come forth unto Gadianton from the records which were delivered unto Helaman; but behold, they were put into the heart of Gadianton by that same being who did entice our first parents to partake of the forbidden fruit.

> 27 Yea, that same being who did plot with Cain, that if he would murder his brother Abel it should not be known unto the world. And he did plot with Cain and his followers from that time forth. (Helaman 6:26-27)

It must be remembered that the definition of an "oath" is a 'cutting' or symbol of death. It can be seen in Moses that these oaths that Cain knew were instituted by Satan in the secret oaths and combinations. This could be done because Cain had at one time participated in covenant making with his father, and knew and understood the penalties of the covenant process and the consequences of the breaking of a covenant.

In verse 26 of Moses, chapter five, Abel had already been chosen as the birthright son and was now Cain's priesthood leader. Cain, in his pride, would not sustain the new patriarchal priesthood authority which his *younger* brother held. "Cain was wroth, and *listened not* any more to the voice of the Lord, *neither to Abel, his brother*, who walked in holiness before the Lord (Moses 5:26). In this he is mimicking the path Lucifer took in the pre-earth life, when Lucifer rejected Adam's (Michael's) priesthood authority and rebelled against the Father's Plan.

The Conspiracy

Cain is not alone in his new religion and organization, but now joins forces with his wife and "his brethren."

> And Adam and his wife mourned before the Lord, because of *Cain and his brethren.* And it came to pass that Cain took one of his brothers' daughters to wife, and *they* loved Satan more than God (Moses 5:27-28).

A *conspiracy* of brothers and sisters working with Cain as their leader ('Master Mahan') plots and organizes the murder of Abel, the chosen priesthood leader and patriarch. This conspiracy with Cain and his "brethren" are mentioned in verse 27 and 29 of Moses, chapter five, and also mentioned in the Book of Mormon and the Doctrine and Covenants.

> 27 Yea, that same being who did plot with Cain, that if he would murder his brother Abel it should not be known unto the world. And he did plot with *Cain and his followers* from that time forth. (Helaman 6:27)

> 16 And from Enoch to Abel, who was slain *by the conspiracy* of his brother, who received the priesthood by the commandments of God, by the hand of his father Adam, who was the first man. (D&C 84:16)

Cain convinced his brethren to rebel against their younger brother Abel who had been chosen as the priesthood leader. Cain reassured himself and his followers that they would be free from the authority and retribution of his father and brother. This promise of freedom from gospel standards and leadership was coupled with the promise of gain in power and wealth with the death of Abel. This was the pattern in the pre-earth councils as Lucifer convinces a third part of the hosts of heaven to rebel against the Father and His choice for the earthly priesthood keys and leadership. Satan's work of rebellion that began before this earth continues in mortality. It is often seen in the *rejection* of priesthood keys and authority, and in the unworthy seeking the power to exercise control and dominion over the souls of men.

Satan's goal is to destroy the eternal opportunities for the family of Adam, which he lost in the pre-earth "war in heaven." Some of the blessings that Satan lost were:

> The priesthood,
> A physical body,
> The power to pro-create,
> The potential to become a son of God,
> The power to become a rightful heir of all that the father hath,
> Exaltation, and
> The Glory of God.

To destroy this for the family of Adam, Satan must set up his counterfeit organizations with his similar oaths and combinations. This requires someone who held the priesthood, has knowledge of the sacred ordinances, and has received their own endowment of power. Cain, in rejecting "the greater counsel which was had from God", is the prime candidate to carry on the war in heaven on earth for Satan.

When Cain and his followers entered into the oaths and combinations, Satan put them under oath using symbols of death or sacrifice to guarantee secrecy upon pain of death.

> 29 And Satan said unto Cain: Swear unto me *by thy throat,* and if thou tell it thou shalt die; and swear thy brethren *by their heads*, and by the living God, that they tell it not; for if they tell it, they shall surely die; and this that thy father may not know it; and this day I will deliver thy brother Abel into thine hands.
> 30 And Satan sware unto Cain that he would do according to his commands. And all these things were done in secret. (Moses 5:29-30)

Joseph Smith taught: "In relation to the kingdom of God, the devil always sets up his kingdom at the very same time in opposition to God."[23] When Adam taught the gospel of Jesus Christ to his children, "Satan came among them, saying: I am also a son of God" and Adam's posterity refused to believe their father Adam (Moses 5:13). They could not see the Son of God that Adam taught about. Satan declaring himself a son of God and appearing as an angel of light (2 Nephi 9:9) convinced the posterity of Adam to reject their father's teaching, with the result that they "loved Satan more than God" (Moses 5:13). As this passage in Moses teaches, Satan was there when the gospel was introduced and explained to Adam. In like manner, Satan was there when Adam's sons received their 'oath and covenant of the priesthood' enabling him to set up (through Cain) *his* 'secret oaths and combinations' using the same signs, tokens, and penalties with which Cain was familiar.

In verse 29 above, it is seen that Cain and his followers "swear by their throats and by their heads" that if they tell it they shall surely die. These oaths of secrecy, 'to swear by their heads and throats,' is common in the Book of Mormon when the signs and tokens of the Gadianton organizations are discussed.

---

23. *TPJS*. p. 365.

Ether:

14 And it came to pass that they all swore unto him, by the
God of heaven, and also by the heavens, and also by the
earth, and *by their heads*, that whoso should vary from the
assistance which Akish desired *should lose his head;* and
whoso should divulge whatsoever thing Akish made known
unto them, the same should *lose his life.*15 And Akish did
administer unto them the oaths which were given by them of
old who also sought power, which had been handed down
even from Cain, who was a murderer from the beginning.16
And they were kept up by the power of the devil to
administer these oaths unto the people, to keep them in
darkness, to help such as sought power to gain power, and to
murder, and to plunder, and to lie, and to commit all manner
of wickedness and whoredoms.18 And it came to pass that
they formed a secret combination, even as they of old; which
combination is most abominable and wicked above all, in the
sight of God. (Ether 8:14-18)

Helaman:

21 But behold, Satan did stir up the hearts of the more part
of the Nephites, insomuch that they did unite with those
bands of robbers, and did enter into their covenants and their
oaths, that they would protect and preserve one another in
whatsoever difficult circumstances they should be placed,
that they should not suffer for their murders, and their
plunderings, and their stealings.22 *They did have their signs,
yea, their secret signs,* and their *secret words; and this that
they might distinguish a brother* who had entered into the
covenant, that whatsoever wickedness his brother should do
he should not be injured by his brother, nor by those who did
belong to his band, who had taken this covenant.23 And thus
they might murder, and plunder, and steal, and commit
whoredoms and all manner of wickedness, contrary to the
laws of their country and also the laws of their God.24 And
whosoever of those who belonged to their band should
reveal unto the world of their wickedness and their
abominations, should be tried, . . . according to the laws of

their wickedness. . . 26 Now behold, those secret oaths and covenants did not come forth unto Gadianton from the records. . . but by that same being who did entice our first parents to partake of the forbidden fruit—27 Yea, that same being who did plot with Cain, that if he would murder his brother Abel it should not be known unto the world. And he did plot with Cain and his followers from that time forth. (Helaman 6:21-24; 26, 27)

The 'oaths and combinations' described in the book of Mormon were established in the beginning by Satan as he teaches Cain and his followers the secrets of the Mahan principles. It should be explained again that there is a difference between 'oath and covenant' and 'oaths and combinations.' A 'covenant' is a promise of obedience and is made with God; it is between the covenant maker and God himself. Only two individuals are party to this covenant making process: God and the initiate. Salvation is an individual accomplishment, not a collective responsibility. Thus, collective righteousness or wickedness has no bearing on the eternal salvation of the individual. In the covenant between Man and God, the 'oath' implies that the covenant and promise of obedience is more sacred and important than death; not that he should lose his life if the covenant is broken.

In contrast, a 'combination' exists between a group of people or a mass of individuals. This covenant combination is one of *secrecy* rather than sacredness, and is administered to the masses and secured by oath for the protection of the 'combination'. The *oath and covenant of the priesthood* is something that takes place between God and the individual as all must work out their own salvation. The *oath and combination* is for the benefit of the group. Each are collectively bound by the "oath." The Covenant "oath" with God is one of sacrifice in similitude of the Only Begotten of the Father. The "combination and oath" administered by Satan include the symbols of the penalties for disobedience ("swear by their head and throats that they tell it not"), which is death.

Following their oath of obedience and silence, Satan binds himself and his power to those who follow his pattern. In Cain's story he swears "unto Cain that he (Satan) would do according to his (Cain's) commands" (Moses 5:30). All was done in secrecy so that Cain's 'father may not know it.'

Cain revels in this new found knowledge and power and proclaims, "Truly I am Mahan, the master of this great secret that I may murder and get gain. Wherefore Cain was called *Master Mahan*, and he gloried in his wickedness" (Moses 5:31). It is interesting that in the Dead Sea Scrolls, Satan is called, in the Hebrew, "*Mas-te-mah*" (too close for coincidence). To *murder for gain* is the "*Mahan Principle*" and is not restricted to human life, but all of God's creations. With the establishment of the secret oaths and combinations, Cain realizes the great benefit of this new organization and brags that he will now be able to 'murder and get gain.' This is the motivating force behind the conspiracy to murder Cain, for he supposes that the possessions of his brother Abel, as well as the leadership and authority, will now belong to him.

In this 'conspiracy' for 'gain,' Cain meets Abel: "And Cain went into the field, and Cain talked with Abel, his brother. And it came to pass that while they were in the field, Cain rose up against Abel, his brother, and slew him" (Moses 5:32).

With the murder of his brother, *Cain gloried* in that which he had done, saying: *I am free; surely the flocks of my brother falleth into my hands*" (Moses 5:33). Free from the leadership of a younger brother, free from the priesthood responsibilities and its obligations of righteousness, free (he supposed) from the guilt and anger of being rejected by the Lord, Cain now believes that all his brother had (i.e. the double inheritance and the birthright) would become his. It cannot be forgotten that Cain felt that he should be the Grand Patriarch for his father's family. One consequence of Abel being chosen as the Grand Patriarch is that the posterity of Abel would then fill that position throughout time. So Cain had much to gain with the death of his brother Abel. Not only did Cain believe his brother's personal property would become his, he also believed Abel's priesthood position would now belong to him and his posterity in perpetuity.

The 'Law of Inheritance' in the days of the Patriarchs stipulated that the eldest and firstborn and birthright son receive a "double portion" of all that his father had as part of his responsibility for the temporal welfare of his father's family (the fatherless, widows, orphans, etc). The birthright son could become not only a patriarch to his family through his marriage and sealing but also the Grand Patriarch by ordinance and the Melchizedek authority. Being the Grand Patriarch and birthright son (not necessarily the firstborn) placed his posterity into that birthright line forever. This is never more evident than in the Book of Mormon as Laman and Lemuel speak about Nephi, their younger brother, who becomes the 'birthright' son chosen by God. The concerns of Nephi's brothers were no doubt some of the same concerns and worries Cain had when Abel was chosen as the birthright son and Grand Patriarch.

> "Yea, they did murmur against me, saying: *Our younger brother thinks to rule over us;* and we have had much trial because of him; wherefore, now let us slay him, that we may not be afflicted more because of his words. For behold, *we will not have him to be our ruler; for it belongs unto us, who are the elder brethren, to rule over this people.*" (2 Nephi 5:3.)

Having murdered his priesthood leader and the birthright son, the Lord questions Cain: "Where is Abel, thy brother?" In answer, Cain reveals the underlying philosophy of Satan and the Mahan Principle, which is opposite of the true priesthood's responsibility. *"Am I my brother's keeper?"* (Moses 5:34). In essence, he's saying it's a dog-eat-dog world and survival of the fittest is the way of life. If this was the pride of Cain, it is no wonder that Abel was chosen as the new Grand Patriarch. The Mahan principle is to "murder and get gain," and to personally prosper at any and all costs. This is the same philosophical force that led to the Nephite destruction, as Mormon explains here:

> Now the cause of this iniquity of the people was this—Satan had great power, unto the stirring up of the people to do all manner of iniquity, and to the puffing them up with pride, tempting them to seek for power, and authority, and riches,

and the vain things of the world.
And thus Satan did lead away the hearts of the people to do
all manner of iniquity. (3 Nephi 6:15-16)

These *four elements of pride* as explained by Mormon are the fundamental attitudes that led to the fall of the Nephites. The same attitudes led to the murder of Abel as described in Moses.

Seek for power,
Seek for authority,
Seek for riches, and
Seek for the vain things of the world.

Pride lies at the foundation of the *Mahan Principle*. This philosophy and doctrine is in stark contrast to the priesthood, which exists to bless and serve others. In the endowment, one covenants to love God and one's fellow man. Instead of selfishness, the meek are selfless and seek not their own. Instead of personal security, the pure in heart sacrifice all. Instead of competition for gain, the merciful consecrate. The character of the righteous (one of "charity, the pure love of Christ") is the opposite of Cain:

And charity suffereth long, and is kind, and envieth not, and
is not puffed up, seeketh not her own, is not easily provoked,
thinketh no evil, and rejoiceth not in iniquity but rejoiceth in
the truth, beareth all things, believeth all things, hopeth all
things, endureth all things. (Moroni 7:45)

The basic differences between the philosophies of Satan and Babylon and that of God and the establishment of Zion are easily seen in scripture. Each has a Motive, Justification, Method Virtue, and a Power and Truth. These are reviewed and compared in their spiritual venue:

	God and Zion	Satan and Babylon
Motive	Consecration	Personal Gain
Justification	Love	Competition
Method	Upheavals of Nature	Violence
Virtue	Repentance	Denial of Guilt
Power	Choice and Agency	Compulsion
Truth	Seeking for Continual Light and Truth	Deception and Control of Knowledge

Cain confirms that the death of Abel came about because of Satan, plus his own "jealousy" of *his brother's possessions and priesthood position.* Cain declares to God: "Satan tempted me *because of my brother's flocks*: And I was wroth also; for *his offering thou didst accept and not mine"* (Moses 5:38). This verse lists two things of which Cain was tempted. First, the possessions of Abel (his flocks) and second, his priesthood position as Abel's offering and priesthood activity was accepted and Cain's was not. Abel was chosen and accepted by God to be the new priesthood leader for Adam's posterity. Cain had failed to learn and understand:

36 That the rights of the priesthood are inseparably connected with the powers of heaven, and that the powers of heaven cannot be controlled nor handled only upon the principles of righteousness.
37 That they may be conferred upon us, it is true; but when we undertake to cover our sins, or to gratify our pride, our vain ambition, or to exercise control or dominion or compulsion upon the souls of the children of men, in any degree of unrighteousness, behold, the heavens withdraw themselves; the Spirit of the Lord is grieved; and when it is withdrawn, Amen to the priesthood or the authority of that man. (D&C 121:36-37)

Scriptural history makes clear that the conflict between Cain and Abel is one of possession, power and priesthood. The rebellious and proud son tries to usurp the title of prophet, priest and king from the chosen younger brother. This is a pattern (the younger chosen over the elder) seen throughout the scriptures as priesthood authority and leadership positions are lost by the unworthy. When the wicked rule, they begin to exercise control and unrighteous dominion, not realizing that priesthood authority ends with their wickedness. The "authority" is to act in God's name is not something the unrighteous can wield. Therefore, Cain is 'left unto himself to kick against the pricks and fight against God' (D&C 121:38).

As touched on previously, the motif of an unworthy firstborn losing his priesthood position to a second-born is repeated throughout the scriptures. Besides Lucifer and Michael in the pre-earth life and Cain and Abel, there is a conflict between Ham, the son of Noah, and the priesthood line that belongs to Shem that resulted in Ham's stealing a priesthood garment and imitating the priesthood ordinances. Ishmael and Isaac are separated by their mothers as they compete for the covenant blessings and the office of prophet, king, and priest. Esau, the elder brother of Jacob, should have had the birthright based on birth order. But Esau does not take the priesthood covenants seriously and sells the priesthood birthright to Jacob, who obtains the blessing from Isaac by wearing the Garments of the Priesthood (Genesis 27:15).

Jacob's sons wrestle with jealousy when Joseph, the first-born righteous son of his second wife, receives the birthright and patriarchal responsibility instead of Reuben (the firstborn son of the first wife), who was unworthy. [The line of authority goes not from first born of the first wife to the second born, but from the firstborn of the first wife to the firstborn of the second wife. Concubinical children follow the natural children.] Jacob gives this authority to Joseph as he gives him the garment of the priesthood, described as the coat of many colors or 'pieces' (Genesis 37:4). Solomon and Adonijah in 1 Kings 1 also strive for the kingship. In the Book of Mormon, Laman and Lemuel, having lost the birthright due to wickedness, constantly murmured that Nephi, their younger brother, sought to rule over them and bind them down (1 Nephi 15:36).

The conflict lies between the 'oath and covenant of the priesthood' (God trying to establish Zion), and the oaths and combinations of Satan (using the pride of the natural man to build up Babylon). The battle continues between Babylon and Zion, the flesh and the spirit, ignorance and light and truth; between the individual remaining a 'son of man' or becoming a 'son of God' by receiving the endowed blessings of posterity, priesthood and inheritance that are promised by an Eternal Father to the obedient and faithful. The covenants and laws that will instill the power of this promise of Abraham upon the faithful are the very covenants that Satan tempts all to break. For, as was the case with Cain, when one fails to live up to the covenants they have made with God, they will be in Satan's power. These covenant blessings have counterfeit counterparts in the oaths and combinations inspired by Satan. The devil seeks to destroy the priesthood of God and usurp God's power by setting up his counterfeit priesthoods to be like the Most High.

> 12 How art thou fallen from heaven, O Lucifer, son of the morning! How art thou cut down to the ground, which didst weaken the nations!
> 13 For thou hast said in thine heart, *I will ascend into heaven, I will exalt my throne above the stars of God*: I will *sit also upon the mount of the congregation*, in the sides of the north:
> 14 *I will ascend above the heights* of the clouds; *I will be like the Most High*. (Isaiah 14:12-14)

This is the goal of Satan and the foundation of the struggle that led to the murder of Abel by his wicked elder brother Cain.

Joseph Smith taught about the origin of sin (see also Moses 6:55) and the character and vanity of man stating:

> ...that Satan was generally blamed of the evils which we did, but if he was the cause of all our wickedness, men could not

be condemned. The devil could not compel mankind to do evil; all was voluntary. Those who resisted the Spirit of God, would be liable to be led into temptation, and then the association of heaven would be withdrawn from those who refused to be made partakers of such great glory. God would not exert any compulsory means, and the devil could not: and such ideas as were entertained by many were absurd. The creature was made subject to vanity. ...all are subjected to vanity while they travel through the crooked paths and difficulties which surround them. Where is the man that is free from vanity? (*TPJS*. p. 187)

Cain murdered his priesthood leader, Abel, in order that he (Cain) and his descendants would have that right to rule over all of humanity. His pride took control, which led to the first murder for gain, seeking the unrighteous exercise control, dominion and power over the souls of the children of men. And thus: "Amen to the priesthood or authority of that man" (D&C 121:37).

Following Cain's response to the Lord's questions about Abel's whereabouts ("Am I my brother's keeper?"), The Lord responds:

35 And the Lord said: What hast thou done? *The voice of thy brother's blood cries unto me from the ground.*
36 And now thou shalt be cursed from the earth which hath opened her mouth to receive thy brother's blood from thy hand.
37 When thou tillest the ground it shall not henceforth yield unto thee her strength. A fugitive and a vagabond shalt thou be in the earth. (Moses 5:35-37)

Many mistakenly assume that skin color was part of the curse of Cain, but these verses make clear that that is not the case. The curse was one of livelihood, lifestyle, and restricted opportunity.

Cain was a "tiller of the ground" (Moses 5:17). A farmer depends on the fruits of the earth to receive his sustenance, his life and livelihood. A farmer is anchored to the land he tends in order to prepare the soil, plant, weed, and harvest. The agrarian cultures realized better than any that their life and livelihood depend upon the grace of God, understanding that the God of nature bestows the blessings of rain, weather and a bountiful harvest. Thus the judgments of God affected the livelihood and very lifestyle of Cain. The implication in scripture is that he is "cursed from the earth" because the earth "opened her mouth to receive (his) brother's blood" therefore the earth "shall not henceforth yield her strength" (Moses 5:36, 37). With the loss of his livelihood, the Lord further addresses the lifestyle of Cain: "A fugitive and a vagabond shalt thou be in the earth" (Moses 5:37). Cain essentially no longer has a place he can call home, and can no longer live the sedentary lifestyle to which he had grown accustomed.

The bands of Gadianton and Kishkumen in the Book of Mormon seemed to be forced into the lifestyle of Cain after they entered into the same secret oaths and combinations established by Satan and Cain. Once recognized in the community, they would be forced to flee to the wilderness (Helaman 2:11; 3 Nephi 1:27). The Gadianton bands, having no real home or livelihood, could only exist by theft, murder and robbery. They had to live in the wilderness, hiding in different places and wandering for survival rather than living in cities. When robbery was not an option they began to starve (3 Nephi 4:1-5) because their lifestyle could not allow for the development of agriculture by the sweat for their brow. This lifestyle continued until they gained control of the government and judges.

Cain's response to the consequences of his actions is first one of fear: "*My punishment is greater than I can bear*" (Moses 5:38). He continues by stating that:

> 39 Behold thou hast driven me out this day from the face of the Lord, and from thy face shall I be hid; and I shall be a fugitive and a vagabond in the earth; and it shall come to pass, that he that findeth me will slay me, because of mine iniquities, for these things are not hid from the Lord.
> 40 And I the Lord said unto him: Whosoever slayeth thee, vengeance shall be taken on him sevenfold. And I the Lord set a mark upon Cain, lest any finding him should kill him.

41 And Cain was shut out from the presence of the Lord, and *with his wife and many of his brethren* dwelt in the land of Nod, on the east of Eden. (Moses 5:39-41)

The phrase *"driven me out from the face of the Lord, and from thy face shall I be hid"* is Cain's recognition that the priesthood rights and blessings are now lost. The consequence and explanatory phrase in verse 41, *"And Cain was shut out from the presence of the Lord,"* again implies this loss of the blessings and rights of the priesthood (see D&C 84:21-22).

Priesthood Restrictions

Traditions and interpretations have taught (in theory, policy and practice) that an ordination to the 'greater priesthood' is a requirement to participate in the ordinances that symbolize the passing through the veil and entering into the presence of God. However, women do not need to hold Melchizedek authority to participate in these ordinances or endowments that are administered by the priesthood. The passage of scripture that has been used to restrict participation based on priesthood could be read and understood differently. Viewed within a contextual deliberation, these verses focus on the fact that the priesthood is *necessary for the* '***administration***' of the blessings described—not that the priesthood is necessary to ***participate*** in the blessings, as in the case of women.

19 And **this greater priesthood** *administereth the gospel* and holdeth the key of the mysteries of the kingdom, even the key of the knowledge of God.
20 Therefore, in the ordinances thereof, the power of godliness is manifest.
21 And *without the ordinances thereof,* **and the authority of the priesthood,** [to administer the ordinances] *the power of godliness is not manifest unto men in the flesh;*
22 For without this [the ordinances and authority to administer] no man can see the face of God, even the Father, and live. (D&C 84:19-22)

Instead of saying that being ordained to the priesthood is necessary to participate in these ordinances, these verses explain that the priesthood is required to administer the gospel and its ordinances to others. This alternate reading may then imply that Cain and his posterity may have lost the right to administrate, but not necessarily the right to participate in these ordinances.

The loss of priesthood rights is not singular to Cain and his posterity. This Section (84) of the Doctrine and Covenants also teaches that the Children of Israel, because of their conscious rejection of the greater priesthood blessings, also lost the right to priesthood administration. The verses above about the priesthood continue below and explain that Israel lost more than just the 'greater priesthood.'

> 23 Now this Moses plainly taught to the children of Israel in the wilderness, and sought diligently to sanctify his people that they might behold the face of God;
> 24 But they hardened their hearts and could not endure his presence; therefore, the Lord in his wrath, for his anger was kindled against them, swore that they should not enter into his rest while in the wilderness, which rest is the fullness of his glory.
> 25 Therefore, he took Moses out of their midst, and the Holy Priesthood also; (D&C 84:23-25)

The Old Testament explains that even the 'lesser priesthood' which remained, was restricted to the males of a *single family line*: The Levites. When Moses came down from the mount, he found that the Children of Israel had fallen away from the Lord and in their nakedness began the worldly worship of the golden calf.

> 25 And when Moses saw that the people were naked (for Aaron had made them naked unto their shame among their enemies);
> 26 Then Moses stood in the gate of the camp and said, Who is on the Lord's side? Let him come unto me. And all the sons of Levi gathered themselves together unto him. (Exodus 32:25-26)

282

Because the Sons of Levi chose to be on the Lord's side amid the wickedness and choice of all the other tribes of Israel, they were selected by the Lord to bear the ministry and priesthood. Like Cain and his posterity, all the other children of Jacob except for the sons of Levi were restricted from holding priesthood responsibilities.

Before the priesthood was restricted and limited to the Levites, the responsibility of priesthood service fell upon the firstborn of each individual family to minister temporally and spiritually, as previously explained. This ancient responsibility of service was patterned after the patriarchal priesthood and authority.

> 12 And I, behold, I have taken the Levites from among the children of Israel instead of all the firstborn that openeth the matrix among the children of Israel: therefore, the Levites shall be mine;
> 13 Because all the firstborn are mine; for on the day that I smote all the firstborn in the land of Egypt I hallowed unto me all the firstborn in Israel, both man and beast: mine shall they be: I am the Lord.
> 41 And thou shalt take the Levites for me (I am the Lord) instead of all the firstborn among the children of Israel; and the cattle of the Levites instead of all the firstlings among the cattle of the children of Israel.
> 45 ...and the Levites shall be mine: I am the Lord. (Numbers 3:12-13, 41, 45)

Thus the Levites were chosen to hold the priesthood, which was *to serve and administer* to the Children of Israel. All the other children of Jacob were *restricted from the administration and outward performance* of sacrifice and other ordinances. Although they were restricted from the responsibility of service for the spiritual welfare of others (administrating), they were not excluded from participating in the ordinances for their own spiritual wellbeing.

In seeking to obtain the priesthood position of Grand Patriarch for himself and his posterity, Cain and his descendants also lost the 'right to' priesthood administration. Abraham explains in his book that this lineage of Cain came through the flood at the time of Noah, as the wife of Ham (Egyptus) was a descendent of Cain. Through her, the blood of Cain and the curse of priesthood restriction was preserved through the flood and remained after the time of Noah.

> 21 Now this *king of Egypt was a descendant from the loins of Ham, and was a partaker of the blood of the Canaanites by birth.*22 From this descent sprang all the Egyptians, and thus the blood of the Canaanites was preserved in the land.23 The land of Egypt being first discovered by a woman, who was the daughter of Ham, and the daughter of Egyptus, which in the Chaldean signifies Egypt, which signifies that which is forbidden;24 When this woman discovered the land it was under water, who afterward settled her sons in it; and thus, *from Ham, sprang that race which preserved the curse in the land.*25 Now the first government of Egypt was established by Pharaoh, the eldest son of Egyptus, the daughter of Ham, and it was after the manner of the government of Ham, which was patriarchal.26 Pharaoh, being a righteous man, established his kingdom and judged his people wisely and justly all his days, seeking earnestly to imitate that order established by the fathers in the first generations, in the days of the first patriarchal reign, even in the reign of Adam, and also of Noah, his father, who blessed him with the blessings of the earth, and with the blessings of wisdom, *but cursed him as pertaining to the Priesthood.* 27 Now, Pharaoh being **of that lineage by which he could not have the right of Priesthood,** notwithstanding the Pharaohs would fain claim it from Noah, through Ham, therefore my father was led away by their idolatry; (Abraham 1:21-27)

The mark of Cain was *not* the curse but a sign of the curse. This "mark" (whatever it was) existed for recognition, and in the case of Cain, as a sign or mark for the *blessing of protection.* After Cain voiced his concern for his life saying, "he that findeth me will slay me" (Moses 5:39) the Lord responded with a form of protection for him: "And I the Lord said unto him: Whosoever slayeth thee, vengeance shall be taken on him sevenfold. And I the Lord set a mark upon Cain, lest any finding him should kill him" (Moses 5:40).

The dark skin may or may not be the "mark" placed upon Cain. However, *hundreds of years later* the land of Canaan, where the descendants of Cain presumably lived, became a climatically difficult and unpleasant place to live, which may have caused the genetic adaptation of a darker skin to appear. It must be remembered that the "mark" (whatever it might be) was a mark for survival and protection, not a curse connected to the murder.

> 6 And again the Lord said unto me: Look; and I looked towards the north, and I beheld the people of Canaan, which dwelt in tents.
> 7 And the Lord said unto me: Prophesy; and I prophesied, saying: Behold the people of Canaan, which are numerous, shall go forth in battle array against the people of Shum, and shall slay them that they shall utterly be destroyed; and the people of Canaan shall divide themselves in the land, and the land shall be barren and unfruitful, and none other people shall dwell there but the people of Canaan;
> 8 For behold, *the Lord shall curse the land with much heat, and the barrenness thereof shall go forth forever; and there was a blackness came upon all the children of Canaan,* that they were despised among all people. (Moses 7:6-8)

There is nothing that proves that the descendants of Cain lived in the land of Canaan. However, the curses of Cain and the verses above imply that the posterity of Cain may have lived in Canaan. Remember that Abraham gives us insight about the curse; namely the loss of priesthood and its connection to the people and blood of those who lived in Canaan prior to the flood. At least one was righteous enough to believe and marry Ham, the son of Noah:

> This king of Egypt was a descendant from the loins of Ham, and was a partaker of the *blood of the **Canaanites*** by birth. From this descent sprang all the Egyptians, and thus the blood of the Canaanites was preserved in the land. Now, *Pharaoh being of that lineage by which he could not have the right of Priesthood...* (Abraham 1:21, 22, 27)

The Burden of Cain and the Land of Canaan

The burden of Cain is seen in the history that follows as Enoch speaks of the linage of Cain and identifies aspects of the punishments a millennium later:

Moses 5, To Cain	Moses 7, Enoch
When thou tillest the ground it shall not henceforth yield unto thee her strength. (Moses 5:37)	The land shall be barren and unfruitful. (Moses 7:7) The Lord shall curse the land with much heat and the barrenness thereof shall go forth forever. (Moses 7:8)
A fugitive and a vagabond shall thou be in the earth. (Moses 5:37)	And I beheld the people of Canaan, which dwelt in tents. (Moses 7:6) (Tents imply a constant movement.)
Cain (and his family) was shut out from the presence of the Lord. (Moses 5:41)	None other people shall dwell there but the people of Canaan. (Moses 7:7) They (the people of Canaan) were despised among all people. (Moses 7:8)
All of them had covenanted with Satan; for they kept not the commandments of God, and it displeased God, and he ministered not unto them. (Moses 5:52)	And it came to pass that Enoch continued to call upon all the people, save it were the people of Canaan, to repent. (Moses 7:12)

It appears from the textual evidence in Moses and Abraham that those who were cursed by the Lord in consequence of the conspiracy and murder of Abel may have lived in the land of Canaan.

The Doctrine and Covenants reveal a statement from the Lord about those who threaten to harm or destroy the priesthood line that was set apart in the council in heaven:

16 Cursed are all those that shall lift up the heel against mine anointed, saith the Lord, and cry they have sinned when they

have not sinned before me, saith the Lord, but have done that which was meet in mine eyes, and which I commanded them.

17 But those who cry transgression do it because they are the servants of sin, and are the children of disobedience themselves.

18 And those who swear falsely against my servants, that they might bring them into bondage and death—

19 Wo unto them; because they have offended my little ones they shall be severed from the ordinances of mine house.

20 Their basket shall not be full, their houses and their barns shall perish, and they themselves shall be despised by those that flattered them.

21 They *shall not have right to the priesthood, nor their posterity after them from generation to generation.*
(D&C 121:16-21)

It can be seen from the above verses that those who "shall lift up the heel against mine anointed" (those foreordained to be priesthood leaders) shall "be severed from the ordinances of mine house" and shall "not have right to the priesthood, nor their posterity after them from generation to generation."

Perhaps the most controversial of Cain's burden was the loss of priesthood rights for his posterity from "generation to generation". But the murder of Abel didn't affect just one person. Abel's righteous posterity were foreordained to be the patriarchs throughout gospel history. The prophet Joseph Smith taught that the patriarchs were foreordained before this earth.[24] It was Abel, the father of this Grand Patriarchal family line, ordained in the pre-earth council, that Cain murdered. He murdered the rightful priesthood leader, Abel, (before he had posterity) thinking to secure for himself and his descendants this priesthood and leadership position throughout time. The sin of "conspiring" to murder the anointed priesthood leader for the sake of position and control for himself and his posterity is what led to the restriction of Cain pertaining to the priesthood.

---

24. *TPJS.* p.365.

That Abel died before any of his pre-earth promised patriarchal posterity were born into mortality is inferred from the birth and naming of Seth:

> 2 And Adam knew his wife again, and she bare a son, and he called his name Seth. And Adam glorified the name of God; for he said: *God hath appointed me another seed*, instead of Abel, whom Cain slew.
> 3 And God revealed himself unto Seth, and he rebelled not, but offered an acceptable sacrifice, like unto his brother Abel. And to him also was born a son, and he called his name Enos. (Moses 6:2-3)

Seth now becomes the replacement for Abel, as Adam declares above. The fact that the priesthood is traced through Abel's line in the Doctrine and Covenants establishes the importance of the Levirate Law of Marriage.

The Levirate Law

The Old Testament outlines what is called the Levirate Law of Marriage. This Levirate Law states that if a birthright son marries and dies before he has sired a son to to whom the birthright and patriarchal authority can pass, his brother's obligation is to marry his widow to provide him that son. The firstborn son of the widow via the brother is considered the sealed descendant and heir of the deceased first husband (meaning, the birthright brother and his widow). The child of this union is then in place to inherit a double portion of his grandfather's possessions as the new and legitimate patriarchal replacement for the first husband of his mother. This thereby continues the patriarchal line in its proper order. The patriarchal priesthood is based on a *"matrilineal patriarchy."*

> 15 Every thing that *openeth the matrix* in all flesh, which they bring unto the Lord, *whether it be of men or beasts,* shall be thine: nevertheless the firstborn of man shalt thou surely redeem, and the firstling of unclean beasts shalt thou redeem. (Numbers 18:15)

The birthright is vested in the firstborn son *of the wife of the firstborn son* [even though he may be dead] (Numbers 3:12) if sired by the brother-in-law or father-in-law (the linage must be from the blood of the previous patriarch; her father-in-law). This explains what is going on and the reason for the somewhat risqué story of Tamar and Judah. The proper order and authority to be the patriarch is *matrilineal* through the wife of the firstborn son. Hence, the children are sealed to the father through the mother. In a "Matrilineal Patriarchy", only the mother can declare who the birthright son is (as in the case of Eve, Sarah, Rebekah, Tamar, etc) since only the mother knows who her firstborn son is and who the father really is. This means that the birthright son and patriarch is chosen by the mother (the matriarch), and ordained and set apart by the father (or patriarch, as in the case of Jacob and Esau and many others). How the Levirate Law of Marriage works within a matrilineal patriarchy is explained in the passage below:

> 5 If brethren dwell together, and one of them die, and have no child, the wife of the dead shall not marry without unto a stranger: her husband's brother shall go in unto her, and take her to him to wife, and perform the duty of an husband's brother unto her.
>
> 6 And it shall be, that the firstborn which she beareth *shall succeed in the name of his brother which is dead*, that his name be not put out of Israel.
>
> 7 And if the man like not to take his brother's wife, then let his brother's wife go up to the gate unto the elders, and say, My husband's brother refuseth to raise up unto his brother a name in Israel, he will not perform the duty of my husband's brother.
>
> 8 Then the elders of his city shall call him, and speak unto him: and if he stand to it, and say, I like not to take her;
>
> 9 Then shall his brother's wife come unto him in the presence of the elders, and loose his shoe from off his foot, and spit in his face, and shall answer and say, So shall it be done unto that man that will not build up his brother's house.
>
> 10 And his name shall be called in Israel, The house of him that hath his shoe loosed. (Deuteronomy 25:5-10)

Though first described in Deuteronomy, this law is evident in the patriarchal narratives found in Genesis. As mentioned above, the Levirate Law is important in the stories of Tamar and Judah (Genesis 38), as well as Ruth and Boaz, and is an integral element in the narrative of Cain and Abel and the priesthood.

Patriarchal linage (through the Matriarch) seems to play a part in almost all the narratives found in Genesis and even the rest of the Old Testament. The question of the Lord to Cain on the whereabouts of his brother Abel initiated this meaningful response from the Lord: "The voice of thy brother's blood cries unto me from the ground" (Moses 5:35). The blood that cries for justice is best explained in light of the Aramaic Genesis.

The Aramaic translation of the Hebrew Bible is called the Targum, and it has the oldest, best, and most complete translations of the Old Testament. In these older manuscripts and translations, the word "blood" is rendered as "bloods" (plural or dual) and should be translated to mean '*bloods*' (bloodline) of the deceased, or the "*descendants that would have been born*" cry from the ground that swallowed, not just blood, but the bloodline and *seed* of Abel. A note in the Targum *Pseudo-Johathan* reads:

> "Ps.-J. differs from all the Targums in its rendering of the phrase "your brother's blood." Onq. Reads: "The voice of the blood of the descendants who would have come forth from you brother," which is essentially the same as the paraphrase which we find in the Pal. Tgs. They take the plur. "*dmy*" "bloods," of HT to refer to Abel's descendants. This midrashic interpretation is well known"[25]

A connection between one's descendants and their blood crying from the ground is seen in the Book of Mormon:

---

25. See footnote #24 in "Notes, Chapter 4," of The Aramaic Bible, Volume 1B, *Targum Pseudo-Johathan: Genesis*, Translated and Notes by Michael Maher, M.S.C., The Liturgical Press, Collegeville, Minnesota, 1987, p. 33.

290

> 40 Yea, why do ye build up your secret abominations to get gain, and cause that widows should mourn before the Lord, and also orphans to mourn before the Lord, and also the blood of their fathers and their husbands to cry unto the Lord from the ground, for vengeance upon your heads? (Mormon 8:40)

The Prophet Joseph Smith taught that "*every man* who has a calling to minister to the inhabitants of the world *was ordained* to that very purpose in the Grand Council of heaven *before this world was.*"[26] This would mean that Abel was ordained before he came here, plus all of those righteous and valiant spirits who would become the Grand Patriarchs for the family of Adam through Abel. Thus, in the oldest translations of Genesis, it is the "bloods" or "descendants" that were to come through the patriarchal line of Abel that cry from the ground for justice.

Under Levirate Law, Seth, the new priesthood line (in name only) becomes a *replacement for Abel*. Moses, chapter six teaches that at the birth of Seth, Adam stated: "God hath appointed me *another seed, instead of Abel*, whom Cain slew" (Moses 6:2). "Seth," in Hebrew means "replacement or substitute" as described by Adam. Seth then marries the widow of Abel (following the Levirate Law of Marriage) and the firstborn son of that union, Enos, is considered the "sealed" descendent and priesthood line of Abel and his wife, even though he was sired by Seth. This is why *the priesthood line is traced through Abel* in the Doctrine and Covenants:

> 14 Which Abraham received the priesthood from Melchizedek, who received it through the lineage of his fathers, even till Noah;
> 15 And from Noah till Enoch, through the lineage of their fathers;
> 16 And *from Enoch to Abel*, who was slain by the conspiracy of his brother, who received the priesthood by the commandments of God, by the hand of his father Adam, who was the first man. (D&C 84:14-16.)

---

26. *TPJS.* p.365.

There is only one way that the priesthood patriarchal line could be traced back through Abel, and that is if Seth became the *"replacement"* for Abel.

Keeping this in mind, remember that Joseph Smith taught, in so many words, that the *'descendants of Cain would not have the opportunity to hold the priesthood until the seed of Abel* (the "bloods" or foreordained patriarchal descendants that cried from the ground) *had a chance to come to the earth."* In other words, since Cain murdered Abel in order that his (Cain's) posterity would become the priesthood line, Cain's descendants were banned from priesthood administration until the foreordained posterity of Abel had a chance to come to the earth and fulfill their responsibility in that patriarchal line.

The teachings of Joseph Smith on the subject are varied in detail but overall express the same idea. Collectively, the rendered idea would be: 'The seed of Cain would not be able to hold the priesthood until the seed of Abel had an opportunity to come to the earth and fulfill their responsibility as the Grand Patriarchs.' As explained, this could only happen by way of the Levirate Law.

> President George Q. Cannon remarked that the prophet taught this doctrine: That the seed of Cain could not receive the priesthood nor act in any of the offices of the priesthood until the seed of Abel should come forward and take precedence over Cain's offspring.[27]

Joseph Fielding Smith concludes from this teaching of the Prophet Joseph that: "The promise was given that this curse, or restriction, will be removed, when the time comes . . . when Abel will have posterity."[28] The reasoning for this conclusion is published in *The Way to Perfection*, chapters 15, 16. Joseph Fielding Smith believed that the birth of Abel's posterity would have to take place elsewhere and in a distant future. Obviously unaware of the purpose and origin of the Levirate Law, it would be difficult to assume anything else. As a

27. Smith, Joseph Fielding, *The Way to Perfection* [Salt Lake City: Genealogical Society of Utah, 1949], 110 - 111.

28. Smith, Joseph Fielding, *Answers to Gospel Questions*, [Deseret Book Co., 1957-1966], 2: 177.

careful study of the scriptures makes clear, the possibility of Abel having posterity after he was murdered could only be accomplished through his 'replacement,' Seth, according to Levirate Law. Elder Smith continues:

> Since Cain slew his brother Abel in order to obtain all the rights of priesthood to descend through his lineage, the Lord decreed that the children of Cain should not have the privilege of bearing the priesthood until Abel had posterity who could have the priesthood and that will have to be in the far distant future. When this is accomplished [on some other world] then the restrictions will be removed from the children of Cain[29]

Again the implication is that the seed of Cain cannot hold the priesthood until the seed of Abel have a chance to fulfill the responsibilities of their fore-ordination in the pre-earth council. Wilford Woodruff recorded the teachings of Brigham Young in his journal when he addressed this subject in a meeting.

> The Lord said, I will not kill Cain, but I will put a mark upon him... it is the decree of God that that mark shall remain upon the seed of Cain until the seed of Abel shall be redeemed, and Cain shall not receive the Priesthood, until the time of that redemption . . . but the day will come when all that race will be redeemed and possess all the blessings which we now have.[30]

Many might question: "Is the loss of these blessings fair for those spirits who are the descendants of Cain? Could it be that those spirits in the pre-earth life wanted to participate in the plan of salvation so much that they agreed to come through that line? Or perhaps, could these spirits be more valiant and faithful, willing to sacrifice earthly opportunities to provide greater blessings for others, with the promise of fulfillment at a later time?" Some individuals have concluded that perhaps the spirits that will come through the line of Cain were

---

29. *Ibid.* 2: 188.
30. *History of Wilford Woodruff*, p. 351. Also quoted in: Smith's, *The Way to Perfection*, p. 106.

somehow less valiant or neutral in the war in heaven. This belief or teaching is ridiculous. President Brigham Young reported on the teachings of Joseph Smith in a meeting held on Christmas Day 1869, in Salt Lake City and stated:

> Joseph Smith had declared that the Negroes were not neutral in heaven, for all the spirits took sides, but the posterity of Cain are black because he (Cain) committed murder. He killed Abel and God set a mark upon his posterity. But the spirits are pure (i.e. innocent See D & C 93:38) that enter their tabernacles and there will be a chance for the redemption of all the children of Adam, except the sons of perdition.[31]

As stated earlier, Enos, born of Abel's wife and his replacement Seth under Levirate Law, is the recognized descendant of Abel. That means that under the Levirate Law, the list of patriarchs in the Old Testament would be the seed of Abel (Remember in D&C 84 the priesthood line is traced back through Abel). This patriarchal line must be remembered in order to understand the timing of the revelation of 1978 that gave the priesthood to all worthy male members. The partial list begins with: Adam, Seth, Enos. Since the Doctrine and Covenants trace the patriarchal priesthood line through Abel, it reads somewhat differently. Under the Levirate Law it would descend in this order: Adam, Abel, Enos (the Levirate son of Seth), followed by the standard Grand Patriarchal list. Seth was in his right, and by his righteousness functioned as a patriarch. The Levirate son, Enos, was also his posterity but was connected or sealed to Adam through the wife of Abel. The key individuals in this Grand Patriarchal line are listed below; however, a complete list of patriarchs may be found in Genesis Chapter Eleven. This partial list includes: Adam, Seth (Abel) Enos, Cainan, Mahalaleel, Jared, Enoch, Methuselah, Lamech, Noah, Shem . . . Abraham, Isaac, Jacob, Joseph, and Ephraim.

---

31. "Journal History", Dec. 25, 1869. quoted in Smith's, The Way to Perfection, p. 105.

The Doctrine and Covenants teaches how this patriarchal priesthood was to be transferred through the ages. In Section 107, it describes how this process was to take place from father to son:

> 40 The order of this priesthood [patriarchal] was confirmed to be handed down from father to son, and rightly belongs to the literal descendants of the chosen seed, to whom the promises were made.
> 41 This order was instituted in the days of Adam, and came down by lineage in the following manner:
> 42 From Adam to Seth, who was ordained by Adam at the age of sixty-nine years, and was blessed by him three years previous to his (Adam's) death, and received the promise of God by his father, that his posterity should be the chosen of the Lord, and that they should be preserved unto the end of the earth; (D&C 107:40-42)

The Book of Mormon contains interesting insights into the lineage of Joseph who was sold into Egypt, bringing this Grand Patriarchal line into the Dispensation of the Fullness of Times and the family of Joseph Smith.

> 6 For Joseph truly testified, saying: A seer shall the Lord my God raise up, who shall be a choice seer unto the fruit of my loins.
> 7 Yea, Joseph truly said: Thus saith the Lord unto me: A choice seer will *I raise up out of the fruit of thy loins*; and he shall be esteemed highly among the fruit of thy loins. And unto him will I give commandment that he shall do a work for the fruit of thy loins, his brethren, which shall be of great worth unto them, even to the bringing of them to the knowledge of the covenants which I have made with thy fathers.
> 8 And I will give unto him a commandment that he shall do none other work, save the work which I shall command him. And I will make him great in mine eyes; for he shall do my work.
> 9 And he shall be great like unto Moses, whom I have said I would raise up unto you, to deliver my people, O house of Israel.

10 And Moses will I raise up, to deliver thy people out of the land of Egypt.

11 But a seer will I raise up out of the fruit of thy loins; and unto him will I give power to bring forth my word unto the seed of thy loins—and not to the bringing forth my word only, saith the Lord, but to the convincing them of my word, which shall have already gone forth among them.

13 And out of weakness he shall be made strong, in that day when my work shall commence among all my people, unto the restoring thee, O house of Israel, saith the Lord.

14 And thus prophesied Joseph, saying: Behold, that seer will the Lord bless; and they that seek to destroy him shall be confounded; for this promise, which I have obtained of the Lord, of the fruit of my loins, shall be fulfilled. Behold, I am sure of the fulfilling of this promise;

15 And his name shall be called after me; and it shall be after the name of his father. And he shall be like unto me; for the thing which the Lord shall bring forth by his hand, by the power of the Lord shall bring my people unto salvation. (2 Nephi 3:6-11, 13-15)

These verses teach that Joseph who was sold into Egypt would have a descendent that would become an instrument in the hands of the Lord and would do a great work of restoration. It is revealed in this passage that the name of this *direct line* seer would be Joseph, and that he would be *named after his father*. This, without question or argument, is speaking of Joseph Smith Jr. and his father Joseph Smith Sr.

The Prophet Joseph Smith Jr. is not the Patriarch in this dispensation, but his father is. Joseph Smith Sr. is the direct line and descendent of the Grand Patriarchs, and is therefore one of this line foreordained to come through Abel. Joseph Smith Sr. and the rest of the patriarchal line were the "bloods" (descendants) that cried from the ground when their father Abel was murdered to stop that lineage.

The Prophet Joseph Smith blesses his Father in this Patriarchal Priesthood and declares his lineage to be that of the Patriarchs of old:

Thus spoke the Seer, and these are the words which fell from his lips while the visions of the Almighty were open to his view, saying:

Blessed of the Lord is my father, for he shall stand in the midst of his posterity and shall be comforted by their blessings when he is old and bowed down with years, and shall be called a prince over them, and shall be numbered among those who *hold the right of Patriarchal Priesthood, even the keys of that ministry: for he shall assemble together his posterity like unto Adam*; and the assembly which he called shall be an example for my father . . .

So shall it be with my father: he shall be called a prince over his posterity, *holding the keys of the patriarchal priesthood over the kingdom of God on earth, even the Church of the Latter-day Saints, and he shall sit in the general assembly of Patriarchs, even in council with the Ancient of Days when he shall sit and all the Patriarchs* with him and shall enjoy his right and authority under the direction of the Ancient of Days. (*TPJS.* p. 38)

Joseph then gives his brother Hyrum a blessing indicating that this priesthood continues through him:

He shall stand in the tracks of his father and be *numbered among those who hold the right of Patriarchal Priesthood,* even the Evangelical Priesthood and power shall be upon him, that in his old age his name may be magnified on the earth. (*TPJS.* p. 40)

Following the death of his father, Joseph Smith received a revelation calling Hyrum Smith to succeed his father. This is not done by ordinance or blessing alone, but *"by right"* (D&C 124:91), or the 'rights of the fathers' as discussed by Abraham (Abraham 1:2-4).

91 ...that my servant Hyrum may take the office of Priesthood and Patriarch, *which was appointed unto him by his father, by blessing **and also by right**;*
92 That *from henceforth he shall hold the keys of the patriarchal blessings upon the heads of all my people,*

93 That whoever he blesses shall be blessed, and whoever he curses shall be cursed; that whatsoever he shall bind on earth shall be bound in heaven; and whatsoever he shall loose on earth shall be loosed in heaven.

94 And from this time forth I appoint unto him that he may be a prophet, and a seer, and a revelator unto my church, as well as my servant Joseph;

95 That he may act in concert also with my servant Joseph; and that he shall receive counsel from my servant Joseph...

96 That my servant Hyrum may bear record of the things which I shall show unto him, that his name may be had in honorable remembrance from generation to generation, forever and ever. (D&C 124:91-96)

Hyrum Smith was ordained and set apart by *ordinance, blessing and by right* to be the patriarch of the church. This is the 'right' that continued from Abel through his posterity, which included the Smith family. This calling is addressed in an article in BYU Studies.

A January 1841 revelation called Hyrum Smith to succeed his father, Joseph Smith Sr., as Patriarch (D&C 124:91-96). The revelation said that Joseph Smith Sr., the first Patriarch, who died in September 1840, had appointed Hyrum to "the office of Priesthood and Patriarch, which was appointed unto him [Hyrum] by his father, by blessing and also by right," implying a chain of Smith family authority over patriarchal blessings, going from the departing Patriarch to his eldest son. In keeping with those words, when Brigham Young ordained John Smith, Hyrum's son, President Young said he acted in the stead of the martyred Hyrum, who had the authority to appoint and ordain the next Patriarch. The tradition of fathers ordaining sons persisted down to 1932, when death prevented Hyrum G. Smith from ordaining his son Eldred as Patriarch.[32]

Speaking at BYU, Patriarch Eldred G. Smith was introduced in these words:

---

32. "BYU Studies," vol. 36 (1996-97), Number 4--1996-97.

Patriarch Eldred G. Smith was born in Lehi, Utah. He is the great-great-great-grandson of Joseph Smith, Sr., the first Presiding Patriarch of the Church. This is the only office in the Church that follows the patriarchal line from father to son, and Elder Smith is the seventh Presiding Patriarch of the Church since it was organized in 1830. ("BYU Speeches of the Year,"1964. p. 1)

The year of 1978 will be remembered by almost all who were alive at that time. It was one of those events that people ask: What were you doing when you heard the announcement? The announcement has become a "Declaration" in the Doctrine and Covenants and canonized as scripture. The declaration changed the doctrine of the Church that had been based on revelation and scripture. Prophet and President Spencer W. Kimball received the revelation that opened all the doors to all those who are worthy.

June 8, 1978

Aware of the promises made by the prophets and presidents of the Church who have preceded us that at some time, in God's eternal plan, all of our brethren who are worthy may receive the priesthood, and witnessing the faithfulness of those from whom the priesthood has been withheld, we have pleaded long and earnestly in behalf of these, our faithful brethren, spending many hours in the Upper Room of the Temple supplicating the Lord for divine guidance.

He has heard our prayers, and by revelation has confirmed that *the long-promised day has come when every faithful, worthy man in the Church may receive the holy priesthood*, with power to exercise its divine authority, and enjoy with his loved ones every blessing that flows therefrom, including the blessings of the temple. Accordingly, all worthy male members of the Church may be ordained to the priesthood without regard for race or color. (Official Declaration - 2)

The revelation about the priesthood was given in June of 1978 and was read to the church on September 30, 1978 at the October General

Conference. Within a year of that announcement another prophetic event happened. President N. Eldon Tanner, under the direction of President Kimball,read a letter to the Church:

> Because of the large increase in the number of stake patriarchs and the availability of patriarchal service throughout the world, we now designate Elder Eldred G. Smith as a Patriarch Emeritus, which means that he is honorably relieved of all duties and responsibilities pertaining to the office of Patriarch to the Church.[33]

The release of Eldred G. Smith as Patriarch to the Church took place *at virtually the same time the priesthood was made available to all worthy males.* President Kimball's inspiration and timing was incredible, as these events unfolded according to the prophecy of Joseph Smith: *'that the seed of Cain would not be able to hold the Priesthood until the Seed of Abel (the patriarchal seed) had a chance to come to the earth and fulfill their responsibility.'* That the Revelation on the Priesthood in 1978 happened in concert with the release of Patriarch Smith was no accident, even if the connection was not fully understood. The important thing to remember is that the change came about not because of pressure or petition but because of revelation and the fulfillment of prophecy. It could have happened no other way.

There were changes made to the Grand Patriarchal Priesthood and Order during the days of Moses. The children of Israel had lived and functioned under this patriarchal law and order during the time of Moses until the time came that the masses were too great to be administered to by family heads alone. Moses was taught by Jethro, his father-in-law, how the Melchizedek Priesthood functioned, and an organization was set up to administer to the needs of the masses more effectively. The Patriarchal priesthood continued to exist in the background within the family but the Melchizedek authority became the administrative authority of the priesthood.

---

33. *Conference Report*, October, 1979

In the same manner, with the growth of the church and the explosion of membership that ensued, it was determined that the duties of the Church Patriarch could best be administered by the Melchizedek authority (which holds all the keys). And with that, the seed of Abel finished fulfilling their responsibility, as Joseph had said.

The Melchizedek authority holds all necessary keys to function in all responsibilities of all priesthoods. Joseph Smith taught that there were three priesthoods: The Melchizedek, the Patriarchal, and the Aaronic. *(TPJS,* p. 323). The Doctrine and Covenants explain that the Greater Priesthood holds all the keys to officiate in all lesser offices:

> 17 But as a high priest of the Melchizedek Priesthood has authority to officiate in all the lesser offices, he may officiate in the office of bishop when no literal descendant of Aaron can be found, provided he is called and set apart and ordained unto this power by the hands of the Presidency of the Melchizedek Priesthood.
> 18 The power and authority of the higher, or Melchizedek Priesthood, is to hold the keys of all the spiritual blessings of the church—
> 19 To have the privilege of receiving the mysteries of the kingdom of heaven, to have the heavens opened unto them, to commune with the general assembly and church of the Firstborn, and to enjoy the communion and presence of God the Father, and Jesus the mediator of the new covenant. (D&C 107:17-19)

> 91 And again, the duty of the President of the office of the High Priesthood is to preside over the whole church, and to be like unto Moses—
> 92 Behold, here is wisdom; yea, to be a seer, a revelator, a translator, and a prophet, having all the gifts of God which he bestows upon the head of the church. (D&C 107:91-92)

The restoration of priesthood blessings and administration that took place in 1978 was because the descendants of Abel had faithfully fulfilled their responsibilities. The statements of Joseph Smith and the scriptures bears witness that the time was right and that the change was done under the inspiration and direction from the Lord. It doesn't matter if President Kimball knew of Joseph's statements and the Levirate Law or not. The inspiration and revelation was there when needed.

The significance of the timing can easily be understood by those familiar with the Scriptures, church history, and the teachings of the Prophet Joseph Smith. The Old Testament and the laws that governed the *Patriarchal Period* such as the levirate law need to be considered in light of these events, for God is the same today, yesterday, and forever. The revelation of 1978 and the prophecy of Joseph Smith and the release of Patriarch Smith all bear testimony of the divinity of this Restored Church and Priesthood Leadership. Even without many understanding the related events of 1978-1979, the Lord fulfilled the prophecies of Joseph Smith while maintaining the integrity of the Laws established in the Patriarchal Age, as explained in the scriptures.

To recap: The blessing of the priesthood to all worthy male members was not due to pressure on the church, from without or from within. It was revelatory in nature and prophesied by Joseph Smith. Earlier contradictory statements made by many general authorities and teachers were simple misunderstandings and misinterpretations of both scripture and the statements made by the Prophet Joseph. Many teachers and even leaders may not have understood the doctrines of the Patriarchal period and how they impacted the true and living Church of Jesus Christ today. The changes made in the Church about priesthood worthiness in 1978 were made by divine will and under divine law, fulfilling prophecy and revelation. These events and all others, from the first man to the last, were taken into consideration when the plan was prepared and presented and the patriarchs were set apart in the pre-earth councils before the foundation of this world.

In summary, the priesthood organization is established for the administration of the Gospel. It is an organization and responsibility of service. The priesthood does not honor the man but the man honors the priesthood. There is no "power" other than the authorization to serve others through the priesthood organization. Cain lost the right to *administer* the ordinances of the Gospel to others, for this is the power or *authority* of the priesthood. According to scripture, Cain and his posterity lost the right of administration, not the right of participation. Many of the past statements from leaders and teachers have proven that there were misunderstandings about the *policies and doctrines* affecting the seed of Cain. It was a doctrine (according to the interpretation of scripture) that the seed of Cain should not hold the authority to administer the gospel. Under the assumption and general understanding that the seed of Cain were black, it became a policy that those with a dark skin color should not hold the priesthood. It was known that not all of similar skin color were the seed of Cain, but, unable to determine who was or was not a descendent of Cain (right or wrong), the policy was created to maintain the doctrine. Priesthood restriction was not because of prejudice against any person or race because of skin color any more than all of the tribes and families of Israel being excluded from the same authorized administration. What if it was believed that the seed of Cain had red hair and were freckled faced? What then would have been the policy and restriction?

Genetic and ancestral lines throughout the Old Testament period have been constrained and restricted from priesthood authority. Restrictions from the service of *administration* should not impact or prevent individual *participation* in a relationship with Christ and the Atonement. The important thing to remember is that any restrictions on 'holding' the priesthood, whether by race, family, or time, have nothing to do with individual or personal righteousness. Nor does skin color have anything to do with the worthiness or the potential for salvation and exaltation. For the 'Lord looks not upon the outward appearance, but upon the heart.'

Chapter 23

Creation: Science and Scripture

I was only eleven years old, and even now remember the perfumed smell of the rich cedar smoke as it drifted through the small and seemingly circular room of the log hogan. It was January, the Navajo reservation was cold and uninviting, and the warmth of the hogan was enticing after walking nearly a quarter of a mile from the truck. In the semi darkness of the fire it seemed like a dream as I stood with the silent members of the Navajo family. I watched in the heat of the haze-filled room as the local shaman or "medicine man" squatted close to the open flame. The colored sand slipped through his fingers, and as if by magic formed an intricate circular design on the earthen floor. This sobering experience made a lasting impression in my mind as I was told when we left the home that the sand painting represented the world, light and darkness, male and female, and the creative forces used in their formation. I will never forget the reverie like feeling as I stepped out of the "white man's" world into an alien environment filled with myth and ritual.

Years later as an undergraduate I began to realize that certain motifs continue to surface in the sea of cultural myth. The most common "myth" in all societies recapitulates elements of the cosmic creation (i.e., the cosmogonic myth) and the formation of mankind by the gods. "This cosmogonic myth serves a single ritual purpose: to connect the two realities of heaven and earth. The process of bringing the visible and invisible worlds into a relationship with each other may be accomplished through the metaphor, symbol, and allegory" of the creation.[34] Knowing that the scriptures contain three accounts of the creation, one must ask those terrible questions, because myth, in a ritual setting, addresses the origins of humanity. It describes the "Golden Age" without death and sin, followed by the introduction of mortality. History is no more than a record of mankind's attempt to find and acquire the glorious pristine era of the past and understand the onslaught of evil to stop that progression. It sometimes seems that all of world history is nothing more than the details of the battle between the forces that seek to establish an earthly Zion and the evil that seeks to create a spiritual black hole of wickedness.

Why Creation Epochs?

In the study of ancient languages, cultures, and religions, 'creation myths' persistently and frequently show up in the ancient documents. Because of their frequency, certain questions naturally follow: *Why are the creation accounts found everywhere? Why are they in every culture? And why are these creation myths repeated so often in an ancient temple setting? What makes the cosmology so important to a people or culture? Why does it show up so often in ancient cultures? What is the relationship between God, the cosmos, and humanity?* These questions are not original. The nostalgia for our beginning lies within every person, religion, and culture. The origin of the world and mankind is the primary focus of the myths of creation found in all cultures of ancient origin. The word "myth" as originally defined means the *true story of a beginning.* Myth is something real, something that happened *ab-origine*: that is, before origins, before our time, or the time of the first time. Mircea Eliade, though non-LDS, defines the term "myth" in words that make sacred connections to the Temple and our creation narratives.

> Myth narrates a sacred history; it relates an event that took place in primordial Time, the fabled time of the "beginnings." In other words, myth tells how, through the deeds of Supernatural Beings. A reality came into existence.

---

34. Heinberg, Richard, *Memories and Visions of Paradise* (Los Angeles: Jeremy P. Tarcher Inc, 1989), p.15.

> ...Myth then is always an account of a "creation" it relates how something was produced, how it began to be. Myth tells only of that which really happened, which manifested itself completely.[35]

Today the word myth is most often used as a synonym for 'fable', a false or fictitious story. As used in this chapter, "myth" will mean the true story of something *real*, especially in regards to the creation epoch.

Researcher and author Barbara Sproul opens her excellent collection of ancient creation stories and myths from around the world with this introductory paragraph about creation accounts:

> The most profound human questions are the ones that give rise to creation myths: Who are we? Why are we here? What is the purpose of our lives and our deaths? These are central questions of value and meaning, and, while they are influenced by issues of fact, they are not in themselves factual questions; rather, they involve attitudes toward facts and reality.[36]

The most important issues faced in mortal life are addressed most directly by the creation accounts found in scripture and the Temple. Understanding these things can provide the observant student an endowment of power, which accompanies the knowledge of important and eternal truths found in these creation epochs. The Western Culture, education, evolutionary theory, and even business have forced thoughts about the creation of our physical world out of the mind of the natural man. The commandment to 'keep the Sabbath day holy' was instituted to *remember and rehearse the creation.* (i.e. man's relationship with God, his fellow man, and the environment in which he must work out his salvation).

12 And the Lord spake unto Moses, saying,

---

35. Eliade, Mircea, *Myths, Rites, Symbols,* Edited by Wendell C. Beane and William G. Doty, Vol. 1, (Harper & Row, Publishers, New York; 1976), p.3.

36. Sproul, Barbara, *Primal Myths.* (HarperCollins, New York, 1991), p. 1, Introduction.

306

> 13 Speak thou also unto the children of Israel, saying, Verily my *sabbaths ye shall keep: for it is a sign between me and you* throughout your generations; that ye may know that I am the Lord that doth sanctify you.
> 14 Ye shall keep the sabbath therefore; for it is holy unto you: every one that defileth it shall surely be put to death. . .
> 15 Six days may work be done; but in the seventh is the sabbath of rest, holy to the Lord: whosoever doeth any work in the sabbath day, he shall surely be put to death.
> 16 Wherefore the children of Israel shall keep the sabbath, to observe the sabbath throughout their generations, for a perpetual covenant. [and the "perpetual covenant" is the connection to the creation]
> 17 *It is a sign between me and the children of Israel for ever: for in six days the Lord made heaven and earth, and on the seventh day he rested,* and was refreshed. (Exodus 31:12-17)

Speaking of keeping the Sabbath a Holy day, the Lord affirms the "perpetual covenant" and blessing of obedience connected to the covenant of the Sabbath, which is directly connected to the creation accounts found in scripture. In the Doctrine and Covenants, the blessing of remembering the Sabbath of creation is explained:

> 16 Verily I say, that inasmuch as ye do this, [keep the Sabbath day Holy] the fulness of the earth is yours, the *beasts of the field* and the *fowls of the air*, and that which climbeth upon the trees and walketh upon the earth;
> 17 Yea, and *the herb*, and the good things which come of the earth, whether for food or for raiment, or for houses, or for barns, or for orchards, or for gardens, or for vineyards;
> 18 Yea, all things which come of the earth, in the season thereof, are made for the benefit and the use of man, both to please the eye and to gladden the heart;
> 19 Yea, for food and for raiment, for taste and for smell, to strengthen the body and to enliven the soul. (D&C 59:15-19; see also Isaiah 58:13, 14)

Sproul again explains the need for a connection to the creation, even for modern man:

"Without it (the creation myth), we cannot determine what things are, what to do with them, or how to be in relation to them. The fundamental structures of understanding what myths provide, even though in part dictated by matter and instinct, are nevertheless essentially arbitrary because they describe not just the real world of fact but our perception and experience of that world.[37]

Any endowment of power from on high that would come from myth and ritual must then contain the elements of the creation and our Heavenly Father's dealings with our first parents. A better understanding of man's role in the cosmos and creation will provide the knowledge one needs to achieve salvation while here on earth. These myths about the creation are not dogmas, but narratives that "describe the work of God and characterize their mutual relations... which are expressive of the relation between God and man."[38]

The man of archaic societies who focused so much on the creation myths, was attempting to make and keep a connection between himself, his world, and the world of the Gods. Mircea Eliade, the father of the History of Religion, speaks of a power that comes from the 'rituals of recitation' of the works of the Gods at the creation of the world. The western culture has basically stripped from modern man the ability to make the necessary connections from this world to the world of the Gods through ritual. Understanding the works of God, especially the relationship of good and evil, gives man a power over all creation. Knowing how something came to be—and that would include Satan and evil—can give us power to control it, and to overcome undesirable influences that exist in the world God created. Knowledge is an endowment of power. Speaking of this endowment of power through knowledge, Eliade surmises that to the man of the ancient cultures (and even the LDS culture):

---

37. Sproul, Barbara C. in *Primal Myths, Creating the World* (New York: Harper and Row, 1979) p. 2,
38. Pedersen, Johns, in his article "Wisdom and Immortality" in *Wisdom in Israel and in the Ancient Near East*, Ed. M. Noth and D. W. Thomas, Sup. *Vetus Testamentum* Vol III (Leiden: E.J. Brill, 1955) pp. 243-244.

308

> ...the essential thing is to know the myths. [the true story of one's beginning] It is essential not only because the myths provide him with an explanation of the World and his own mode of being in the World, but above all because, by recollecting the myths, by reenacting them, he is able to repeat what the God, the Heros, or the Ancestors did ab origine. ...For knowing the origin of an object, an animal, a plant, and so on is equivalent to acquiring a magical power over them by which they can be controlled, multiplied, or reproduced at will. ...In most cases it is not enough to know the origin myth, one must recite it; this, in a sense is a proclamation of one's knowledge, and displays it. But this is not all, He who recites or performs the origin myth is thereby steeped in the sacred atmosphere in which these miraculous events took place. ...By reciting the myths, one reconstitutes that fabulous time and hence in some sort becomes "contemporary" with the events described, one is in the presence of the Gods. ...By "living" the myths, one emerges from profane, chronological time and enters a time that is of a different quality, as "sacred" Time at once primordial and indefinitely recoverable.[39]

The ritual repetition and recitation of the creation epoch, the works of God, and the activities of the first man, symbolically places the initiate in the presence of the Gods and in an environment of "real time". That means one is connected in the present tense with the events and characters that 'created' the world and life as it is known today. Knowledge is power, and with an understanding of *the relationship that exists between God, man, and the environment in which man must live and work out his salvation, the individual obtains a power over the natural evils of life and the dark door of death.* There is a particular structure and function to these creation epochs, which Eliade explains, along with the answer to why it is central in all ancient cultures. In the quote below Eliade explains the 'endowment of power' that comes through the knowledge of, and ritual participation in, the creation of the world and God's involvement with the first man.

39. Eliade, Mircea, *Myths, Rites, Symbols*, Vol. 1, pp. 5, 6.

Defining comments will be placed within this text surrounded by [brackets].

These creation myths and epochs:

> (1) Constitute the History of the Acts of the Supernaturals; [the Gods and the first man]. (2) Are considered to be absolutely true (because it is concerned with realities) and sacred (because it is the work of the Supernaturals [Gods]); (3) Are always related to a "creation," it tells how something came into existence, or how a pattern of behavior, an institution, a manner of working were established; this is why myths constitute the paradigms for all significant human acts: (4) Teach that by knowing the myth, one knows the "origin" of things and hence can control and manipulate them at will; this is not an "external," "abstract" knowledge but a knowledge that one "experiences" ritually, either by ceremonially recounting the myth or by performing the ritual for which it is the justification; (5) In one way or another allow one to "live" the myth, in the sense that one is seized by the sacred, exalting power of the events recollected or re-enacted."Living" a myth, then, implies a genuinely "religious" experience, since it differs from the ordinary experience of everyday life. The "religiousness" of this experience is due to the fact that one re-enacts fabulous, exalting, significant events, one again witnesses the creative deeds of the Supernaturals; one ceases to exist in the everyday world and enters a transfigured, auroral world impregnated with the Supernaturals' [Gods] presence. What is involved is not a commemoration of mythical events but a reiteration of them. The protagonists of the myth are made present, one becomes their contemporary. This also implies that one is no longer living in chronological time, but in the primordial Time, the Time when the event first took place. …To re-experience that time, to re-enact it is often possible, to witness again the spectacle of the divine works, to meet with the Supernaturals and relearn their creative lesson is the desire that runs like a pattern through all the ritual [Temple] reiterations of myths. In short, myths [the Temple] reveal that the World, man, and life have a supernatural origin and

history, and that this history is significant, precious and exemplary. . .[40]

The summary offered as this quote concludes distills the purpose of these creation myths or epoch accounts, and why they are rehearsed and re-enacted in ancient and modern Temples. This endowment of knowledge 'reveals,' in the words of Eliade, 'that the world, man, and life, have a God-given origin and history, and that this history is significant, exalting, and exemplary.'

LDS Temple rituals are often participated in by patrons as a matter of rote responsibility and action. Many participants of an endowment of power seek nothing other than the feel-good feeling resulting from; "that's what I should do" because "that's what I'm told to do." For some, the creation account that is repeated and rehearsed in Temples is often nothing more than just that. Many members talk and even boast of their calling to "work" in the Temples and exult in how spiritually blessed they feel, which are legitimate feelings that all should seek. Though spiritually satisfied in their Martha-like service, many fail to see the purpose for which Temples were established: to teach light and truth, endowing the initiate and patron with the power of knowledge.

Some self-described scholars and individuals seek with a spiritual zeal to find symbols behind every door and in every nook of the Temple and its surrounding grounds. There are symbols that exist, but only so far as the scriptures and God has revealed. Some symbols seen in the temple are nothing more than decoration and architectural detail. Nobody knows the meaning of a symbol except the person who created it, or required it to be made. If the origin of the symbol is not known, then every interpretation could be correct; conversely, every interpretation could potentially be wrong. All temples are constructed to maintain sacred space so that *revealed knowledge*—not hidden and subtle symbols—could be taught. The Lord delights in plainness, not the gnostic secrecy that can only be found by a select few.

---

40. *Ibid.* pp. 6, 7.

The sacred knowledge provided in the Temple, reveals an 'endowment of power' to those seeking light and truth. The real message of this endowment power is found not in the symbols and metaphors, but in the message that is clearly taught and plainly explained as God creates the world. What happens to the first man and woman happens to everyone. The plan of salvation and exaltation that was prepared for the first parents through the Atonement of Jesus Christ is the same for all today. Sometimes the forest cannot be seen because of the trees. The message of the creation epoch will often remain *unseen,* because so many books have shrouded the real and fundamental meaning of the endowment searching beyond the mark in symbols, metaphors, opinions, and private interpretations. These authors seek to explain Temple symbolism to the 'lay member' who has not been trained for a ministry of metaphor and symbol. If a knowledge of symbol, metaphor, architecture, ancient cultures, or education is necessary to understand the *information presented* in the Temple, then spiritual perfection is forever out of reach. Not only would the 'lay member' fail terribly, but God would be partial toward the learned, blessing only those who have been trained to understand metaphor and symbol.

There are some members on the other end of the spectrum who take the creation epochs so literally that they employ the information presented as finite detail to explain all the works of God in this physical environment. They think to hold all science and religion to the details of creation as presented, failing to realize that even though the creation accounts are presented in a scriptural account, they are still ritual in purpose. These zealots suppose that the concepts and descriptions found in the creation account are literal and must be accepted as the unquestioned truth of the timetable of creation. For example, some hold to the idea that the 'six days' of creation are six twenty-four hour periods that conform to our understanding and standard of time. Others have determined that these six days were in reality six thousand years, based on the belief that one day with God is *as* a thousand years.

The trend by many is to surmise that all of creation and the world in which we live, with mountains, fossils and fossil fuels, dinosaurs, cave dwellers and mountains and canyons etc. were created in the six thousand years before Adam is placed on the earth. They believe that the earth and its solar system is no older than twelve thousand years. Some members spend an inordinate amount of time and money trying to prove their interpretation of the scriptural creation epoch in order to bring scientific and religious communities around to their point of view. Not surprisingly, they tend to be partial to the single creation account that best substantiates their theories. If life is a probationary state, then sin is the misuse of time. These zealous fundamentalists, in their dogged failure to comprehend the true purpose of the creation accounts, unwittingly limit their own understanding and vision.

There are four primary accounts of the creation used in the church. These are: Moses, Genesis, Abraham, and the Temple accounts. Each differs in significant ways because they are presented for a particular reason and from a particular point of view, which will be explained in detail later in this chapter.

The creation accounts found in Moses and Abraham are written accounts of their endowment of power (not just the ritual but the reality). Abraham, in the first four verses of the first chapter, explains in his colophon that he was seeking for light and truth and the blessings of the fathers. Abraham then spends the rest of the record explaining how he received his endowment from the fathers. Both Moses and Abraham include a creation accounts because the creation epoch is a required element in the endowment of power that they are receiving. The *Pearl of Great Price* is truly that, as it records the knowledge that these prophets and patriarchs received from God as they were blessed with the light, truth, and the blessings that they had been seeking. It is from these texts that our most sacred rituals and ordinances are derived for those willing to live a higher law in order to receive further light and truth.

Relationships

The scripture are replete with the purpose of the creation. The Lord declares to Moses: "this is my work and my glory—to bring to pass the immortality and eternal life of man" (Moses 1:39). This statement establishes a purpose for the creation of the universe as well as the heavens and the earth, making a connection between the creation and the salvation of man. If this connection between the work and glory of God and the physical environment exists, one might reasonably ask 'why' the creation accounts exist. Is it so that man might have a 'scientific explanation' about the world around him? Or does it exist in order to establish an understandable relationship? The creation epochs are not detailed enough to be considered a scientific treatise of any sort, so we must consider the likelier possibility that they are included in ritual and scripture in order to *establish a relationship*: a relationship between God, man, and the environment in which mankind will live.

To assume that the creation accounts found in scripture are meant to (or could be used to) establish scientific fact is foolish. While these accounts contain truths, even some orderly scientific truths, they are not written to become a point of scientific discussion, argument, theory, or fact. Wherever a creation account exists in the ancient world, it is presented in the framework of an ordinance or initiation and is meant to establish a relationship between God, man and the environment in which man will exist.[41] That means it doesn't address the environment that existed before the earth was fit for man (more about this later). If one were to approach the creation epochs looking to prove the theory of intelligent design to the scientific community that God exists "with disregard of their possible ritual and cultic settings, it may lead to the most fearful misinterpretations."[42] This lone and dreary world is the created environment in which mankind will need to learn and work out their own salvation in 'fear and trembling' (Mormon 9:27). Creation accounts exist to help us understand relationships, not science. They establish that God is the creator of the world and consequently our lives, lifestyles, and livelihoods, reinforcing our understanding that without God, nothing is possible.

41. I. Engnell, "Knowledge and Life in the Creation Story" in *Supplements to Vetus Testamentum* (1955) vol. III p. 105, 106.
42. *Ibid.*

The scriptures can enlighten our understanding about the creation of the earth. Addressing *marriage* and the potential of *children*, the Lord creates another connection between creation and mankind, linking the two together.

> 16 Wherefore, it is lawful that he should have one wife, and they twain shall be one flesh, and all this that the earth might answer the end of its creation;
> 17 And that it might be filled with the measure of man, according to his creation before the world was made.
> (D&C 49:16-17)

The Prophet Isaiah teaches the same thing in the Old Testament as he purposely explains why the creation accounts exist and were given to the Children of Israel through Moses. This same account is found in our Book of Moses and is recounted in the Pearl of Great Price for the same reason that Isaiah infers.

> 18 For thus saith the Lord that created the heavens; God himself that formed the earth and made it; he hath established it, he created it not in vain, he formed it to be inhabited: I am the Lord; and there is none else. (Isaiah 45:18)

Like Isaiah, Nephi, the son of Lehi, also concludes as did Isaiah that there is a connection between the creation and the salvation of mankind, as he states: "Behold, *the Lord hath created the earth that it should be inhabited; and he hath created his children that they should possess it*" (1 Nephi 17:36).

These few scriptures explain that the Creation accounts that are rehearsed and explained *in history and in ordinance* exist to establish a purpose of creation and a relationship between God, man, and the environment in which man will live. The definition of "man" is that being who is created in the image and likeness of God and *who has the potential to become like God.*

Creation Epochs and the Endowment of Power

The 1828 dictionary defines the word 'endowment' as:

> "That which is given or bestowed on the person or mind by the creator; gift of nature; any quality or faculty bestowed by the creator...Natural vigor of intellect is an endowment of the mind."

The Endowment of Power lies not in any ordinance but in knowledge. The Prophet Joseph Smith taught that "a man can be saved no faster than he gains knowledge", which is echoed in the Doctrine and Covenants:

> He that keepeth his commandments receiveth truth and light, until he is glorified in truth and knoweth all things. (D&C 93:28)

> That which is of God is light; and he that receiveth light, and continueth in God, receiveth more light; and that light groweth brighter and brighter until the perfect day. (D&C 50:24)

Without a change of character, there is no power in the ordinances of salvation or exaltation. An individual could participate in every priesthood ordinance the church has to offer and not one ordinance has any power to force the reality of the ordained blessing unless the person, by using their agency, has changed their character to become worthy of that reality. Alma explains the purpose of Melchizedek ordinances:

> Now these ordinances were given after this manner, that thereby the people *might look forward* on the Son of God ... it being his order, and this that they *might look forward* to him for a remission of their sins, that they might enter into the rest of the Lord (Alma 13:16).

The ordinances provide *the hope of a future reality*, 'to look forward' to that reality. To reiterate, the real power of the ordinance lies not in the priesthood that performs the ordinance or in the ordinance itself, but in the agency of the individual that receives that ordinance. The power of the ordinances lies in the individual choice to change one's character in a way that will foster the relationship with God that is needed to make the ordinance a reality.

> For the natural man is an enemy to God, and has been from the fall of Adam, and will be forever and ever, unless he yields to the enticings of the Holy Spirit, and *putteth off the natural man and becometh a saint through the Atonement of Christ the Lord,* and becometh as a child, submissive, meek, humble, patient, full of love, willing to submit to all things which the Lord seeth fit to inflict upon him, even as a child doth submit to his father. (Mosiah 3:19)

Repentance is simply the process of changing one's character. The more an individual knows and understands about their life, surroundings, and potential, the more perfect will be the decisions and actions, all of which are reflected in the character and nature that is developed.

The creation accounts are rehearsed in scripture ritual and ordinances to establish character-changing relationships. King Benjamin makes this connection between the change of character and the creation accounts in a way that defines the purpose of these creation accounts in the temple and scripture.

> 20 I say unto you, my brethren, that if you should render all the thanks and praise which your whole soul has power to possess, *to that God who has created you,* and has kept and preserved you, and has caused that ye should rejoice,
> 21 I say unto you that *if ye should serve him who has created you from the beginning,* and *is preserving you* from day to day, by *lending you breath,* that ye may live and move and do according to your own will, and even supporting you from one moment to another—I say, if ye should serve him with all your whole souls yet ye would be unprofitable servants.

22 And behold, *all that he requires of you is to keep his commandments;* and he has promised you that if ye would keep his commandments ye should prosper in the land;

23 And now, in the first place, *he hath created you, and granted unto you your lives, for which ye are indebted unto him.*

24 And secondly, he doth require that ye should do as he hath commanded you; for which if ye do, he doth immediately bless you; and therefore he hath paid you. And ye are still indebted unto him, and are, and will be, forever and ever; therefore, of what have ye to boast?

25 And now I ask, can ye say aught of yourselves? I answer you, Nay. *Ye cannot say that ye are even as much as the dust of the earth; yet ye were created of the dust of the earth; but behold, it belongeth to him who created you.*
(Mosiah 2:20-25)

The real endowment of power, then, is knowing and understanding the concepts that King Benjamin taught, as well as other key doctrines of life and salvation. This knowledge that endows one with power over mortality might be summarized in a few simple statements:

- That God lives,
- That God created this world for mankind,
- That our separation from God can be reversed,
- That we have an eternal nature and spirit,
- That there is a plan of progression toward God,
- That there is a purpose to this life that endures past death,
- That our potentials are as limitless as God's,
- That the trials of mortality have purpose and are necessary,
- Where evil comes from and how to control it,
- That death is not an end but a beginning, and
- That a Son of God, provides an Atonement and resurrection.

Knowing the truth of these things endows an individual with a power over this mortal life of sin, suffering, death and evil. This life changing knowledge can provide the joy and happiness of redemption and the hope of a better resurrection, establishing a purpose in life that will motivate us to want to return to the presence of God. To understand the power this knowledge imparts, imagine how one would navigate this temporal sphere without it. The longing to understand the meaning of life is universal. In the creation accounts one begins to find the answers. For this reason all ancient cultures had creation epochs that gave them a place in this world and a relationship with the creator, and an understanding that what the first man did and experienced, all mankind must do. Hence, the purpose of the ritual repetition is to realize and remember that divine and eternal relationships exist between God and man, and to understand the potential of life in the immortal world of the Gods.

The three pillars of the Gospel are The Creation, The Fall and The Atonement, which also happen to be the primary messages the creation accounts ritually convey. In short, *God's work and message in scripture is not to provide a scientific treatise on the creation, but to furnish the spiritual* (not scientific) *truths needed to bring to pass the immortality and eternal life of man.*

Creation

The Doctrine and Covenants teach that an eternal truth is a "knowledge of things as they are, and as they were, and as they are to come" (D&C 93:24). This definition of truth implies that to have a complete, or a more perfect understanding of truth, one must comprehend all aspects and points of view in all timeframes; i.e., the past, present, and the future of a particular truth.

In the Latter-day Saint world, there are four 'creation accounts' that are considered scripture or inspired. They are found in Genesis, Moses, Abraham, and the Temple. The creation account in Moses is the 'inspired version' of Genesis, prepared by Joseph Smith; therefore, the three accounts considered here will be Moses, Abraham, and the Temple. These three accounts are remarkable in that they present different points of view in origin and presentation. The creation account found in Moses, written for the Children of Israel, and what God did for them presents the creation as a historical event that happened in the past: *"Things as they were"*. The Temple account presents the creation as something that is happening right now, real time, in the present tense, or *"Things as they are."* Patrons symbolically become the man Adam and the woman Eve, participating in the events and ordinances that are discussed in 'real time'. Abraham records the creation epic from a view of the intelligent spirit before the creation has taken place. It is something that has not yet happened and is yet to come: *"Things as they are to come."* Thus these three creation accounts present the reader with scriptural points of view of the creation from all three time frames: *as they are* (the Temple), *as they were* (Moses), and *as they are to come* (Abraham). Seen from these three perspectives, the reader will come away with a fuller, more accurate understanding than could be obtained from focusing on a single account. Using one account at the exclusion of the others could easily lead to errors. Each account differs in key ways, owing to their respective points of view, but all are true and correct.

Remember, these three accounts are not meant explain the science of creation. Nor are they written to explain or even imply how long it took to create the world. They were given to mankind as part of an ordinance and an initiation, and always show up in this context. Each creation account begins with the general geologic information (water and dry land) and then moves into the astro-geologic (the sun, moon and stars) creation. These geologic and astro-geologic creations are generally defined as the creation of the "heavens and the earth." This creation of the heavens and the earth are mentioned as fundamental facts without any detail about how, when, or how long the geologic and astro-geologic creation took place, forming the general framework or setting for what follows. As the biologic creation begins (the creation of the plants, fouls, fish and land animals), the detail, though sparse, is expanded a hundredfold compared to the generality of 'heavens and earth.' This expansion in discussion and detail is found in scripture for a specific reason and is connected to the structure and purpose of 'myth and ritual' as described previously in this chapter.

Geological Creation

Of the three creation accounts in the church, there are two readily available in scripture. Readers and researchers tend to focus on the account in the Book of Moses (inspired version of Genesis) in preference to the account in the Book of Abraham, which is unfortunate because the Book of Abraham account is better, more complete, and provides a better understanding of the creation than that of Moses. The Abrahamic account will be the main focus in this chapter because of its point of view and the expanded detail.

Remember that Moses is writing for the stubborn Children of Israel. His account is trying to establish a relationship between them, their God and the world in which they lived. He is teaching them about the creation as something that happened in the past. That being the case, it is rehearsed in such a way that the necessary connection that should exist is established. This basic understanding is required to begin a relationship with God for the advancement of their salvation (D&C 84:19-24).

It's in the details that the Abrahamic account enlarges and clarifies one's understanding. Moses speaks of God in the singular; Abraham refers to Gods in the plural. This is an insight recognized and confirmed by Joseph Smith. Moses speaks of the "first day"; in Abraham it is rendered as the "first time", eliminating the concept of 24 hours or 1,000 years as a period of creation. These and other key refinements of detail can clarify our understanding of the creation. Abraham and Joseph Smith provide a number of insights into the creation by the "Gods" and the council of which they are a part. The statements of Joseph imply that at the head of the council are those who created the geological and astro-geological creation, seemingly independent of the biological creation that took place much later. Joseph Smith states that "In the beginning the head God called together the Gods and sat in grand council to bring forth the world."[43] Decisions were made and "the head God organized the heavens and

---

43. *TPJS*, 1843-44, p. 348.

the earth"[44] and then, "the heads of the Gods appointed one God for us."[45]

The Gods begin with the creation of the Heavens and the Earth as a general aspect of the creation—the framework, so to speak; not one of the "days or times" of the creation account. Letting the scriptures speak for themselves may require an open mind that is unencumbered by the thoughts and traditions of the past.

The events in the first five verses are discussed in a general and informative way, introducing the creation account. To view these first five verses from a 'textual studies' point of view, one might recognize the colophonic (content summary) character of these verses. This is easily seen in verse one of Moses. This first verse is the 'summary' of what is to follow—the 'trailer', if you will, and the title of the text: "*God formed the heavens and the earth.*" Period. Statement of fact, introduction, and title.

The first five verses of both Abraham and Moses seem to be the colophon (the introduction and explanation of what is coming up) for the creation account that begins in verse six of each record. This will be seen in greater detail below with the introduction of the sun, moon and stars as the *causation* of light and darkness. Keeping in mind that these creation accounts are for the purpose of establishing a relationship between God, man, and the world in which man will live. Therefore it should not be surprising that, the environment or elements in which man will *not* live (the heavens and an empty and desolate earth) are addressed in a general fashion, as in the astro-geologic creation that follows. These elements are general because they are always there and were there before any man was placed here.

---

44. *Ibid.* 1843-44, p.372

45. *Ibid.*

Abraham 4	Moses 2
1 And then the Lord said: Let us go down. And they went down at the beginning, and they, that is the Gods, organized and formed the heavens and the earth. 2 And the earth, after it was formed, was empty and desolate, because they had not formed anything but the earth; and darkness reigned upon the face of the deep, and the Spirit of the Gods was brooding upon the face of the waters. (Abraham 4:1-2)	1 And it came to pass that the Lord spake unto Moses, saying: Behold, I reveal unto you concerning this heaven, and this earth; write the words which I speak. I am the Beginning and the End, the Almighty God; by mine Only Begotten I created these things; yea, in the beginning I created the heaven, and the earth upon which thou standest. 2 And the earth was without form, and void; and I caused darkness to come up upon the face of the deep; and my Spirit moved upon the face of the water; for I am God. (Moses 2:1-2)

In verse one Abraham adds information about this geologic creation as he states that the Gods "organized and formed," whereas Moses states "I created" (remember Moses is writing for the Children of Israel). In verses 2 Abraham explains that '*after*' the earth was created it was "*empty and desolate*" while Moses reports that the "earth was without form and void." Moses in verse two states that "my spirit moves upon the face of the water" while Abraham states that the "Spirit of the Gods was 'brooding' upon the waters." The word "brood" as used here conveys a different emotion or meaning than "my Spirit moved" upon the waters. To 'brood' means to watch over, to incubate, while protecting, preparing, and nurturing, like a hen might do over her eggs.

"And they (the Gods) said: Let there be light; and there was light." (Abraham 4:3; Moses 2:3 "God")

Abraham 4	Moses 2
4 And they (the Gods) comprehended the light, for it was bright; and they divided the light, or caused it to be divided, from the darkness. 5 And the Gods called the light Day, and the darkness they called Night. And it came to pass that from the evening until morning they called night; and from the morning until the evening they called day; and this was the first, or the beginning, of that which they called day and night. (Abraham 4:4-5)	4 And I, God, saw the light; and that light was good. And I, God, divided the light from the darkness. 5 And I, God, called the light Day; and the darkness, I called Night; and this I did by the word of my power, and it was done as I spake; and the evening and the morning were the first day. (Moses 2:4-5)

Both, Abraham and Moses speak of the light being divided from the darkness. However, Abraham informs us that the Gods "*caused* it to be divided", implying that there were laws, action, and obedience taking place. Verse 5 of each text explains that the division of light and darkness needed a designation, but in Abraham's account it was not necessarily meant to be a time period. "From evening to morning it was called night" and from the "morning to the evening it was called day." This became the beginning of the use of the terms "day and night." Moses implies that the introduction of light and darkness was the "first day", whereas Abraham states that this division was the "beginning" of that which was called day and night. The terms "day and night" are designations of light and darkness, and were never meant to be time periods of either 24 hours or 1,000 years.

In the next few verses, the creation of the sun, moon and stars is introduced. Keep in mind the distinctions that were made above in verses 4-5 of Abraham about light and darkness, day and night, and pay attention to the word "*caused*" in connection to the division between the light and darkness.

Abraham 4	Moses 2
14 And the Gods organized the lights in the expanse of the heaven, and **caused them to divide the day from the night**; and organized them to be for signs and for seasons, and for days and for years; 15 And organized them to be for lights in the expanse of the heaven to give light upon the earth; and it was so. 16 And the Gods organized the two great lights, the greater light to rule the day, and the lesser light to rule the night; with the lesser light they set the stars also; 17 And the Gods set them in the expanse of the heavens, to give light upon the earth, and to rule over the day and over the night, **and to cause to divide the light from the darkness.** (Abraham 4:14-17)	14 And I, God, said: Let there be lights in the firmament of the heaven, to divide the day from the night, and let them be for signs, and for seasons, and for days, and for years; 15 And let them be for lights in the firmament of the heaven to give light upon the earth; and it was so. 16 And I, God, made two great lights; the greater light to rule the day, and the lesser light to rule the night, and the greater light was the sun, and the lesser light was the moon; and the stars also were made even according to my word. 17 And I, God, set them in the firmament of the heaven to give light upon the earth, 18 And the sun to rule over the day, and the moon to rule over the night, and to divide the light from the darkness; and I, God, saw that all things which I had made were good; (Moses 2:14-18)

Only from one point in space does it appear that our sun and moon are the same size. When viewed from the earth, and in the same arc, the sun and the moon appear to be the exactly the same size. One to rule the day and another to rule the night. Coincidence or design?

Viewing the introductory verses of both accounts in parallel columns allows one to see the differences within the texts and provides for a better understanding of how the lights that were set in the firmament became the 'cause' of the seperation. Abraham again gives the best account, but the vocabulary is revealing in both accounts. God creates the sun and moon (lights in the expanse) and then sets the earth spinning which then *causes* light to be "divided" from the darkness.

Abraham 4	Moses 2
3 And they (the Gods) said: Let there be light; and there was light. 4 And they (the Gods) comprehended the light, for it was bright; and they divided the light, or *caused it* to be divided, from the darkness.	3 And I, God, said: Let there be light; and there was light. 4 And I, God, saw the light; and that light was good. And I, God, divided the light from the darkness.

Reviewing these accounts to this point, it is implied by the text itself that the first five verses of Abraham 4 and Moses 2 are the introduction of the creation of the heavens and the earth, and the introduction of light by the sun and darkness because of the earth rotation. As explained, the *cause* of the separation of light from the darkness is the introduction of the sun, moon and stars in verses 14-17 of Moses. The heavenly luminaries are in place "for signs, and for seasons, and for days, and for years" (*rotations*) and with this placement, there can be the division of "light and darkness' and the 'day and night' that is introduced in verse 5 of Moses 2, and Abraham 4. The creation and placement of the sun, moon and stars becomes the '*causation*' of the phrase "let there be light" (i.e. division between light and darkness), in the introductory verses 3 and 4 of the corresponding chapters.

Abraham 4	Moses 2
14 And the Gods organized the lights in the expanse of the heaven, and *caused them to divide the day from the night*; and organized them to be for signs and for seasons, and for days and for years; 17 And the Gods set them in the expanse of the heavens, to give light upon the earth, and to rule over the day and over the night, *and to cause to divide the light from the darkness.*	14 And I, God, said: Let there be lights in the firmament of the heaven, *to divide the day from the night,* and let them be for signs, and for seasons, and for days, and for years; 18 And the sun to rule over the day, and the moon to rule over the night, and *to divide the light from the darkness;* and I, God, saw that all things which I had made were good;

Many teachers have been asked: "When God said, before the sun was created, 'Let there be light,' what was the source of the light?" What these accounts are establishing: In the very beginning the Gods created the heavens and the earth, and in the heavens they placed the sun and moon and stars to give light to the earth. They then spun it around so that part of the time it was light and part of the time it was dark, and the Gods call the light 'day' and the darkness they called 'night'. This is intentionally general as the creation of these elements is the same and will be same throughout the existence of the earth. Every 24-hour period there is day (light) and night (darkness). There is a heavenly expanse with a sun and a moon and stars. There is an earth with dry land to walk on and there is water. There is a sun, a moon and stars to see each day. The general geologic and astral-geologic creation must be in place to continue the preparation of the earth for mankind.

Because there are always those who cannot let go of a belief in the six days of creation, the proverbial 'dead horse' must continue to be beat. It just doesn't matter if it took six days, six thousand years, six million years, or six billion years. These accounts are not meant to set the scientific community straight, and are *not* lessons in science, physics, biology or astronomy. The creation epochs exist to establish individual spiritual relationships between Deity, the cosmos, and mankind. To think that science should be reconciled to scripture—or scripture to science—based on these scriptural accounts, is not only narrow-minded but a waste of time. One is sure to miss the beautiful forest of relationships when the trees of interpretation are blocking the real view. These creation accounts are not meant to establish scientific facts for the fundamentalist, or fundamental fiction for the scientist. Any endeavor or argument to *prove or disprove* the creation accounts via scientific process, theory or inquiry is also a waste of time and effort. The details are not there, nor are they meant to be found within the texts.

To review, the purpose of the creation accounts is to establish the relationship between God, man, and the environment in which he is to live and die as he works out his own salvation. It is always rehearsed in the context of an ordination or initiation, and provides the framework or setting for an endowment of power, which is the knowledge needed for the process of salvation and exaltation.

Biological Creation

Given that the creation epochs found in scripture are rehearsed to establish a relationship between God, man, and the environment man will live in, the descriptive rehearsal of the biological creation (plants and animals) must have the same fundamental purpose. In other words, the flora and fauna introduced are described as being created *'for the use of man.'* These are the plants and animals that will be on the earth *when Adam is placed on it*, when it is prepared for him and his posterity. This biological creation is not talking about anything that could not coexist or that lived before the earth was prepared for Adam, Eve and their posterity.

> 19 For, behold, the beasts of the field and the fowls of the air, and that which cometh of the earth, *is ordained for the use of man for food and for raiment*, and that he might have in abundance. (D&C 49:19)

> 16 Verily I say, that inasmuch as ye do this, the fulness of the earth is yours, the beasts of the field and the fowls of the

air, and that which climbeth upon the trees and walketh upon the earth;

17 Yea, and the herb, and the good things which come of the earth, *whether for food or for raiment, or for houses, or for barns, or for orchards, or for gardens, or for vineyards;*

18 Yea, *all things which come of the earth, in the season thereof, are made for the benefit and the use of man, both to please the eye and to gladden the heart;* (D&C 59:16-18)

10 And again, verily I say unto you, all wholesome herbs *God hath ordained for the constitution, nature, and use of man—*

12 Yea, flesh also of beasts and of the fowls of the air, *I, the Lord, have ordained for the use of man with thanksgiving;* nevertheless, they are to be used sparingly; (D&C 89:10, 12)

These verses make it clear that the fruit trees and herbs, the fish and fouls, and all manner of beasts and life on earth that are described in the creation accounts are those that will be on the earth when it is prepared for the introduction of the man Adam into the new world. Thus, the biological creations recounted in Moses and Abraham includes only the plants and animals that will be on the earth during the time Adam and his posterity will possess it. Beyond knowing about the general creation of the heavens and the earth, there is no need to know about the plants and animals that might have lived prior to the advent of Adam *to establish the necessary relationships* these accounts are intended to forge. Therefore, the creation accounts would *not by nature* and should *not by purpose* include that which may have existed before it was prepared for Adam. *Nor do these creation accounts limit life to that which is described within the text.*

Remember, "Mankind" is defined and limited to *those beings that are created in the image and likeness of God and have the potential to become like God.* It is an important distinction when considering the varieties of life that this earth may have supported before the advent of man.

How Long?

The Book of Abraham is again the text of choice as it presents a better view of the biological creation and how it took place as the earth was 'prepared' for Adam and his posterity. The scriptures presented below clearly imply that the plants and animals that will accompany Adam and his posterity during their temporal sojourn were prepared, ordered, and 'organized'. Abraham clearly describes the works of the Gods and the preparation of the earth to sustain the necessary flora and fauna for mankind. How long could the preparatory period be? As long as need be, states Abraham, for "the Gods watched those things which they had ordered until they obeyed" (Abraham 4:18).

> 11 And the Gods said: *Let us prepare the earth* to bring forth grass; the herb yielding seed; the fruit tree yielding fruit, after his kind, *[while mankind is on it]* whose seed in itself yieldeth its own likeness upon the earth; and **it was so, even as they ordered**.
> 12 And **the Gods** *organized the earth to bring forth* grass from its own seed, and the herb to bring forth herb from its own seed, yielding seed after his kind; and the earth to bring forth the tree from its own seed, yielding fruit, whose seed could only bring forth the same in itself, after his kind; and **the Gods saw that they were obeyed.** (Abraham 4:11-12)

The time it might take to prepare the earth to bring forth the grass, herb, and the fruit trees that will be on the earth when Adam is placed upon it is indeterminable. The account in Abraham makes it clear that the Gods were *preparing* the earth for the plants that would be used by mankind. Once ordered, prepared, and organized, the "Gods saw that they were obeyed"; that is, they watched to know that their plan was good and was going to work for the benefit of mankind. The length of this preparation period could be as long as was needed to prepare the soil with the necessary organic material (carbon based life) that would make the ground fertile and thus prepared for the plants (and animals) that would be used by man. Below, the Gods address Adam's needs as they organize the plants that will be available to him:

> And the Gods said: Behold, *we will give them* every herb
> bearing seed that shall come upon the face of all the earth,
> and every tree which shall have fruit upon it; yea, the fruit of
> the tree yielding seed to them we will give it; it shall be for
> their meat. ...and all these things shall be thus organized
> (Abraham 4:29-30).

The preparation of the earth continues for the animals that will be *on
the earth* during the time that Adam and his posterity will inherit this
environment.

> 20 ...abundantly the moving creatures that have life; and the
> fowl, that they may fly above the earth in the open expanse
> of heaven *[while mankind is on it]*.
> 21 And **the Gods *prepared the waters*... And the Gods saw
> that they would be obeyed,** and that their plan was good.
> 24 And **the Gods *prepared the earth to bring forth the
> living creature after his kind*,** cattle and creeping things, and
> beasts of the earth after their kind; and it was so, as they had
> said.
> 25 And **the Gods *organized the earth to bring forth the
> beasts after their kind*,** and cattle after their kind, and every
> thing that creepeth upon the earth after its kind; *[while
> mankind is on it]* and **the Gods saw they would obey.**
> (Abraham 4:20-21; 24-25)

There are two key questions that arise from these verses: 1) What
preparation was needed; and 2) How long did that preparation take?

Given that the soil would need to be rich and fertile enough to sustain
the plant life that man and his animals would require for sustenance,
the soil would need to be prepared with all manner of organic material
and minerals. Organic material within the soil implies that there had
been 'carbon based' life (plants and or animals) that lived and died
over a long period of time as the soil was readied for Adam's use.

Death before the Fall?

The *traditions* in the LDS community have created the belief that nothing, including plants or animals, died before the fall of Adam. In reality, the scriptures teach that Adam and Eve were immortal, rather than all life forms. The only life form that could transgress, sin, or fall from the presence of God is that creature who has the potential to become like God (Adam and his posterity). That means that nothing less than man can fall. The brute beast, for example, can fulfill the measure of its creation and reach its full potential without a knowledge of the plan of salvation. This applies to all lower forms of life that are incapable of sin because they are ruled and act by instinct.

The first traditional argument that there was no death of anything before the fall is based on the assumption that the whole world (the physical sphere called earth) was in a *"terrestrial"* state and that fell from the presence of God (which was somewhere near Kolob) when Adam partook of the fruit, hence causing the "fall" of the earth and Adam. This tradition is not scriptural (remember the standard), only conjecture and opinion. For this to be true, the fall of the earth itself would, of scriptural necessity, include not only our solar system but also our universe, as the sun, moon, constellations, and stars were set in their position before man was ever created, for "signs and for seasons, and for days and for years" (Abraham 4:14; Moses 2:14).

This tradition is founded upon an interpretation of one passage of scripture that seems to imply that there was no death before the fall. It is upon this one verse that the traditions and opinions have been built:

> 22 And now, behold, if Adam had not transgressed he would not have fallen, but he would have remained in the garden of Eden. And all things which were created must have remained in the same state in which they were after they were created; and they must have remained forever, and had no end. (2 Nephi 2:22)

At first look it is easy to see why the tradition of 'no death before the fall' gained a foothold. But when studying the scriptures there are sometimes words that need to be examined within the context. For example, when the word "therefore" is read, one should discover what therefore is "there for." The greatest need is to find out within the context *who* is being spoken about; that is, who '*they*" are (or might be) within a given text. It is only in the context of the scripture that these discoveries might help explain the inspired, written word. Scripture is the best commentary on scripture and is more reliable and sound than the respected arm of flesh. Even Joseph Smith stated that his "key" to studying the scriptures and that was to "try and discover the question that provoked the response or answer from the Lord."[46]

In 2 Nephi 2:22 there are three places where the word "they" is used. The key to understanding this passage and its meaning is to *discover who "they" are*. This can only be done by examining the context of the verses in question (below). The passage is somewhat lengthy but should be seen in its entirety for a better understanding of who "they" are. The *object of discussion*, from beginning to end, is Adam and Eve. The scene opens with *Adam and Eve* partaking of the forbidden fruit.

2 Nephi 2:19-25

> 19 And after *Adam and Eve* had partaken of the forbidden fruit
> *they* were driven out of the garden of Eden, to till the earth.
> 20 And
> *they* have brought forth children; yea, even the family of all the earth.
> 22 And now, behold, if *Adam* had not transgressed
> *he* would not have fallen, but
> *he* would have remained in the garden of Eden.
> And all things which were created must have remained in the same state in which
> *they* were after
> *they* were created; and
> *they* must have remained forever, and had no end.

46. *TPJS*, p. 276.

23 And

> **they** *would have had no children*; wherefore
> **they** *would have remained in a state of innocence,*
> having no joy, for
> **they** *knew no misery; doing no good, for*
> **they** *knew no sin.*

24 But behold, all things have been done in the wisdom of him who knoweth all things.

25 **Adam** fell that men might be; and men are, that they might have joy. (2 Nephi 2:19-25)

This passage recounts not only the consequences of Adam and Eve partaking of the forbidden fruit, but also what might have been had they not transgressed. There is only one "object" of discussion in this passage of verses (19-25) and that object of discussion is Adam and Eve. The "they" of verse 23 without question is Adam and Eve, and therefore must be the same "*they*" referred to in verse 22—*not* all plants and animals.

In matters of scripture interpretation, all have agency and the freedom to form their own conclusions or adopt and adapt them from favorite commentaries or the statements of general authorities. But nonetheless, the scriptures remain the best commentary on the scriptures.

It should be kept in mind that the 'sanctification' at the end of creation, i.e. the Sabbath day, does not take place until after it has been fully prepared for the man Adam and described as 'good' (Abraham 5:3; Moses 2:31-3:3). As mentioned in scripture, the 'sanctification' at the culmination of creation *could be* the beginning of a time without death. However, this process did not take place until after *all was prepared* for those who have the potential to become like God (Adam and his posterity). Thus the "Gods prepared the earth" to bring forth the plants and animals that will live upon the earth through the duration of humankind, and when thus prepared, and finished, they blessed it. The earth, once prepared for man, does not limit or eliminate the possibility of the death of plants or animals that might exist before the earth is ready for man. These plants and animals, possessed of a spirit, would need to be free to act for themselves in the 'sphere' in they are placed, with a physical body created such to allow their spirit to fulfill the measure of their creation and reach the full potential (intelligence) of their spirit.

Therefore, the life and death of plants and animals before the fall could be part of the preparation of the earth for Adam, while also giving them a time, place, and purpose to live. Time (as we know it) is limitless when the "Gods prepared the earth to bring forth" the plants and animals that will be on the earth while Adam and his posterity are here. How long might it take to prepare the necessary organic material on the earth? The obvious answer: As long as needful; as long as it takes. The creation epoch in the Book of Abraham allows for this open-ended timeline. Not just six days, or six thousand years: for the "Gods prepared the earth" for the plants and animals that would be on the earth with Adam, and "they watched until they saw that they would be obeyed" and then the Gods moved forward. Relationships, not science, are the purpose of the creation accounts.

Something else to consider: The definition of death before the fall— including the time Adam and Eve are in the Garden—is uncertain, for the bark on trees is composed of dead cells; likewise the hair and nails and claws of the animals are composed of discarded cells. Did the plant life that was consumed by Adam and Eve and the animals in their environment die as it was consumed? The second that any fruit is ripe, it begins to rot and die. The flowering plants that need to bud, blossom, and then produce 'seed in themselves' must die to do so. If there were no death, there could be no growth, for the growing process requires death and change.

The scriptures present a clear picture of only a few things pertaining to death before the fall. The main clear and sure doctrine is Adam and Eve's immortality in the presence of God before they partook of the forbidden fruit.

The Doctrine and Covenants teaches that by the command of God, there was no death (for mankind) after the fall for at least three generations (see Moses 5:2-13).

> 42 But, behold, I say unto you that I, the Lord God, gave unto *Adam and unto his seed, that they should not die as to the temporal death*, until I, the Lord God, should send forth angels to declare unto them repentance and redemption, through faith on the name of mine Only Begotten Son. (D&C 29:42)

Age After Age

Elder James E. Talmage delivered an address in the Tabernacle in August, 1931 that was published in the "Deseret News" and then created into a pamphlet by the church to be distributed throughout the wards and stakes. It was again published for the members in "The Instructor" in 1965.[47] According to Elder Talmage's understanding, this important talk addresses the idea and doctrine of death before the fall. Speaking of the fossil record of plants and animals that were once living organisms, and the fossil fuels of coal oil and gas, Elder Talmage stated that this fossilized carbon based life "*lived and died, age after age, while the earth was yet unfit for human habitation.*"[48]

Talmage notes that life and death before the fall is a vital part of the earth's preparation for the advent of man. He posits that even the fossil fuels needed to already be in the earth and ready to use when Adam was placed on it, so that he could progress as fast as his intellect and righteousness might allow. This discourse by Talmage supports the interpretation that there must have been death before Adam, just as the fossil record testifies. Again the *creation accounts are for relationships not details.* They establish no sure facts about the earth

---

47. Talmage, James E., Address Delivered in the Tabernacle, Salt Lake City, Utah Sunday, August 9, 1931, Titled "The Earth and Man" This address was originally published in the "Deseret News," Nov. 21, 1931; subsequently published as a pamphlet by the Church of Jesus Christ of Latter-day Saints, 1931; later published in "The Instructor," vol. 100, no. 12 (Dec. 1965), pg. 474-477; continued in vol. 101, no. 1 (Jan. 1966), pg. 9-15.
48. *Ibid.*

between the general creation of the heaven and the earth and the
arrival of Adam, other than to confirm that it was prepared for him
with the plants and animals that will co-exist with him. Adam, as
Talmage points out, was the first man and the first flesh on the earth
that *has the potential to become like God*. That's what sets man apart
from all other creatures. That means that all else falls into the realm of
the plant or animal kingdoms that could have lived and died before
Adam. This concept is especially important to keep in mind in any
discussion or deliberation over dinosaurs and cave dwellers
(mistakenly called 'cave *man*').

The Spiritual Creation

The LDS tradition of a "spiritual creation", derived from the creation
narrative in Moses, holds that the spiritual creation is the creation of
the animating spirit of every living thing before it is created physically.
Although contrary to scripture and the statements of Joseph Smith, this
tradition has become the accepted LDS view, largely on the strength of
the narrative hint in Moses, even though it conflicts with Abraham's
more expansive account. Abraham is seeing the creation from a pre-
earth and pre-creation point of view, as he describes being in the
council of heaven and being chosen as one of the 'great and noble
spirits' prepared to be a priesthood and patriarchal leader (Abraham
3:22-23). Abraham expands upon and clarifies what Moses is just
hinting at, while LDS commentaries run rampant with explication that
neglects the explanation found in the Book of Abraham.

Moses' account of the so-called 'spiritual creation', which has become
the traditional doctrine:

> 5 And every plant of the field before it was in the earth, and
> every herb of the field before it grew. For I, the Lord God,
> *created all things, of which I have spoken, spiritually, before*
> *they were naturally upon the face of the earth.* For I, the
> Lord God, had not caused it to rain upon the face of the
> earth. And I, the Lord God, had *created all the children of*
> *men; and not yet a man to till the ground*; for in heaven

created I them; and there was *not yet flesh upon the earth*,
neither in the water, neither in the air; (Moses 3:5)

It is easy to see how the traditional notion of "spiritual creation" was derived from this one verse. Abraham, however, provides us with a better understanding. The creation account presented in the Book of Abraham, and especially chapter five, specifically addresses the 'spiritual creation' as *the planning meeting of the Gods that were in counsel about the creation of the earth.* In his account, Abraham may not only be recording the work of the Gods in the creative process, but he could also be seeing and describing the grand counsel of heaven where the plan of salvation and exaltation is presented to all the spirits that are to come to this earth. Abraham chapter three ends with an account of this Grand Counsel choosing the future spiritual leaders (the "noble and great ones") from amongst the spirits that were to come to this world. This takes place prior to the beginning of the creation epic in chapter four. Chapter five offers the expanded version of the spiritual creation hinted at in Moses 3:5. The corresponding verse in Abraham of the spiritual creation found in Moses 3:5 is Abraham 5:3. However, Abraham's discussion of the spiritual creation includes verses 2-5, which provides a better understanding of what the spiritual creation really encompassed.

Abraham 5	Moses 3
2 And the Gods said among themselves: On the seventh time we will end our work, which we have counseled; and we will rest on the seventh time from all our work *which we have counseled*. 3 And the Gods concluded upon the seventh time, because that on the seventh time they would rest from all their works which they (the Gods) *counseled among themselves to form; and sanctified it.* And thus were their decisions *at the time that they counseled among themselves to form the heavens and the earth*. 4 And the Gods came down and formed these the generations of the heavens and of the earth, when they were formed in the day that the Gods formed the earth and the heavens, (Abraham 5:2-4)	2 And on the seventh day I, God, ended my work, and all things which I had made; and I rested on the seventh day from all my work, and all things which I had made were finished, and I, God, saw that they were good; 3 And I, God, blessed the seventh day, and sanctified it; because that in it I had rested from all my work which I, God, had created and made. 4 And now, behold, I say unto you, that these are the generations of the heaven and of the earth, when they were created, in the day that I, the Lord God, made the heaven and the earth,

Abraham 5	Moses 3
5 According to all that which they had said concerning every plant of the field before it was in the earth, and every herb of the field before it grew; for the Gods had not caused it to rain upon the earth *when they counseled to do them*, and had not formed a man to till the ground	5 And every plant of the field before it was in the earth, and every herb of the field before it grew. For I, the Lord God, created all things, of which I have spoken, spiritually, before they were naturally upon the face of the earth. For I, the Lord God, had not caused it to rain upon the face of the earth. And I, the Lord God, had created all the children of men; and not yet a man to till the ground; for in heaven created I them; and there was not yet flesh upon the earth, neither in the water, neither in the air;

As seen above, Abraham makes clear that what is really going on is the planning meeting (Council) of the Gods that were in counsel about the creation of the earth (a super activity), not a "spiritual creation" of all things to be physically created later, as tradition holds. The word 'counseled', as Abraham uses it, conveys deliberation, instruction, direction, and guidance.

Accepting the premise that the creation accounts are provided to establish a relationship between God, mankind, and the environment in which man must live and work out his salvation *opens the door* for a better relationship between science and religion. Death before the fall is no longer an issue. Likewise, the amount of time to prepare the earth for Adam and his posterity can be as long as needed.

With this understanding then, the thorny questions about cave dwellers and dinosaurs can be explained without scriptural problems. The Abrahamic creation epoch opens possibilities that cannot be seen through the traditional cosmological view found in the Book of Moses alone. The only scientific issues not accepted within the scriptural standard are the commonly accepted theories about the evolution of man and animals (addressed later in this chapter).

Spirits

Scriptures teach that all living creatures have a spirit, which animates their physical body, giving life to the organized elements of the earth. The Doctrine and Covenants teach that the spirit and body are in the likeness of each other:

> ...that which is *spiritual being in the likeness of that which is temporal; and that which is temporal in the likeness of that which is spiritual*; the spirit of man in the likeness of his person, as also the spirit of the beast, and every other creature which God has created. (D&C 77:2)

A spirit that is in the 'likeness' of their physical body animates the bodies of man and beast. This also has a bearing on the theory of evolution, which claims to adapt the physical attributes of a creature into a different form. If evolution could change the physical body, then the spirit must also be reformed or changed through evolution. This is incompatible with our understanding that 'every man, every creeping thing, and every animal' has a spirit in the likeness of their physical bodies.

Every spirit must be free to act within its created and assigned environment. The Doctrine and Covenants speaks of the free nature of the spirit and the agency that must exist. The Lord states, "All truth is independent in that sphere [environment] in which God has placed it, to act for itself, as all intelligence [spirits] also; otherwise there is no existence" (D&C 93:30). Thus a spirit, in its body, must be capable of fulfilling the measure of its creation and reaching its full potential. The Lord has taught in scripture and through the Prophet Joseph Smith that spirits are eternal and were not created, but have and will exist forever.

> 18 ...if there be two spirits, and one shall be more intelligent than the other, yet these two spirits, notwithstanding one is

more intelligent than the other, *have no beginning; they existed before, they shall have no end, they shall exist after, for they are gnolaum, or eternal.* (Abraham 3:18)

29 Man was also in the beginning with God. Intelligence, or the light of truth, *was not created or made, neither indeed can be.* (D&C 93:29)

There are two theories concerning the intelligence of spirits. The first is the 'globular theory' in which all spirits are in a pool and the larger the amount of intelligence that is used the greater the potential the spirit might have (these theories have been taught in almost every LDS educational venue and class). The second theory, more in line with scripture, is the individual intelligence of spirit. This would teach that each spirit has the intelligence to be what it is capable of becoming. In other words, there are spirits that can only be man, and spirits that can only be monkeys; likewise cows, dogs, or even beetles.

If the spirit exists, it must at some time receive a body and a temporal life, and have the opportunity to live and die, and have seed in itself to reproduce after its kind in order to fulfill the measure of its creation. Therefore, the spirit must have the physical body that would allow that spirit to act and react in the environment or 'sphere' in which it is placed. As an example, the spirit of a dog, with which all are familiar, is able to love, protect, play, run, and jump. Man's best friend even has a personality that can display love, affection, and bonding. If that same spirit were placed in the body of a beetle or bird, the dog spirit would not be able to reach its full potential and fulfill the measure of its creation.

As stated earlier, the body a spirit is placed in must be capable of fulfilling the measure of its creation and reaching its full potential. This would extend to man, who has the potential to become like God. With that potential, he must be created in the image of God *because the measure of his creation is to become like God*, who is an exalted man.

342

Before Adam

Anything manlike that lived prior to Adam is less than man—and does not have the potential to become like God, who is an exalted man. The monkey, only a few chromosomes different from man, is still not a man. A cave dweller, genetically closer to man than monkey, is still not the offspring of God with the potential to become like God. Every being that is less than man is animal and cannot act upon their environment, but must react to, or be acted upon by that environment. For man it is possible to travel, live in space, walk on the moon, live under the oceans or on the ice caps of the poles, creating a habitation in a less hospitable environment. Anything less than man is not capable of living in an environment which is not suited to the requirements of its body. The penguin would die in the desert, just as the lizard would quickly freeze in Antarctica. Mankind alone has the capability at act upon his environment and make it habitable.

The cave dweller, with his intelligence of spirit, could react to his environment in limited ways: the creation and use of a few tools, living in caves or forming crude shelters, making coverings from animal skins, etc. However, as all anthropologists will explain, this lasted throughout their time and tenure on earth (about 40,000 years). There was no change, no progression, no language, and the new theory now is—no evolution. The explosion of language, metallurgy, recorded history, farming and more, began with the first man Adam and his posterity, for whom the earth was prepared.

> 34 And *the first man of all men have I called Adam*, which is many. (Moses 1:34)

> 3 ...even the right of the firstborn, or *the first man, who is Adam, or first father*, through the fathers unto me. (Abraham 1:3)

> 16 And from Enoch to Abel...who received the priesthood by the commandments of God, by the hand of his father *Adam, who was the first man*— (D&C 84:16)

The cave dweller, without language or civilized abilities, nevertheless required a physical body that allowed his spirit (similar to man's) to reach its full potential. Because their spirits exist and have always existed, they, like any other form of animal, needed a time and place to receive a physical body in which they could fulfill the measure of their creation and reach their full potential, whatever that might be, based on the intelligence of their spirit.

One key difference between man and beast is the human ability to *act in futurity*, as explained by the Lord in the Doctrine and Covenants.

> 78 That every man may act in doctrine and principle pertaining to futurity, according to the moral agency which I have given unto him, that every man may be accountable for his own sins in the day of judgment. (D&C 101:78)

This states that all men (who have the potential to become like God as descendants of Adam) have the ability to 'act pertaining to futurity' with a 'moral agency' that would make them accountable for their sins. This is speaking of an ability and necessary freedom required for mankind, and not the animal kingdom, which cannot act in futurity. Only mankind is capable of making a decision in life with no expectation of return on earth, only in futurity (at some point after death). All animal life reacts to its environment, while mankind can act upon life's experience, making decisions that have eternal consequences. None but man is capable of comprehending the concept of a God. Who but man can 'conceive' of a God that cannot be seen by the natural eyes, but is known in the heart, mind, and spirit as a consequence of relationship to Him? Who but man is able to recognize spiritual impressions and make moral choices by agency and not by instinct? Who but man has the ability and potential to repent and forgive, to change their character, while making decisions that will render consequences after death?

Adam was the first being created in the image of God, that has the potential to become like God. He was created to have seed—to procreate physical bodies that can house the spirits that have prepared themselves to progress toward exaltation—spirits that are possessed of the spiritual intelligence to understand the plan of salvation and the sacrifice of Jesus Christ. By exercising faith unto repentance (which no animal can do), coupled with the grace and mercy of God, they are provided with the potential of an endowment of 'power to become the sons of God' (John 1:12).

As Elder Talmage explained, when Adam was placed on the earth it was perfectly prepared for him. All that he or his posterity would ever need or use was already there on the earth. All the fossil fuels, coal, oil, and gas were already in place, prepared for the time man would need them, when the first parents were placed in the Garden of Eden.

Remember, Abraham records that they, the Gods, ordered these things to be, and then *watched until they saw that they would be obeyed.* This preparatory period could take as long as was necessary, perhaps millions and millions of years. During this period, preparing for the appearance of man, the spirits and bodies of the creatures that could not co-exist with man, like the dinosaurs and, later, cave dwellers, could come and live in their turn and their time, fulfilling the measure of their creation and reaching their potential. These beings could, as Talmage explains, "live and die age after age while the earth was yet unfit for mankind."

Once on the earth, Adam is "blessed" (Moses 2:28; Abraham 4:28) with the potential to multiply and fill the earth; blessed with the capacity to "subdue the earth" in order to carve out an inheritance for his family. He was also given the spiritual intellect to bless others through priesthood authority, having "dominion over every living thing" upon the earth. These potential blessings given to Adam in the beginning are the same blessings given to man by God as we receive the 'blessings of the fathers' or 'covenants of the fathers.' These consist of 'priesthood, posterity, and inheritance' in an endowment of eternal duration.

A Brief Look at Evolution

The evolutionary theory of the biological world in which man exists is just theory—and that particular theory does not seem to have scriptural support. As time progresses, it has less scientific support, too. There are many who have decided that God could accomplish His designs by way of evolution, or perhaps via a combination of creation and evolution. The argument between those who believe in evolution and those who hold fast to the scriptural account of creation will go on forever. So much of what we believe and accept is determined by who we place in authority over us, i.e. our 'sources.' Only the individual can give the authority over their beliefs to a prophet or scripture. The same is true for those who place their 'faith' in a biology professor or their own education (arm of the flesh). The authority the individual accepts (chooses) becomes the foundation for their standard of truth, no matter if it is right or wrong, and is reflected in their opinions and beliefs. The Doctrine and Covenants declare that we should "seek learning by study and also by faith" (D&C 88:118), which seems to suggest a combination of education and faith in God and his words found in scripture.

The non-evolutionary premise presented here may cause some to stop reading at this point, but the author has chosen the scriptures as his authority and standard of truth; therefore they are used as the measuring rod for truth in his research and conclusions. The scriptures rise as the bedrock, or primordial mound, from the waters of creation as a standard in doctrine and truth. Many church leaders have spoken about the scriptures and the power and place that they should take in the lives of each member in determining truth

Many who accept the theory of evolution find no incongruities or conflicts between the basic concepts and principles of evolution and scripture. When conflicts arise, the intellectual will often determine the theory of evolution to be more correct and of far more value than the 'antiquated scriptures.' Their assumption is that modern man is more qualified to determine man's relationship with his environment than the simple-minded prophets and patriarchs of old that claim to have spoken with God about the creation. History, especially recent history, should remind the best and brightest of scientists and intellectuals that trusting in the educational arm of flesh for 'non-compromised truths' is a precarious business. While science has made some great strides in explaining our world, scientific conclusions, in general, cannot be trusted for more than six months before a new theory is advanced that promises to 'end all debate.' On the other hand, scriptures are true whether one agrees with them or not. As Joseph Smith stated "one's opinion will not make the truth without effect."[49]

Evolution theory demands that over time, more complex genetic mutations must develop for evolution to exist. This theory readily accepts that the animal kingdom evolved because of these mutations, but at the same time does not recognize the same process within the plant kingdom, as the mushroom should, over time, turn into the mighty redwood and Sequoia forest. Evolution is founded upon the 'law of uniformitarianism.' This law states that things that evolve always evolve at the same rate, and that this time rate must remain constant to allow for the evolution to take place. Another basic premise is that there must be a need for the evolution of the parts for the creature to survive. In other words, for an eye to evolve, the creature will need an eye to see food to survive or for protection. Following this premise, during the time required for this need to evolve (which could be eyes, ears, olfactory development, teeth, limbs, etc.), the creature would have starved to death or been eaten. Another consideration often left out of the argument about evolution is that of catastrophes that could effect and nullify the law of uniformitarianism.[50] Be it evolution or catastrophes, it is the genetic seed that would have to effect (or cause) a change in offspring. That is, the creature would have to produce offspring carrying a new genetic code for the changes (new eyes, limbs, tails, etc) to take place

Once science grasps a theory, there is often no letting go— professional reputations and livelihoods are often built and staked on a

---

49. *TPJS*, 1976, p.352.

50. *Catastrophes and Evolution: Astronomical Foundations*, ed. S.V.M. Clube, Papers presented at the meeting of the 'Royal Astronomical Society at Oxford'; Cambridge University Press, Cambridge, 1989.

particular premise. There is scientific 'fact,' scientific theory, and scientific ego that must be overcome. This creates a 'black hole' where everything in a given discipline is governed only by accepted theories. This black hole often allows for no other ideas to be entertained, which in turn consumes any light and truth that might be made available by other discoveries and insights, even when the new idea might be more correct. The Darwinian black hole has consumed almost all biological sciences, and after a century, the idea of "Intelligent Design" is just now gaining ground.

In every account of the creation that is used in the church, reproduction in the animal or plant kingdom is explained as being *after* "their kind" or with "*seed in itself.*" This is done with such repeated emphasis that it would seem that the scriptures are addressing a modern need for clarity and understanding.

Abraham 4:11-12	Moses 2:11-12
11 And the Gods said: Let us prepare the earth to bring forth grass; the herb *yielding seed*; the fruit tree *yielding fruit, after his kind, whose seed in itself yieldeth its own likeness* upon the earth; and it was so, even as they ordered. 12 And the Gods organized the earth to bring forth grass *from its own seed, and the herb to bring forth herb from its own seed, yielding seed after his kind*; and the earth to bring forth *the tree from its own seed, yielding fruit, whose seed could only bring forth the same in itself, after his kind*; and the Gods saw that they were obeyed.	11 And I, God, said: Let the earth bring forth grass, the herb yielding seed, the fruit tree yielding fruit, *after his kind*, and the tree yielding fruit, *whose seed should be in itself* upon the earth, and it was so even as I spake. 12 And the earth brought forth grass, every herb *yielding seed after his kind, and the tree yielding fruit, whose seed should be in itself, after his kind*; and I, God, saw that all things which I had made were good;

In the Book of Abraham, the Lord makes sure in verse 12 and verse 25 that it is understood that the "*seed could only bring forth the same in itself, after his kind.*" The animal kingdom reproduced after "*their kind*" the same as the plant life. The plant life had seed in itself which "*yieldeth its own likeness* upon the earth" which produced "after his kind, ... whose *seed should be in itself,* after his kind."

Abraham 4:21-22, 24-25	Moses 2:21, 24-25
21 And the Gods prepared the waters that they might bring forth great whales, and every living creature that moveth, which the waters were to bring forth abundantly *after their kind*; and every winged fowl *after their kind*. And the Gods saw that they would be obeyed, and that their plan was good. 22 And the Gods said: *We will bless them, and cause them to be fruitful and multiply*, and fill the waters in the seas or great waters; and cause the fowl to multiply in the earth. 24 And the Gods prepared the earth to bring forth the living creature *after his kind,* cattle and creeping things, and beasts of the *earth after their kind;* and it was so, as they had said. 25 And the Gods organized the earth to bring forth the beasts *after their kind, and cattle after their kind, and every thing that creepeth upon the earth after its kind*; and the Gods saw they would obey.	21 And I, God, created great whales, and every living creature that moveth, which the waters brought forth abundantly, *after their kind*, and every winged fowl *after his kind*; and I, God, saw that all things which I had created were good. 24 And I, God, said: Let the earth bring forth the living creature *after his kind*, cattle, and creeping things, and beasts of the earth *after their kind,* and it was so; 25 And I, God, made the beasts of the earth *after their kind*, and cattle *after their kind*, and everything which creepeth upon the earth *after his kind;* and I, God, saw that all these things were good.

In both accounts, following the introduction of plant and animal life, man (that being who has the potential to become like God) is introduced. Man is created in their "own image" and in the "image of the Gods" and is created from the elements of the sphere where he must be governed by natural law, even the dust of the earth. As mentioned above, the Doctrine and Covenants states that the spirit and body are alike in image: *"that which is spiritual being in the likeness of that which is temporal;* and that which is temporal in the likeness of that which is spiritual; *the spirit of man in the likeness of his person, as also the spirit of the beast, and every other creature which God has created."* (D&C 77:2)

According to this passage, if the body of the beast is evolutionary then the spirit must be also. This is counter to what we are taught in D&C 93:30, that every spirit has an *intelligence* that must have the freedom "to act for itself, and the physical body must be created such to allow the individual spirit to fulfill the measure of its creation and reach its full potential.

One key deterrent to the theory of evolution is called a "law" because *it has never been seen to be otherwise in our observable universe.* Science has determined that "entropy" should be considered a "law" and not "theory". The Law of Entropy states that everything left unto itself will digress, devolve, dissolve and decompose; moving from a state of order to disorder, and will continue to do so without the infusion of outside energy. So to move from a single cell to a multiple-celled entity of a higher form will take an energy outside of and independent of itself. To move from a less complex life-form to a more complex life-form is, according to the law of entropy, impossible. The basic law of entropy and the newer view of *"maximum entropy"* is explained in simple terms using the loss of heat:

> Swenson & Turvey provided the example of a warm mountain cabin in a cold snow-covered woods with the fire that provided the heat having burned out. Under these circumstances there is a temperature gradient between the warm cabin and cold woods. The second law tells us that over time the gradient or potential will be dissipated through

walls or cracks around the windows and door until the cabin is as cold as the outside and the system is in equilibrium. We know empirically though that if we open a window or a door, a portion of the heat will now rush out the door or window and not just through the walls or cracks. In short, whenever we remove a constraint to the flow (such as a closed window) the cabin/environment system will exploit the new and faster pathway thereby increasing the rate the potential is minimized. Wherever it has the opportunity to minimize or 'destroy' the gradient of the potential (maximize the entropy) at a faster rate, it will – exactly as the Law of Maximum Entropy Production says. Namely, it will "select the pathway or assembly of pathways that minimizes the potential or maximizes the entropy at the fastest rate given the constraints." Once this principle is grasped, examples are easy to recognize and show in everyday life.[51]

It is worth remembering that God is capable of doing whatever he wants to do. He may, if he so chooses, provide or infuse any amount of energy necessary to accomplish his work. Abraham explains that the Gods: "prepared the earth" to bring forth the living creature" and "organized the earth" to do the same, and then "watched those things which they had ordered until they obeyed" (Abraham 4:18-25) implying that if it didn't work they might have done something else. As can be seen, these verses could be used to argue for or against evolution; however, the verses in Moses and Abraham (quoted above), state that the biological creations—plants and creatures—had 'seed in themselves to produce *only* after their kind.' And the Gods "*watched* ... until they were obeyed."

These few pages are not meant to initiate an argument for or against physical evolution. The main purpose here is to explore the origin of the spirit that animates the physical body, and in particular, the human body. Physical bodies animated by the spirit must be created from the

51. http://www.lawofmaximumentropyproduction.com/ See also: 6. Swenson, R. and Turvey, M.T. (1991). "Thermodynamic reasons for perception-action cycles. Ecological Psychology", 3(4), 317-348. Translated and reprinted in *Perspectives on Affordances*, in M. Sasaki (ed.). Tokyo: University of Tokyo Press, 1998 (in Japanese).

dust or from the natural elements of the 'sphere' in which they are placed in order to be governed by the laws of nature. Hence, Adam should be created from the "dust of the earth" on which he will dwell, to be governed by the laws that govern the elements of which his physical body is comprised. This places all mankind descending from Adam and Eve into a physical relationship we call a genetic 'family tree,' consisting of fathers, mothers, sons, and daughters.

The Prophet Joseph Smith, in the "Inspired Version" of the Bible (the familiar "Joseph Smith Translation") (JST) changed the King James Version to emphasize the physical body of Adam and its relationship to the elements of the earth on which he will live. The genealogies found in chapter three of Luke's gospel shows this change when compared with the JST.

King James Luke 3:38	Joseph Smith Translation Luke 3:38
38 Which was the son of Enos, which was the son of Seth, which was the son of Adam, which was the son of God.	38 And of Enos, and of Seth, and of Adam, who was formed of God, and the first man upon the earth.

This creation of the "first man upon the earth", formed from the "dust of the earth", is a phrase and doctrinal concept used throughout the scriptures and is found in all the standard works. In the verses listed below, it can be seen that the text is *not* using similes or metaphors or words such as "like" or "as" to imply a symbolic meaning. Each statement is definite in the context of the scripture and therefore definite in the meaning and understanding.

If a statement is to be taken in a symbolic or metaphorical sense, then to whom should one look to explain the metaphor? If the symbols were not *at the very least* founded on an historical event, there could be no wrong interpretation, and probably no right interpretation either of the sure and real meaning of the symbol. If the 'creation of man from the dust' is just metaphor, then the scriptures are either not entirely true or God is trying to keep information from all but the learned (the ministers of metaphor and symbol). If the creation of Adam from the dust (elements) of the earth (as all scripture claims) is not true, then where will the guesswork end? We would have to ask: what else is there in scripture that we should not believe? If 'God cannot and did not create Adam from the elements of the earth as one might make an adobe brick,' as some have said, then the notion of a resurrection from the dust of the earth ("for dust thou art, and unto dust shalt thou return") becomes a real concern for the believer.

Old Testament

Genesis 2:7, And the Lord God *formed man of the dust of the ground*, and breathed into his nostrils the breath of life; and man became a living soul.

Genesis 3:19, In the sweat of thy face shalt thou eat bread, till thou return unto the ground; for out of it wast thou taken: for dust thou art, and unto dust shalt thou return.

Job 10:9, Remember, I beseech thee, that thou hast made me as the clay; and wilt thou *bring me into dust again*?

Job 34:15, All flesh shall perish together, and *man shall turn again unto dust*.

Psalm 103:14, For he knoweth our frame; he remembereth that *we are dust*.

Ecclesiastes 3:20, All go unto one place; all are of the dust, and all turn to dust again.

Ecclesiastes 12:7, Then shall *the dust return to the earth as it was*: and the spirit shall return unto God who gave it.

New Testament

1 Timothy 2:13, For Adam was first formed, then Eve.

Book of Mormon

Jacob 2:21, Do ye not suppose that such things are abominable unto him who created all flesh? And the one being is as precious in his sight as the other. And *all flesh is of the dust*; and for the selfsame end hath he created them, that they should keep his commandments and glorify him forever.

Mosiah 2:25, And now I ask, can ye say aught of yourselves? I answer you, Nay. Ye cannot say that ye are even as much as the dust of the earth; yet *ye were created of the dust of the earth*; but behold, it belongeth to him who created you.

Mosiah 2:26, And I, even I, whom ye call your king, am no better than ye yourselves are; for I am also of the dust. And ye behold that I am old, and am about to yield up this mortal frame to its mother earth.

Mormon 9:17, Who shall say that it was not a miracle that by his word the heaven and the earth should be; and *by the power of his word man was created of the dust of the earth*; and by the power of his word have miracles been wrought?

Doctrine and Covenants

D&C 77:12, Q. What are we to understand by the sounding of the trumpets, mentioned in the 8th chapter of Revelation?A. We are to understand that as God made the world in six days, and on the seventh day he finished his work, and sanctified it, *and also formed man out of the dust of the earth*, even so, in the beginning of the seventh thousand years will the Lord God sanctify the earth, and complete the salvation of man. . .

D&C 138:17, *Their sleeping dust was to be restored unto its perfect frame*, bone to his bone, and the sinews and the flesh upon them, the spirit and he body to be united never again to be divided, that they might receive a fullness of joy.

Pearl of Great Price

Moses 3:7, And I, *the Lord God, formed man from the dust of the ground,* and breathed into his nostrils the breath of life; and man became a living soul, the first flesh upon the earth, the first man also; nevertheless, all things were before created; but spiritually were they created and made according to my word.

Moses 4:25, By the sweat of thy face shalt thou eat bread, *until thou shalt return unto the ground*—for thou shalt surely die—*for out of it wast thou taken: for dust thou wast, and unto dust shalt thou return.*

Moses 6:59, That by reason of transgression cometh the fall, which fall bringeth death, and inasmuch as ye were born into the world by water, and blood, and the spirit, which I have made, and *so became of dust a living soul,* even so ye must be born again into the kingdom of heaven, of water, and of the Spirit, and be cleansed by blood, even the blood of mine Only Begotten; that ye might be sanctified from all sin, and enjoy the words of eternal life in this world, and eternal life in the world to come, even immortal glory;

Abraham 5:7, And the Gods formed man from the dust of the ground, and took his spirit (that is, the man's spirit), and put it into him; and breathed into his nostrils the breath of life, and man became a living soul.

Without exception, these verses and all others teach that God not only created the physical bodies, but that they were created out of the dust of the earth or sphere upon which they will live. Should we as Latter-day Saints let the scriptures speak for themselves or try to correct the word and work of God found in the scriptures.

In order to be governed by the laws of nature in a temporal state—in particular the law of entropy—the physical body must be formed from the elements of the 'sphere in which God has placed it.' The elements (dust) of the earth from which mankind is created are eternal, and therefore, by ordinance and power (contrary to entropy), the bodies of all mankind shall eventually be resurrected and inseparably connected to the spirit. "For man is spirit. The elements are eternal, and spirit and element, inseparably connected, receive a fullness of joy; And when separated, man cannot receive a fullness of joy" (D&C 93:33-34).

One dimension that is required for entropy to exist is that of "time." Without time, nothing could move from a state of order to disorder; therefore, they would remain in the "state in which they were after they were created" forever (2 Nephi 2:22). That strongly suggests that it's the absence of 'time' that distinguishes the immortal environment, as was the case with Adam before the fall: "for as yet the Gods had not appointed unto Adam his reckoning of time" (Abraham 5:13).

Chapter 24

Plural Marriage

A person can only be held accountable for sins (if that term might be used) in the time in which they live, as all would hope to become free and clean from the sins of their generation. None can be held accountable for things that might have been considered sins in the previous generations of Abraham, Moses *or even Joseph Smith's day*. Likewise, the ancients could not be accountable for sins that did not exist in their day but may exist today. If this were not so, then most would stand condemned for not living the Law of Moses, and be held bound by the dietary laws, sacrificing those succulent dishes of "crab and lobster." Men would also be justified in carrying out blood feuds living the law of "an eye for an eye and a tooth for a tooth." Consequently, the individual may ONLY be held accountable for the *laws and commandments* given by God in the day in which one lives. Thus, the primary need for modern revelation and living prophets through all generations and dispensations of the gospel, are to declare the sins of *their* generation to the people of the Church of Jesus Christ that live during the prophet's tenure (Ezekiel 3:17-21).

In the church there are 'doctrines' and there are 'church policies.' The doctrines of salvation and exaltation will not change; however, the policies that govern the teaching and administering of the doctrines and ordinances may change based upon the social, environmental, and cultural needs—and sometimes the spiritual tendencies of the members of the church which may have a power and consequence to close the heavens. The Lord may desire that young men serve a mission, but whether they serve two years or eighteen months is a matter of policy. Latter-day Saints are commanded to meet together often to partake of the sacrament with a request to attend Sunday School, Priesthood, and Relief Society meetings. This could be split-up during the day or week, or it could be accomplished in a three-hour block. The commandment or doctrine is kept but the policy of administration may change in every generation based on the needs of a particular time or place.

There are, however, certain commandments, and ordinances that are required in every dispensation. In the order of battle, there are 'general orders' and 'specific orders.' General orders would include common commandments viable in every dispensation, such as the Ten Commandments. Specific orders may be for a single dispensation or given time during a single dispensation of the gospel. For instance, the "gospel" (i.e. Faith, Repentance, Baptism, and the reception of the Holy Ghost), must take place in the life of every individual for salvation. There are also moral commandments connected to the ordinances of salvation and exaltation that seem to prevail in all time periods, such as the charge to care for each other, with scriptural and God-given prohibitions against adultery, fornication and homosexuality, to name a few.

One important "doctrine of exaltation" is that of "eternal marriage." This *doctrine* is found in section 131:1-3 of the Doctrine and Covenants. It states:

> In the celestial glory there are three heavens or degrees; And in order to obtain the highest, (the highest is only for those to be exalted) a man (or a woman) must enter into this order of the priesthood [meaning the new and everlasting covenant of marriage]; And if he does not, he cannot obtain it.

This passage, as well as the following section, states that an *ordinance* of "sealing" between a male and a female must take place preparatory to exaltation. Thus, a man cannot become exalted without a perfect woman at his side. Likewise, a woman cannot be exalted without a celestial man at her side. That means, as we understand it, that

Godhood or exaltation in the highest degree must consist of two people, a "sealed couple".

The Doctrine and Covenants teach that the purpose of the creation and the earth itself is securely connected to the doctrine of marriage and the children of that necessary union.

> 15 And again, verily I say unto you, that whoso forbiddeth to marry is not ordained of God, for *marriage is ordained of God unto man.*
> 16 Wherefore, it is lawful that **he should have one wife**, and they twain shall be one flesh, and *all this that the earth might answer the end of its creation*;
> 17 And *that it might be filled with the measure of man*, according to his creation before the world was made.
> (D&C 49:15-17.)

The purpose of the creation, then, is for a man to have "*one wife*" so that the earth might be filled with the measure of men that were prepared to come to this earth as spirits before the earth was even created. (This scripture, doctrine, and concept also holds the answer to the Church's position on same sex relationships, covered in chapter 26.)

In a lengthy discussion, the Apostle Erastus Snow described the idea of deity and the exaltation of the male and female in the light of scripture and modern revelation:

> "And God said, let us make man in our own image, after our likeness, and let them have dominion over the fish of the sea, and over the fowl of the air, and over the cattle, and over all the earth, and over every creeping thing that creepeth upon the earth.

> "So God created man in his own image, in the image of God created he him; male and female created he them. And God blessed them, and God said unto them, be ye fruitful and multiply and replenish the earth, and subdue it, and have dominion over the fish of the sea, and over the fowl of the

air, and over every living thing that moveth upon the earth." (Genesis 3:26-28)

We also read, "This is the book of the generations of Adam: In the day that God created man, in the likeness of God made he him, male and female created he them, and blessed them and called their name Adam in the day when they were created."

The being we call man, in the original language of the scriptures written by Moses, was called Adam, "male and female created he them, and called their name Adam." There was no effort at distinguishing between calling one man and the other woman. This was an after-distinction, but initially he called their name Adam. He created them male and female, for they were one. He said not unto the woman multiply, and to the man multiply, but he said unto them both, multiply and reproduce your species, and replenish the earth.

He speaks unto them as belonging together, as constituting one being, and as organized in his image and after his likeness. The apostle Paul, treating upon this subject in the same way, says that man was created in the likeness of God, and after the express image of his person. John, the apostle, in writing the history of Jesus, speaks in the same way; that Jesus was in the likeness of his Father, and the express image of his person.

If the revelations that God has made of himself to man agree and harmonize upon this theory, and if mankind would be more believing and accept the simple, plain, clear definition of Deity and description of himself which he has given us instead of hunting for some great mystery and seeking to find out God where he is not and as he is not, we all might understand him. There is no great mystery about it. No more mystery about it than there is about ourselves and our own relationship to our father and mother and the relationship of our own children to us. That which we see before our eyes, and which we are experiencing from time to time, day to day, and year to year, is an exemplification of Deity.

"What?" says one, "Do you mean we should understand that deity consists of man and woman?" Most certainly I do. If I believe anything that God has ever said about himself, and anything pertaining to the creation and organization of man upon the earth, I must believe that Deity consists of man and woman. Now this is simplifying it down to our understanding. The great Christian world will be ready to open their mouths and cry, "Blasphemy! Sacrilege!" They will open wide their eyes and wide their mouths in the utmost astonishment. "What! God is a man and woman?"

Then these Christians – who say he has no form, neither body, parts nor passions – will object. One party may say he is a man, and the other may say he is a woman. I say he is both. How do I know? I only repeat what he says of himself; that he created man in the image of God, male and female created he them, and he called their name Adam, which signifies in Hebrew, the first man. So that the beings we call Adam and Eve were the first man placed here on this earth, and their name was Adam, and they were the express image of God.

Now, if anybody is disposed to say that the woman is in the likeness of God and that the man was not, or vice versa, I say you are both wrong, or else God has not told us the truth. I sometimes illustrate this matter by taking up a pair of shears or scissors, if I have a pair, but then you all know they are composed of two halves. They are necessarily parted, one from and they joined to another to perform their work for each other, as designed. They belong together and neither one of them is fitted for the accomplishment of their works alone. And for this reason says St. Paul, "the man is not without the woman, nor the woman without the man in the Lord." In other words, there can be no God except he is composed of the man and woman united, and there is not, in all the eternities that exist, nor ever will be, a God in any other way. I have another description: There never was a God, and there never will be in all eternities, except they are made of these two component parts: a man and a woman; the male and the female. (Erastus Snow, March 3, 1878, *JD* Vol 19, pp. 267-272.)

Elder Snow explains that God is two people, not a single man, nor a married man, but a man and woman sealed together by the power and authority of God in an ordinance of exaltation. The rules of Hebrew grammar require the noun to agree in number, gender, and definiteness, except for the word "God." The word "Elohim" is a plural word used in a singular context. Indeed, the Prophet Joseph said that "Elohim" should be translated in the plural throughout the Bible (*TPJS*, p.372).

The scriptures explain the creation of man and woman in these words: "Let us make man in our image, after our likeness... and I, God, created man in mine own image... male and female created I them." The creation of Adam and Eve was patterned after God, in the image and likeness of the perfect and exalted husband and wife, male and female.

It would be foolish to think of an exalted male God going off to 'creative priesthood meeting' in order to learn how to judge, create and destroy worlds, while the female Goddess joins a society to learn how to crochet eternal doilies or fix celestial meals or keep the heavenly home a perfect place for her omnipotent, omniscient and omnipresent spouse. Foolish thoughts like these are surely blasphemous to the doctrine of exaltation. God is two people; the sealed couple become God, as Elder Snow explained above.

The Equality of Male and Female

Chapter two of the Book of Moses, records the creation of Adam and Eve and how they were made in God's "image" and "likeness." Created like God in looks and in substance, they were formed, God said, "in mine own image...male and female created I them" (Moses 2:26-27). Before proceeding further, a few points about the creation so far as the man and woman are concerned should be reviewed. The Hebrew word for our English translation 'help meet' comes from '*kenegdo*', meaning a 'helper meet for him.' The root '*neged*' means to be 'in front of' or 'counterpart' and connected with the preposition as it stands in scripture '*ke-negdo*' means '***corresponding to him, equal to, and adequate to himself.***' In short, it is to be worthy of each other and be a "helper meet," one who will 'match' and not to be unequal (in a greater or lesser degree) to the spouse. This "help mate" is understood to be equal, a "mate" the same as one might mate socks. Equal in size, wear, and color, a mate in all aspects of creation, potential, and blessing. Before the fall, (and this must be kept in mind) this verse *establishes an anthropology of equality and "grounds a relationship of mutuality between the sexes."*

Polygamy

In scripture, one requirement for exaltation is the 'sealing ordinance' of one man to one woman. Nowhere in scripture does it state that 'polygamy' is a necessary requirement for exaltation. This discussion will likely be contrary to many of the traditional teachings that Latter-day Saints are familiar with. This article is not meant to correct the church or any doctrine espoused by its members or leaders, but instead present a point of view that is based on the scriptures rather than commentary.

The scriptures give only two reasons for polygamous marriages and relationships. The first is found in the Book of Jacob. The Nephites were desirous to have more than one wife like many of the peoples and cultures in the ancient near east. Because of the brass plates, the Nephites knew that not only the patriarchs of Genesis but also the kings of Israel had multiple wives and concubines. In the passage below, Jacob addresses the general orders and law of all dispensations, yet explains that there are times that this law may be adjusted by policy for temporal needs.

> **23** But the word of God burdens me because of your grosser crimes. For behold, thus saith the Lord: This people begin to wax in iniquity; they understand not the scriptures, for they seek to excuse themselves in committing whoredoms,

because of the things which were written concerning David, and Solomon his son.

24 Behold, David and Solomon truly had many wives and concubines, which thing was abominable before me, saith the Lord.

25 Wherefore, thus saith the Lord, I have led this people forth out of the land of Jerusalem, by the power of mine arm, that I might raise up unto me a righteous branch from the fruit of the loins of Joseph.

26 Wherefore, I the Lord God will not suffer that this people shall do like unto them of old.

27 Wherefore, my brethren, *hear me, and hearken to the word of the Lord*: For *there shall not any man among you have save it be one wife;* and concubines he shall have none;

28 For *I, the Lord God, delight in the chastity of women.* And whoredoms are an abomination before me; thus saith the Lord of Hosts.

29 Wherefore, this people shall keep my commandments, saith the Lord of Hosts, or cursed be the land for their sakes.

30 For *if I will, saith the Lord of Hosts, raise up seed unto me, I will command my people;* **otherwise they shall hearken unto these things**.

31 For behold, I, the Lord, have seen the sorrow, and heard the mourning of the daughters of my people in the land of Jerusalem, yea, and in all the lands of my people, because of the wickedness and abominations of their husbands. (Jacob 2:23-31)

Verse 26 states: *"Wherefore, I the Lord God will not suffer that this people shall do like unto them of old."* The Lord, through his prophet, told this generation that they were not to live the law of polygamy, and that He (the Lord) delights in the "chastity of women." But he continues, (in verse 30) *"For if I will, saith the Lord of Hosts, raise up seed unto me, I will command my people; otherwise they shall hearken unto these things."* Here the Lord states that "if" He decides or determines that it is necessary to live the law of polygamy to raise up a righteous seed on earth, He will command it for that time period. Otherwise all are to live the monogamous doctrine and law.

In 1832 the Prophet Joseph speaking to Levi Hancock told him: "Brother Levi, the Lord has revealed to me that it is his will that righteous men shall take righteous women even a plurality of wives that a righteous race may be sent forth upon the earth preparatory to the ushering in of the Millennial Reign of our Redeemer." (Levi Hancock Diary). Notice that Joseph Smith explains that the plurality of wives was for this temporal life and time "preparatory" to the coming of Christ. Not many years ago if someone asked in a Sacrament meeting (in the Mormon axis of Idaho, Utah, and Arizona) for a raise of hands of those who descended from polygamist families, almost 80% would raise their hands. What would be the membership of the church today if that righteous seed and not been raised up during the early days of the Church?

In this dispensation, in Section 132:63 of the Doctrine and Covenants, the Lord reaffirms the use of polygamy for raising up a righteous posterity and adds a second reason:

> ...for they (multiple wives) are given unto him to *multiply and replenish the earth (raise up seed unto me)* according to my commandment, and to fulfil the promise which was given by my Father before the foundation of the world, and for **their exaltation in the eternal worlds,** *that they may bear the souls of men;* for herein is the work of my Father continued, that he may be glorified. *(D&C 132:63)*

This verse, like the one in Jacob, indicates that the law of polygamy could be instituted to raise a righteous people unto the Lord, and also for the woman's "exaltation in the eternal worlds." This second reason is for ordinance only. This is true because no person, male or female, can be exalted without the ordinance of eternal marriage (D&C 131). Polygamy was a dispensational policy and therefore could be changed according to the needs of the church.

There will be a time when men are few and the ordinance of exaltation might only be available to righteous women in this manner. This does not mean in any way that the numerous women sealed to a particular man will be his wives in the hereafter. A righteous woman who has had the opportunity to receive the ordinance of eternal marriage, and is worthy of celestial glory, will be sealed "by the holy spirit of promise" to a man worthy of her. They together, the two, will become God. Statistics indicate that many more male children die before the age of eight than female children. We know that those who die before the age of eight are immediately taken into the presence of God. In order for that person to receive his or her exaltation, they must participate in a sealing. It will be an easy task for the perfect man to love a perfect woman with perfect love and vise-a-versa. The important thing to keep in mind is that exaltation is being sealed to someone who is worthy of the same glory. Women sealed in the earthly ordinance to a man have participated in the ordinance and are now prepared, if found worthy, to be sealed by the Holy Spirit of Promise to an eternal mate and companion into the "image of God." This ratification by the Holy Spirit of Promise must follow the earthly ordinance of temple marriage when we have been found true and faithful in all things. Thus Adam and the Lord may declare that "a man must leave his father and mother and be sealed (by the Holy Spirit of Promise) to his wife (singular)."

In a personal letter sent to a missionary, a loving parent taught that President Woodruff stated that he had 'been sealed to 700 good women,' not with a view of claiming them as his wives, but to 'afford them the chance of spiritual advancement thru the sealing ordinance, that was necessary for them.' President Woodruff then referred to the millions of unmarried soldiers slain in the battles of the world from earliest times, stating that they would have their temple work done by their descendants and 'then be eligible to choose a wife from among those for whom the sealing ordinance had been performed' (as in the case of the 700 women sealed to him). President Woodruff made it clear that he did not 'expect to claim them as his wives in the hereafter,' but that they would be elevated to a place where 'they would meet and choose their own worthy celestial mate.'

Many have been taught that polygamy is a requirement for exaltation, believing that all in the celestial kingdom must be willing to live in polygamous and eternal relationships, however this is not necessarily a doctrine according to scripture and the statements of Joseph Smith. So the question must be asked: How did this notion get entrenched in Mormon tradition?

After the westward movement of the saints, polygamist unions were outlawed for those living in the governed territories of the United States. As there were many saints living in Canada and Mexico who were still living in polygamist marriages, there was a code word that was used when the leaders wanted to speak to those still living a polygamist lifestyle. This code word was "celestial marriage." During conference, when a leader would say something similar to: "I would like to talk about celestial marriage," it would be the code phrase indicating that they were about to address those who were still living in polygamy outside the United States. After a generation, polygamy and 'celestial marriage' became synonymous, and it was just a matter of time before this idea took on the weight of doctrine.

If polygamy were necessary for exaltation, then only a few people throughout time would be exalted. Polygamy, in scripture, becomes necessary only "to raise up seed unto the Lord" and to provide the ordinances necessary for exaltation in the next life.

This law is difficult to understand fully without keeping in mind that God is two people: the "twain" become sealed, or "cleave" unto a spouse—a sealed husband and wife—equal in all aspects, working for their own immortality and eternal life as well as that of their children. The word "help meet" which Eve was called, means "one equal to and worthy of in every respect." This concept would disallow more than one wife to one husband *in the exalted sphere* unless the woman is not and could never be equal to her husband, which is not so. As it is stated in scripture:

> Then shall *they* be gods, because *they* have no end; therefore shall *they* be from everlasting to everlasting, because *they* continue; then shall *they* be above all, because all things are subject unto *them*. Then shall *they* be gods, because *they* have all power, and the angels are subject unto *them*. (D&C 132:20)

The cultural Church has evolved through three doctrinal phases. Many instructors quote from the 23 volume *Journal of Discourses* when it comes to the purpose and doctrine of polygamy. In many ways this collective tome could be viewed as the "Journals of Research and Development." Following the death of Joseph Smith, many of the early brethren were trying to determine "why" particular things were taught and restored by the Prophet Joseph. In process of this, there was much conjecture and opinion presented by the leaders that wasn't necessarily congruent with scripture, but which represented their best answers to the questions. During this era of doctrinal discovery, many traditions, opinions, and interpretations became cemented as doctrines—rather than using scripture as the standard of doctrine. Hence, many beliefs were contradicted within the Journals in answering why polygamy exists, leading to multiple opinions that are still being taught—from one leader stating that multiple wives are needed to populate worlds without number, to another proclaiming that each world requires a separate wife, and so on.

After the turn of the century, the church moved into a 'do or die' phase as the doctrines from the research and development age became set in an acceptable concrete. Unlike the present, where they offer mostly 'entertaining fiction of men, mingled with scripture', forty years ago Deseret Book published nothing but doctrinal books about LDS beliefs, doctrines, and answers to difficult questions.

During this period, many missionaries were taught that if a door was slammed in their face, that person would never get another chance— and his entrance into the celestial kingdom was damned forever. The non-member, it was commonly believed, would have no chance in the next life: it was the LDS way or no way. Sins were categorized and numbered according to the level of wickedness and ability to receive forgiveness. The Lesser Law rose to the top like cream, as members were told what was good and what was evil. Many felt like they were told what movies to watch and what food and drink would be acceptable, rather than teaching the higher law as taught by Joseph Smith, which is: to teach correct principles but allow them to govern themselves. During this era, excommunications were rampant as bishops were counseled that if they didn't take care of the sins in their wards, they would suffer for, and be accountable for, those very sins. This second phase lasted from the opinions and writings of B.H. Roberts until the beginning of the presidency of Ezra T. Benson.

The third phase became one of 'loving and rescuing', accepting that individuals have weaknesses rather than trying to purge the church of any and every unclean thing, burning the wheat along with the tares in the process. For those living through that era, there was a noticeable move from the doctrinal hard line to one of perfecting the saints through love and acceptance and service, heralding a generational change during the lengthy tenure of President Hinckley.

In summary, the Lord sets the standard in scripture and through the prophet and president of the church during his time of responsibility. In this life, God may command and revoke according to His will and knowledge of all things (D&C 56:4). The eternal doctrine of exaltation requires the ordinance of sealing, but the policy and practice of polygamy may come and go as God sees fit for the benefit of his church and kingdom *on earth*. Polygamy is not an accepted practice for the Church of Jesus Christ of Latter-day Saints, and those who believe or practice so will not be able to maintain their membership. Time, place, and need all play a part in the policies of any organization and particularly in the Church of Jesus Christ, as its founders and leaders are inspired to do the work that the Lord requires, despite their personal weaknesses in body, mind, or spirit.

Chapter 25

Women and the Priesthood

One of the current issues and concerns of many who seek to change the church revolve around "Women and the Priesthood." Those who believe that it is time that women be ordained to the priesthood need first to understand the priesthood and address the answers to a few questions, such as: What is Priesthood? What is the purpose of the priesthood? Is there a "power" bestowed with the priesthood? What is the difference between power and authority? These issues will be addressed later in this chapter; however, a basic understanding of the priesthood should precede any discussion as to why the priesthood has been limited to male members.

This chapter will include a brief history of the priesthood, a discussion of the Patriarchal Priesthood and the Melchizedek Priesthood, with a brief mention of the Aaronic Priesthood and their corresponding "authorities" or responsibilities.

What is Priesthood? The stock response is "the power and authority to act in God's name." The priesthood organization (sometimes called "the church") is the organization that administers the gospel and makes available the ordinances to those who desire and are worthy to participate in the gospel of Jesus Christ.

The "Priesthood" itself: is an *authority* that is given, passed or transferred. The word "hood" implies '*a responsibility given and accepted*' often by covenant. A *"priest" is one who serves and ministers to man for and in-behalf of God.* The word *"hood"*, connected to that of *"priest"*, becomes *"Priest-hood"* which is the *"authority to serve and minister to mankind for and in-behalf of God."* Service is truly the activity arm of the priesthood.

Many view the priesthood as a miraculous God-like "power" that is invested or bestowed upon an individual that can move mountains and raise the dead. Man cannot actually hold the power that makes God, God, let alone view His works.

> 5 Wherefore, no man can behold all my works, except he behold all my glory; and no man can behold all my glory, and afterwards remain in the flesh on the earth. (Moses 1:5)

The power that belongs to God is inherent in God himself (D&C 121:36) but there is an authority ("rights of the priesthood") that are "connected to the powers of heaven," which "right" is to serve and bless others as an authorized ambassador of God. The authority that exists in the church must be provable by a certificate of ordination and worthiness through record keeping and the church organization. The Priesthood has no inherent "power" in and of itself, for *"no power* or influence __can__ or ought to be maintained by virtue of the priesthood" (D&C 121:41) or priesthood position.

Nowhere in scripture is the priesthood invoked as a power to initiate a miracle or healing. All miracles are done in the name of Jesus Christ and by faith. It is by faith that one is healed or may heal; it is power of faith that moves the mountain. The vocal mention of the authority of the priesthood holder in the administering of an ordinance is for the record keeping that is required of an ordination or blessing within the organization of the church and its community of saints (D&C 20:63-64). An individual that performs a gospel ordinance within the church must vocally recognize (state) their authority as part of the record keeping process, but the authoritative power behind that ordinance is faith and the name of Jesus Christ.

Abraham is told that the "rights of the priesthood" (D&C 121:36) is the "right" (authority) to administer the "rites" (ordinances) of the gospel. The priesthood is an adopted linage and an organization of administration. Abraham was so righteous that he wanted a posterity that could and would serve God by serving and blessing all of mankind.

> 11 And I will bless them that bless thee, and curse them that curse thee; and in thee (that is, in *thy Priesthood*) and in thy seed (that is, *thy Priesthood*), for I give unto thee a promise *that this right* shall continue in thee, and in thy seed after thee (that is to say, the literal seed, or the seed of the body) *shall all the families of the earth be blessed,* even with the blessings of the gospel, *which are the blessings of salvation, even of life eternal.* (Abraham 2:11)

There is no '*power*' in the priesthood (the 'Power of the priesthood' is the authority to administer) that performs the ordinance, nor any power in the ordinance itself. The real power of any ordinance lies in the character change initiated by the *power of hope.* A loving Father has made sure that no priesthood power is able to defy one's spiritual agency. For this reason, Satan was cast out of heaven (Moses 4:3). One could be baptized a million times or participate in any ordinance of the gospel multiple times over, yet these ordinances have no *power* over the individual receiving them if the person receiving the ordinance chooses not to change his character. The power behind any ordinance lies in the agency of the person who receives it. There is no ordinance that can 'repent' you, no ordinance that can 'faith' you, nor is there any ordinance that can perfect you or change your will into God's will. The ordinances exist for a "hope." Speaking of all Melchizedek Priesthood ordinances, Alma explains what the priesthood ordinances are for:

> 16 Now these ordinances were given after this manner, *that* thereby the people **might look forward** on the Son of God, it being a type of his order, or it being his order, and this *that* **they might look forward** to him for a remission of their sins, *that they might enter into the rest of the Lord.* (Alma 13:16)

The ordinances are a hope of a future reality **IF** the receiver chooses to change his character and begins to exercise faith unto repentance. It could be a hope of being washed and becoming clean, or a hope of rising in the first resurrection, or a hope of having the Holy Ghost as a constant companion. The reality of the power lies within the individual, not the priesthood holder or the ordinances of the priesthood. The "power" is wholly in the agency and change of the individual, 'acting in futurity' (D&C 101:78) in the hope of a future reality. However, the ordinances must still be administered by someone who is authorized by the church as part of their record keeping responsibility.

The following pages will address the authority and responsibilities of the different priesthoods as defined by Joseph Smith and scripture. Addressed in light of the standards found in scriptures, the issue of women and the priesthood can be understood and put in proper perspective.

Three Grand Orders

Joseph Smith taught that; "There are three grand orders of priesthood referred to [in the Epistle to the Hebrews]" and then outlines them as "the Melchizedek, the Patriarchal, and the Aaronic" (*TPJS*, p. 322-23; HC 5:554-55). Each of these different 'orders' of priesthood have selective and separate responsibilities that would govern their use and authority in the administration of the gospel of Jesus Christ.

Patriarchal Priesthood

The Book of Genesis is the priesthood manual for the patriarchal priesthood. Under the patriarchal order, mentioned throughout the Book of Genesis, the patriarch or father was *prophet, priest, and king* to his family. He would give inspired direction and provide the priesthood ordinances for the salvation and exaltation of his wife and children, while providing food and shelter for their proper growth, nourishment, and protection.

The government of God is Patriarchal. It consists of the Patriarch acting as *Prophet, Priest, and King.* Anciently, the authority and calling of a father and patriarch as a *"prophet"* would be to provide the inspired direction and guidance to those for whom he was responsible. As the *"priest,"* the father was to stand as a mediator between his family and God, providing the ordinances of salvation and exaltation for those in his immediate care. Acting as a *"king"* in the ancient world, the patriarchal responsibility was to take care of the temporal needs of his family (subjects). He (the King) was to provide for and protect his people. This truth is taught in the address of King Benjamin in the first few chapters of Mosiah. The patriarchal priesthood authority has the authority to administer the gospel and provide *direction* to his family line and to none others. Speaking of this patriarchal order, the Doctrine and Covenants teaches that this authority passes only from father to son. The "order of this priesthood" in the quote below refers to the Patriarchal Priesthood as Adam the patriarch of the race provides the blessings to his direct line of righteous posterity and future 'grand patriarchs.'

> 40 The order of *this priesthood was confirmed to be handed down from father to son,* and rightly belongs to the literal descendants of the chosen seed, to whom the promises were made.
> 41 This order was instituted in the days of Adam, and came down by lineage in the following manner:
> 42 From Adam to Seth, who was ordained by Adam at the age of sixty-nine years, and was blessed by him three years previous to his (Adam's) death, and received the promise of God by his father, that his posterity should be the chosen of the Lord, and that they should be preserved unto the end of the earth;
> 44 Enos was ordained at the age of one hundred and thirty-four years and four months, by the hand of Adam.
> 48 Enoch was twenty-five years old when he was ordained under the hand of Adam; and he was sixty-five and Adam blessed him. (D&C 107:40-42, 44, 48)

There are patriarchs and 'grand patriarchs.' As described, every father is a patriarch for his immediate family, becoming a prophet, priest, and king, as described, for his wife, children, and grandchildren in a direct line. A 'grand patriarch' is one who has been chosen to assist his father – becoming responsible for the temporal and spiritual salvation of all his father's children.

Every grand patriarch would ordain his first-born son or first righteous born son to become a co-regent or co-patriarch, with ordained authority to function outside of his own family line. Adam blessed and ordained the early patriarchs to this authority (see D&C 107:40-48). This ordained authority is Melchizedek.

> 3 For this Melchizedek was ordained a priest after the order of the Son of God, *which order was without father, without mother, without descent,* having neither beginning of days, nor end of life. And all those who are ordained unto this priesthood are made like unto the Son of God, abiding a priest continually. (JST Hebrews 7:3)

Modern scripture reveals that the Melchizedek authority is conferred upon the "grand patriarchs" to minister outside of their family lines. Prophet Joseph explains that: "The Melchizedek Priesthood holds the right from the eternal God, and *not by descent from father and mother*" (*TPJS*, p. 323) unlike the patriarchal priesthood which "*was confirmed to be handed down from father to son*" (D&C 107:40). Therefore, the grand patriarch needed to be ordained to a Melchizedek authority to perform ordinances outside of family lines.

Following the death of Joseph and his brothers in Egypt, the patriarchal authority becomes dormant during the falling away that occurs as the dispensation changes from Abraham to Moses. It is during this time that the children of Israel fall from the ways and teachings of the patriarchs and the priesthood of their fathers, becoming enamored in the splendors of Egypt. Without righteous fathers in the home, the necessary blessings and ordinances normally administered by the father must now be administered under another authority that is "without father or mother."

Jethro, the father-in-law of Moses recognized the differences between the patriarchal and Melchizedek authorities and responsibilities. instructs Moses about priesthood organization and councils. When Moses thinks to act in a patriarchal manner, Jethro (who ordained Moses to the Melchizedek Priesthood – see D&C 84:6-7) tells Moses that he (Moses) is not the Patriarch to the Children of Israel, and then counsels him about his Melchizedek priesthood responsibilities.

Moses acts like he is the Patriarch of all Israel:

> 13 And it came to pass on the morrow, that Moses sat to judge the people: and the people stood by Moses from the morning unto the evening.
> 14 And when Moses' father in law saw all that he did to the people, he said, What is this thing that thou doest to the people? Why sittest thou thyself alone, and all the people stand by thee from morning unto even?
> 15 And Moses said unto his father in law, Because the people come unto me to inquire of God:

Jethro tells Moses that "this is all wrong:"

> 16 When they have a matter, they come unto me; and I judge between one and another, and I do make them know the statutes of God and his laws.
> 17 And Moses' father in law said unto him, The thing that thou doest is not good.
> 18 Thou wilt surely wear away, both thou, and this people that is with thee: for this thing is too heavy for thee; thou art not able to perform it thyself alone.

Jethro tells Moses that he is the "Prophet and Priesthood Leader" and what his responsibilities are:

> 19 Hearken now unto my voice, I will give thee counsel, and God shall be with thee: Be thou for the people to God-ward, that thou mayest bring the causes unto God:
> 20 And *thou shalt teach them ordinances and laws, and shalt shew them the way wherein they must walk, and the work that they must do.*

Jethro then explains to Moses about the Melchizedek organization of administration. Setting up assignments and quorums:

> 21 Moreover *thou shalt provide out of all the people able men, such as fear God, men of truth, hating covetousness; and place such over them, to be rulers* of thousands, and rulers of hundreds, rulers of fifties, and rulers of tens:
> 22 And let them judge the people at all seasons: and it shall be, that every great matter they shall bring unto thee, but every small matter they shall judge: so shall it be easier for thyself, and they shall bear the burden with thee.

Moses listened to his Father-in-law, his priesthood leader:

> 23 If thou shalt do this thing, and God command thee so, then thou shalt be able to endure, and all this people shall also go to their place in peace.
> 24 So *Moses hearkened to the voice of his father in law, and did all that he had said.*
> 25 And *Moses chose able men out of all Israel, and made them heads over the people,* rulers of thousands, rulers of hundreds, rulers of fifties, and rulers of tens.
> 26 And they judged the people at all seasons: the hard causes they brought unto Moses, but every small matter they judged themselves.

Jethro says: "You've got it and I'm out a' here:"

> 27 And Moses let his father in law depart; and he went his way into his own land. (Exodus 18:13-27)

Jethro, in his wisdom and priesthood understanding, teaches Moses that he is not the father and patriarch of the children of Israel; rather, he is the prophet and high priest of the Melchizedek Priesthood. As such, he may help take care of every family's spiritual and temporal needs through the Melchizedek and Aaronic priesthood organizations. As the patriarchal era come to an end, with the rejection of the higher priesthood and its ordinances, the responsibilities of prophet, priest and king are divided. In the Old Testament, this division of responsibility is executed thusly: the *prophet* gives direction from God to the *king*, and the *High Priest* administers the temple ordinances and sacrifices that were required by the Lord under the Law of Moses. An example of this is seen as the kingship is about to be passed to Solomon: David is the king of Israel, Nathan is the Prophet, and Zenock is the Priest.

Melchizedek Priesthood

Because the responsibility of the Patriarchal Priesthood is to take care of the temporal and spiritual needs of one's family, the priesthood authority also divides these two responsibilities as it serves and ministers to the family. Spiritual needs are provided for by Melchizedek authority; temporal concerns are addressed by the Aaronic authority. Thus the umbrella of Melchizedek authority has the power to preside over both spiritual and temporal needs, which it does through the Stake (Melchizedek) and Ward (Aaronic) organizations. The Aaronic authority will not be addressed here as it does not pertain to the immediate discussion

The Savior fulfilled the Law of Moses and introduced the Melchizedek Priesthood and the Ordinances of Godliness back to the earth beginning with the Sermon on the Mount. The combined responsibility of prophet, priest, and king was given back to the worthy man and woman through the Melchizedek authority and the ordinances (D&C 84:19-22) and endowment of power found only in the Temple. Through the sacred ordinances performed in the Temple, a couple may be sealed and enter into the patriarchal order of the priesthood, becoming a patriarch and matriarch, a king and queen, a priest and priestess unto God and their family.

Temple marriage is the ordinance that bestows the patriarchal priesthood upon the sealed couple.

> 1 In the celestial glory there are three heavens or degrees;
> 2 And in order to obtain the highest, *a man must enter into this order of the priesthood [meaning the new and everlasting covenant of marriage]*;

380

3 And if he does not, he cannot obtain it. (D&C 131:1-3)

A couple, upon being sealed, enters into the patriarchal "order of the priesthood." Each spouse, equal in all things and responsibilities, holds this most important priesthood together as a patriarch and matriarch to their family. They have entered into "this order of the priesthood, meaning the new and everlasting covenant of marriage." There can be no patriarch without a matriarch and each has separate responsibilities in this order of father and mother. This is the same priesthood that Adam and Eve were blessed with before the fall (Gen. 1:28).[52] It is the same priesthood that they had after the fall, with divided responsibilities in mortality. This "order of the priesthood" is the order of heaven and inherent in the couple who have been sealed together, with the same commission in life as our first parents was given in the Garden of Eden. The main responsibility of this patriarchal priesthood, which the married couple jointly holds, is to bring to pass the immortality and eternal life of their children, by instruction and ordinance.

As the examples throughout Genesis teach, the matriarchal responsibility in this priesthood is to prepare and present her children to her husband. The one primary responsibility of the matriarch is to choose the new 'grand patriarch' and present him to her husband for his ordination and blessing, as in the case of Rebekah and Jacob. Only the mother knows who her firstborn is and who the father is. Under the patriarchal priesthood, the selection of the new patriarch is the responsibility of the mother and matriarch. This is called a *Matrilineal Patriarchy*.

---

52. *The Personal Writings of Joseph Smith*, Compiled and Edited by Dean C. Jesse, (Salt Lake City: Deseret Book, 1984), pp. 92, 132. The Prophet Joseph Smith remarks in a marriage ceremony that "marriage was an institution of heaven instituted in the Garden of Eden." Following the ceremony, he pronounced them Husband and Wife and "in the name of God" blessed them with the "blessings that the Lord conferred upon Adam and Eve in the garden of Eden" in Gen. 1:28. Joseph remarked that the 'dominion' given to Adam & Eve was the Priesthood. The Lord was speaking to them, Adam & Eve. He gave unto them—dominion. When a man and woman enter into the New and Everlasting Covenant of Marriage, they enter into the covenants of the Patriarchal Priesthood.

The authority to administer over people outside of a family line is a power reserved for the Melchizedek priesthood. For example; a father *could* bless his children under the authority of the Patriarchal priesthood which he jointly holds with his wife, having been sealed in the temple. However, to perform the same ordinance or blessing for his home teaching families, he must perform the ordinance under the authority of the Melchizedek priesthood. It should be kept in mind that "all authorities or offices in the church are appendages to this (Melchizedek) priesthood" (D&C 107:5). Therefore, the Melchizedek priesthood is the greater priesthood and becomes the 'umbrella authority' over the church, having "power and authority over *all the offices in the church* in all ages of the world, to administer in spiritual things" (D&C. 107:8). Therefore, all ordinances and blessings are pronounced and performed under this Melchizedek authority, as the church and record keeping is recorded and governed by the Melchizedek priesthood. Since the church functions under the Melchizedek authority, patriarchal authority is seldom if ever mentioned, and the Aaronic authority is invoked only when ordinances (such as a baptism) are performed by those holding only the Aaronic priesthood.

The responsibility of the patriarch and matriarch is to prepare and assist their children in their personal quest of salvation and exaltation. The Melchizedek priesthood exists to assist the fathers and mothers in these patriarchal responsibilities. The church, under the direction of the Melchizedek Priesthood leadership, has as a primary goal and purpose to make sure *every man woman and child, (alive and dead)* have the opportunity to receive, if so desired and worthy, the ordinances of salvation and exaltation in an organized and orderly way. The administration of the gospel by the church or priesthood organization is done for the sake of order and record keeping. Thus, all ordinances performed that are for salvation and/or exaltation must be done under the direction of the member of the Melchizedek priesthood leader who "presides" (has the authority and responsibility to assist and record the ordinance) for the person involved.

The church organization or Melchizedek Priesthood leadership's primary purpose is to *minister* to (serve) and *administer* the gospel, assisting the father and mother in their responsibilities. This they do by teaching the gospel via classes, talks and other activities, and by providing opportunities to serve others and to learn to love others. The patriarch and father of the family has the inherent authority and responsibility to provide the spiritual and temporal needs of his family. This is true no matter if the father is a member or not as the patriarch is the authority of the home. The priesthood organization works for the father and patriarch, making sure the ordinances of the gospel are made available to his family when needed—like baptism and the sacrament. The priesthood leadership provides council and direction to help perfect the saints and edify the body of Christ.

The priesthood organization fundamentally works for the father and mother. The church organization, with its auxiliaries, aids and assists in the ministry (responsibilities) of the father and mother, and, if needed, administers the ordinances of the gospel by substitution. Ordinances of salvation and exaltation are administered by the authority of the priesthood on those who stand in proxy for the dead. Likewise, saving ordinances may be administered to the living by the authority of the priesthood who officiate as proxy for the father and patriarch of the fatherless, widows, and orphans.

Why the Priesthood is Male

The oldest form of authority is connected to the authority and government of heaven, which is patriarchal. The Father has no priesthood. He has authority and power by virtue of being God. It is not given ('hood') to Him. The power of God lies inherent within him as the Father of all. This authority is patriarchal in its very nature as it is the authority of the Father and fathers to provide the spiritual and temporal needs of their family. When the patriarch has a son, that first born son will usually become the 'birthright son,' chosen because of his righteousness and ordination. That chosen son, by virtue of birth position and righteousness, has an *inherent authority* or responsibility to become *as a* patriarch and priesthood leader for the temporal and spiritual welfare of all his father's family (see Numbers Chapter Three).

Christ is the Firstborn and Only Begotten Son of the Father and therefore has an *inherent authority* and responsibility for the temporal and spiritual needs of all of His Father's children. Christ is the temporal creator and the spiritual redeemer. According to scripture, Christ's inherent authority is called: "The Holy *Priesthood, after the Order* of the Son of God" (D&C 107:3). This Holy Priesthood, after the Order of the Son of God, is now called the Melchizedek Priesthood. It's the authority to *serve and minister to man for and in-behalf of Christ* the Firstborn, and is the authority to administer ordinances *outside* of the immediate family lines. Thus the "Grand Patriarchs" from Adam, Seth, Enos, and Canaan down through Abraham, Isaac, Jacob, and Joseph hold not only the patriarchal priesthood to administer to their direct family line but also hold the Melchizedek authority to provide, as needed, the necessary ordinances and temporal sustenance for their father's other children (extended family) in the event a patriarch may physically be unable, unrighteous, missing, or dead.

To put it succinctly and simply, the Melchizedek priesthood holder becomes an assistant or substitute to the husband, father and patriarch in the temporal and spiritual care of his family. Thus, the priesthood holder may only act only under the direction of the father [patriarch], if present, or the matriarch of the family in the absence of the father. The injunction within scripture to take care of the "fatherless, widows, and orphans" all have one thing in common, which is the absence of a father, husband and patriarch. For this reason, the priesthood responsibility rests on the male, who acts with the authority of ***God the Father*** using the authority inherent in the Firstborn Son of God.

Those who continue trying to change the church's position on the issue of women holding the priesthood do not understand the standard that governs the church. The scriptures are the standard of truth and the Standard Works determine all doctrine. A system of beliefs that is not founded upon scripture or a standard of God-given rules that do not change is not a religion. Without a standard of truth, every system of belief becomes nothing more than a club, existing without any power, doctrine, or truth capable of providing salvation. Thus those who seek to change the rules to suit their personal interests and desires fail in their assessment and vision of a church and religion. There are other options. Organizations and religions exist that will allow and accept female ministers. There are religions where the rules and standards may be changed by vote or petition, like a club. Those who do not agree with standard church doctrine are not forced in any way to compromise their agency.

Joseph Smith said the following in regard to those who believe they have a right to tell the priesthood leaders when changes need to take place:

> I will inform you that it is contrary to the economy of God for any member of the church, or any one, to receive instructions for those in authority, higher than themselves; therefore, you will see the impropriety of giving heed to them; but if any person have a vision or a visitation from a heavenly messenger, it must be for his own benefit and instruction; for the fundamental principles, government, and doctrine of the church are vested in the keys of the kingdom. (*TPJS*, p 21)

There would be no revelation (from God) that an individual lay member would or could receive that would cause or effect a change in church doctrine or policy. God does not work that way. He is not a God of confusion. A person will never receive from God inspiration or a revelation that should ascend the leadership ladder higher than themselves and their own responsibility. Instruction from God will come from the top down to avoid confusion and a lack of faith in leadership. Because of the *checks and balances of quorum authority* as outlined in the Doctrine and Covenants (D&C 107:22-29) there will never be a revelatory change or instruction that will come from any single individual without the authority and keys of administrative responsibility. The only one who holds all keys of administration is the sustained president of the Church; he alone may speak for the whole

Church and to the whole Church, for that is his authority, office, and priesthood responsibility.

Priesthood Authority

The priesthood cannot be conferred without an ordination to an office and responsibility. The conferral of the priesthood without ordination to office of responsibility has no inherent value and no authority. Hence the question: Is the priesthood then a *power*? The priesthood cannot be conferred upon anyone without also ordaining them to an office of responsibility, otherwise the "power" of priesthood would not need an office in which to function—it would be a power or authority in and of itself.

When priesthood is conferred and one is ordained to an office, then the priesthood becomes a responsibility of service inherent within that office. Any power of the priesthood lies in *the power to act on the accepted responsibility* by the individual. The authority to function in the priesthood is not given by ordination. It is given to the individual by common consent, i.e. being accepted by the community of saints where the responsibility will be filled, and is ultimately confirmed by ordination by the correct or presiding authority in that ward or stake.

> 63 The elders are to *receive their licenses from other elders, by vote of the church* to which they belong, or from the conferences.
> 64 Each priest, teacher, or deacon, who is ordained by a priest, *may take a certificate from him at the time, which certificate, when presented to an elder, shall entitle him to a license, which shall authorize him to perform the duties of his calling,* or he may receive it from a conference. (D&C 20:63-64)

IF there were a *power* of the priesthood then an individual would not lose that power when released from responsibilities, or when moving from a one ward or stake to another.

> 19 And now, verily I say unto you, let every elder who shall give an account unto the bishop of the church in this part of the vineyard be recommended by the church or churches, *in which he labors,* that he may render himself and his accounts approved in all things (D&C 72:19)

In short, to serve in a priesthood position, a recognized authority and priesthood leader must call a person, with the acceptance of the responsibility voiced and agreed upon by the individual being called. The *authority to function* in any priesthood office or position actually comes from the people they will serve. In 'sustaining' the individual in a position of responsibility, they (the members) bestow the authority to administer to them by common consent. The Doctrine and Covenants explains the purpose of priesthood and describes how common consent works:

> 143 The above offices I have given unto you, and the keys thereof, *for helps and for governments, for the work of the ministry and the perfecting of my saints.*
> 144 And a commandment I give unto you, that you should fill all these offices *and approve of those names which I have mentioned, or else disapprove of them* at my general conference; (D&C 124:143-144)

To recap, the priesthood and the priesthood position *does not* honor the man; the man honors the responsibility by service. The work of the priesthood is the work of a loving God and is predicated on loving and serving others. This is the law upon which all the law and the prophets hang. *There is no rank in the kingdom, only responsibility!* The priesthood ordination *is not* one of power, but an authorized responsibility of service that is received by acceptance and recognition from those that will be served. For this reason, when the priesthood is conferred, the individual must also be ordained to an office, which is an ordination to a responsibility. The priesthood is a responsibility to serve others in the administration of the gospel of Jesus Christ, to assist the father in his temporal spiritual responsibilities. In family units without a worthy father to administer the temporal and spiritual needs of life, the priesthood becomes the substitute and/or assistant to the family's patriarch by invitation only. The priesthood and the father have the right and *responsibility* to administer to the needs of the family, temporally and spiritually.

Chapter 26

Same Sex Attraction

This topic is one that invokes high anxiety from many members of the church whose opinions are more often based on emotion rather than understanding the standard of scripture. The ideas discussed in this chapter no doubt will offend many good Latter-day Saints on both sides of this precarious fence. As the author I would ask that you force your way through the whole chapter to better understand the scriptures and the doctrines contained in them concerning this topic. To begin any gospel discussion, there are some basics doctrines and a scriptural picture that must be re-viewed to appreciate any answer that could be given or provided for a better understanding of the issue. To that end, please read the first chapter in Part II of this book, "A Standard of Doctrine."

All good parents love their children. They not only hope and pray for their wellbeing, but also want to help them find happiness in this life. In a family, every child should be able to find love, acceptance, help and support no matter what problems or issues may arise. The old cliché that "a mother can be no happier than the worst pain of her children" is not so much an antidote as it is a truth. Parents should support their children and love them in all their weaknesses. All have heard of 'tough love' where a punishment may be used against the will of a child to help change the child's actions. Parents who allow their children to misbehave sometimes become enablers of a destructive course.

The great call of scripture and every prophet since Adam has been the gospel call of: faith, repentance, baptism and the gift of the Holy Ghost. The first two principles are the responsibility of the individual and the church and priesthood administer the first two 'ordinances' for those who have "exercised their faith unto repentance" (Alma 34:15-17). Faith, as used and defined in scripture can only be faith if it is in something that cannot fail, i.e. Jesus Christ and his Atonement. According to Amulek in the Book of Mormon, the way to exercise faith in Christ and the Atonement is to repent.

Repentance

Repentance is a word that has been misinterpreted and misunderstood. It often conjures a mental image of suffering and sorrow. The repentance process can also invoke the pain and embarrassment of confessing a sin to a priesthood leader. Some view repentance as saying 'sorry' without any real determination to change. In fact, repentance is a word that means *'the process of changing character,'* i.e. being better than one was before. Repentance is the process upon which exaltation is founded.

The word 'repent' in both Hebrew and Greek is an archery term that means to 'take aim again' having 'missed the target' which is the definition of the word 'sin'. To 'take aim again' is practice, trying to improve by recognition and habit, allowing for the change of character as our ability changes. Recognizing the need to 'take aim again' is an integral part of repentance. If the need for change is unrecognized, there will be no "will" or reason for the change of character.

Satan's Powers of Control

Scripture explains that Satan has two sure methods to entice mankind to "sin." The first is by the temporal environment in which all live and the flesh of which all are made. This 'flesh' or mortal body is hardwired with desires, appetites, and passions that are contrary to a character that may dwell with God. King Benjamin uses the term *"natural man,* he describes as an "enemy to God and always will be unless he puts off the natural man" (Mosiah 3:19; see also D&C 67:12). Lehi also speaks of the temporal flesh or 'natural man' and the power of Satan.

> 28 And now, my sons, I would that ye should look to the great Mediator, and hearken unto his great commandments; and be faithful unto his words, and choose eternal life, according to the will of his Holy Spirit;
> 29 And not choose eternal death, according to the **will of the flesh and the evil which is therein,** *which giveth the spirit of the devil power to captivate,* to bring you down to hell, that he may reign over you in his own kingdom. (2 Nephi 22: 28-29)

It is this fight that rages between the flesh and the spirit that Paul speaks of throughout his letters in the New Testament (See Galatians 5:16-26; Galatians 6:8; Romans 8:1-23, etc.). Between the teachings of a corrupt and immoral society and the collusion of hormones, ego and pride, the desires of the flesh are often the catalyst that will lead an individual down a path of spiritual peril. This might include immorality, drugs, alcoholism or other excesses of the flesh that will separate man from God.

The Second dictum that gives Satan power over humanity is ignorance – not knowing the laws of God and why He commands the way He does. The individual without a knowledge of truth will have no other place than their own ignorance in which to base their opinion.

> 29 —because of the many plain and precious things which have been taken out of the book, which were plain unto the understanding of the children of men, according to the plainness which is in the Lamb of God—*because of these things which are taken away out of the gospel of the Lamb, an exceedingly great many do stumble, yea, insomuch that Satan hath great power over them.* (1 Nephi 13:29)

> 11 And they that will harden their hearts, to them is given the lesser portion of the word *until they know nothing* concerning his mysteries; and *then they are taken captive by*

the devil, and led by his will down to destruction. Now this is
what is meant by the chains of hell. (Alma 12:11)

When one doesn't know or understand the doctrines of the church, popular opinion will often fill the void, becoming the standard of doctrine. As explained in 1 Nephi above, when truths are absent, Satan rules. For this reason, the attitudes and morals assimilated from a godless culture and point of view, pervasively promoted as right or true from kindergarten through college, should always be suspect when not founded on a standard of truth.

The greatest threat to a culture is the culture itself. When there is no accepted standard of truth, no standard exists, and opinions, traditions, and interpretations will rule the day. When an opinion becomes one's standard, the argument ends and truth is lost. These *opinions are most often embraced* because of the flesh and the weaknesses described in scripture as 'desires, appetites, and passions,' when coupled with a lack of knowledge about the purpose of life.

To begin a discussion of same sex relationships, be it genetic or by choice, a scriptural definition of sin should be addressed and discussed first. This definition, as found in scripture, may come as a surprise to many in the church when compared to the traditional view of sin. Following this discussion, a few pages will be used to review the doctrines in scripture about the plan of salvation and the purpose of creation and our life on this earth. As this discussion of sin and the purpose of creation is expanded, keep in mind that Satan gains control of mankind **first** by the desires, appetites, and passions of the flesh, which one usually embraces willingly because of the instant gratification. The **second** weakness that gives the Devil influence and power over humanity is associated with the individual's ignorance of God's law, purpose, and plan of salvation. Since most people don't know what they don't know, they can only trust in their own emotions, experience, and knowledge if they do not have a standard of truth to rely on.

The Definition of Sin

Many members of the church have mentally categorized sins into lists from the least to the worst. For example, is it worse to smoke cigarettes or drink alcohol? Is viewing pornography a worse sin than taking drugs? Is cheating in business worse than cheating on your spouse? In everyone's mind there are sins that top the list and are considered more grievous than others, and some sins that don't seem to matter that much. Not surprisingly, the sins or weaknesses that an individual is most tolerant of are those of which he or she is most familiar or guilty. The weaknesses of a loved one are also often accepted because of that familiarity and love.

Joseph Smith stated that for an individual 'to dwell with God one must have developed the character of God' (*TPJS* P. 216). This teaching implies that it is the character and nature of the individual that is most important in achieving the goal of being with our loved ones in the presence of God, for "no unclean thing can dwell in the presence of God" (1 Nephi 10:21). The change of character is a product of agency and choice, not miracle or ordinance. The improvement and development of character is the power of exaltation, as one will choose to put off the natural man and become a saint. Nevertheless, there is a tendency to rationalize sin and guilt into an accepted lifestyle because of a belief that God is 'loving and merciful.' Again, the Prophet Joseph taught:

> ...he that has made no improvement will be cast out as an unprofitable servant, while the faithful will enjoy everlasting honors. Therefore, we earnestly implore the grace of our Father to rest upon you, through Jesus Christ His Son, that you may not faint in the hour of temptation, nor be overcome in the time of persecution. (*TPJS*, p. 68).

Christ gave us important insights into sin when confronted by the Pharisees who sought to convict Him by the Law of Moses. They tempted Him by asking which commandment was the most important to keep, seeking to get Christ to categorize the commandments as many Latter-day Saints do. The response of the Savior not only explains the purpose of the commandments, but also defines sin

> 36 Master, which is the great commandment in the law?
> 37 Jesus said unto him, *Thou shalt love the Lord thy God with all thy heart, and with all thy soul, and with all thy mind.*
> 38 This is the first and great commandment.
> 39 And the second is like unto it, *Thou shalt love thy neighbor as thyself.*
> 40 *On these two commandments hang all the law and the prophets.* (Matthew 22:36-40)

Christ explains that *all commandments* have only two purposes: to develop the character that will (1) 'love God' and (2) 'love' mankind. These two commandments—loving God and loving mankind—are so fundamental that Christ declares that *upon these two* "hang **all** *the law and the prophets.*" That means that all the commandments that could be broken (therefore all sin also) hang upon these two *laws*. Thus everything the *prophets teach* or have taught must also be connected to the same two laws. Putting it simply: all the commandments and the teachings of every prophet are structured to develop, through obedience to the commandments, the individual character and nature that will love God and love mankind. This love of God is much more than declaration; it is a love with "all thy heart, and with all thy soul, and with all thy mind"—the complete and whole person, in nature and character. The second is similar, as a person should by nature love others as they love themselves.

This, then, is the purpose of commandments, prophets, religion, and life: to develop the character that loves God and our fellow man. Christ expands upon this as he gives His last commandment before His death:

> 34 A new commandment I give unto you, That ye love one another; as I have loved you, that ye also love one another.
> 35 By this shall all men know that ye are my disciples, if ye have love one to another. (John 13:34-35)

Notice: the Christian responsibility to love others shifts from 'loving your neighbor as yourself' to loving others as "Christ loved," with a willingness to give one's life for others. Christ emphasizes in verse 35 that those who don't love others with this pure love of God are not disciples of Christ and therefore not Christian.

The apostle John stresses the connection between loving God and loving other in his letters by stating:

> 20 If a man say, I love God, and hateth his brother, he is a liar: for he that loveth not his brother whom he hath seen, how can he love God whom he hath not seen? (1 John 3:14)

Based on the words of Christ and the "Law and the Prophets," the definition of sin would be: ***That which distracts one from developing the character that loves God and loves all mankind.***

Moroni taught about the character of those who love others in his description of charity, the pure love of Christ:

> And charity *suffereth long*, and *is kind*, and *envieth no*t, and is *not puffed up, seeketh not her own*, is *not easily provoked, thinketh no evil*, and *rejoiceth not in iniquity* but rejoiceth in the truth, beareth all things, believeth all things, hopeth all things, and endureth all things (Moroni 7:45).

Christ explains better than anyone what it means to Love God. In His last sermon to the apostles, He states that "*if ye love me keep my commandments*" (John 14:15). The overt way of expressing our love of God is to keep the commandments and love all others around us as He loved us. If the work and glory of God is to bring to pass the immortality and eternal life of man (Moses 1:39), then the individual's necessary contribution to the Atonement is to develop the love and character that Christ had for all of mankind. 'For God so loved the world that He gave His only Begotten Son, that whosoever might believe on Him *and keep his commandments* shall have eternal life' (John 3:16).

The Prophet Joseph Smith taught about the purpose of commandments
that originate from God.

> We believe that God condescended to speak from the
> heavens and declare His will concerning the human family,
> *to give them just and holy laws, to regulate their conduct,*
> and guide them in a direct way, that in due time He might
> take them to Himself, and make them joint heirs with His
> Son. But when this fact is admitted, that the immediate will
> of heaven is contained in the scriptures, are we not bound as
> rational creatures to live in accordance to all its precepts?
> *Will the mere admission that this is the will of heaven ever
> benefit us if we do not comply with all its teachings?* Do we
> not offer violence to the Supreme Intelligence of heaven,
> when we admit the truth of its teachings, and do not obey
> them? Do we not descend below our own knowledge, and
> the better wisdom which heaven has endowed us with, by
> such a course of conduct? For these reasons, if we have
> direct revelations given us from heaven, surely those
> revelations were never given to be trifled with, without the
> trifler's incurring displeasure and vengeance upon his own
> head if there is any justice in heaven. This must be admitted
> by every individual who confesses the truth and force of
> God's teachings, blessings, and cursings as contained in the
> sacred volume.
>
> Here, then, we have this part of our subject immediately
> before us for consideration: God has in reserve a time, or
> period appointed in His own bosom, when *He will bring all
> His subjects, who have obeyed His voice and kept His
> commandments, into His celestial rest.* This rest is of such
> perfection and glory, that *man has need of a preparation
> before he can, according to the laws of that kingdom, enter it
> and enjoy its blessings.* This being the fact, G*od has given
> certain laws to the human family, which, if observed, are
> sufficient to prepare them to inherit this rest.* This, then, we
> conclude, was the purpose of God in giving His laws to us: If
> not, why, or for what were they given? ... It would be
> nonsense to suppose that He would condescend to talk in
> vain: for it would be in vain, and to no purpose whatever (if

the law of God were of no benefit to man): because, *all the commandments contained in the law of the Lord, have the sure promise annexed of a reward to all who obey,* predicated upon the fact that they are really the promises of *a Being who cannot lie,* One who is abundantly able to fulfill every tittle of His word: and if man were as well prepared, or could be as well prepared, to meet God without their ever having been given in the first instance, why were they ever given? for certainly, in that case they can now do him no good. (*TPJS.* pp. 54, 55).

So how do we love God? This is accomplished by learning His word and keeping His commandments while participating in the necessary ordinances. As he said in John 14:15, "if ye love me keep my commandments." It doesn't get any plainer than that. This obedience, motivated by love, is required to develop the character necessary to dwell with God.

The Pre-Earth

The Lord declared to Moses, "this is my work and my glory—to bring to pass the immortality and eternal life of man" (Moses 1:39). This statement establishes a fundamental purpose for the creation of the universe as well as the heavens and the earth, thus forming a connection between the creation and the salvation of man. It is here and now, in this created environment, that mankind will need to learn to work out their own salvation in 'fear and trembling' (Mormon 9:27). Creation accounts are for relationships, not science. They establish that God is the creator of our life, lifestyle, and livelihood, with an understanding that without God, nothing is possible. God's goal, His work and His glory, is the eternal happiness and joy of each individual spirit.

Latter-day Saint doctrine teaches that all spirits were given an opportunity to hear and accept the plan of salvation and happiness before we ever came to this dreary world. All the spirits that were to come to this earth were gathered and were taught about this earth and how bad mortality could be. All the problems of the flesh and an earthly existence were explained before any came to earth. All were taught about the spiritual fall that would take place on earth because of the flesh and about the ignorance that would plague all mankind.

Every spirit in that heavenly council would need to know how bad this life could be: the suffering and pain, both emotional and physical. All had to understand perfectly that there would be diseases and sicknesses that would plague the bodies all would have. All knew perfectly that there would be *weaknesses of the flesh*, some of which were the consequence of imperfections developed over generations in the genetic code. Every spirit understood perfectly, without any misunderstanding or misconception, how bad this life could be and what those weaknesses might be that could cause some to rebel against God because of the flesh. All spirits understood with the same perfection how it would feel to suffer physically and emotionally through sickness, cancer, and diseases of all kinds. Everyone had to know how it would feel to lose a child or spouse in death, both physically and spiritually. If the spirits of mankind did *not understand all things about mortality with a perfect understanding and comprehension* before accepting or rejecting the opportunity to participate in this world, *agency would have been compromised* and God would cease to be God.

Once all knew and understood what this life had to offer, with all its physical, mental and emotional imperfections, a choice was made. Every spirit that has come or that will come to this earth chose the plan of joy and exaltation that was offered, and the immortality and eternal life promised (Abraham 3:25). It was a choice made with a full knowledge of the conditions one might grapple with in this mortal sphere. Understanding this, one may come to realize that are no trials and tribulations here, only a life—a life that every individual spirit has actively chosen, with the goal to return to that God that gave them life. Agency reigns supreme, even in the heavens, as all those who chose not to participate in this plan of salvation were not forced to submit. Fully aware of the consequences, they rebelled against the plans of God in the pre-earth environment, led by Lucifer, and were cast out to seek their own kind of misery.

In this temporary mortal life, replete with the weaknesses of mind and body, all have the agency to turn those weaknesses into strengths with the help of a loving God and Father. Moroni outlines a plan and pattern to do just that.

27 And if men
(1) come unto me
I will show unto them their weakness.
I give unto men weakness (because of life and the flesh)
that they may be humble; and
my grace is sufficient for all men
(2) that *humble themselves before me*; for
if they humble themselves before me, and
(3) have faith in me,
then will I make
weak things become strong unto them. (Ether 12:27)

The important instruction is that weaknesses are given to help humble the individual enough to turn to God for help. It is the recognition of one's weakness and need for God that leads to humility. When this humble recognition is coupled with faith and a desire to come unto God, the grace of Christ will provide the power to overcome *any and all* weaknesses of the flesh. *Pride* is seeking one's own will using a weakness as a reason or rationale. *Humility* is seeking to keep God's will within their weaknesses. Having a weakness or genetic tendency does not make one a victim of circumstance by God or man. The gospel and the Atonement provide the power to overcome the weaknesses that one might have. A loving God will not and cannot place us in a position where our agency ceases to exist becoming a spiritual victim or casualty. God had promised a way out for every temptation:

There hath no temptation taken you but such as is common to man: but God is faithful, who *will not suffer you to be tempted above that ye are able; but will with the temptation also make a way to escape,* that ye may be able to bear it.
(1 Corinthians 10:13)

> Verily, thus saith the Lord unto you whom I love, and whom I love I also chasten that their sins may be forgiven, for with the chastisement I prepare a way for their deliverance in all things out of temptation, and I have loved you— (D&C 95:1)

According to the passages above, no one is a victim of their physical body (except for the physically or mentally handicapped). Agency is the freedom to choose and act—not to be acted upon because of their weaknesses. If this were not the case there could be no judgment according to works. Those who demand the *freedom* to satisfy the desires, appetites, and passions of the body will in time lose their freedom of choice and be acted upon, becoming enslaved to the demands of the body.

> 27 Wherefore, *men are free according to the flesh*; and all things are given them which are expedient unto man. And *they are free to choose liberty and eternal life*, through the great Mediator of all men, *or to choose captivity and death, according to the captivity and power of the devil;* for he seeketh that all men might be miserable like unto himself.
> 28 And now, my sons, I would that ye should look to the great Mediator, and hearken unto his great commandments; and be faithful unto his words, and *choose eternal life, according to the will of his Holy Spirit;*
> 29 And *not choose eternal death, according to the will of the flesh and the evil which is therein, which giveth the spirit of the devil power to captivate,* to bring you down to hell, that he may reign over you in his own kingdom. (2 Nephi 2:27-29)

Righteousness is choosing good in the presence of evil. It is having the spiritual strength to do that which is right while at the same time the opportunity to choose and do evil as an option. Without opposition there can be no righteousness or wickedness. Everyone has been given the strength and opportunity to make the choice that will separate temptation from sin.

Satan realizes that the person who claims to be a 'victim' will never progress spiritually. The rationalization to break the commandments will often lie in the 'victim mentality:' "It's not my fault, I can't help it, the devil made me do it, God made me this way." As long as the finger is pointed at someone else there can be no responsibility, and in the mind of the victim, there should be no condemnation. Nephi warned that a sign of apostasy among members of the Church in the Last Days would be a trust in the love of God rather than the Redemption of God.

> 8 And there shall also be many which shall say: Eat, drink, and be merry; nevertheless, fear God—*he will justify in committing a little sin;* yea, lie a little, take the advantage of one because of his words, dig a pit for thy neighbor; *there is no harm in this;* and do all these things, for tomorrow we die; and if it so be that we are guilty, *God will beat us with a few stripes, and at last we shall be saved* in the kingdom of God. (2 Nephi 28:8)

Purpose of Creation

Scriptural accounts of the 'council in heaven' inform us that all spirits must come to a physical world with a physical body. There are spirits waiting their turn to come to this earth to begin the process that leads to eternal joy and exaltation. In the creation of man and woman, a loving Father has provided a way that these spirits may come to this earth and receive a physical body.

The scriptures enlighten our understanding about the purpose of the creation of the earth. Addressing marriage and the potential for children, the Lord establishes the true purpose of creation and links it to a pre-earth awareness of that purpose.

> 16 Wherefore, it is lawful that he should have one wife, and they twain shall be one flesh, and all this that the earth might answer the end of its creation;

17 And that it might be filled with the measure of man, according to his creation before the world was made. (D&C 49:16-17)

The Doctrine and Covenants explains that a man should have one wife 'that the earth might answer the end of its creation' this that the earth would be 'filled with the measure of man' i.e. those who were spirits in that grand council 'before the world was made.'

The Prophet Isaiah teaches the same concept in the Old Testament as he explains why creation accounts exist and why they were given to the children of Israel through Moses. This same account is found in our Book of Moses and recounted in the Pearl of Great Price for the same reason that Isaiah infers.

18 For thus saith the Lord that created the heavens; God himself that formed the earth and made it; he hath established it, he created it not in vain, *he formed it to be inhabited:* I am the Lord; and there is none else. (Isaiah 45:18)

Likewise, Nephi, the son of Lehi, teaches that there is a connection between the creation and the salvation of mankind. He states: "Behold, the Lord hath *created the earth that it should be inhabited;* and he hath created his children that they should possess it" (1 Nephi 17:36).

The habitation of the earth is designed to take place as described in D&C 49 above. One man is to have one wife, cleaving to one another (sealed) in order to have physical children that will house the spirits that were prepared and waiting to come to this earth. This is the plan of God, according to scripture, which will enable all spirits to progress and develop the godlike qualities worthy for exaltation.

These few scriptures confirm that the creation accounts that are rehearsed and explained in history and in ordinance exist to establish a purpose of creation and a relationship between God, mankind, and the environment in which salvation is secured. All the spirits that come to this earth were in the pre-earth council and knew and understood this plan of salvation. These chose to participate in mortality with all the physical weaknesses that might hinder that salvation. This choice could only be made with a promise that they would eventually understand the Gospel of Jesus Christ and learn to be obedient to the commandments that would allow them to return to a loving Father and God.

Same Sex Attraction

To begin a discussion of same sex attraction and same sex relationships, a few points need clarification. Historically the main argument for same sex attraction has been based on genetics. The phrase, 'God made me this way,' historically was meant to justify and rationalize same sex attraction as a function of genetic mandate. Without doubt, there are individuals with visible and/or invisible genetic variations or differences that may lend support for this argument in both women and men. If same sex attraction is due to genetic makeup then clearly this attraction is no fault of the individual. However, the decision to act on the attraction is always a function of choice. One must remember that in the next life there will be no physical handicaps or genetic defects. As Alma says, "this corruption will put on incorruption" (Alma 5:15).

During the last two decades, same sex relationships have been defended and advanced in public schools and the western culture as a "*lifestyle choice*" without regard or connection to a genetic compulsion. These lifestyle choices, now rebranded as '*alternate lifestyles*,' reinforce the idea that *some* same sex relationships are a function of choice and free will rather than a genetic burden from nature or God. In any case, whether the attraction is a function of genetic 'wiring' or not, the choice to engage in a same sex relationship *is always a choice*.

The secular education everyone is exposed to has an overwhelming power over the acceptance or rejection of the mores of any given time or culture. History and scripture have shown that this notion is true, as the divergent and abnormal tendencies of a culture always increase

404

over time. This entropic motif is attributed to a disconnect from religion and faith in God, and an intellectual separation from the faith and traditions of the family values of preceding generations.

> 1 Now it came to pass that there were *many of the rising generation that could not understand* the words of king Benjamin, being little children at the time he spake unto his people; and *they did not believe the tradition of their fathers.*
> 2 They did not believe what had been said concerning the resurrection of the dead, *neither did they believe concerning the coming of Christ.*
> 3 And now *because of their unbelief they could not understand the word of God*; and their hearts were hardened. (Mosiah 26:1-3)

This movement away from what was once considered a moral 'mainstream' to a new mainstream with the absence of sexual morality is a product of a cultural downshift that uses all forms of education including schools and textbooks, media and music, among other things, to coarsen the public landscape. Behaviors and attitudes that are scripturally aberrant are shrouded in words like *rights, choice, alternate lifestyles and toleration.* Language is important because recasting an immorality as a 'right' lends the behavior a legitimacy that fosters acceptance over time. Once immoral behaviors are cast as rights and given legal protection, schools are forced to fall into line, spouting the party line and promoting acceptance of the behavior. The cultural and social impact on our children can be significant. The education system is a powerful tool of change, powerful enough to transform sins into a civil right within a single generation. Given the time between kindergarten and a university degree, teachers wield the power to mold and shape the morals of a rising generation that will one day become the political leaders that craft the laws for future generations, and religious leaders that will accept politically correct tolerances.

> 10 And also all that generation were gathered unto their fathers: and there arose another generation after them, *which*

knew not the Lord, nor yet the works which he had done for Israel.

11 And the children of Israel did evil in the sight of the Lord, and served Baalim:

12 And *they forsook the Lord God of their fathers,* which brought them out of the land of Egypt, *and followed other gods, of the gods of the people that were round about them,* and bowed themselves unto them, and provoked the Lord to anger. (Judges 2:10-12)

Children are taught in the public school system from the age of six until they finish high school. Given this long-term accessibility, teachers could advance the idea that cannibalism is an accepted way of life and nothing more than a menu choice. This is true with any other philosophy or lifestyle choice, be it moral, religious, or political. Remember, Adam and Eve were cast out of Eden because they were convinced to expand their menu choice.

"Mugulu, how often have I told you not to play with your food?"

For decades now, the schools have been teaching children about alternative lifestyles from first grade through high school graduation and beyond. For thirty to forty years, prime time television and theatrical movies have overtly and covertly taught that any alternate lifestyle is okay and a choice that anyone may make without repercussions. In the media (all forms) people living alternative lifestyles or behaving immorally are presented sympathetically, as nice people who are no different than the rest of us, thus normalizing the behavior. This is "so well done" that children who have ostensibly been raised to know the difference argue with parents about the acceptability of these lifestyle choices.

The chart below depicts of percentage of college graduates sampled over nearly 4 decades who believe that extramarital, homosexual, and premarital sex is "always wrong." Of the three main 'alternate' lifestyle choices offered, notice which one has become most acceptable over time. LGBT and Pre-marital sexual activity is now taught in schools and presented in the media as a recreational activity and choice rather than a religious or moral obligation. The accepted alternate lifestyle has become more acceptable at an increasing rate compared to the other two statistics.

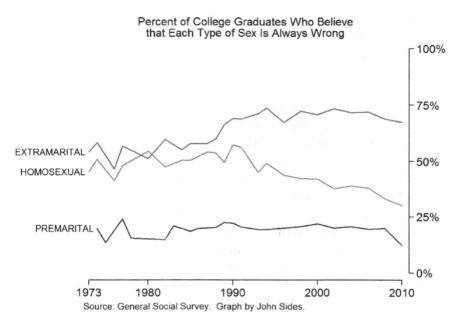

Percent of College Graduates Who Believe
that Each Type of Sex Is Always Wrong

Source: General Social Survey. Graph by John Sides.

No doubt there may be some genetic reasons for same sex attraction, but there is now clearly something else in play. Whether for shock value or attention, it has become fashionable and trendy on high school and college campuses today to be 'bi-sexual' (disproportionately among young women), which means that the alleged attraction AND its practice *is a chosen lifestyle*. Girls are basically "trying on" sexual lifestyles like the latest fashions, with obvious disregard for traditional sexual morality. This fluid attitude can be traced directly to the activism and advocacy of the homosexual movement within our schools and the media, which promotes the normalization of same sex attraction. It is more than a fad—"it is symptomatic of a confusion that reaches the core of human identity."[53] The natural attraction between boys and girls has been so 'confused by public celebration of homosexuality and other sexual acting out that young people are now confused about something as simple and basic as heterosexual identity.'[54] By law in some states a person can change their sexual identity—whether they identify as a male or a female—simply by

53 http://www.albertmohler.com/2004/01/27
54 *Ibid.*

saying so, depending on how they feel from one day to the next. Were someone to challenge a person's right to determine their chosen sexual identity on whatever basis they choose, that person would be labeled 'intolerant' and would be in violation of state law.

There is much more to this trend than can be explored here, except to point out that over time, these choices will become more acceptable to an ever-increasing age group. The young are the most pliable and accepting due to the incessant social indoctrination they receive. In twenty years time, one could expect the bulk of society to be infected with a tolerance for every sexual behavior. Moreover, as shown repeatedly in the Book of Mormon, the decline in obedience and righteousness in the rising generation has a negative and contaminating effect on the attitudes and practices of an *ever-increasing age group*. The acceptability moves from the teachers to the youth and from the youth to the parents and future parents (see 3 Nephi 1:30).

The bottom line is, man cannot pick and choose what God will accept. Despite our wants and desires, God tells man what is expected of him in order to qualify for an eternal lifestyle of happiness. That someone adopts a lifestyle that is contrary to the will of God does not nullify the doctrines or scriptures that have explained God's will concerning such a lifestyle. Thus, sexual expression must be kept within the bounds the Lord has set (within marriage between a man and a woman), no matter how we are 'wired' here in mortality. In that regard, the attraction or desire for someone of the same sex is fundamentally no different than a man's attraction for his neighbor's wife, or the babysitter. One might not choose the biological or physical attraction, but one certainly has a choice whether or not to act on it.

Keeping the commandments is how an individual manifests his or her love of God, the first of the two great commandments. Many view God as someone who will love all mankind in their sins, which he does. But hoping that the 'unchangeable God' will make an exception for one's special flavor of indiscretions because of His perfect love is a vain hope. There are laws that even God must obey, and His mercy is connected directly to the change of character (being penitent).

> 23 But God ceaseth not to be God, and *mercy claimeth the penitent,* and mercy cometh because of the Atonement; and the Atonement bringeth to pass the resurrection of the dead; and the resurrection of the dead bringeth back men into the presence of God; and thus they are restored into his presence, to be judged according to their works, according to the law and justice.
> 24 For behold, justice exerciseth all his demands, and also mercy claimeth all which is her own; and thus, *none but the truly penitent are saved.*
> 25 What, *do ye suppose that mercy can rob justice? I say unto you, Nay; not one whit. If so, God would cease to be God.* (Alma 42:23-25)

Of course laws or commandments that personally effect individuals and families will often seem antiquated, unfair, or unjust. Some will want the church to change the doctrines of God and accept lifestyles that are not condoned in scripture. Because of justice, as Alma declares above, *God cannot save anyone in their sins.* Because God loves all humanity, God seeks to help all turn from their sins.

> 37 And I say unto you again that he cannot save them in their sins; for I cannot deny his word, and he hath said that no unclean thing can inherit the kingdom of heaven; therefore, how can ye be saved, except ye inherit the kingdom of heaven? Therefore, ye cannot be saved in your sins. (Alma 11)

The War in Heaven was fought to preserve the agency of the individual. Satan sought to take away the agency to sin. In contrast, God's plan was to make sure everyone could sin if they chose. A thoughtful question connected to that war: Could or would God hold someone accountable, or punish someone, for using the agency that the heavens fought to preserve? Standing before the judgment bar of God, those who have decided not to change their character and not to keep the commandments are not cast out of His presence; they themselves will "shrink from the presence of God." All become the judges of their own selves, not God. For this reason the judgment is just.

Commandments are not given as restrictions or restraints, but recipes for happiness in this world and the next. Commandments exist because a loving God knows what will make His children happy, and what will bring joy in this life and the next. God loves all, but at the same time He wants all to repent (change their character) and sin no more so that they will be able to participate in that eternal happiness, which is His work and His glory. A parent's love for their children cannot be greater than the love God has for them, and by virtue of being God, He cannot command (whether one agrees or disagrees) anything that will not be for their eternal benefit and glory. Many believe that the church and consequently God should change for the 'better.' God cannot change for the better because He is already perfect and He will not change the perfect to make life and eternity worse.

In John Chapter Eight the woman taken in adultery was left without accusers. Christ showed His earthly love by saying "Neither do I condemn thee." The Savior did not judge or condemn her for using the agency He insured, protected and for which He fought. Christ displayed His Godly redemptive love and desire by stating, "Go, and sin no more" (John 8:1-11). This passage is often quoted but seldom understood. Christ does not condemn the adulteress for her use of agency; He just asks her to change her lifestyle. He knows how true happiness and joy is achieved. Based on the knowledge of truth that one might have, each individual will have joy or sorrow, happiness or misery, condemn or exalt themselves because of their agency, choice, and chosen nature and character.

There are sins or weaknesses that exist because of the flesh. They are perpetuated because of pride and a desire to use our God given agency to do according to our own will. But no one is a victim of God. Those who have neither a standard of truth nor an understanding of eternal truths or the plan of salvation are vulnerable to being carried about on every wind of doctrine, fashion and fad. But the choice to act on our impulses still belongs to the individual and not God. He will not control the agency of man, but neither is His mercy able to rob justice of her due.

There are those who have chosen an alternate lifestyle contrary to the scriptures upon which the church must rely as a standard. Many who struggle with same sex attraction, or are sympathetic to it, hope the church will change its position on the acceptability of this practice. Others actively seek to change the church's perception and acceptance of this practice by protest and vigil. This the church cannot do.

Some will condemn the policies of the church and label the church and its members 'intolerant' and 'bigoted' for not sanctioning their chosen lifestyle. God himself has guaranteed agency and personal choice and action and the church cannot take that away from the individual. Nevertheless, the doctrines founded in scripture become the standards of the Church of Jesus Christ, which are NOT based on sexuality, but on the moralities of eternal happiness

A religion must be founded on an unchangeable God and a standard of truth from which to build the faith of its members.

> 9 For do we not read that God is the same yesterday, today, and forever, and in him there is no variableness neither shadow of changing?
> 10 And now, if ye have imagined up unto yourselves a god who doth vary, and in whom there is shadow of changing, then have ye imagined up unto yourselves a god who is not a God of miracles. (Mormon 9:9-10)

If God or His Church could change doctrines and beliefs based on the wish or whim of its members, or change its truths by vigil, petition or vote, it would cease to be a religion and would become a club. If one does not like the position of the Latter-day Saint beliefs, there are many organizations and even religions that accept the alternate lifestyle in their membership and leadership. The standards of the church are the scriptures, which must be a final word on the doctrines and beliefs of the organization. Again, the commandments found in the scriptures are not restrictive, but are the path to eternal happiness and joy. Of what value is a religion or church that would not have as its goal the *eternal happiness* of its individual members? All are free to act for themselves, free to create the character that they will want and have for eternity. This everyone can do without the condemnation from a loving God, who will allow each spirit to be what he or she may want to be and where they want to be for eternity. Our loving God has provided a path and road map to happiness and joy, but none are forced to walk that path or obey the warning signs along the way. The Standard Works are the standards for happiness, in and out of this world. If a church did not maintain the *rules of eternal joy* (commandments) there would be no purpose of faith or religion, for that church would have no power to save. Without a standard there is no set of unchangeable rules. How could faith be built or maintained on something that could be changed by vote based on special interests or weaknesses? There are other options and organizations for those who do not want to live by the standards that are set in Latter-day scripture.

When one seeks to change the doctrines and scriptural standards of the church, they are subtly expressing specific beliefs about the church which they hope to change. Implied but rarely articulated in their forceful desire for change are these core beliefs:

- This is not a religion.
- This organization is not founded on scripture and doctrine from God.
- The church organization is not directed by Christ.
- This church organization is only a culture, social organization or club that can be changed, manipulated and pressured.
- The priesthood leadership is not inspired and cannot be considered prophets, seers, and revelators.
- God needs to conform to personal opinion, desires and whims.
- This is not the true church or priesthood.

Below are a few of the scriptures in the standard works that address same sex relationships along with other unacceptable activities and character traits that would lead one away from eternal happiness.

> Genesis 19:5; Leviticus 18:22; 20:13; Deuteronomy 23:17; Isaiah 3:9; Romans 1:27; 1 Corinthians 6:9; 1 Timothy1:10; 2 Timothy 3:3; Jude 1:7; 2 Nephi 13:9.

In Scripture, same sex relationships are listed together in the context of other sins such as adultery, fornication, family incest and other weaknesses of the flesh and character that are considered unacceptable behavior (Leviticus 20:10-16). When reviewing the list of scriptural passages above, as well as the few verses below, the question must arise: Which is the greatest offence? For example:

> 9 Know ye not that the unrighteous shall not inherit the kingdom of God? Be not deceived: neither fornicators, nor idolaters, nor adulterers, nor effeminate, nor abusers of themselves with mankind,
> 10 Nor thieves, nor covetous, nor drunkards, nor revilers, nor extortioners, shall inherit the kingdom of God.
> 11 And such were some of you: but ye are washed, but ye are sanctified, but ye are justified in the name of the Lord Jesus, and by the Spirit of our God. (1 Corinthians 6:9-11)

When reviewing the passage above, which is the worst sin? Which sin will keep the individual out of the kingdom of God? Often the acts that people are most forgiving and accepting of are the ones with which they are most familiar, including personal weaknesses or the weaknesses of loved ones. It follows then that the greatest sin, the worst sin, is the one that restricts each individual person from the presence of God and from the full potential of happiness and joy, *whatever that weakness may be.* One does not trip over the mountain, but a neck can be broken from a crack in the sidewalk.

Perhaps a look at what should be acceptable or what God should be blamed for (*with tongue in cheek*) might help make a point. The mother that is upset with the church for not accepting her alternate lifestyle child and wanting the church to change its policies should ask themselves a few questions logically connected to these verses above (as well as many others). If one wants the church to accept the gay and lesbian lifestyle, why not also demand that the church accept the adulterous lifestyles of husbands and priesthood leaders? Perhaps a petition could be passed or a vote taken to repeal the Word of Wisdom as a commandment, thus removing it as a requirement for Temple attendance. By vote we could make the cultural hall the smoking section for Sacrament Meeting. And with the economic difficulties of today, perhaps a petition for 5% tithing would be prudent.

The point is, if pressure and petition can force any doctrinal or moral change, then any change is possible. There could be "NO TRUE CHURCH" if personal opinion, society or cultural norms determine the accepted doctrines and moral laws of a religion rather than a standard of scripture and unchangeable doctrine.

Those who believe that an alternate lifestyle should be accepted because "God made them that way" must also accept individual entitlements of those who may claim genetic reasons for acting on other personal weaknesses. For example, a person may claim to have an overactive libido that makes them unable to control or limit themselves to a monogamous physical relationship with a spouse. If one accepts that God made them that way, these adulterous actions could not be wrong or called sins, since they cannot help but cheat on their spouses. If they have no control, they have no agency, and therefore no responsibility to be obedient to any. Another individual, because of genetic makeup, might be susceptible to alcoholism and therefore not responsible for his or her drinking or the drunken stupor and irresponsibility that follows. One may be over weight through no fault of their own. Can pornography be wrong if God created mankind with two eyes and overwhelming sexual desires? Where might the rationalization ever end?

Thus, to accept one justification or 'entitlement' to sin, one must be prepared to accept them all. There is a standard, and that standard is found in the scriptures and the declarations of the prophets of God.

415

Again, commandments are not restrictive in nature, but recipes for happiness.

Life is nothing more than the battle or fight that exists between two forces, the flesh and the spirit. Eternal happiness and reward is determined by which force is allowed—*by personal choice*—to win that war.

> 16 This I say then, Walk in the Spirit, and ye shall not fulfil the lust of the flesh.
> 17 For the flesh lusteth against the Spirit, and the Spirit against the flesh: and these are contrary the one to the other: so that ye cannot do the things that ye would.
> 18 But if ye be led of the Spirit, ye are not under the law.
> 19 Now the works of the flesh are manifest, which are these; Adultery, fornication, uncleanness, lasciviousness,
> 20 Idolatry, witchcraft, hatred, variance, emulations, wrath, strife, seditions, heresies,
> 21 Envyings, murders, drunkenness, revellings, and such like: of the which I tell you before, as I have also told you in time past, that they which do such things shall not inherit the kingdom of God.
> 22 But the fruit of the Spirit is love, joy, peace, longsuffering, gentleness, goodness, faith,
> 23 Meekness, temperance: against such there is no law.
> (Galatians 5:16-23)

God Lives! His commands and His will has not changed. There is a life after death! Therefore, there exists a purpose to this life! Whether we see or understand that purpose does not negate the existence of God, life after death, or its purpose!

All spirits were perfect when they came to earth through a physical birth, having no desire for sin or wickedness. Every spirit was pure and whole when they entered mortality.

> 54 ...the children, for they are whole from the foundation of the world.

> 55 And the Lord spake unto Adam, saying: Inasmuch as thy children are conceived in sin, (in a sinful world) even so when they begin to grow up, sin conceiveth in their hearts, and they taste the bitter, that they may know to prize the good. (Moses 6:54-55)

> 8 Wherefore, little children are whole, for they are not capable of committing sin; wherefore the curse of Adam is taken from them in me, that it hath no power over them;
> 12 But little children are alive in Christ, even from the foundation of the world; if not so, God is a partial God, and also a changeable God, and a respecter to persons; for how many little children have died without baptism!
> (Moroni 8:8, 12)

The dichotomy of mortality lies in the fact that every individual begins with a perfect and pure spirit without any spiritual handicap. Through birth into a temporal world, that pure spirit must inhabit an imperfect physical body. Because of the fall of Adam, the spirit had no other option than to receive and endure this fallen body. Therefore, a loving Father in Heaven promised, through the power of the resurrection—initiated by the grace, sacrifice and resurrection of Christ—a perfect and immortal physical body. Thus the time will come that every spirit, good or bad, will receive a perfected and incorruptible body for eternity. The spirit that inhabits and animates that perfect body will be the same spirit that began in perfection, but now it will possess the nature and character that was molded and cast through the exercise of agency in mortality.

> Ye cannot say, when ye are brought to that awful crisis, that I will repent, that I will return to my God. Nay, ye cannot say this; for that same spirit which doth possess your bodies at the time that ye go out of this life, that same spirit will have power to possess your body in that eternal world.
> (Alma 34:34)

Therefore, during this life the spirit will use the agency it has been given to either become more like God (character matters!), or it will choose to succumb to the imperfections and worldly desires of the flesh. Mortality is the probationary period where the spirit will either learn to control the imperfect body or allow the body to control, create and cast the nature of the spirit. The eternal spirit that either submitted its will to God or the flesh will be inseparably connected to that perfect body. It is the spirit's quality of character and nature that will determine and choose its most comfortable habitation and happiness in the eternities, not the quality of the immortal body.

God has provided everyone with the rulebook for eternal happiness. Every individual spirit may choose that happiness by keeping the commandments God has instituted, or they may gamble on the hope that they will be satisfied in eternity without family and without relationships. President Joseph Fielding Smith taught that outside of the Celestial kingdom, there will be no recognition of any previous earthly relationships. Moreover, every relationship based on a physical relationship or attraction will be absent in all but the Celestial kingdom.

> For, behold, I create new heavens and a new earth: and the former *shall not be remembered, nor come into mind.* (Isaiah 65:17)

There is only one kingdom and glory set aside for a continuation of relationships, a place reserved for those whose worthiness is created by the personal desire (through the use of agency) to exercise faith in Christ and repent (change one's character), thus developing the character and love that has made God who He is. The judgment of a character developed by choice and works in mortality can be nothing but perfect and righteous. All judgment is "just" because any condemnation or punishment is not issued from God but from the individuals themselves.

> These are they that are redeemed of the Lord; yea, these are they that are taken out, that are delivered from that endless night of darkness; and thus *they stand or fall*; for behold, they are their own judges, whether to do good or do evil. (Alma 41:7)

> 29 And this to the intent that whosoever will believe might be saved, and that whosoever will not believe, *a righteous judgment might come upon them; and also if they are condemned they bring upon themselves their own condemnation.*
> 30 And now remember, remember, my brethren, that *whosoever perisheth, perisheth unto himself;* and whosoever doeth iniquity, doeth it unto himself; for behold, ye are free; ye are permitted to act for yourselves; for behold, God hath given unto you a knowledge and he hath made you free. (Helaman 14:29-30)

For one to become 'their own judge', they must comprehend the magnitude of what their full potential was. Each will understand not only the character and nature they have chosen, but also the nature and glory of God. When the time comes that all will 'see as they are seen, and know as they are known' (D&C 76:94) either their 'confidence will wax strong in the presence of God' (D&C 121:45) or they will shrink from His presence, by choice and with a perfect knowledge:

> For behold, when *ye shall be brought to see your nakedness* before God, *and also the glory of God*, and the holiness of Jesus Christ, it will kindle a flame of unquenchable fire upon you. (Mormon 9:5)

> Therefore, if that man repenteth not... *the demands of divine justice do awaken his immortal soul to a lively sense of his own guilt*, which doth *cause him to shrink from the presence of the Lord*, and doth fill his breast with guilt, and pain, and anguish, which *is like* an unquenchable fire, whose flame ascendeth up forever and ever. (Mosiah 2:38)

> And if they be evil *they are consigned to an awful view of their own guilt and abominations, which doth cause them to shrink from the presence of the Lord...* (Mosiah 3:25)

Each individual will become their own arbiter and judge, *placing themselves* in the eternal environment that they have selected by their preparation and agency. Hell is where one does not belong and that could be in the celestial kingdom and the presence of God:

> 3 Can ye behold the Lamb of God? *Do ye suppose that ye shall dwell with him under a consciousness of your guilt? Do ye suppose that ye could be happy to dwell with that Holy Being, when your souls are racked with a consciousness of guilt that ye have ever abused his laws?*
> 4 Behold, I say unto you that ye would be more miserable to dwell with a holy and just God, under a consciousness of your filthiness before him, than ye would to dwell with the damned souls in hell. (Mormon 9:3-4)

In summary, the War in Heaven was fought to preserve the agency of the individual. Contrary to common perception, those who decline to change their character (repent) and keep the commandments are not cast out of the presence of God. In fact, they "shrink from the presence of God." All become judges of their own selves, not God. Thus, the Judgment of God is just. With a perfect recollection of one's works and choices, possessed of the eternal nature and character they have developed, each person will choose the presence or absence of Deity. All will choose to be where they are comfortable for eternity. Agency is supreme, and the exercise of that agency, ensured by God himself, will determine one's glory or condemnation. It is only in the Celestial environment that any earthly relationships will continue with loved ones, and they too must be worthy of the same celestial glory.

Whether our dispositions toward sin are genetic or the result of choice, it must be remembered that the moral codes and commandments found in scripture are not meant to be restrictions of one's agency. Like all weaknesses of the flesh, from sexual desire to overeating, the goal in mortality is to create—by agency, choice, and actions—a spirit that someday will inhabit a perfect body and worthy to be in the presence of God. The weaknesses of mortality can become strengths through repentance (character change) and the gospel of Jesus Christ; ensuring that every spirit is free from becoming a victim of their body, mind or circumstance.

420

Conclusion

Only those who have a broken heart and contrite spirit may be taught or instructed by the spirit. All the words in the world will not change the mind of those who do not want to know or understand. The best and most important decisions in life are made by being objective and impartial, looking at all points of view without preconceived notions or preferences. However, this objective mindset is often difficult to acquire or instill in another because of personal desires, education, and the filters of prejudices that have been learned through education or experience. One cannot teach the person who doesn't want to know.

The information in this book is not meant to be comprehensive in its scope, nor is it expected that it will change the mind and hearts of those who have chosen to separate themselves from the faith of their fathers. That choice belongs solely to the individual and their agency. The faith and testimonies of parents, loved ones, friends, leaders, prophets, (modern day and those found in the scriptures) serve as righteous examples, but have no power to change the minds and hearts of those who have chosen to fall away. To a loving and faithful parent, the falling away of their child is akin to the child's death. In life someone else exercising his or her agency, over which we have no control, generates almost all of the emotional pain that one suffers. Nevertheless, no human spirit may be condemned by God or themselves until they know and understand the plan of salvation and the gospel of God perfectly.

True agency cannot exist without a full and perfect knowledge of how and why, along with the knowledge of options and consequences of the choice. Any judgment without this standard is unjust and will compromise the agency of the individual. Parents may be assured that their children or loved ones will not be consigned by God or themselves until they understand the gospel and the plan of salvation perfectly and comprehend the doctrines of exaltation with a perfect knowledge, void of any misunderstandings, misconceptions or misinformation. The required space between death and the resurrection is necessary for the learning and understanding of this gospel plan of salvation. No one in mortality understands it perfectly, thus, a time or "space" (Alma 40:9, 21) must exist to learn and then accept or reject the plan of salvation. It is only with this full and perfect knowledge that any judgment of eternal consequence may take place. Again, if this were not so, one's agency would be compromised. The time in the spirit world is a time to reflect and repent, to learn and embrace the gospel. A time to come unto Christ as taught by righteous parents in mortality and family members in the spirit world. Nevertheless, each may "choose for themselves" to begin that process of progression and joy or accept a simple and single satisfaction.

Just as families exist here on earth to teach the principles and ordinances of the gospel, the same sociality will exist in the spirit world for the same reason. Who better to teach the gospel, here or there, than those who love and care for each other? Agency cannot be compromised. Everyone will know and understand perfectly before any judgment takes place.

An apostasy and falling away from the faith with eternal consequences *cannot* take place until a comprehensive knowledge and understanding is acquired. This perfect knowledge and full rejection is not something that will take place in mortality, as Moses was taught:

> Wherefore, no man can behold all my works, except he behold all my glory; and no man can behold all my glory, and afterwards remain in the flesh on the earth. (Moses 1:5)

Though this book may not change those who have fallen away, it is hoped that it will arm parents and teachers with an increased vision and understanding of the ideas concepts and scriptures that establish doctrine. Despite the questions and answers or issues surrounding the church and its priesthood organization; each testimony should be centered in Christ and his Atonement. The strength to endure the temptations of faith will be found only in Christ.

> And now, my sons, remember, *remember that it is upon the rock of our Redeemer, who is Christ, the Son of God, that ye must build your foundation;* that when the devil shall send forth his mighty winds, yea, his shafts in the whirlwind, yea, when all his hail and his mighty storm shall beat upon you, *it shall have no power over you to drag you down* to the gulf of misery and endless wo, *because of the rock upon which ye are built, which is a sure foundation, a foundation whereon if men build they cannot fall.* (Helaman 5:12)

It is the gospel of Christ that must be understood, not necessarily the organizational hierarchy of administration. Every home and parent should feel as did Nephi when he discussed the testimonies of their children:

> And we *talk of Christ*, we *rejoice in Christ*, we *preach of Christ*, we *prophesy of Christ*, and we write according to our prophecies, *that our children may know to what source they may look for a remission of their sins.* (2 Nephi 25:25)

This is the faith that should be taught to the youth as they begin to grow in the church. Their faith should be pointed first toward Christ and the gospel rather than focusing on the organization of administration. There is no other name but Christ that has the power to save:

> 7 Your hearts are changed through faith on his name; therefore, ye are born of him and have become his sons and his daughters.
>
> 8 And under this head ye are made free, and there is no other head whereby ye can be made free. There is no other name given whereby salvation cometh; therefore, I would that ye should take upon you the name of Christ, all you that have entered into the covenant with God that ye should be obedient unto the end of your lives. (Mosiah 5:7, 8)

Because salvation comes only through Christ and the Atonement, the faith that will lead to salvation must be placed in Christ and none else. It is not the power or position of a priesthood leader that can save. Paul taught:

> 12 Now this I say, that every one of you saith, I am of Paul; and I of Apollos; and I of Cephas; and I of Christ.
>
> 13 Is Christ divided? Was Paul crucified for you? Were ye baptized in the name of Paul? (1 Corinthians 1:12-13)

As the title page of the Book of Mormon instructs, the text exists for "the convincing of Jew and Gentile that Jesus is the Christ, the Son of the Living God." This is the message and witness of all scripture and of the prophets who have recorded their testimonies of Christ. As the Book of Mormon begins, with the dream of Lehi and the Tree of Life, the message of the fruit and pure Love of Christ permeates the text from beginning to end.

It is to this end that this book is written. My objective as an author and teacher has been to show why our faith and hope should be in Christ, while explaining how the church and priesthood organization has been divinely authorized to administer His gospel, even the gospel of Jesus Christ. My message to those who would seek to separate themselves from the LDS faith would be to remember that the primary purpose of the church organization is to assist the individual in their efforts to "come unto Christ," finding joy in their redemption through a personal relationship with Christ and the Atonement.

Life is a Threshing Floor where choices are made and character is developed, made manifest by the words, works and thoughts of every individual. It is at the threshing floor of life that one learns about their place in creation and their relationship with God and humanity. The goal in life is to create a nature and character worthy to be in the presence of God. Because of the eternal truths learned from an endowment of power in this lone and dreary world, we can 'act in futurity'. This endowment of knowledge and truth and reality will provide the power to *endure to the end,* overcoming the trials and tribulations of spirit, mind, and body that all must experience and endure.

Eternal joy depends upon the acceptance of Jesus Christ as the redeemer. As we exercise faith unto repentance, we gain access to the mercy guaranteed by the atoning sacrifice of Christ.

Solomon constructed the first temple recorded in scripture on a Threshing Floor, and within the walls of that temple were carved images of the Tree of Life that were overlaid in gold. The sacred spot of the Threshing Floor encased the central message and symbol of the fruit from the Tree of Life. It was on the Threshing Floor that the chaff was separated from the life-giving grain. Because of position, purpose and place, the ancient Threshing Floor of Faith became the center of spiritual instruction, a place where faith and testimonies could be strengthened. A place where truths were presented to enable the individual to endure mortality, providing an endowment of power for all who will come to the Tree of Life and partake of the fruit of the Pure Love of Christ.

Scripture Index

Old Testament

Genesis
1: 28	380
2: 7	352
3: 19	352
3: 26-28	359-360
4: 4	260
15: 6-18	249-250
19: 5	413
27: 15	276
31: 51-55	250
37: 4	276

Exodus
18: 13-27	377-378
18: 21	185
20	116
31: 12-17	306
32: 25-26	281
32: 26, 29	153

Leviticus
18: 22	413
20: 10-16	413
20: 13	413

Numbers
3:	383
3: 12-13	282, 288
3: 41, 45	153, 282
8: 9-25	153
18: 1-7	153
18: 15	287

Deuteronomy
6: 6-9	128
17: 6	158
19: 15	158
23: 17	413
25: 5-10	288

Judges
2: 10-12	101, 405

Ruth
1: 16-17	251

1 Samuel
15: 22-23	261

2 Samuel
24: 14-25	19

1 Kings
1	276

1 Chronicles
21: 13-30	19

Job
10: 9	352
34: 15	352

Psalms
15	226
15: 4	252
24:	226
103: 14	352

428

New Testament

Book of Mormon

Doctrine and Covenants

Pearl of Great Price

Made in the USA
Middletown, DE
05 November 2023

41857861R00245